Religious Statecraft

COLUMBIA STUDIES IN MIDDLE EAST POLITICS

COLUMBIA STUDIES IN MIDDLE EAST POLITICS

Marc Lynch, Series Editor

Columbia Studies in Middle East Politics presents academically rigorous, well-written, relevant, and accessible books on the rapidly transforming politics of the Middle East for an interested academic and policy audience.

The Arab Uprisings Explained: New Contentious Politics in the Middle East, edited by Marc Lynch

Sectarian Politics in the Gulf: From the Iraq War to the Arab Uprisings, Frederic M. Wehrey

From Resilience to Revolution: How Foreign Interventions Destabilize the Middle East, Sean L. Yom

Protection Amid Chaos: The Creation of Property Rights in Palestinian Refugee Camps, Nadya Hajj

RELIGIOUS STATECRAFT

The Politics of Islam in Iran

MOHAMMAD AYATOLLAHI TABAAR

COLUMBIA UNIVERSITY PRESS *NEW YORK*

Columbia University Press
Publishers Since 1893
New York   Chichester, West Sussex
cup.columbia.edu
Copyright © 2018 Columbia University Press
Paperback edition, 2019

Library of Congress Cataloging-in-Publication Data
Names: Tabaar, Mohammad Ayatollahi, author.
Title: Religious statecraft : the politics of Islam in Iran / Mohammad Ayatollahi Tabaar.
Other titles: Columbia studies in Middle East politics.
Description: New York : Columbia University Press, 2018. |
Series: Columbia studies in Middle East politics
Identifiers: LCCN 2017014876 | ISBN 9780231183666 (cloth) | ISBN 9780231183673 (pbk.) |
ISBN 9780231545068 (e-book)
Subjects: LCSH: Islam and politics—Iran—History—20th century. | Islam and politics—Iran—
History—21st century. | Shiʻah—Iran. | Iran—Politics and government—1979–1997. | Iran—Politics
and government—1997–
Classification: LCC BP173.7 .T32 2017 | DDC 322/.10955—dc23
LC record available at https://lccn.loc.gov/2017014876

Cover Image: Atefe Alemrajabi. Photograph of Molla Ismael Mosque (built circa 1800), Yazd, Iran.

Dedicated to those who have been persecuted in the name of Islam
or
for being Muslim

Contents

CONTENTS

Preface

I was in the second grade when the Iranian Revolution occurred. The subsequent "Islamization" of the society, the hostage crisis, the civil wars, the Iran–Iraq War, the economic and political reform eras, and other events pushed me and many of my peers to study the social sciences. This book is perhaps above all a personal attempt to decipher what my generation went through. I only hope that I provided an impartial analysis of a country whose local politics continues to influence global politics.

This book is rooted in my high school and college years, when I was first exposed to many of the ideas discussed in the coming chapters. My thinking branched out into term papers in the early years of my long graduate student career at the New School for Social Research and the University of Chicago, as well as into my dissertation at Georgetown University. It further evolved as I straddled the academic, policy, and media worlds at this time. The intensity of the "Iran debate" in the United States, as well as the ever-changing political landscape inside Iran itself, challenged me to develop a lucid framework that could explain the intricacies of factional politics, foreign policy, and the role of religion. I then re-examined the earlier (pre)revolutionary phases as if they were happening in "real time" to better identify the contingencies and options that actors faced at particular moments.

Throughout this voyage, many individuals and institutions helped ensure the completion of this book.

My adviser, Charles Kupchan, as well as Thomas Banchoff, José Casanova, and Abdolkarim Soroush provided immeasurable support and feedback at Georgetown University, and this work benefited tremendously from their guidance.

I have been particularly privileged to enjoy the mentorship and friendship of Abdolkarim Soroush over the past three decades. He is an intellectual powerhouse behind the movement that introduced religious pluralism and "civil" Islam to the Iranian polity and society.

For the development of the original manuscript, I owe a great deal to Marc Lynch, who encouraged and supported me in his various capacities at George Washington University, the Project on Middle East Political Science (POMEPS), *Foreign Policy*'s Middle East Channel, the *Washington Post*'s *Monkey Cage* blog, and Columbia University Press's Middle East Politics Series.

I presented early drafts of this book at the POMEPS-Yale University Book Seminar and the Hushang Ansary Book Conference at Texas A&M University's Scowcroft Institute of International Affairs. I benefited from critical comments provided by Nathan Brown, Greg Gause, Nader Hashemi, Elizabeth Shakman Hurd, Ellen Lust, Jack Snyder, and other participants.

I was fortunate to receive constructive feedback on various chapters of the manuscript from Ariel Ahram, Ali Banuazizi, Farideh Farhi, John Gledhill, Peter Krause, Nadejda Marinova, Mohsen Milani, Will Norris, Gabriela Thornton, and Kadir Yildirim.

Reyko Huang has been a big-hearted colleague and a de facto mentor of mine since we both joined Texas A&M University's Bush School of Government and Public Service. She read through several drafts of the manuscript and each time offered insightful pathways to improve it. My other colleagues— particularly Don Bailey, Leonard Bright, Ann Bowman, Joe Cerami, Greg Gause, Chuck Hermann, Valerie Hudson, Wendi Arant Kaspar, Ren Mu, Larry Napper, Andrew Natsios, Ron Szabo, Bill West, and Janeen Wood—gave me extraordinary levels of support.

I am indebted to my former BBC colleagues Sina Alinejad, the late Afshin Mobasser, and Kambiz Fattahi. Kambiz read the manuscript carefully and never hesitated to share with me the thousands of invaluable documents he had tirelessly collected from various archives in recent years.

Veteran Iranian analysts and activists, including Ahmad Salamatian, Mohsen Sazegara, and Hassan Shariatmadari, gave precious insights that sharpened my arguments.

Many of the ideas in this book emerged in long conversations with Laura Secor over the past decade. While working on her book *Children of Paradise: The Struggle for the Soul of Iran*—an unsurpassable intellectual history of Iran—Laura remained profoundly engaged with this book project.

Caitlin Elizabeth Browne was a key and sharp reader throughout as well as a loyal friend.

My visiting positions at George Washington University's Institute for Middle East Studies, the University of Cambridge's Centre of Islamic Studies, Columbia University's Saltzman Institute of War and Peace Studies, Harvard University's Center for Middle East Studies, and Rice University's Baker Institute for Public Policy provided me with vibrant intellectual homes at critical stages of the writing process. I am grateful to Edward Djerejian, Françoise Djerejian, Bill Martin, and Allen Matusow for their ceaseless and warm support at the Baker Institute.

Generous grants from the Bodman Foundation, the Bush School, and the Scowcroft Institute enabled me to conduct much of the archival research.

I thank the staffs of Texas A&M University's Evans Library and Policy Sciences and Economics Library; the University of Texas at Austin's Perry-Castañeda Library; Harvard University's Widener Library; Columbia University's Butler and Lehman Libraries; the University of Chicago's Regenstein Library; Stanford University's Green Library; the Hoover Institution Library and Archives; Rice University's Fondren Library; the Jimmy Carter, Ronald Reagan, George H. W. Bush Presidential Libraries; and the Library of Congress.

For research assistance, I am indebted to Shira Babow, Leslie Cohen, Colton Cox, Marlee Kingsley, Jessica Koloini, Meghan McCaffrey, Ramin Naderi, Adan Obeid, Jared Skidmore, Sumer Wachtendorf, Richard Wilbur, and others who shall remain anonymous.

I thank the editorial and production team at Columbia University Press for its professionalism and for providing permission for the excerpts of the hostage crisis and the Iran–Iraq War chapters to be published in *Security Studies* and the *Journal of Strategic Studies*. I am grateful to Mary McGovern, Joanna Bruso, and Lianne Hart for their tremendous help in copyediting the manuscript. Alissa Levin, Vahid Vahdat, and Jeff Cox provided valuable input in the cover design.

My parents, sisters, nieces, and nephews from afar provided much of my daily writing vigor. Like countless others who have become unfortunate hostages of U.S.–Iran tensions, my family accepted my decision to study abroad and patiently came to terms with its unpredictable consequences. I am eternally beholden to my parents and my late grandparents for everything they taught me in life. My interest in politics and religion started with the books, journals, and free debates that surrounded me as a child.

I fear that I have forgotten to mention many more names that were crucial in this endeavor. This, however, does not include those others whose love and support shall not be forgotten.

Religious Statecraft

Introduction

The Politics of Islam

IN FEBRUARY 1979, Ayatollah Ruhollah Khomeini sat at the helm of God's Government in Iran. While history has remembered him as a man of unbending principle, he charted a complex and contradictory course—from defender of the constitutional monarchy in 1961, calling on Mohammad Reza Shah to reign, not rule; to developing a doctrine of supreme clerical rule, *Velayat-e Faqih* (Guardianship of the Jurist), to replace the monarchy; to reverting to advocating a progressive constitutional government minus the Shah on the eve of the Iranian Revolution in 1978–79; to institutionalizing *Velayat-e Faqih* in the new constitution, putting himself at the top of the combined supreme religious and political authority. On his deathbed, he revised even *Velayat-e Faqih*, no longer requiring his successor to possess the highest possible clerical qualifications but instead endowing the position with ultimate political authority—Absolute *Velayat-e Faqih*.

Before ascending to power, Khomeini pledged freedom to the opposition to unite under his Islamist banner, made alliances with nationalists, attracted leftists to his political cause, endeared himself to the Iranian army, and promised the monarch's American patron unobstructed access to oil. Once in power, he and his followers would "break the pens" of the dissidents, uproot the nationalists, liquidate the leftists, decapitate the army, install their own Islamic Revolutionary Guard Corps (IRGC), and bring the entire state apparatus under the Islamists' control. He had vowed friendship with the United States but then blessed the seizure of the American embassy.

He sought a united Shi'a authority to capture the state, only to end its independence and bring it under the state's control. Khomeini preached the establishment of an Islamic state to implement Islamic law but reversed the means and ends when he sanctioned the abrogation of Islamic law to protect the state.

His followers were no less fickle. After Khomeini's death in 1989, they split into two groups and took his ideological legacy down opposite paths. The radical Islamist leftists who had structured their faction around statism and anti-imperialism, and seized the U.S. embassy in 1979, later reinvented themselves in 1997 as proponents of reformist Islam, human rights, and better relations with the United States. By contrast, the conservative Islamist right, which was considered more "moderate" in the early years of the revolution, evolved into a more statist, ultraconservative, anti-American faction. Khomeini's successor, Ali Khamenei, initially downplayed his predecessor's preference for the Absolute Guardianship of the Jurist, only to further expand it once he himself became the Guardian Jurist; he then went from a middling title, *Hojjat al-Islam*, to Ayatollah, before ultimately claiming to be a grand ayatollah. Former president Akbar Hashemi Rafsanjani, who played a critical role in institutionalizing *Velayat-e Faqih* in 1979 and then tailoring that robe for Khamenei in 1989, backed the popular pro-democracy Green Movement in 2009 and strove to weaken the position of the Guardian Jurist to the clerical equivalent of the British monarchy. His reformist successor, Mohammad Khatami, symbolized the transformation of a staunchly anti-imperialist faction into one that would advocate better relations with the United States. Former president Mahmoud Ahmadinejad and his circle spoke of wiping Israel off the map, but later declared friendship with the Israeli people. His anti-American position was followed by numerous unsuccessful attempts to open a secret channel to the White House.

The story of post-revolutionary Iran is one of ideological and political contradictions—often articulated by the same actors. Religion is a ubiquitous and yet mercurial feature of contemporary Iranian politics. "Islam" has taken a wide range of quietist, revolutionary, reformist, nationalist, and secular manifestations in contemporary Iran. Scholars and policymakers have not paid sufficient attention to how elites have constructed and used religious narratives[1] for political purposes, and changed these narratives in the process. Religion is often described as either a mask for Iranian leaders' hunger for power or a determinant of their behavior. Lost between the two is an analysis of how religion is instrumentally crafted, negotiated, and contested in the political sphere. If elites unremittingly develop and deploy religious discourse, scholars should study this continual development and deployment. Just as social scientists examine elites' electoral and nuclear politics, so should they examine their religious politics.

Ignoring the role of religion in political analysis, Clifford Geertz once prudently observed, "is not so much to stage the play without the prince as without the plot."[2] Conversely, one can argue that ignoring politics is to stage a play that—despite having a plot—leaves out the prince and the rest of the cast. Beneath the façade of a seemingly static, consistent, and ideological political system is a dynamic, fast-paced underworld of bold, ideational impresarios unabashedly comfortable with supplying any religious commodity necessary to control the state.

In this book, I demonstrate that Iranian politics revolve around instrumentally constructed religious doctrines and narratives. Interactive and embedded in daily politics, these doctrines and narratives shift as the positions of their carriers change within the political system. Actors develop and deploy religious narratives to meet their factional and regime-level interests, depending on their locus in the system and their subsequent threat perceptions.[3] Rather than the driving force behind behavior, religious ideas are the constructs of actors seeking to meet the challenges of elite competition. In an uncertain climate, political actors are prone to become ideational entrepreneurs,[4] reformulating their goals according to ideological references that capture the popular imagination and bring them closer to dominating the polity. The state is not "a means for the production of meaning,"[5] but the opposite. *Meaning production is a means for capturing the state.* A monopoly over the legitimate use of religion is a sine qua non of an "Islamic" state.

Before proceeding, a critical caveat is in order. This book does not seek to uncover the "real" Khomeini or, for that matter, any political actor that appears in this account. Rather, it studies him and his fellow Islamists as rational actors without making unfalsifiable assumptions about their "true" ideological dispositions. The Islamists' instrumental use of religion neither negates nor confirms their sincerity. One could claim that Khomeini was *not* a true believer in Islamist ideology, since he continuously used and bent religious rules to ascend to power. One could also posit that Khomeini *was* a genuine believer precisely because he was determined to make his vision work, even if it required certain tactical adjustments. Neither can be proven or disproven. To ascribe strategic thinking to a religious actor is not to call into question his or her beliefs.[6]

Religion, Political Uncertainty, and Agency

The central claim of this book is that there is no such thing as "political Islam." There is, however, a *politics* of Islam. I argue that *religious narratives can change, change rapidly, change frequently, and change dramatically* in accordance with elites' threat perceptions. That is not to say that religion holds no explanatory value in seeking to understand political action. On the contrary, the following chapters show that religious ideas, ideals, and ideologies play a critical role in generating mass support and elite cohesion. However, religion is not wholly malleable, either. Political actors must understand the religious market and consumers' preferences before innovatively overcoming doctrinal and institutional constraints and crafting new religious narratives.[7]

In Iran, the societal turn toward Islam was palpable by the 1960s. Even Marxist thinkers such as Jalal Al-e Ahmad (1923–1969) came to acknowledge its potential superiority over other ideologies as a means to bring about fundamental social and political changes in the country.[8] But this turn required appropriating and activating specific political properties in Islam in general and in Shi'a in particular. It took powerful figures such as the French-educated sociologist Ali Shariati (1933–1977) to turn a quietist Shi'a theology into a revolutionary ideology.[9] By reconstructing Islamic history in terms of another popular ideology of the day, Marxism, he turned an anomaly in Shi'a—the revolt of only one out of the Twelve Imams—into a rule, proposing what he called "Red Islam." Similarly, it was Khomeini who appalled the traditional clerical establishment in both Qom and Najaf by proposing a "theory" of the state for the Shi'a. Thus, it was not Shariati's revolutionary Islam or Khomeini's *Velayat-e Faqih* that propelled the Islamic Revolution of 1979; rather, it was a popular aspiration for political change, if not revolution, that led both figures to reconstruct the history of Islam accordingly.[10] In other words, revolution came first and "Islam" followed. Simply studying Shi'a theology would not predict or even explain the revolution.[11]

Unlike studies that take ideational factors as exogenous, this book demonstrates that religious narratives are endogenous to elite competition and factional politics. Actors are not solely driven by—nor do they simply use—the ideas that are *available* to them; rather, they *craft* their own narratives for political ends. Providing a revisionist reading of Iranian politics since 1979, I argue that these studies get the causal link between religious ideology and political order perilously backward. Instead of viewing religious ideology as a determinant of an actor's political objectives and interests, I examine the religious consequences of politics. Political behavior that many experts interpret as an outcome of an ideology should rather be examined as a cause of that particular ideology. I process trace half a century of doctrinal changes against the backdrop of domestic and international politics and locate "political Islam" at the heart of elite politics in Iran. In this micro-level analysis, I claim that Islamist ideology was not only used, but also—more importantly—constructed and institutionalized strategically by elites in response to changing opportunities and threat perceptions. The more closely I have studied the evolution of religious narratives, the more strongly I detect a strategic logic behind them. My constructivist-interpretivist method has brought me to a rationalist conclusion.

Scholarship remains confused over the causes and consequences of Iranian politics. The occupation of the U.S. embassy in Tehran was not driven by the Islamists' inherent anti-Americanism, as is often claimed. This book shows that the Islamists' internal competition with the Marxists dictated the anti-American shift culminating in the hostage crisis. The Iran–Iraq War did not last eight years because of an essential culture of martyrdom in Shi'a Islam. Rather, the Islamist government employed a variety of religious narratives and doctrines to achieve its internal political objectives and simultaneously resist the Iraqi army. Similarly, Khomeini's "fatwa" against the British author Salman Rushdie was not simply the result of his religious fanaticism, as we are often told. Rather, in the aftermath of a devastating war with Iraq, the embarrassment of the Iran–Contra affair, and the growing reaction to Rushdie's novel, *The Satanic Verses*, in the Muslim world, he used the fatwa as a way to silence enemies, outbid rivals, and restore his ideological credibility.

In each instance, politics drove religious ideology, not the other way around. Iran's pragmatic turn after Khomeini's death was not only a result of his conservative successors' learning from the negative experiences of their revolutionary excesses in the 1980s. Rather, they *had* to "learn" how to selectively moderate their foreign and economic policy to succeed in their practical goal of reconstructing the war-torn country. Khomeini's marginalized radical followers did not return to power in 1997 solely due to their intellectual journey to reformism; instead, they realized they had to reinvent themselves as Muslim democrats and proponents of "civil Islam" in order to simultaneously challenge the electoral process and the establishment's "political Islam." Ahmadinejad's sudden shift from expediting the return of the Hidden Imam to praising Cyrus the Great was not a spontaneous appreciation of Persian nationalism. It was a calculated, albeit unsuccessful, move to cultivate public support against his old conservative allies. Similarly, Ayatollah Khamenei's purported fatwa against the use of nuclear weapons can be explained as an effort to signal commitment, help the subsequent nuclear agreement in 2015, and save the Islamic Republic from political collapse.

This book is not only about religion and Iranian politics; it makes specific arguments about religious ideology with respect to individual Iranian leaders, not least of all the founder of the revolution, Ayatollah Khomeini. Scholars and observers of Iranian politics often describe Khomeini either as an ideological actor with a fixed goal of establishing an Islamic state to challenge international norms, or as a rational but deceitful leader, the Ayatollah Realpolitik,[12] whose religion was only a façade covering his ruthless desire to ascend to and stay in power. Both groups refer to his treatise, *Islamic Government*, as strong evidence at least a decade before the Iranian Revolution of the blueprint he had in mind to bring the state under clerical control. Yet these teleological arguments conceal both the driving forces behind the evolution and institutionalization of Islamism in Iran and the unintended consequences that followed. If the final product of Khomeini's vision was so unambiguous, the obvious question is, why did no one detect it before it was well established? How did a wide range of actors, from the United States, which had analyzed his writings, to the Iranian opposition forces that allied with him, fall into this "trap" and view him as a Gandhi?

These analyses suffer from several problems. First, by inferring intentions from observed behaviors and religious rhetoric, they overlook other empirical evidence that can lead to alternative explanations for the post-revolutionary order. Second, by taking the emerging political order for granted and linking it to its religious foundation, scholars often overlook other contingencies as well as the factors that blocked alternative paths a post-revolutionary Iran could have taken. What seems predetermined in hindsight is simply one possible scenario among others ex ante. Presuming otherwise overlooks the interactive nature of politics, the intra-elite dynamics at critical junctures, and the unintended consequences of each step. The actual Islamic Republic that emerged in 1979 was more the product of uncertainties than the straightforward materialization of Khomeini's *Islamic Government* lectures a decade earlier.

Scholars often take Islamist ideology as a given, as they do the notion that the mosque was a built-in institution ready to be deployed for the revolution. However, as Charles Kurzman argues, the mosque network "was not controlled by the Islamists at the outset of revolution," but by the mainstream traditional clergy.[13] Fixation on Khomeini's "immutable" ideological worldview as a goal keeps us from recognizing the strategies that he and his allies had to employ to weaken their clerical rivals and unseat the Shah. Khomeini's religious "vision" was as much a goal as it was an evolving means to a political objective. Conversely, ignoring the ideological component would divest our perspective of the mechanisms through which such strategies became effective. Khomeini's religious credentials and discourses brought him credibility to forge alliances, generate mass mobilization, and undermine regime cohesion. It was partly due to his effective use of religion that key players such as the chief of staff of the Imperial Army; the head of the much-feared secret service, SAVAK; and even U.S. officials facilitated the political transition, intentionally or unintentionally. They believed that their positions within—or leverage over—the state would remain intact under the new regime. The Shah, too, deployed Islamic narratives as a counterstrategy by installing "religious-friendly" officials, reducing public demonstrations of Western culture, and liberalizing the political arena. But in doing so, he fatally entered a territory in which he had little authority to compete with Khomeini, despite his attempts to muffle his rival. He sent Khomeini from Qom to be marginalized among the quietist clerics in Iraq. When this failed, he asked Saddam Hussein to expel Khomeini from the Shi'a-majority country to an "infidelistan" (France), where he only ended up attracting the world's attention. Finally, the Shah's last prime minister permitted Khomeini to return to Qom in the hope that there he would be "drowned" among the clergy. But instead, his political movement engulfed the clerical establishment.

At each turn, Khomeini masterfully averted what could have been serious blows to his movement by adjusting his strategies and employing new discourses. In Najaf, his anti-Shah speeches eventually overcame his isolation as the demonstrations in Iran spread; in France, the "cradle of freedom," he made powerful pro-democracy promises that helped bring him out of seclusion and break the French ban on his media coverage. He portrayed himself as a seminarian with no personal ambition other than removing the Shah and restoring the nation's dignity. He repeatedly claimed that he would neither hold any position nor allow any cleric to leave the seminaries. All of this would change beyond anyone's imagination—including Khomeini's own—once the monarchy ended. He returned to Iran, and a range of new actors competed for political power. Each move shaped the scope of options ahead.

Upon landing in Tehran, Khomeini ordered his militant clerics to serve as judges and summarily execute the army's top generals and other remnants of the old regime for "sowing corruption on Earth" and "declaring war on God," invoking these Quranic lines to swiftly and legitimately eliminate any potential military coup, even though some of these generals had worked with him to ensure a smooth regime transition. But toppling the monarchy also unleashed an existential threat to him and his appointed nationalist Provisional Government, not from the army or the United States, but from the mushrooming Marxist groups with their appealing anti-American ideologies and strong organizational capabilities. The institutional network, mobilizing capacity, and extensive popularity of these groups among students, workers, middle-class intelligentsia, and other anti-imperialist forces posed an overwhelming challenge to a nascent Islamist–nationalist government.

Out of fear of becoming the Alexander Kerensky—the moderate chairman of the post-revolutionary Russian Provisional Government who was overthrown by the Bolsheviks in 1917—of the Iranian Revolution, Khomeini transformed from a Gandhi into a Lenin. He and his disciples stole the Left's anti-imperialist narrative and organizational structure. Although they had not initially sought a confrontation with the United States, they calculated that outbidding their rivals' anti-Americanism in such a threatening climate would generate new constituencies at the expense of the communist Left.

When radical Islamist students preemptively seized the U.S. embassy in November 1979, even U.S.-friendly Islamist clerics reluctantly ended their burgeoning communication with American officials. Anti-Americanism had become the new game in town, and the Islamic Republic had to play along to survive against its internal challenges. Surprised by the turn of events, President Jimmy Carter sought out Muslim theologians in an effort to understand Khomeini's worldviews. By projecting a committed, ideological, irrational, anti-imperialist image, Khomeini perplexed the United States, divided the Marxist Left, isolated the nationalist rivals, and paralyzed his orthodox clerical nemeses.

State-Building: Monopoly Over the Use of Religion

Khomeini's political gambit depended on his ability to institute and maintain a monopoly on the legitimate use of religion—which has in effect come to define the Iranian state since 1979. Doing so was a precondition to establishing a Weberian monopoly of the legitimate use of violence. In other words, to Islamicize the state, Khomeini first had to statize Islam.

Thus, he strove to order power[14] in the mosque before doing so in the state. Concerned about the political ramifications of his theological isolation, Khomeini and his militant disciples relentlessly campaigned—from early on and particularly after the revolution—to make new institutional arrangements to intimidate and co-opt the clerical establishment. It was a daunting task to subjugate the Shi'a clergy, which had enjoyed centuries of institutional independence. The very brand of the project—the "Islamic" state-building enterprise aimed at implementing *shari'a* under the leadership of the now-titled *Imam* Khomeini—increased the cost of clerical opposition to the new political order. It silenced senior traditional clerics and co-opted many of their students. Dissenters and defectors were dealt with through multiple institutions, including the Special Court for the Clergy (SCC), which was established even before the ratification of the new constitution. The SCC operated outside the lines of judicial authority, under the more political auspices of the Imam's office. Any senior cleric who opposed Khomeini, including Grand Ayatollah Kazem Shariatmadari, was branded pro-American and silenced.

Many scholars mistakenly treat the clerical community as a monolith, largely opposed to the Shah and in favor of the "Islamic Government"; they also portray Khomeini's own disciples as homogenous and blind followers. Their accounts thus overlook the critical role that Khomeini and his lieutenants played in expanding *Velayat-e Faqih* and capturing the state. As I explain in the following chapters, recently released documents reveal Khomeini's outbidding political strategies to overcome his senior clerical rivals before the revolution. Moreover, his close clerical associates pressed him to endow them with more power than he had originally anticipated. He initially resisted the establishment of the Islamic Republican Party (IRP), fearing an anti-clerical public backlash. He approved the first constitutional draft that contained no privilege for the clergy and no reference to *Velayat-e Faqih*. But facing threats from competing clerics, nationalists, and leftists, he eventually consented and funded the formation of a clerical Islamist "party" in 1979.

After the IRP's electoral success in the Constitutional Assembly, his disciples impatiently institutionalized *Velayat-e Faqih* as a bulwark against the growing internal threats. Khomeini put the militant clergy in charge of both the legislative and judicial branches of the government but deliberately prevented his ambitious followers from capturing the presidency. He was concerned that clerical involvement in the daily politics of the executive branch would compromise their religious—and ultimately political—authority. But after the defection of one lay president to the Marxist Islamists, and the assassination of the second lay president by them, Khomeini finally gave in and approved the candidacy of a cleric, Ali Khamenei, for president. Eight years later, Khamenei would succeed Khomeini as the new Guardian Jurist, despite his low religious credentials. For that political transition to take place, Khomeini had to significantly alter his own doctrine of *Velayat-e Faqih* shortly before his death. Otherwise, the state would have fallen into the hands of theologically more qualified competitors who did not adhere to his Islamist ideology.

Despite four decades of relentless efforts to control the clergy and institutionalize a politicized theology as the only legitimate interpretation of Shi'a Islam, Iran's Guardian Jurist remains existentially threatened by the millennia-old theological schools that oppose *Velayat-e Faqih* as a modern and even heretical invention. This perceived threat has shaped Iran's domestic and foreign policy from the prosecution of the war with Iraq and the nuclear program to the ongoing "defense of [Shi'a] shrines" in Syria and Iraq.

The Islamic Republic of Iran, with all its modern institutions and evolving religious character, is a relentlessly changing product of inter- and intra-elite rivalries. To this day, Iranian political elites respond to internal or external conflicts by devising ideational interpretations and innovations and attributing them to Khomeini, the Twelve Shi'a Imams, or Prophet Mohammad. The logic of political competition compels unanticipated ideological twists and turns, because threat perceptions and strategic interests continually shift as the positions of actors within the system change. This is the story of modern Iranian politics—imbued by a wide spectrum of debates ranging from seventh-century Islamic theology to contemporary, democratic and nondemocratic Western political thought. These dialogues are designed to constrain political rivals, change their strategic calculations, and reverse their preferences.

Contributions, Methodology, and Roadmap

This book aims to understand how and why religious discourses evolve in reaction to elite politics. I do not examine them as causes but as outcomes, as well as processes through which elites act, interact, and compete for power. The empirical basis for this argument consists of a detailed period-by-period revisionist account of Iranian politics made possible by copious documents, primarily from Iranian media, multiple archives, and memoirs of key figures of the ruling elite. This is therefore a work of both social science and historical revisionism. I do not propose a theory to explain the Iranian Revolution, the Iran–Iraq War, Iran's domestic politics, foreign policy, nuclear program, or regime durability. Instead, I offer a new framework within which to analyze them. This leads us to revise how we understand these events and issues. Using this new framework, I debunk some existing claims while offering alternative explanations for why events unfolded as they did.

Examining the religious consequences of politics has important theoretical, empirical, and policy implications. Theoretically, this book contributes to the broader rationalist-constructivist debate in political science on the relationship between religion and politics by demonstrating how religious narratives and ideologies are constructed to correspond with the vicissitudes of elite competition in an uncertain climate. It exhibits the contradictory and multidirectional paths that religious narratives can simultaneously embark upon. At any given time, these narratives may take a combination of observable turns to manage the masses from below, elites from the left and right of the political spectrum, and international actors from above. Both international relations and comparativist scholars of religion and politics have largely ignored this colorful collection of properties that ideas can concurrently acquire. Building on international relations and comparative politics literature, I offer a factional level of analysis—distinct from state- and regime-level explanations—to account for the politics of religion. This framework allows me to more accurately analyze the domestic roots of Iran's foreign policy, as well as the international sources of domestic politics and the linkage between this two-level game[15] and ideological discourses.

Empirically, this work sheds light on otherwise overlooked evidence to reveal the extraordinary level of ideational entrepreneurship necessary to preserve elite cohesion and generate mass support in Iran. Breaking binaries such as secular/radical, it aims to show that the emergence of religious narratives is neither accidental nor unidirectional, nor does it occur after behavioral change. Rather, religious ideology is a strategic tool, crafted and deployed intentionally along with, if not before, behavioral change to advance the elites' interests at a given time and place.

Finally, looking at religion as a commodity instrumentally configured to meet specific threats and opportunities can help policymakers better assess the causes and longevity of various ideological narratives, as well as the threat perceptions of their purveyors. I argue that (trans)national groups are not permanently wedded to an ideology. As their positions within the political system change, so too do their threat assessments and consequently the content (not the façade) of their ideological discourses. Understanding the nuances of their ideational trajectories can help us better comprehend these actors' calculations and responses.

Media as a Method

In addition to archival research, theological and military journals, political memoirs, and other original sources, this book relies systematically on the media to follow the development of elite politics in parallel with the process of religious construction in Iran. Daily accounts allow me to unearth the debates, doubts, perceptions, and contingencies that scholars may have overlooked or, more importantly, later considered a given. It is often surprising to see that what is now perceived as a fait accompli was previously only one of several possible outcomes.

Ironically, the media can be a uniquely rich source of information in authoritarian regimes where there is little space for viable civil societies and alternative political parties. The Iranian media often plays the role typically filled by political activists in a more democratic polity. Despite massive censorship and crackdowns, the media (both "old" and "new") remains a critical vehicle for the opposition and dissidents to reach their constituencies and challenge the state by writing "between the lines." Moreover, scholarship on the Iranian media in particular frequently considers the state a monolithic entity and thus views state-controlled media as a unitary actor and mouthpiece of the government. It also focuses on dissident media and the "democratizing" role of the Internet in anti-government protests and the war of narratives with the regime.[16] Iran's contentious factional politics in fact furnish one of the most dynamic media environments among autocracies. While the regime brutally cracks down on dissident media outlets, hundreds of government and semi-governmental papers, websites, blogs, and other social media tools are engaged in highly combative debates on a wide range of issues. These elite media outlets are distinct from the mass media, including state-controlled television and radio, whose function is often limited to that of a traditional government propaganda mouthpiece. Rather than telling people "what to think," the elite media are part of the factional war over "what to think *about*."[17] They discuss specific issues, test certain ideas, and present particular views. Many of these writers and contributors are former or current officials, such as members of parliament, ministers, etc., while others may not hold office but are directly linked to top officials—effectively unofficial officials. Both groups, particularly the latter, play a critical role in promoting certain policies at the elite level.

These media outlets constitute the extension of the fourth branch of the government. Instead of acting as a link between citizens and leaders, they serve as mediators between state elites. They are also unofficial traders of information, policies, and debates with other states. Having a ubiquitous presence in major policymaking decisions, they chronicle ongoing debates in the highest offices and often signal what will ultimately become the state's official policy. Thus, the elite media are less interested in shaping public opinion than in forming the strategic interests of the state, regime, or factions.

This is a cost-efficient method of promoting policies because it allows the players to prepare the audience for a policy while leaving the door open for reinterpreting or backtracking on a proposed change. Therefore, even state media should not be dismissed as mere propaganda but rather viewed as a dynamic platform through which ruling factions debate, dispute, demote, or promote particular policies. The media is thus an invaluable source of information and analysis for social scientists, who too often neglect it in favor of personal interviews, secondary sources, or public polling to develop or test theories in autocracies.[18] It is an especially crucial source for studying elite-level politics in Iran.

Much of my work relies on four decades of post-revolutionary Iranian media from a wide range of political perspectives, including nationalist, Marxist, Islamist, and reformist groups. Complemented by other primary and secondary sources—including theological writings, state-owned and independent academic journals, declassified documents from U.S. archives, and other materials—I construct a metaphorical motion picture whose scenes will be examined frame by frame. This approach allows me to highlight new empirical evidence with significant theoretical implications that should point to the endogeneity of religion.

This book offers a within-case study of the instrumentalization and evolution of religious discourses by political elites across six decades of Iran's domestic and international politics. Employing process tracing,[19] I closely examine the locus of ideas in a causal sequence. Studying elites in the same political environment allows me to more effectively isolate causality and explain their multifinality and divergent ideological paths while controlling for exogenous factors.[20] In addition to the aforementioned overarching argument, each chronologically ordered chapter provides a revisionist account of a specific period of Iran's recent history, presenting a stand-alone argument for that period and shedding new light on various aspects of the country's domestic politics and foreign policy. Although religious narratives are the unifying theme throughout the book, some chapters concentrate less on discursive politics and pay more attention to the logic of factional politics at specific critical junctures.

Chapter 1 lays out the theoretical argument at the intersection of comparative politics and international relations on the one hand, and rationalism and constructivism on the other. Chapters 2 and 3 examine state–mosque relations in Iran and Khomeini's constitutionalist and Islamist discourses aimed at uniting the clergy, forging an alliance with the nationalists, and establishing his religious authority leading up to the 1979 revolution. Chapter 4 focuses on how the intensification of the competition with the nationalists and orthodox clergy prompted the Islamists to unearth *Velayat-e Faqih* after the revolution and institutionalize it via the constitution. Chapter 5 looks at the communist threat to the new political order in the immediate wake of the revolution, the Islamists' subsequent adoption of anti-Americanism, and the seizure of the U.S. embassy in November 1979. Chapter 6 details the factional sources and ideological consequences of the Iran–Iraq War (1980–1988), revealing how the Islamist–nationalist rivalry and the IRGC-army competition eventually turned into an intra-Islamist competition between the Islamic Republican Party and the IRGC. Chapter 7 traces the unintended discursive consequences of the war, including the formulation of Absolute *Velayat-e Faqih*.

Chapter 8 argues that Khomeini's successors used his *Velayat-e Faqih* selectively to remain in or return to power. A fruit of this political rivalry was constructions of new ultraconservatism and religious pluralism, which led to the confrontation of political Islam and civil Islam. If the political competition over religious ideas had been rooted in academic, theological, or intellectual circles in the late 1980s and early 1990s, it permeated the media and public discourse with the reform movement in 1997. Chapter 9 proposes that the reformists and conservatives endeavored to bring those discussions and, more importantly, their daily social and political implications to debates in the public sphere in order to expand their popular support and further open the electoral process in the lead-up to the 2009 Green Movement. Chapter 10 examines the simultaneous ideational threat that the reformists, a Turkish "moderate" Islamist government, and the then-ruling Egyptian Muslim Brotherhood posed to the incumbent conservatives in Iran. Chapter 11 discusses how new factional coalitions reinterpreted *Velayat-e Faqih* and adopted Persian nationalism before reentering the realm of internal and international politics to shape Iran's regional and nuclear policies and relations with the United States. The final chapter concludes with a discussion of the book's empirical findings, theoretical contributions, and policy implications.

ONE

The Factional Causes and Religious Consequences of Politics

HOW CAN WE EXPLAIN "religious" politics without either essentializing or bypassing religion? Scholarship on religion and politics tends to vacillate between these two extremes. Essentialists and primordialists ascribe to religious actors a set of fixed theological and overpredictive characteristics that determine their behavior,[1] while rationalists focus on strategic interests and view ideology as a "poor predictor" of action.[2] The first group explains political outcomes in terms of the actors' religious doctrines; the inflexibility of religious doctrines leads to radical actions. These studies in general focus on the causal role of religion in the security arena. The second group examines internal political upheavals and religious transformations—particularly the ideological "moderation" of actors—in the context of party politics. They posit that doctrinal changes are a contingent byproduct of the electoral process.

In many of these studies, religious ideology is either a mover or an accidental product of politics. The first considers doctrine as exogenously induced; the second views it as endogenous to electoral politics. The essentialists are concerned with political theology as an independent variable but do not account for observable ideological shifts: political theology consists of long-held static beliefs rather than interpretations that can change in short order. Many rationalists, on the other hand, address it as an outcome of behavioral change. Absent in the literature is a micro-level causal analysis of theological shifts. This theophobia has led to a number of shortcomings. Falling into one-dimensional spectrums and binaries such as radical/moderate, social scientists often study religious ideologies as unitary and unidirectional. They do not account for the collection of contradictory attributes that religious discourse can possess.

This book studies religion and politics by studying both religion and politics instead of fixating on one at the expense of the other. It aims to explain how elites strategically construct religious doctrines in an uncertain environment. It focuses on religion not as an independent variable, nor a constitutive factor, nor an accidental outcome, but as a strategic construct with which political actors strive to capture the state.

I use an "extreme" case whose politics have been deeply imbued with religious ideology for the last half century. As an "instance of a class of events,"[3] Iran is often employed by social scientists to demonstrate the resurgence of religion and its undeniable role in international politics. Because it is an "Islamic" state led by "God's representative on earth," Iran can provide us with a unique analytical edge to study the role of religion in politics. Therefore, it should be the least likely case in which religious doctrines alter. Yet religious discourse in Iran has taken a variety of quietist, revolutionary, statist, reformist, pragmatic, and ultraconservative turns. These narratives have emerged or faded in direct response to inter- and intra-elite rivalries during the 1979 revolution, the post-revolutionary civil wars, the Iran–Iraq War, the reform era, the Green Movement, the nuclear negotiations, the conflicts in Iraq and Syria, etc.

This chapter lays out my argument on the strategic construction and deployment of religious doctrines by political elites, which has been a dominant yet overlooked feature of Iranian politics since the revolution. I introduce a factional level of analysis and argue that political actors, be they incumbents or challengers, employ a diverse range of religious ideologies to capture the state through various means, including generating mass mobilization and preventing elite defections. I begin with an overview of the literature on the role of religion in politics before examining the rationalist and constructivist explanations of ideological change.

Religion: A Sticky Model or a Plastic Tool?

Religion may be considered divine and immutable, but its interpretation is fluid and subject to human susceptibility to fear and greed. Religious symbols and narratives may solve what Max Weber called the masses' "problem of meaning,"[4] but they can also help elites overcome the collective action problem.[5] These "cultural subsystems" may be a "blueprint" for action as well as a "model of" and "model for" reality.[6] They can also be manipulated by elites who seek to challenge the givenness of one political order and give meaning to another. In other words, religious ideology is what elites make of it.

This tension between the devout yet utility-maximizing masses and the elites has shaped much of the primordialist, constructivist, and rationalist studies of religion and ethnicity in recent decades. Going beyond "thick description," scholars have endeavored to wed nonmaterial factors with positivist methodology to arrive at generalizable conclusions. Ann Swidler analyzes culture as a "tool kit" and an independent variable that shapes action.[7] David Laitin looks at how an externally imposed hegemony determines which cultural subsystems, including religion, will be politically salient and thus used instrumentally by elites.[8] Lisa Wedeen conceptualizes culture as meaning-making practices that "produce observable political effects" such as compliance.[9] Sheri Berman traces how different "programmatic beliefs" resulted in diverging institutions and polities in Europe after World War I.[10] Even scholars who ignored ideational factors were forced to make theoretical adjustments in reaction to real-world events. Theda Skocpol, facing criticism in the aftermath of the Iranian Revolution of 1979—the very year her book, *States and Social Revolutions*, was published—struggled to explain why her theory could not account for an urban-based movement that toppled a strong state whose fifth-mightiest army in the world remained intact.[11] Although Skocpol had initially dismissed any role for ideology, she later conceded that "Islam was both organizationally and culturally crucial to the making of the Iranian Revolution against the Shah."[12]

In the four decades since the Iranian Revolution and more recently, particularly after the September 11 attacks in 2001, a new wave of studies has emerged to examine the "resurgence" of religion. Many scholars and policymakers have sought to account for the role of ideology but have gone to the other extreme, perceiving religious actors (from the Islamic Republic of Iran to the Islamic State of Iraq and Syria) as primarily driven by doctrines and dedicated to replacing the international order with their own divine outlook. They argue that religious groups pursue interests and goals constitutively different from those the rest of the world has seen. These scholars strive to unearth the roots of each group's actions from its doctrinal claims and theological rhetoric to explain its resilience and success. In other words, what scholars claim is often similar to what these groups claim about themselves.

Even rationalist and institutionalist studies often view actors as constrained or motivated by institutionalized doctrines. Daniel Philpott posits that institutional differentiation and long-held political theology are the two independent variables that explain why some actors resort to violence while others pursue democratic goals.[13] Monica Toft argues that civil wars in the Muslim world are particularly violent because "Islam has Jihad."[14] Elites outbid each other by manipulating the built-in violent elements of religion; thus, "religion often leads to uncompromising demands."[15] Despite their differences, these explanations take ideational factors as exogenous. Political elites use ideas that are *available* to them rather than *crafting* their own. There is an inherent limitation in "available" ideas, this literature postulates: "[e]ven given some liberty in translation over time, religious texts and interpretations circumscribe the conduct of followers in important ways."[16]

These works focus on the restrictive and yet explanatory power of culture, religion, or ideology—how they produce different institutions or regime types, contribute to their survival, or mobilize the masses. But few scholars have traced the ideational implications and consequences of these phenomena. If religion was a cause of the Iranian Revolution and later contributed to one of the longest wars of the twentieth century with Iraq, did the revolution and war themselves shape Islamic narratives as well? Were the leaders of the revolution aware of the political utility of Islam? If yes, how did this self-awareness play into the Iranian politics during the revolution and war? Just as scholars are cognizant of the power of ideas, so are the actors on the ground.

It is precisely this reflexive step that many scholars do not account for: the agential power of political actors who intentionally develop and deploy ideas despite the limitations of their cultural toolkits and religious blueprints, as well as any structural or path-dependent obstacles. As Laitin points out, actors—particularly during times of crisis—move away from ready-made cultural tools toward strategic calculations.[17] In other words, increased "uncertainty breeds rationality"[18] and induces further ideological shifts. Consider Iranian activists, such as Ali Shariati and Ayatollah Khomeini, who turned Shi'a Islam from a passive and quietist religion to a revolutionary ideology in the 1970s. Of the Twelve Shi'a Imams, only one revolted against an oppressive ruler in the seventh century. The rest (with the exception of the Hidden Imam, who is presumed to be in occultation[19] since 941 A.D.) remained silent and even made peace with an unjust caliph. Yet Iranian Islamists turned the anomaly (Imam Hossein's uprising) into a rule, providing a revolutionary reading of Islam that appealed to the population at large in 1979. It is this level of analysis that forces us to study ideas as a variable shaped by goal-oriented actors to bring about structural transformations. In contrast to what Berman demonstrates in the post–World War I European cases[20]—in which ideas predict actors' choices even when the political environment shifts—ideational factors did not automatically dictate actors' choices in Iran. Rather, ideologies themselves changed in response to the available strategic options and were effectively deployed to generate the desired institutional outcomes.

Ideationist theories become even more problematic when analyzing the post-Khomeini order, both internally and internationally. They do not adequately explain why Khomeini's disciples split and arrived at diametrically opposed ideological destinations. Why did the radical Islamists who occupied the U.S. embassy and brought down the nationalist Provisional Government in 1979 become avid proponents of democracy and rapprochement with the United States two decades later? Why did the conservatives who initially advocated more pragmatic foreign and economic policies later adopt their radical leftist rivals' anti-Americanism? Some scholars' responses to these questions often revolve around intellectual learning processes at critical junctures as a result of new experiences.[21] Social constructivists maintain that elites' preferences are driven by their ideational exposures,[22] asserting that it is the content of their cognitions, exogenous to material features, that influence their actions. Political actors' cognitive systems remain stable even when their material interests change. Iranian radicals matured after the revolution, learned from the negative experience of the Iran–Iraq War, and transformed after the collapse of the Soviet Union and the "end of history," so the argument goes. They went back to school, studied liberal philosophy, delved into a democratic literature, and thus put aside their revolutionary excesses, emerging as reformists. But several empirical questions remain unanswered. What explains the variation in the learning processes? All political factions were exposed to similar aforementioned systemic experiences (i.e., the Iran–Iraq War) and ideas—why did only some "learn" while others did not? In fact, the conservatives "un-learned" and "un-moderated," even though they were immersed in the same political environment. While in some cases ideas may predict an actor's choices even when the political environment shifts,[23] I argue that actors also craft specific ideas targeting the available choices, particularly when circumstances on the ground change. The same actors develop dissimilar ideas when positioned in a different environment. In other words, *the strategic options available to political actors in a given context predict their ideological dispositions.*

Ideationist and Rationalist Explanations of "Moderation"

In recent years, rationalist scholars of ethnic politics have incorporated analytical tools from the constructivist literature to study ethnicity as a consequence, not a cause, of political violence. Rejecting primordialist views, they argue that while ethnicity has no explanatory power for ethnic violence, the social construction of ethnicity does. Bringing constructivism into a rational choice framework, James Fearon and David Laitin point out a path in which intergroup rivalry may lead to redefining the boundaries and content of the ethnicity and the construction of antagonistic ethnic identities.[24] In this context, the construction of ethnic identity is merely strategic. Similarly, Stathis Kalyvas shows how incumbent states encourage rebel defections by manipulating and adding new political dimensions to ethnic identities. He focuses on the "identity consequences of civil war" and demonstrates the "multidirectional empirical prediction (i.e., toward both hardening and softening of ethnic identities)."[25]

This framework has yet to penetrate the study of religion and politics, particularly of the Middle East. Ironically, in his own work on religious parties, Kalyvas adheres to a strict rationalist perspective to explain what he considers a unidirectional and accidental outcome: religious "moderation." Referring to the European Christian Democrats in the nineteenth century, he argues that in reaction to electoral and nonelectoral institutional constraints, religious parties generally tend to move to the center. When in the minority, they join a secular coalition to win elections. When in the majority, powerful institutions such as the military may overthrow them if they do not put aside their religious identity. Therefore, they compromise with diverse political groups to create a centrist, cohesive, and united coalition. According to his theory, the politicization of religion leads to the unintentional secularization of religion. This contingent outcome is not the result of an "exogenously induced adaptation" but rather a response to "endogenous constraints."[26] Kalyvas shares Skocpol's view that ideology, including religious ideology, is a "poor predictor" of political events and actions.[27] By considering religion without its theological baggage, Kalyvas and other rationalists uncover the ideological roots of secular parties and movements, as well as the economic foundation of religious pluralism.[28]

Scholars of authoritarianism, too, have broken away from long-held Orientalist explanations, applying similar rationalist-institutionalist frameworks to the Middle East. Following in Kalyvas's footsteps, Vali Nasr has explained that the rise of "Muslim democrats" in Turkey was similar to that of the Christian Democrats in Europe. He argues that "it is the imperative of competition inherent in democracy that will transform the unsecular tendencies of Muslim Democracy into long-term commitment to democratic values."[29] These parties moderate to take advantage of new political opportunities and reduce state repression. The scholarly focus here is on street-level pragmatic actors rather than religious interpreters:

> Muslim democracy rests not on an abstract, carefully thought-out theological and ideological accommodation between Islam and democracy, but rather on a practical synthesis that is emerging in much of the Muslim world in response to the opportunities and demands created by the ballot box.[30]

Although they focus on the role of ideas, "inclusion-moderation" theorists likewise posit that in nonliberal democratic polities, behavioral change precedes ideological modification. They assert that factors such as political opportunity structures, internal practices and organizations, the emergence of new ideas and narratives, and state–mosque relations explain which Islamist parties are inclined to moderate. Jillian Schwedler considers internal debate to be a critical factor in the embrace of pluralistic principles by Islamist parties.[31] Democratic structures and the existence of a level of tolerance within Jordan's Islamic Action Front (IAF) led this party toward ideological moderation. In contrast, because Yemen's Islah party did not enjoy a united moderate leadership, it could not take advantage of the state's political opening to become behaviorally moderate and, eventually, ideologically moderate.

Although some scholars, including Nathan Brown and Schwedler,[32] emphasize both political opportunity structures and ideological debates, many others view moderation as a possible outcome of political participation. In short, while religious parties matter, religion itself does not. Tarek Masoud pleads "guilty" that his book, *Counting Islam: Religion, Class, and Elections in Egypt*, does not focus on religion at all:

> This book aims to treat Islamist parties not as "ideas or tides" or as elements of a diffuse social movement seen only obliquely in patterns of headscarf wearing, beard growing, or mosque attendance but as *political organizations* with strategies and resources that can be observed directly and measured with precision.[33]

But, as I argue below, religious ideas are part and parcel of the strategies and resources that religious parties—precisely as political organizations—use, thereby meriting serious study.

Depicting one-dimensional spectrums, the rationalist literature tends to view religious ideologies as unitary and their evolution as unidirectional and unintentional. This perspective does not account for the collection of contradictory attributes that religious discourse can alternatively, simultaneously, and strategically possess. Indeed, many scholars have recently acknowledged the compartmentalized nature of "moderation" and questioned its sequencing logic.[34]

In their struggle for power, Islamist actors can appropriate, deappropriate, and reappropriate a variety of often conflicting principles from liberalism and authoritarianism to secularism, "fundamentalism," anti-Americanism, capitalism, socialism, nationalism, etc. What scholars often call secularization or "moderation" can be a combination of inconsistent, selective, compartmentalized, and reversible attributes that accompany, not follow, behavioral change. For instance, the journey of Iran's radical Islamists toward establishing a reformist party headed by former president Khatami began with a gradual appreciation and incorporation of religious pluralism while simultaneously maintaining antagonism toward American imperialism and liberal economic policies. They were "moderate" in domestic political affairs but remained initially "radical" in their foreign and economic policy. By contrast, Iran's pragmatists—led by former president Rafsanjani—initiated a state-capitalist economic program, relaxed restrictions on social issues, and moved toward improving relations with the West, but remained autocratic. The two camps, initially rivals, eventually united in appearing as proponents of both liberal economic and democratic policies. Their coalition brought the reformist Khatami and pragmatist Hassan Rouhani to the presidency in 1997 and 2013, respectively.

Between 2005 and 2013, Iran's conservative president Mahmoud Ahmadinejad went from touting an apocalyptic plan to expedite the return of the Hidden Imam to espousing a nationalist invocation of the founder of the Persian empire, Cyrus the Great; his advocacy of women's rights reflected parallel fluctuations. Vacillating between conflicting policies and narratives, each of these factions displayed some elements of moderation by tolerating certain pluralistic or nonreligious characteristics but not others. Therefore, "moderation" is a fluid and yet narrow (indeed, normative) term that does not capture the multitude of fickle features a party can simultaneously possess—at any given time as well as across time. Perhaps more than anything else, the term reflects the preoccupation of academics and policymakers with particular readings of secularization and liberalization.[35]

Equally salient, elites' adoption of pluralistic values is not a one-way street. As the internal political landscape shifts, so do elites' perceptions of their interests and threats. They may "regress" just as they "progress." Ayatollah Khomeini's interpretation and use of Islam radicalized drastically as he was challenged, particularly by communist and armed groups. In the late 1970s, he promoted a democratic and peaceful version of Islam to unite opposition groups against the Shah and convince the United States to cease supporting the monarch. Once he came to power and nationalist, communist, and separatist groups challenged his new regime, Khomeini pivoted to a violent brand of Islam that justified liquidating all those who "declared war against God." A decade later, his revolutionary Islam morphed into "pragmatism" that sanctified any action deemed necessary to preserve the Islamic state, even those breaching Islamic law. Fearful that rivals would inherit such power, conservative figures such as then-president Ali Khamenei attempted to downplay Khomeini's declaration that the survival of the state (and by definition the authority of the Leader) superseded all laws, including Islamic law. But when Khamenei became the Supreme Leader himself, he (now *Ayatollah Khamenei*) expanded the authority of the Guardian Jurist beyond his predecessor's claims and even into the citizens' private spheres.

On the international level, constructivists and rationalists struggle to explain Iran's behavior as well. Constructivists claim that Iran's foreign policy is a manifestation of its mixed religious, nationalist, and anti-Western identity,[36] a "historically driven way of perceiving the world."[37] Thus, Iran's anti-Americanism was the result of the Islamists' hatred of the West. Mohammad Khatami's moderate foreign policy era should "reflect a broader transformation in the political articulation of Iranian post-revolutionary identity that was generated by the convergence of Khomeini's death and the war's conclusion and accelerated by the unfettering of public debate via the Khatami-era media renaissance."[38] Likewise, the rise of the neoconservatives led by Mahmoud Ahmadinejad in 2005 heralded a new era of regional adventurism for Iran.[39] An extreme essentialist view ascribes Iran's nuclear program to its leaders' purported messianic beliefs. To Princeton historian Bernard Lewis, because Iranian clerics "are religious fanatics with an apocalyptic mindset . . . mutually assured destruction is not a deterrent—it's an inducement."[40] A dovish constructivist version, on the other hand, describes the nuclear program as a manifestation of Iran's historical quest for independence, self-sufficiency, and dignity.[41] Although this literature on ideological changes can be immensely rich, it can suffer the pitfall of an essentialist explanation of Iranian politics, failing to accurately explain the mechanism of ideational change or account for variation in the adoption or rejection of an ideology by the same political actors.

For realists, Iran may pose an ideal hard case with which to prove that ideology does not matter and that all states are driven primarily by their security interests.[42] Contradicting its religious rhetoric, Iran has purchased weapons from Israel in its war against its fellow Muslim Iraqis,[43] allied with Christian Armenia against Shi'a Azerbaijan, worked with the secular Tajik government against an Islamist opposition, and remained silent while its Russian and Chinese partners cracked down on their Muslim populations.[44] But if ideology is irrelevant, what explains the massive and costly production—and ceaseless use—of religious ideologies and narratives by Iranian elites in the foreign policy arena? Why, for example, the overwhelming presence of ideology in Iran's strategic war planning and tactical battlefield operations against Iraq in the 1980s and ISIS in the 2010s?

Granted, rationalists have not ignored ideology altogether. Some international relations scholars have studied the role of ideational factors in shaping actors' threat perceptions. Expanding on Stephen Walt's balance of threat theory,[45] Gregory Gause goes beyond the state and examines threat perceptions on the regime level.[46] He accounts for the role of religion and identity in Middle East politics by making a distinction between regime security and state interests. Gause argues that transnational and ideological factors such as Islam and Arabism can pose even more direct and immediate threats to the legitimacy of the region's leaders than can military power. He finds that states in the Middle East "overwhelmingly identified ideological and political threats emanating from abroad to the domestic stability of their ruling regimes as more salient than threats based upon aggregate power, geographic proximity, and offensive capabilities."[47] Bringing ideational factors within the realist framework, he demonstrates that for Third World rulers, regime security can take precedence over state security. These leaders use identity, culture, and religion to have "access to the domestic politics of their neighbors"[48] and "expand their influence and at times their territory, appealing to citizens of other states for support against their own governments."[49] Thus, Iran posed a threat to Sunni Saddam Hussein in Iraq by provoking its Shi'a population. In this analysis, religious identity and sectarianism are viewed as a source of power for states. Although this literature lends explanatory power to ideology, it takes it as exogenous and does not account for change in the content of ideology and activation of certain ideational attributes over time. Moreover, the treatment of regimes as monolithic does not capture the highly factional nature of Iranian politics, whose elites have demonstrated remarkable differences over time in their threat perceptions as well as their construction and use of religious identity both internationally and domestically.

Arguments of the Book

Building on the strengths of the previous theories, I situate my arguments at the intersection of international and domestic politics on the one hand and rationalist and constructivist theories on the other: how factions assess threats and seek to craft ideologies to meet their political objectives. This requires expanding the playing field beyond local dynamics to include external causes, catalysts, and contingencies, all of which affect the actors and their interests—and thus their strategic use of religion. I study religion as a subset of ideas that is central to constructivist studies of international relations. However, I employ the theoretical tools of comparativist scholars to "denaturalize"[50] the concept of religious doctrines and capture the malleable, strategic, contingent dimensions of ideas that correspond to elites' threat perceptions in the realist sense.

I borrow the rationalist conceptualization of ideological threat perception and apply it to political factions to account for Iranian elites' behavior in both internal and international arenas. I employ the concept of political faction—a network of loosely connected formal and informal organizations and coalitions—to explain the complexities of threat perception in an authoritarian context where genuine parties cannot properly function. A political faction can be any group of elites, institutions, or parties that targets key elected or appointed bodies to capture the state. I argue that in Iran, factional interests, in addition to overall regime and state security interests, help define foreign and domestic policies. This argument may potentially apply to other electoral autocracies as well.

Factions view ideology as a potent force that can be used to expand popular support, trap competing elites, gain social and political leverage, and thus control the state. War-making and peacemaking decisions, economic measures, and other critical issues often serve to defend the ruling groups and institutions against internal rivals. A ruling faction may opt for foreign policy decisions that are harmful to the state but protect the regime or the ruling faction. Rulers can use international conflicts to marginalize domestic rivals and monopolize other branches and institutions of the (parallel)state. However, these decisions have an important ideological component. For example, Iranian Islamists adopted and maintained a costly anti-American rhetoric, eventually seized the U.S. embassy, and then used the Iran–Iraq War to remove their formidable leftist, liberal, and orthodox clerical rivals from the political scene throughout the 1980s. These events brought hardship, sanctions, and isolation to the state, but they helped consolidate the Islamist faction within the regime. Even though factional, regime, and state interests can be interwoven, if they are at odds, a faction's security concerns can shape its ideological outlook and may take precedence over the interest of the state and regime. Examining both threat perceptions and ideological transformations through this factional lens allows us to more accurately account for contradictions and seemingly irrational foreign and domestic policies.

The international system may force the ruling faction to shift its ideology and pursue pragmatic policies simply to survive. Similarly, internal conflicts can motivate a faction to modify its religious ideologies to maximize its interests at the expense of its rivals. In both circumstances, elites must craft new religious narratives that create political latitudes and opportunities. Islamist parties adjust and institutionalize their religious doctrines to correspond with these shifting, multilevel interests and threats.

However, activists cannot pivot to new ideologies overnight because ideological shifts entail transaction and audience costs, including charges of opportunism and loss of constituencies.[51] This poses additional challenges for ideational entrepreneurs, who must seek to present the façade of their discourse as constant and its development as a natural evolution if they are to reduce conversion costs. One may not recognize the extent and intension of changes that the religious foundation of Iran's political system, *Velayat-e Faqih*, has experienced without a micro-level analysis of both the doctrine itself and its political context over time. In short, transaction costs do not necessarily prevent political actors from making ideological shifts.

In any complex, strategic, interactive, and unpredictable "political and social life,"[52] actors vie not only to anticipate their rival's next move but also to control its range of actions, perceptions, and calculations. Each move is influenced by possible countermoves and the potential impact on the environment as a whole. As Robert Jervis argues, "many of an individual's preferences stem from her position in the social system."[53] Likewise, actors develop discourses that match and advance their position in the political system. Consequently, they engage in a war of narratives to impose "norms" and other ideational restrictions on their competitors and the masses. Thus, ideas and norms are endogenous to interactions: they are not merely social interactions,[54] but also strategic interactions.[55] It is through these processes that such norms are formed, debunked, or sustained.

Process tracing religious narratives against the backdrop of domestic and international politics, I argue that religious ideas provide elites with unmatched resources to demonstrate the legitimacy of a political cause, their ability to deliver, and their commitment to action as well as to instill discipline in the masses in an uncertain climate. Elites generate these discourses in a wide range of circumstances to support their ambitions for regime durability, foreign policy objectives, war conduct, peacemaking, etc. Far from being taken "as if" by nonbelieving, degraded, deconstituted, passive, and complicit people,[56] these ideas are "natural" constructs, presented *as is* to conform with the masses' most potent beliefs and cognitive systems. They do not kill, but rather generate politics; do not depoliticize but mobilize citizens.

Actors re-create specific religious scenes and rituals that speak to the internal or external "imagined community,"[57] its collective memory, past experiences, and ongoing grievances, and generate meaning, purpose, and solidarity for the masses.

These narratives are designed to limit competing elites' choices and trap them into acting accordingly. Consider the reenactment of the battle of Karbala during the revolution and the war. By depicting the Shah as the historically vilified Yazid who martyred Imam Hossein and his followers in 680 A.D., Khomeini induced doubt and fear in the regime's military and political elites, warned soldiers against killing demonstrators, increased the cost of crackdown, and thereby created an opportunity for mass protests that eventually led to the revolution.

Khomeini was nimble in deploying narratives as needed. If for the internal audience, he himself played the revolutionary Hossein, simultaneously he acted as a Gandhi for the international audience to signal a lack of political ambition and a peaceful Islamic nationalist mission for the post-victory era. Later, he emerged as a Lenin to expand his constituencies to include the anti-imperialist leftists. When the pope intervened on behalf of the American hostages in Tehran, Khomeini silenced him by asking why he did not act like Jesus and condemn American crimes against Iran. Later, he shifted back to the battle of Karbala to mobilize hundreds of thousands of volunteers to fight against the Iraqis.

In each case, it was the preferences of the target audience that dictated the specific roles. But it was Khomeini's (the actor's) threat perception that shaped the content of the script. Such image-making would impose not just shame but actual costs on individuals who challenged it. So instead of social norms and symbols entrapping the actors and constituting their strategic interests,[58] it is the actors' strategic interests that determine the salience of their religious norms. Unlike many rationalist social scientists, Khomeini believed in the power of ideas to bring about political change in short order. Unlike many ideationists, he believed in the power of individual agency to construct those ideas to serve specific political objectives. As a result, each scholarly camp has remained troubled by either the rational or the ideational aspect of his strategic construction of religion.

My argument can be summed up as follows. First, elites instrumentally craft and deploy religious ideologies for political gain. Second, these ideologies take various observable twists and turns, and acquire contradictory attributes in different settings corresponding to actors' changing threat perceptions. Third, ideational shifts are not permanent or unidirectional. They are reversible and multidirectional and correlate with changes in elites' locus within the system. Fourth, ideational changes are not the accidental result of political opportunities and (non)electoral constraints, nor are they always natural outcomes of specific learning processes. Rather, elites change religious discourses deliberately and in response to the relative distribution of power within the domestic political system and their position within it. Fifth, elites use religion to manage factional politics. Religious doctrines are relentlessly generated, contested, negotiated, invented, archived, renewed, borrowed, and diffused by competing elites. Political actors reach out to independent intellectuals or incubate their own powerhouses, seeking the development of new suitable ideas, the repair of bruised ones, and the renewal of old ones. Elites adopt alternative jurisprudential, theological, philosophical, and social scientific concepts, methods, and theories to expand the content or boundaries of doctrines and thus deepen or expand constituencies.

TWO

A Shi'a Theory of the State

IN THEIR QUEST to capture the state, Iran's Islamist actors aspired to attain a monopoly over the use of religion. Only the *indisputability* of the "sacredness" of their political cause could guarantee its realization. However, achieving this discursive monopoly necessitated a seamless ecclesiastical concord, a tall order in the decentralized and apolitical Shi'a theology. Led by the Qom-based Ayatollah Khomeini and backed by urban religious and nationalist dissidents, an Islamist faction unleashed a series of political actions that polarized Iranian politics, forcing the clerical establishment as well as the secular opposition to unite behind it. In the process, the Islamists transformed the public understanding of religion's role in politics and governance.

Observers often argue that Iran's clerical movement emerged as a reaction to the Shah's modernizing White Revolution after the 1961 death of Grand Ayatollah Hossein Borujerdi, Qom's Supreme Marja'-e Taqlid (the highest level of Shi'a authority, and the ultimate "model" and "source of emulation"). They also claim that Khomeini was already an established religious scholar before choosing "politics as a vocation"[1] to challenge the Shah's anti-Islamic reforms.[2] However, the empirical evidence suggests that the internal clerical competition to succeed Borujerdi and establish a united religious authority is an overlooked force behind the emerging mosque-state conflict. Khomeini's own confidants now point to both his *political* project and his junior status relative to other clerics and argue that the *disputability* of his jurisprudential credentials informed his political action, which in turn elevated his religious authority.

Khomeini's lack of marja'iyyah credentials compelled him to reach out to reluctant marjas to build a united front against the monarchy. His anti-government political leadership unconventionally helped establish his own marja'iyyah in two stages: first, he led a constitutionalist opposition to the Shah's reforms after Borujerdi's death, culminating in the June 1963 uprisings and the subsequent protest against the immunity granted to U.S. forces stationed in Iran; and second, he presented *Velayat-e Faqih* after the death of Grand Ayatollah Mohsen Hakim (1889–1970), positioning himself to lead an anti-Shah coalition that deposed the monarch in 1979. Khomeini's alternating instrumental adoption of constitutionalism and Islamism corresponded to various phases of these movements, the goal being to institute a coherent religious authority willing to challenge the political authority. These doctrinal maneuverings sought to reduce the likelihood of clerical resistance to the Islamists' opposition to the Shah.

This chapter argues that religion was not only a visionary set of principles with which to establish an "Islamic" state; more importantly, it was an integral part of Khomeini's strategic calculations and daily political struggles. His instrumental use of religion brought him protection against the state and attracted new allies. The nationalists, in search of clerical partners, forged an alliance with Khomeini to leverage his ability to mobilize the masses. In return, they shared their organizational capacity, including a vast network that disseminated his message, channeled religious taxes, and created an opposition formidable enough to undermine the monarchy's international linkages and elite cohesion. He and his Islamist disciples countered every move of the orthodox clergy and the Shah by masterfully deploying religion to create a coherent narrative "obvious" enough for the masses to comprehend, Islamic enough to constrain his clerical enemies, and revolutionary enough to compete with the leftist opposition for young recruits.

Khomeini's depiction of the Shah as "anti-Islam" appealed to the masses and trapped the silent clergy into acquiescence, lest they pay the heavy cost of being the dictator's de facto collaborator. In a classic case of overcoming what the economist Timur Kuran calls "preference falsification,"[3] the Islamists called for demonstrations on religious holidays, which provided immunity and made participants less afraid to come out. There were others whose participation in the uprisings did not necessarily constitute preference revelation, but they were boxed into joining the *Islamic* demonstration. The point here is not to explain the complexity of individuals' motivations but to emphasize how religion played a double role: it provided immunity for anti-Shah elements and compelled bystanders to join.

The chapter begins by examining state–clergy relations before Khomeini's rise. It sheds light on the institutional access the Shah granted the clerical establishment under Borujerdi to shape government policies in return for their endorsement. It then delves into the post-Borujerdi challenges Khomeini faced in disrupting this modus vivendi—disarming the orthodox Shi'a clergy and outmaneuvering competing moderate clerics and other opposition groups—and foreshadows his path to delinking the United States and the army from the Shah and eventually abolishing the monarchy. Finally, it discusses the development of his theological case for clerical control of the state.

The formation of a modern state in Iran prompted the emergence of a strong Shi'a establishment in the country. Reza Shah's (1878–1944) state-building project, centered in Tehran, paralleled Sheikh Abodulkarim Ha'eri-Yazdi's (1859–1937) seminary-building venture in Qom.[4] Located 120 kilometers southwest of Tehran and near the Shrine of Fatima Masumeh (790–816 A.D.; sister of the Eighth Imam, Ali ibn Musa al-Ridha, 765–818 A.D.), Qom has been a center of Shi'a scholarship for centuries. Ha'eri-Yazdi reestablished the seminary in Iran in 1922, but this time primarily with the support of traditional merchants (*bazaaris*) and not through state patronage.[5] Although the secular government usurped much of the clerics' traditional control over law, education, and endowments, the security and development it extended throughout the country contributed to the prosperity and elevation of Qom. As Roy Mottahedeh points out, "Iranians were becoming more nationalistic, and many Iranian mullahs wanted an Iranian center of Shi'a learning on a par with or superior to Najaf, in Iraq."[6] Bitten by the negative experience of the involvement of some Shi'a clerics in the anti-British colonial uprisings in Iraq as well as in the British-backed constitutional movement in Iran, Qom's seminaries would become a quietist center of Shi'a scholarship.

There emerged a new but tumultuous modus vivendi between political and religious authorities in Iran. Reza Khan eschewed his Kemal Ataturk–inspired secular republicanism and vowed to protect the Shi'a nation against communists, Baha'is, and other ideological threats once he took power as Shah in

1925. In the ensuing anti-clerical environment, leading religious figures remained outside politics and quietly strove to forge working relations with
the government that would respect the ecclesiastical institutions' traditional
independence from the state. This strategic decision was consistent with the
doctrine of *mahdaviat*, which repudiated any legitimate government in the
absence of the Twelfth Imam.

Following Ha'eri-Yazdi's death (1937) and Reza Shah's abdication (1941),
Khomeini—who had accompanied the former to Qom as a young student—
joined a campaign to preserve the city as a Shi'a capital and prevent the
seminary's collapse into tribalism.[7] Together with prominent clerics and *bazaaris*, they pleaded with Borujerdi, one of the most prominent sources of
emulation in the Shi'a world, to leave the city of Borujerd in the western province of Lorestan for Qom. Reza Shah's son and successor, Mohammad Reza
Shah, also visited Borujerdi when the latter was hospitalized in 1944. He recognized Borujerdi's spiritual authority and promised to accommodate his religious concerns. "They needed each other, as they were both within a year or
two of assuming real power; they were both worried about the virtual occupation of parts of Iran [by the Allies] and they both disliked the Communists."[8]

Borujerdi accepted the invitation, topped Qom's "Triangle of Ayatollahs,"[9]
and with the death of the Najaf-based Supreme Marja Ayatollah Seyyed Abolhassan Esfahani in 1947, emerged as the Shi'ites' ultimate source of emulation. Once again, Qom became a center of Shi'a theology. The new Shah
granted Borujerdi institutional access[10] to the state to shape policies on the
role of the clergy and the influence of the Baha'i religious minority. As the
Shah nostalgically remembered three decades later on the eve of the revolution, "[a]n understanding between the clergy and the monarchy existed
until the death of Borujerdi. We even postponed agricultural reform during
his lifetime because he disapproved of it."[11] In the following decades, the
clerical establishment remained quietist and united. Even the anti-British
nationalization movement (1951–1953) could not politicize Qom's senior
clergy. Borujerdi congratulated the Shah after the United States' Central Intelligence Agency–led coup brought the king back to power in 1953. The
lower-ranking politically active cleric, Ayatollah Abolghasem Kashani
[1882–1962], who played a leading role in backing Prime Minister Mohammad Mosaddeq's nationalization of oil, later switched to support the Shah as
well. The clergy was the monarch's bulwark against communist and nationalist oppositions.[12]

Borujerdi kept the mosque and the state strictly separate from each other. He established a "board of governance" to settle internal conflicts in Qom and prevent the state's interference in clerical affairs.[13] He often sent his associates, including Khomeini, to convey his requests to political authorities, including to the Shah himself.[14] Qom's seminarians thus jokingly called Khomeini "Borujerdi's foreign minister"[15] in describing their relations. However, this modus vivendi gradually came under attack by both politically informed clerics such as Khomeini and the ascending U.S.-backed Shah. Khomeini urged Borujerdi to stop the state's aggressive secularization policies, first and foremost by purging from the seminaries "pseudo-clerics"—a reference to pro-government seminarians. Khomeini said, "This is like the enemy has attacked you, but someone has handcuffed you from behind . . . If you want to do something, to take over the government, to get the Majles [parliament] to stop corruption, they [pro-regime clerics] will undermine you in society. You first have to deal with them."[16] Khomeini's advice fell on deaf ears. Borujerdi maintained order in Qom's seminaries when several clerics revolted against controversial undertakings such as the possibility of Iran recognizing Israel.[17]

Borujerdi, however, struggled to resist the challenge that young Islamist clerics such as Seyyed Mojtaba Navvab-Safavi (1924–1955) posed to his authority. Influenced by Egypt's Islamist Muslim Brotherhood, Navvab-Safavi was a low-ranking cleric when he cofounded the Militant Society Against Anti-Religiousness—later establishing the Society of Islamic Devotees (Fadayian-e Islam)—to implement what he called "Islamic law." He and his followers plotted and killed Ahmad Kasravi (1890–1946), a prominent secular intellectual and historian, for writing a book on Shi'ism that they deemed offensive. Navvab-Safavi then successfully mobilized the clergy to pressure the Shah into freeing the actual killers. Emboldened, his group assassinated Minister of Court Abdol-Hossein Hajir in 1949 along with several other politicians in the following years.

Navvab-Safavi's fiery speeches against moral corruption and the silence of the clergy soon attracted followers in Qom, Tehran, and other major Iranian cities, who in turn proceeded to disrupt the quietist seminaries. In his book, *Guidelines for Truths*, Navvab-Safavi viciously attacked Borujerdi, accusing him of "using the Prophet's position and Islam's marja'iyyah" to "forge anti-Islamic laws and implement the plots of Islam's enemies."[18] He wrote, "I swear to God that a loyal dog has more dignity than a disloyal person like you!"[19] Navvab-Safavi called for purifying the clergy and removing the marjas who collaborated with the enemies of Islam. Although he was based in Tehran, his supporters swiftly dominated the campus of Qom's prominent Feyzieh Theological School.[20]

Struggling to maintain authority, Borujerdi expressed no tolerance for Navvab-Safavi's demands and ordered his students to beat the young Islamists and banish them from Feyzieh; the seminaries and seminarians had to be cleansed from politics. Borujerdi deliberately did not call the police and the army, partly to protect the independence of his territory and partly to neutralize Navvab-Safavi's charges that he was co-opted by the regime. The chaos ended and order was reestablished without the need for government intervention in this internal clerical affair. Navvab-Safavi and his militant followers were eventually arrested and sentenced to death for assassinating those whom they called "anti-Islamic" officials and "heretic" intellectuals. Borujerdi's determination to keep Qom neutral alienated some of his associates, including Khomeini, who had pleaded with him to intervene and ask the Shah to commute the Fadayians' sentences. As Khomeini's daughter, Zahra Mostafavi, recalled forty-three years later in a newspaper interview, her father came home, angrily threw his garb (*aba*) on the floor, and said to his wife that he could not convince Borujerdi to protect Navvab-Safavi: "He [Borujerdi] said, 'I have nothing to do with these [government-related] affairs.' "[21]

The remaining Fadayians went to prison or fled underground, but they would join Khomeini's movement several years later. Khomeini's successor, Supreme Leader Ayatollah Ali Khamenei, has claimed that attending Navvab-Safavi's sermon at a seminary in Mashhad when he was only fourteen "lit the first fire" of an Islamist movement in his heart.[22] The execution of Navvab-Safavi—a "descendant" of the Prophet—by the secular Shah had a chilling effect on the clergy, particularly the fiery younger generation. However, the Fadayian movement demonstrated to the increasing number of restless seminarians and even lay activists the effectiveness of deploying religion to challenge the state. Outside the quietist seminaries, anti-Shah resentment was growing among nationalists, leftists, and traditional *bazaaris*.

Nevertheless, Khomeini, who had closely observed or even personally knew the leading clerical figures of the constitutional and nationalization eras (namely Hassan Modarres [1870–1937] and Kashani), reluctantly remained quiet and in the shadow of Borujerdi for years. Relations between the two deteriorated to the point that Khomeini was not even welcome in Borujerdi's home. In addition to administrative conflicts over curriculum development within Iran's network of Shi'a seminaries,[23] Borujerdi reportedly viewed

Khomeini as a co-conspirator behind the Fadayians' activities.[24] In one incident, Khomeini was ignored for hours in Borujerdi's waiting room, after which he promised to "never set foot in this house again."[25] Yet according to one of Khomeini's students, he was prudent enough to continue attending Borujerdi's classes and not isolate himself.[26] The young Khomeini would not join a political movement without the blessing of a marja, let alone confront a marja.

The Islamists' (Anti-)Clerical Movement

In March 1961, Borujerdi died, and with him the centralized Supreme Marja. With the disappearance of a united quietist religious authority, the incumbent monarch, Qom's divided clerics, and the fragmented nationalist opposition began strategizing for a new religious order. Within the state, there emerged debate on (a) whether the marja'iyyah should stay in Iran or be transferred back to Iraq and (b) whether it should remain central under a single Supreme Marja or be divided among several ayatollahs. The Shah had reduced the nationalist and communist threats through co-optation and elimination. He concluded that the benefits of keeping the prestigious and lucrative institution in Qom no longer outweighed the conservative cost it imposed on the regime's modernizing efforts.[27] His condolences to Najaf-based Ayatollah Hakim were largely interpreted as a shift in his preferences toward both moving the Shi'a epicenter to Iraq and splintering Iran's clerical establishment.

Unable to agree on the next religious authority, a new "triangle" of competing ayatollahs emerged from Borujerdi's shadow: Ayatollahs Mohammad Reza Golpayegani, Shahab al-Din Mar'ashi-Najafi, and Kazem Shariatmadari, each with followers derived from their respective home regions. The majority of senior clerics hoped for a new understanding with the mighty Shah. They were particularly fearful that communists would claim the clerical establishment's moral authority and penetrate Iranian society with their powerful ideology.

But public reactions to Borujerdi's death were so overwhelming that even Qom's seminarians and U.S. officials were taken aback. One young theologian remembered how the heartfelt sorrow evident throughout the country was a "slap on the mouth of Marxist-communist propaganda" by demonstrating Islam's—and thereby the clergy's—continued popularity.[28] The forty-day mourning for Borujerdi "brought religion forward by 40 years and pushed communism back by 40 years."[29] Similarly, the U.S. consul in Tabriz noted that Borujerdi's death led to "the most impressive public reaction of recent years" in Azerbaijan. He downplayed its political significance but added that "the speed with which [black] flags appeared and groups gathered at appointed places demonstrated the local discipline as well as the zeal of Shi'a Islam."[30] Relying on the perceived deeply rooted popularity of Borujerdi's legacy, the orthodox establishment remained adamant in following his apolitical footsteps and maintaining the old modus vivendi with the Shah. This preference, however, did not bode well given the increasing discontent in urban religious circles; nor did it correspond to the Shah's upcoming social and economic plans.

Those in nationalist opposition and affluent urban religious circles expected a more politicized religious authority against the political, social, and economic encroachments of the state. Borujerdi's death coincided with the establishment of the Freedom Movement by a group of young religious activists who split from the secular National Front opposition. Led by a French-educated engineer, Mehdi Bazargan, and Ayatollah Mahmoud Taleqani, and blessed by the exiled hero of the nationalization movement, Mohammad Mosaddeq, the Freedom Movement looked for a strategic partnership with Qom's new marjas against the Shah. At a time when the Shah had successfully cracked down and divided the opposition, this group of religiously oriented Iranian nationalists viewed the clergy as the last remaining force with a historically proven ability to mobilize the masses.

In a 1962 national award-winning edited volume that predated and paralleled Khomeini's future doctrine of *Velayat-e Faqih*, Bazargan and several other lay and clerical activists pressed the sources of emulation to enter the political realm. In his own chapter, Bazargan argued that there was a dangerous imbalance between what the nation demanded and what the Islamic jurists supplied. While the people expected decisive political leadership, the clerics were occupied with the minutiae of religious interpretation surrounding praying, ablution, and breastfeeding. He argued that the comprehensive religion of Islam, which pays attention to such detailed personal matters, must have plans for macro social and political issues as well. He called for a "real Islamic government" that was national, democratic, and under the clergy's supervisory leadership.[31] Naming and shaming pro-regime clerics as the gravest threat to Islam, he deliberately increased the cost of any clerical association with the monarchy or any tolerance of its policies. He wrote that if the clergy is "divine, it has to be useful to society."

In the midst of a debate and competition over the direction of marja'iyyah, Bazargan was carefully presenting Qom's seminary with two options: (a) rupture with the past and leap into the modern world to lead a restless society; or (b) become increasingly archaic and irrelevant. He effectively signaled readiness to bring the nationalists' political machinery and financial resources behind the next generation of sources of emulation. Their decades-old organizational experience, comparable only to that of the communists, could disseminate the clerics' messages and attract religious taxes and political support from the urban lower and middle classes, the merchants, and the educated professionals. This could in turn provide more stipends for seminarians, more representatives throughout the country, more followers, and more power to the anti-Shah clergy.

Similar tensions were simmering in Qom. A few senior clerics, including Shariatmadari and Khomeini, viewed the power vacuum as an opportunity to establish a new religious authority that met the above-mentioned external demands. Unlike Shariatmadari, an established first-rate marja with followers and vast financial resources, Khomeini was low ranking in terms of scholarly reputation, number of students, and religious donations.[32] As President Hassan Rouhani, a young seminarian at the time, acknowledges in his memoir, few considered Khomeini a source of emulation.[33] Khomeini had gained prominence as a learned cleric, but not quite a mainstream theologian. He taught primarily not jurisprudence but philosophy and mysticism, both of which were looked down upon—or even considered heretical—by many of his orthodox colleagues. People flooded the homes of well-established ayatollahs in Qom, including Golpayegani, and escorted them to mourning ceremonies for Borujerdi. No one stepped into Khomeini's home except his protégé, Hossein-Ali Montazeri.[34] Due to his philosophical, mystical, and political tendencies, many students avoided his classes.[35] By Qom's scholastic standards, it would take Khomeini decades to match his superiors' authority, if it were possible for him to do so at all. Perhaps his junior status and concerns over how senior clerics might react contributed to his reluctance to publish a *resalah*, a treatise essential for any aspiring marja.

Notwithstanding these deficiencies, Khomeini would rise to lead the clerical establishment, and eventually the broader opposition to the Shah. Backed by an extensive network of religious and nationalist opposition groups, he would establish his marja'iyyah by compensating for his low jurisprudential status with political activism. He would unleash a series of protests against the

Shah's reforms, generating political action and new alliances that would bring prominence and unity to religious authority under his leadership. As described in the next section, his outbidding moves would drag other clerics into an unwanted confrontation with the state and attract veteran urban oppositions.

Prime Minister Assadollah Alam's controversial 1961 local council elections bill consisted of enfranchising women and permitting officials to be sworn in on any holy book, not just the Quran. Ayatollahs Golpayegani, Mar'ashi-Najafi, Shariatmadari, and Khomeini met at Ha'eri-Yazdi's (the founder of Qom's modern seminary) house to develop a strategy against the government's "un-Islamic" acts. Shariatmadari and Khomeini were more eager than the other two to challenge the state. Unable to reach an agreement, they decided to issue separate statements condemning Alam's decree.

Although Khomeini took a constitutionalist approach to maintain the minimum clerical unity,[36] he outbid the others by sending more assertive telegrams to the government demanding the law's repeal. Not only did he send audacious letters to the Shah and Prime Minister Alam, but with limited access to copy machines, he stayed up night after night, writing hundreds of letters to other clerics all over the country and the region to inform them of the new calamity against Islam.[37] The Shah responded to others, but not to Khomeini, by dismissively addressing them as *Hojjat al-Islam*, a significantly lower ranking title than ayatollah, implying that the site of religious authority was now in Najaf.[38] He reminded them that as a devout Shi'ite, he was no less concerned with religious duties, and that the clergy was well advised to notice that the world had changed thanks to science and technology. He also ended the telegram by wishing them divine help in their duty to work with the "commoners." Qom's clerics perceived this line to be particularly offensive, since many interpreted it as suggesting that statesmanship and governance were the realms of modern elites, technocrats, and scientists, not backward clerics.[39]

Several senior clerics softened their position but privately emphasized that they could not remain silent if Khomeini was speaking up.[40] Khomeini issued a fatwa banning quietist citizens from practicing *taqiyya* (loosely translated as dissimulation) as justification for their inaction.[41] Meanwhile, urban-based Islamist activists mushroomed to pressure quietist clerics to join Khomeini and other radical clerics, distribute their messages in cities, and coordinate, if not enforce, worker strikes.[42]

After a series of concessions, Alam eventually withdrew the entire bill. This brought credibility to Qom's clerical establishment and above all to Khomeini, whose unanswered telegram to the Shah had already increased his popularity, as evidenced by a dramatic rise in religious taxes and donations he received. While few had paid Khomeini religious taxes before, many—particularly from Tehran—turned to him in the aftermath of the local council controversy.[43] According to SAVAK (the Shah's secret service) documents, Khomeini's "sahm-e imam" [imam's share] jumped from thirty thousand to four hundred thousand tomans in the first month after the state–clergy conflict began. In the same time frame, Ayatollah Ahmad Khansari's quietist stance reduced his alms by 50 to 75 percent.[44] Even army colonels secretly visited Khomeini and paid him religious taxes.[45] With the rise in his fame, followers, and flowing cash, his associates quickly put together his *resalah* and arranged stipends for seminarians.[46] The nationalist Freedom Movement began to notice not just Shariatmadari but also the more politically savvy Khomeini.

Emboldened by the victory, Khomeini was determined to "keep the oven [of struggle against the Shah] hot" by generating religiously motivated political action.[47] In a traditional environment in which the clergy considered listening to radio to be anti-religious, Khomeini gave money to his student, Akbar Hashemi Rafsanjani, to secretly purchase a radio and inform him of the latest political developments.[48] He aspired to consolidate the emerging religious unity by opposing the Shah's White Revolution, a series of economic and social reforms initiated in 1963, partly under pressure from U.S. president John F. Kennedy.

Some of the provisions of the White Revolution, particularly land reforms, angered the clerics, who had already lost control—even over religious endowments—to the state. They could not sanction measures against landowners, many of whom followed their obligations to pay religious taxes. Clerics themselves were landowners or beneficiaries of endowed lands, and they received religious taxes from landowners. Because of the unified clerical opposition in Qom under Borujerdi, the Shah waited until after the Supreme Marja's death to implement reforms. Starting first with the introduction of land reforms, he planned to follow with other measures, including enfranchising women, nationalizing forests, and establishing literacy, health, and religious corps. As Ayatollah Montazeri (a young seminarian at the time) acknowledged later, a few clerics—including his mentor Khomeini—feared that opposing White Revolution provisions such as land reform and the literacy corps would lead peasants and the more progressive urban population to rebel against the clergy.[49] After all, it is widely recognized among Muslims that true Islam backs poor peasants against rich landowners, and its prophet instructed followers to "seek knowledge even in China." So instead, Khomeini invoked a constitutional argument against the referendum itself, not the provisions: as long as there was the Majles (parliament), the Shah had no right to call for a national referendum to legitimize the White Revolution. His appeal entailed the revival of a specific provision of Article 2 of the Constitution's Supplementary Law that gave veto power to a council of clerics. It also sought to outbid the secular nationalists, whose banner, "reform yes, dictatorship no," posed only a weak challenge to the White Revolution's progressive agenda. He confided to his followers that despite his constitutionalist tone, he would neither endorse nor reject constitutionalism, lest the ossified clergy accuse him of being Westernized or the intellectuals label him caliphate-minded.[50]

Several clerics warned Khomeini against confronting the Shah directly, arguing that unlike the previous time, the monarch would not back down.[51] To weaken the clergy's cohesion, the Shah used his private clerical channel to inform Qom's religious authorities of the importance of these reforms for the survival of the world's only Shi'a-majority state, arguing that without these reforms, the communists would take over and bring down the mosques "on the clergy's head."[52] But knowing that Khomeini and a few others planned to oppose the White Revolution, many clerics feared that their own inaction in the face of such "threats" against Islam would seriously damage their legitimacy. This apprehension brought the divided senior clerics together in a rare moment, and they called for a boycott of the White Revolution referendum. The Shah, however, had no tolerance for what he audaciously called "the untouchable animals" and "black reactionaries" who, together with the communist traitors, were undermining his modernizing efforts. In response, he sent hundreds of commandos to raid the Feyzieh seminary on March 22, 1963; dozens of students were killed and many more were injured.

Shariatmadari and other shocked clerics appealed to Khomeini to join them in toning down the rhetoric, but he responded that it was in fact time to up the ante and "exploit" this tragedy,[53] telling his associates that the regime's disproportionate reaction unintentionally created "20 thousand preachers" to promote his movement.[54] He argued against repairing the damage to the Feyzieh building so the people would continue to see the regime's "savagery" against Islam.[55] Both Khomeini and Shariatmadari then opened bank accounts and called for donations to rebuild the school. The

massive flow of money to reconstruct Feyzieh from ordinary citizens—
including even "unveiled women" in major cities—surprised the clergy and
lent more weight to the anti-Shah opposition.[56]

The Shah privately assured American officials that his determination to
"break" the clergy and pull their "political teeth" was "irrevocable."[57] As of
May 1963, the U.S. embassy in Tehran saw no sign of unrest in the country. It
concluded that the absence of a hierarchy among the clerics prevented any
organized mass uprising in reaction to the White Revolution. But the embassy
acknowledged that "the possibilities of such foolish steps are always present when volatile religious emotions are engaged by demogogery [sic]."[58]
Khomeini, too, was aware of both points.

As the Shah ratcheted up the pressure on the clerics, Khomeini embraced it
as an opportunity to box them in; he specifically welcomed the termination of
the clerics' exemption from military service, as it would reduce the seminarians' fear of guns and soldiers.[59] He told his pupils, "I know very well how to
shoot. I have been in battles myself, too. Once the feudal landowners came to
loot [the city of Khomein], I was one of those who took arms and fought against
them."[60] Future president Rafsanjani was among those who were picked up
on the street and drafted, although he deserted the army a few months later.

With the arrival of the holy month of Ramadan, Khomeini sent specific instructions to his students throughout the country to fuse the bloody attack on
the Feyzieh seminary with the story of Karbala—an epic battle (680 A.D.) in
which Prophet Mohammad's grandson Imam Hossein and his followers were
massacred by the Caliph Yazid. Khomeini and less senior clerics attacked the
Shah in their lectures and sermons for endangering Islam and making Iran sub-
servient to the United States and Israel. He and several other ayatollahs aimed
to incite new protests across the country within the Shi'a mourning cycle of
Muharram (the first month of the lunar Arabic calendar), a tactic he would
implement again in the 1978–1979 revolution. According to Rouhani, Khomeini coordinated with like-minded clerics and was confident of a mass uprising to overthrow the Shah.[61] Most competing clerics were reluctant to sign any
joint declaration with Khomeini, but their individual declarations ended up
following Khomeini's lead anyway, as they could not afford to take a neutral
approach against the Shah.[62] After each statement Khomeini issued, activists
would press his peers to either sign it or issue their own. One activist remem-
bers that some, like Ayatollah Mar'ashi-Najafi, complied easily like a "lamb";
others, such as Shariatmadari, had to be pressed hard to issue a declaration.[63]

On June 3, 1963, Khomeini and a few other clerics delivered a historic speech in Qom, taking advantage of Ashura (the tenth of Muharram), the anniversary of the battle of Karbala. Comparing the monarch to Yazid, Khomeini declared Feyzieh to be the bloody scene of a new Karbala, and harshly advised the Shah to listen to the clergy rather than Israel. SAVAK immediately dispatched security agents to arrest Ayatollahs Khomeini, Seyyed Hassan Tabatabaei Qomi, and Baha al-Din Mahallati, who had made similar anti-Shah speeches. Major Seif al-Din Assar led the military team to capture Khomeini and was so anxious that he made a vow in the middle of the mission: if all went smoothly, he would sacrifice a lamb for Imam Hossein's brother Abbas, who died in the same battle of Karbala.[64] Terrified of touching an ayatollah, the Imperial Army officer was appealing to Abbas, a master of all ayatollahs, for help. In the event, Khomeini was transferred to prison safe and sound.

However, the arrest of Khomeini and other clerics subsequently sparked a mass protest in Qom, Tehran, and other cities on June 5, 1963 (Khordad 15, 1342, according to the Iranian calendar). The five-thousand-member, urban-based religious networks distributed statements and pictures and even carried wooden clubs to force the *bazaaris* to shut down their stores and join the demonstrations;[65] they had already preempted the regime by co-opting mobs, such as those led by the infamous anti-Mosaddeq thug, Tayyeb Haj-Rezaei.[66] But security forces brutally crushed the uprising, imprisoned many clerics and activists, and later executed agitators, including Tayyeb. Khomeini claimed that fifteen thousand were massacred, although most estimates suggest that a few hundred were killed or injured.[67]

What became known as the 15th of Khordad Movement, however, catapulted Khomeini to the center of the political scene. A newborn clerical religious opposition movement took a seat at the table with Iran's veteran nationalists and Marxists. Viewing the clergy as their only channel to the masses, Bazargan's Freedom Movement officially welcomed their arrival.[68] With the rise of Khomeini's stock, nationalists who had previously had their eyes on Ayatollah Shariatmadari moved to provide their political machinery to the detained, lower-ranking but more fiery Ayatollah Khomeini.[69] Even Marxist intellectuals such as Bijan Jazani (1938–1975), the legendary founding father of the armed struggle against the Shah, later recognized Khomeini as a powerful minority within the "reactionary," "compromising," "pro-regime," and "pro-feudal" clerical establishment.[70]

Nevertheless, Khomeini was vulnerable to a fate similar to that of Navvab-Safavi. As a preventive measure, Montazeri and other pro-Khomeini seminarians began a campaign to establish him as a marja, which, if successful, would bring him constitutional immunity. Montazeri went to Qom's sources of emulation and senior lecturers, and insisted that the reluctant senior clerics sign petitions or issue statements that acknowledged Khomeini as a marja. But they were particularly alarmed by his political activities, which put them in the dangerous position of choosing between his leadership and the Shah's. They worried that political activism would prompt the U.S.-backed monarch to eradicate Qom's seminary altogether. At one point in a meeting of prominent clerics, one negated Khomeini's marja'iyyah credentials and asked who on earth followed him. Montazeri quickly responded, "I do."[71] The resolute student blocked the exit door and did not let anyone out before they all came on board. The senior clerics feared that their lack of support of the imprisoned Khomeini would be portrayed by their followers and students as collaboration with the secular, repressive Shah and his foreign sponsors.

After intense discussion and debate, a statement was prepared, discussed, edited, and agreed upon. Pressed by the *bazaaris*[72] and dreading the consequences for the Shi'a establishment should Khomeini be executed, several ayatollahs, including Shariatmadari, also went to Tehran and issued statements declaring him a marja. In an ironic twist of history, Khomeini would isolate both Shariatmadari and Montazeri years later after coming to power. But for now, he escaped prosecution and possibly death. He also officially gained the politically useful special immunity and financially lucrative title of marja. The importance of this event for the Islamic Republic was revealed decades later, when Iranian clerics would fight to receive recognition for helping Khomeini gain marja'iyyah after the June 1963 uprising.[73] Contrary to what some observers have claimed, Khomeini clearly established his religious credentials after, *not* before, entering the political arena.

The new title emboldened Khomeini in his aspiration to further challenge the government and achieve the mantle of the Supreme Marja. He would soon take advantage of his status for political gain. If in the past he had hesitated to join a movement without the support of the marjas, he was now one himself and faced no such limitation.

Indeed, in the following months, the main preoccupation of the clergy, the monarchy, and the United States was Khomeini's potential ascendance to Supreme Marja'iyyah. Prime Minister Alam told U.S. diplomats that several clerics secretly asked him to "disregard" their public appeal to release Kho-meini, fearing his domination of Qom.[74] Khomeini and Shariatmadari were now particularly competitive with each other in taking over the Supreme Marja'iyyah and had already begun sending their representatives to attract followers throughout the country and the Shi'a world.[75] Various reports sug-gested that Khomeini had become popular among the *bazaaris* and lower classes in Tehran,[76] receiving "the bulk" of their tithes.[77] In some cities, he was declared the lead marja. Leftist students, including the Marxist-leaning Islamist Mojahedin-e Khalq Organization (MKO), began visiting him in Qom. Noting that he was the "front runner" to succeed Borujerdi with a potential linkage to Fadayian-e Islam, the U.S. and Iranian governments dreaded the eruption of a "campaign of terror and assassinations." A possible solution was sending him to exile in Iraq, where he would "be imbroiled [*sic*] in Shi'a politics in the holy cities of Najaf or Karbala."[78] Neither the United States nor the Shah took the nascent alliance between Khomeini and the nationalists seriously. The latter was too divided, while the former was too "reaction-ary" to form an effective partnership. The Islamists' opposition to reforms would only isolate them, as the nation was looking to step fully into the twen-tieth century—or so the United States and the Shah hoped. The U.S.-backed White Revolution was designed to "bypass the middle class and appeal to the peasantry as the new political base of the regime."[79] Washington saw no need for the Shah to accommodate the opposition.

In the post–June 1963 environment, the Shah seemed to have successfully crushed the religious opposition. Nevertheless, the upcoming holy month of Muharram posed a dilemma for the regime. Khomeini's continued detention or even exile could lead to a new round of agitation as anti-Shah preachers could once again assign the Yazid and Imam Hossein roles to the monarch and the ayatollah, respectively. Alternatively, his release could be seen as a victory for the rising Islamists. Indeed, Khomeini's subsequent release and return to Qom in April 1964 boosted his popularity.[80] "The fact that he man-aged to come out of the prison of 'Pharaoh' alive had given him the enigmatic quality of a Moses," a Khomeini biographer notes.[81]

But he was surprisingly quiet, perhaps due to the climate of fear and the fact that senior clerics adamantly refused to follow him this time.[82] The regime's bloody crackdown stunned the clergy[83] and brought regret to those who felt that Khomeini had dragged them into a bloody confrontation. On several occasions, Shariatmadari angrily charged Khomeini and his followers with pressuring him into costly political actions.[84] In a private meeting, Shariatmadari accused Khomeini of pursuing politics instead of religion, warned him against undermining the security of the only Shi'a state in a Sunni-majority region, and admonished him for acting in the name of the entire clergy and thus endangering the institution of marja'iyyah.[85] Qom's senior clergy refused to join any anti-Shah protests. Various ayatollahs rejected Khomeini's appeal to issue a declaration on the anniversary of the Fayzieh massacre. Political activism was neither desired nor possible.

However, silence or collaboration with the Shah could undermine the clergy's legitimacy in Iranian society as well. Shariatmadari took a third path. By establishing a cultural center, Dar al-Tabligh, he created a safe substitute for political action. Khomeini and his followers were concerned that Dar al-Tabligh would further divide Qom's religious authority by attracting money and seminarians into apolitical arenas.[86] SAVAK reported that Khomeini increased stipends and other religious payments to prevent his students' attrition and to attract Shariatmadari's seminarians and representatives.[87]

Isolated from his peers, Khomeini first turned to and then against the Shah's key external patron, the United States. During the period in which he was under house arrest, Khomeini reportedly sent a message to the Kennedy administration through a University of Tehran theology lecturer. According to a recently declassified U.S. intelligence document, "Khomeini explained that he was not opposed to American interests in Iran. On the contrary, he thought the American presence was necessary as a counterbalance to Soviet and possibly British influence. Khomeini also explained his belief in close cooperation between Islam and other world religions, particularly Christendom."[88] Khomeini was perhaps aware of the rocky relations between Kennedy and the Shah. But his quiet attempt to undermine American support of the monarchy failed, thus forcing him to play the anti-American card to galvanize popular support.

By September 1964, SAVAK was confident that "the religious situation" no longer posed a security threat.[89] However, Khomeini's failure to revive clerical support pushed him to look for new secular allies among the nationalists and Marxist-Islamists. This required a change of tone to more strongly oppose "world colonialism" and "the West."[90]

In October 1964, the Majles was secretly debating a bill that would grant immunity to U.S. military personnel in Iran. For many, it was reminiscent of a humiliating capitulation treaty imposed on Iran in 1828 by Russia (and later other European powers) for ninety-nine years. After establishing a modern secular judiciary, Reza Shah abrogated the treaty in 1928, but now his son was seen as enacting a similar law. Upon learning about the bill through his brother, Khomeini acquired a copy and promised to reveal it.[91] In a provocative speech that coincided with the anniversary of the Shah's coronation, the birthday of Fatimah (Prophet Mohammad's daughter), and incidentally his own birthday (based on the lunar Arabic calendar), Khomeini denounced the monarchy and carefully framed the attempt to give immunity to the U.S. military as an insult to nationalist and religious principles: "They sold us. They sold our independence . . . They destroyed our dignity. Iran's glory is gone! They destroyed the glory of Iran's army!"[92] As the audience was crying, in a thundering denunciation he added: "They brought the Iranian nation beneath the American dogs. If a person runs over an American dog, they will prosecute him. If the Shah runs over an American dog, they will prosecute him. But if an American cook runs over the Shah, a source of emulation, or a high official, no one can prosecute him!"[93] Khomeini shouted that if there were a single cleric in the parliament, this law would not have been passed, and that the Shah kept the clergy out of politics so he could enslave the country to foreign powers. Overnight, tens of thousands of pamphlets based on Khomeini's speech were published and distributed in major cities.[94] Several clerics issued declarations against the bill, although they were cautious not to target the Shah. But the anti-capitulation move did not generate Khomeini's anticipated revolt, nor did his instantaneous arrest breed any strong reactions in Qom or major cities. Two explanations for the failure of this gambit may be in place: first, his inability to make a strong religious case for the anti-capitulation cause and second, the massive crackdown in the aftermath of the June 1963 uprising.[95]

Khomeini was promptly sent into exile in Turkey and eventually to Iraq. He settled in Najaf, the quietist "Oxford" of Shi'a theology, where—it was hoped by the Shah, the United States, and the orthodox clergy—he would be overshadowed by the top ayatollahs.

"The Islamic Government"

The quietist establishment in Iraq received Khomeini cautiously as the troublemaker from Qom. Najaf's Ayatollah Hakim, and other senior clerics such as Ayatollah Abolghasem Khoei, had long opposed Islamism and clerical involvement in politics despite their hostility toward the Iraqi government, particularly after the ascendance of the socialist Ba'ath Party in 1963. In a meeting, Khomeini pressed Hakim to move to Iran, unite the clergy, and rise up against the monarchy as Imam Hossein did against Yazid. Hakim snapped back, "What would you say about Imam Hassan [Hossein's elder brother]? He did not revolt [but instead made peace with Yazid's father]."[96] Khomeini alleged that Imam Hassan tried but did not have enough popular support. Iranian society was ripe for revolt. He referred to the June uprising as an enormously popular movement in Iran and promised to be the first to support Hakim if he led an uprising, but to no avail.

After failing to stir the Iraqi-based ayatollahs against the Shah, Khomeini remained quiet in the city he called "the den of snakes"—a reference to its vicious clerical rivalries.[97] Najaf's clerics accused him of working with the Godless Iraqi government while attacking the Shi'a Shah. Khomeini seemed subdued and frustrated. "Whatever step I take, I face opposition from a group of Najaf's clerics," he complained to his associates.[98] His marjai'yya was under question. His few students were known for their political activism, not for their scholarship. They were isolated as well and reportedly could not even find wives in Najaf because of their association with him. Khomeini soon entered a bidding war with other sources of emulation to increase the seminarians' stipends. Thanks to his followers' religious taxes (mostly from Iran), his students received stipends several times higher than their peers.[99] In Qom, his followers unsuccessfully pressed sources of emulation to launch a campaign to bring him back from exile. Shariatmadari furiously dismissed their pleas, telling them they had better worry about their own shameful conduct of gay sex ("*lavat*") instead of political affairs—a shocking reference to rumors about the all-male clergy.[100]

Once again, the illness and death of the most senior marja—this time Hakim in 1970—permitted Khomeini to revitalize his political machinery. His son, Mostafa Khomeini, and other followers reinvigorated their efforts to promote him as the most senior marja.[101] But to their dismay, senior Shi'a clerics in Iraq and Lebanon promoted Khoei instead. They would not mention Khomeini even as the second marja after Khoei. So Khomeini himself renewed the drive to build a supreme religious authority to capture the state.

In January and February 1970, Khomeini delivered a series of lectures in Najaf that constituted the most comprehensive doctrine of the state—

Velayat-e Faqih or the Guardianship of the Jurist—in the history of Shi'a theology. The political order after Prophet Mohammad's death had endured for millennia, but Khomeini began by questioning its assumptions. He strongly rejected the prevalent Shi'a view that the community had no political responsibility before the return of the Hidden Imam. Boldly challenging the millennia-old doctrine that any theory of the state was a heresy, he rhetorically asked, "So far, more than a thousand years have passed since the Lesser Occultation, and it is possible that another hundred thousand years go by and it would still not be expedient for His Excellency to return. Should Islamic laws be left on the ground in this long period and not be implemented and anyone can do anything as they wish? Is it supposed to be chaos? Were those laws that Islam's Prophet suffered 23 years to articulate, promote, spread, and implement only for a limited period?"[102]

Secret agents of SAVAK reported that the exiled cleric discussed the challenges that Islam had faced since its advent: "As soon as Islam rose, it had to deal with Jewish propaganda [against the Prophet Mohammad], which continues to this day."[103] Then the Christian crusaders and later the colonizers aspired to infiltrate the Muslim world. According to Khomeini, Islam had deviated as a result of these conflicts such that even the educated and many of the senior clerics no longer knew the core meaning of the religion. The Prophet's creed had been reduced to ordinances about "women's menstrual and birth blood."[104] But, according to Khomeini, Islam was not only a set of laws, values, and prayers; above all, it was about establishing a state. And it was this basic notion—forcibly forgotten through a litany of foreign conspiracies, according to Khomeini—that needed to be reconstructed and brought back.

The claim was so "obvious" that Khomeini did not believe he had to provide much reasoning. But he embarked on making a theological and historical argument for his political case: "Islam has a few books about ordinances, but the rest are about laws, economics, and politics. At a time when America's occupants were barbaric redskins, and [the Persian empire of] Iran was afflicted with a lawless autocracy, divine laws were brought forth by the Prophet."[105] Mohammad established the state and executed those advanced laws with his own hands. With such a clear precedent, how could Muslims separate religion from politics? Islam was not the few apolitical prayers that Najaf's "rotten" clerics had presented for centuries, Khomeini lectured his audience. Rather, it was an all-inclusive blueprint that guided human beings from womb to tomb.

Islamic jurists were therefore obliged to follow their Prophet's true path and directly run the state and its executive branch.

He stressed that the enemies of Islam had made Muslims see their own religion the way they, its enemies, had wanted—as apolitical. This was a calamity, and the only antidote was to unearth the real Islam: "They started from zero to get here. You should start from zero, too."[106] Once Muslims realized that the Prophet was a statesman who gave Islamic jurists the same power and obligation to implement his religion's comprehensive political and judicial teachings, their fate would no longer be the same. It was time to believe that the clergy's main place was not inside a mosque but as head of the state: "God damn those who assigned us this [praying] duty. Our duty is to form a government!"[107]

No Shi'a marja had ever made a political claim over the state. Even those senior clerics, including Molla Mohammad Kazem Khorasani (1831–1911), who had led anti-government protests during the constitutional movement did so based on the Quranic concept of "enjoining the good and forbidding the wrong."[108] A few clerics, such as Mohammad Hossein Na'ini (1860–1936) and Sheikh Fazlollah Nouri (1843–1909), conditionally advocated the *faqih*'s limited supervision of the legislature and the judiciary.[109] In fact, Iran's first constitution (1906) included an ecclesiastical advisory committee consisting of five clerics to ensure that no law passed by the parliament was against Islam.[110] In an earlier work, Khomeini himself expanded this committee into a Majles of marjas who would choose a "just Sultan."[111] His activism in Iran after Borujerdi's death revolved around constitutionalism. But Khomeini was now arguing for much more comprehensive and direct involvement of the clergy in the executive branch. Government was to be the prerogative of the Islamic jurists. He contended that the Prophet Mohammad was sent by God not only to expound and promulgate law but also to *implement* law: "He cut off the hand of the thief and administered lashings and stonings."[112] Moreover, Khomeini argued, the obligation to execute the law did not end with the Prophet's death. "The successor to the Prophet must do the same; his task is not legislation, but the implementation of the divine laws that the Prophet has promulgated."[113]

This divine form of government could be run only by someone who understood the law, since "it is only the just *fuqaha* [jurisprudents] who may correctly implement the ordinances of Islam and firmly establish its institutions, executing the penal provisions of Islamic law and preserving the boundaries and territorial integrity of the Islamic homeland."[114] Thus, the *faqih* had the same authority as the Prophet because government was not about the divine status of the office holder but the implementation of divine laws. "God has conferred upon government in the present age the same powers and authority that were held by the Most Noble Messenger (the Prophet) and the Imams (peace be upon them) with respect to equipping and mobilizing armies, appointing governors and officials, and levying taxes and expending them for the welfare of the Muslims."[115] Therefore, a state—the means to reach the goal of implementing the law—was needed to apply those divine ordinances. Although Khomeini despised the modern state system as a foreign plot to divide the Ottoman Empire and the rest of the Muslim world, he understood its paramount importance for his project. As he explained, "if the Islamic order is to be preserved and all individuals are to pursue the just path of Islam without any deviation, if innovation and the approval of anti-Islamic laws by sham parliaments are to be prevented, if the influence of foreign powers in the Islamic lands is to be destroyed—government is necessary. None of these aims can be achieved without government and the organs of the state."[116]

Unsurprisingly, these lectures did not cultivate much support in Najaf, where more senior clerics, such as Khoei, rejected any special privileges, let alone leadership, for Shi'a jurists in political spheres.[117] Khomeini's associates attempted to distribute his written lectures throughout Najaf's seminary classes, only to be barred by the vast majority of lecturers and marjas.[118] Very few seminarians debated his jurisprudential proposition. But, back in Iran, Khomeini's Islamist disciples in the seminaries, including Rafsanjani, secretly gathered to listen to the taped speech four weeks later. The words of their source of emulation brought tears to their eyes, SAVAK's highly classified documents noted.[119] Perhaps they were astounded to hear such a definitive political manifesto. As Khomeini's protégé, Montazeri, later recalled, his mentor had never claimed that clerics had to lead the state during his prior decades of teaching in Qom. Once, Montazeri had asked Khomeini about his view on the Shi'a concept of sovereignty in the absence of the Hidden Imam: do Shi'ites agree with the Sunnis that the ruler should be selected by the community as opposed to being divinely appointed? Khomeini's response was vague but negative: if the Hidden Imam had not returned, it was the people's fault, and they had to follow their religious obligations until he came. The faithful were not obliged to do anything else in order to bring about divine sovereignty, Khomeini declared during his constitutionalist years in Qom, prior to his exile in 1964.[120]

In the years following his *Velayat-e Faqih* lectures, Khomeini relentlessly increased his onslaught against not only the Shah but the senior clerics. Once again, his rhetoric made it costly for others to disagree with him. He provocatively condemned the lavish celebrations of the 2,500th anniversary of the Persian empire in 1971 and expressed astonishment at Najaf's silence on the matter. He asked that at a time when people were dying of hunger, the country's oil was being sold to the "Occupiers of Jerusalem," and the regime's security forces were throwing protesting seminarians from the rooftops of Qom's schools, how could the clergy acquiesce to the celebration of a group of oppressive ancient kings? Was it enough to pray, go to the shrine, and live off of the religious taxes of Muslims? One hundred telegrams from Najaf's scholars and mass protests of one hundred fifty thousand seminarians in Iran could make a difference, Khomeini angrily said in his lectures in Najaf, according to SAVAK documents.[121] He urged senior clerics throughout Iran to speak out and "enlighten" the people. How could the regime tell clerics they should not interfere in politics? Didn't Moses come to uproot the Pharaoh's unjust rule? "Did God not realize that Moses was interfering in politics!?"[122] Khomeini assured the clergy that the Shah would not dare to harm them: "How could the regime throw us all into prison or kill us? If it could, it would have gotten rid of me by now."[123] He forcefully defined *taqiyya* as a passive submission to and collaboration with an unjust ruler.

Despite SAVAK's vigilance and censorship, Khomeini's students and sympathizers ensured that the senior clerics, their seminarians, and their followers would not remain oblivious to these carefully crafted anti-Shah messages. Their objective was to limit the clergy's options such that no one could afford to be quiet—or worse, to have public ties with the monarchy—without being ostracized in religious circles. They calculated that those clerics who preferred to camouflage themselves under the banner of religion while staying out of politics would be delegitimized. The "true" Islam would require action, dissent, and opposition to the new Pharaoh.

In 1975, the Shah required Iranians to choose between joining his newly established National Rastakhiz (Resurrection) Party and leaving the country. Khomeini immediately issued a fatwa banning Iranian citizens from the party's membership. He declared that Rastakhiz was created to cover the failure of the Shah's reforms; if the White Revolution was as successful and popular as the Shah claimed, "why is there a need to impose a party on the people?"[124] The land reforms only made the country more dependent on foreigners for its basic agricultural needs, Khomeini claimed. The Shah had thus destroyed Iran's economy and was now selling oil to buy useless weapons and import wheat and rice. Warning of the consequences of establishing Rastakhiz, Khomeini pressed his peers to declare membership haram (forbidden) for any true Iranian Muslim.[125] In the same fatwa, Khomeini took a shot at the tactical advice moderate clerics had privately provided the monarchy—that the Shah take a religious turn and demonstrate more respect for Islamic rituals to undermine the Islamists' appeal. Khomeini warned, "The nation should not be deceived by the regime's empty propaganda. While they oppose Islam and its ordinances, their propaganda shows the Kumeyl prayer and chest beating, and chain lashing [on the Shi'a commemoration of Imam Ali and Imam Hossein's deaths]. They publish the Quranic ordinances and they themselves violate them."[126] Soon, SAVAK intercepted a large mailing of Khomeini's fatwa to top clerics, leading academic institutions, and government agencies throughout the country.[127] Its agents reported that because Khomeini's supporters had disseminated his message widely and effectively, senior clerics, including Shariatmadari and Mar'ashi-Najafi, would not express their supportive view of the National Rastakhiz.[128]

A Turn Toward the United States and Alliance with the Nationalists

Khomeini understood that the Shah was at the helm of an oil-rich state with powerful Western supporters who considered Iran a strategically important ally in countering Soviet influence in the Persian Gulf. To overthrow the Shah, he needed not only to build a formidable opposition, but to placate the West's qualms about a post-Shah Iran. He had to tactically forge an alliance with influential opposition groups and carefully present a peaceful, democratic, anti-communist, and human rights–friendly Islam that could coexist with international institutions and norms.

Promoting a clerical government based on Velayat-e Faqih would do the opposite: it would divide the opposition and unite the United States, the Shah, and his army. Therefore, the idea of a clerical government remained a hypothesis in Shi'a theology, not just by default but also by design. Khomeini's

Velayat-e Faqih lectures and subsequent book did not receive much attention beyond seminary circles and he did not promote them. In fact, *Velayat-e Faqih* was almost completely absent from any political debate, including Khomeini's own speeches, throughout the 1970s and until well after the revolution had succeeded. Knowing its provocative implications, Khomeini was perhaps practicing *taqiyya* himself. Instead, he shored up support to overthrow the Shah throughout the 1970s, working with Western-educated intellectuals, sending messages to Iranian students abroad, and fomenting dissent inside the country. Khomeini's vague references to the role of the clergy remained limited, seemingly intended merely to convince the public that the path to freedom and independence could only be accomplished through Islam and the clergy.

As discussed earlier, the religious offshoot of the nationalist opposition (the Freedom Movement) had already noticed and established links with Khomeini in the 1960s. The June 1963 movement had brought his name out of Qom's isolated seminaries and into the urban centers of politics. At this time when most clerics were either quietist or pro-Shah, the Freedom Movement shared its invaluable resources with Khomeini. For instance, the Texas-based pharmacologist Ebrahim Yazdi, a prominent nationalist activist, promoted Khomeini's messages and collected and distributed his religious charities throughout North America.

However, Khomeini's efforts to establish a supreme religious authority with a monopoly over the use of religion now faced powerful rivals in the opposition, many of whom had already begun deploying religion for political gain. Islamism had become the new game in town, often at the expense of the clergy. From Egypt to Iran to Pakistan, local and lay intellectuals, nationalist dissidents, and communist activists looked to Islam as a new political force, following what they perceived to be the failure of the constitutional movement, nationalism, and leftist ideologies to rid them of dictatorship and foreign domination.

In Iran, Jalal Al-e-Ahmad, a former member of the communist Tudeh Party, argued that only Islam had the potential to avert the "earthquake" and "flood" of the Western cultural blitz. In his seminal book *Gharbzadegi* ("Westoxification"), he wrote that he regretted that the clergy, despite being the "last fortress"[129] against the monolithic entity called the "West," had forfeited its historically leading role and hidden in its "cocoon" since the constitutional movement. Al-e-Ahmad was followed by Ali Shariati, a French-educated sociologist whose Islamicized Marxism made religion an attractive commodity for the restless youth of the 1960s and 1970s. He reinterpreted the history of Islam and reconstituted a passionate and powerful Shi'a-inspired revolutionary ideology that helped bring down the Shah in 1979. By invoking the battle of Karbala, Shariati, like Khomeini, turned an anomaly into a rule. Even though Hossein was the only Imam who revolted against an unjust ruler, he claimed that Shi'ism, in essence, was a Red ideology and a "comprehensive political party."[130] It was a robust political force with the necessary tools to generate mass mobilization and a "permanent revolution" toward a classless utopia.[131] Unlike Al-e-Ahmad, Shariati believed that religion was too important to be left in the hands of the clergy.

To the conservative clerical establishment's dismay, these Western-educated, Marxist-existentialist-inspired intellectuals helped construct a politicized form of Islam in Iran and the broader Muslim world that appealed to the modern strata of society. If Reza Shah had robbed the clerics of their leading role in education, endowments, and the judiciary, now the secular leftist intellectuals were weakening their monopoly over religion itself. The clerical establishment detested these lay activists far more than the monarchy.

While most clerics responded by returning to their texts and seminaries in Qom and Najaf, Khomeini took full advantage of the rising appreciation of Islam as a political force among dissidents from Marxist communists to liberal nationalists. Ultimately, this would allow him to reclaim not only the religious realm but also the state. Under his leadership, the clergy would come to control Iran's army, foreign policy, nuclear program, and even the remotest and most specialized corners of the polity. But in the moment, he had to recalibrate his discourse to compete for new recruits in the leftist–Islamist market of the opposition.

In direct response to mounting international pressure on the Shah to relax the political atmosphere, particularly after Jimmy Carter became the U.S. president in January 1977, communist, nationalist, and religious associations, publications, and soon pockets of protests emerged throughout Iran.[132] Khomeini incorporated his rivals' modern language and naturally harvested their converts, as he was the legitimate symbol of militant Islam. As a result, many of the youth Shariati attracted away from various socialist and communist organizations to his Red Islam would eventually join the ranks of Khomeini's Islamist supporters.

In his widely disseminated speeches and lectures in Najaf, Khomeini and his Islamist followers appealed to intellectuals as well as nationalist figures, urging them to join forces with the clergy. Mildly criticizing Shariati and others who made a case for "Islam minus the clergy," he reminded them of the clerics' mobilization capacity. "Do not say that we want Islam, but not the mullah. This is irrational. This is not politicking. You should embrace them with open arms. If they are not politically informed, inform them. They are the ones who are influential among the people."[133] Then he advised the clergy to be more tolerant of activists and intellectuals with religious affinities:

> At a time when all pens and measures and propaganda are against us; when we have no radio to deliver our message, no free press to write a word, when we have no propaganda, no choice; then we need every person. Those [intellectuals], who pick a pen and promote Shi'a, even if they make four mistakes, they should not be dismissed. Correct them! Do not push them away! Do not dismiss the university! These academics will take over the country tomorrow. You and I are not becoming ministers. Our vocation is different. Tomorrow, our country's fate is in the hands of the university graduates. They are the ones who will become representatives or ministers . . . They, too, are in prison. They, too, have suffered. They, too, are in exile. They, too, cannot go back to the country.[134]

Khomeini intended to both politicize the younger seminarians and link them with the wider secular opposition. In messages to Iranian organizations abroad, including the Union of Islamic Associations of Students, he attacked the Shah for violating Islam's "progressive" laws. Sent a year before the revolution, these communications declared that only by marginalizing religion could the Shah give the country's entire resources to "looters," allow Israel to "monopolize" the bazaar, deprive the "freedom" of girls in school by turning them into sex objects, and try to change the Muslims' Friday holiday to the Christians' Sunday. He ended these messages by reminding the "intellectuals and youth" to ensure that religion had "a role" in governance.[135] A few years later, however, after the revolution, he would deride these same intellectuals and give religion and the clergy not merely *a* role in government, but *the* leading role.

In the late 1970s, as the movement against the Shah was gaining momentum in major cities across Iran, Khomeini made a stronger case for the politicization of the clergy and began laying the foundation for its political ascendance. His tone became more reminiscent of his forgotten book, *Islamic Government*. In a speech before the seminarians in Najaf, he attacked those who claimed religion and politics were separate: "What is politics? Relationships between the ruler and the nation, relationships between the ruler and other governments . . . Islam has more political laws than worshiping laws. Islam has more books about politics than about worshiping."[136] In another speech in Najaf the following month, Khomeini claimed that Shi'a Islam has the "richest" jurisprudence and laws in the world.[137] He introduced a role model, Seyyed Hassan Modarres, a cleric and member of the parliament who had resisted the Shah's father, secular politicians, and foreign powers before government agents killed him. In reference to Modarres's courage in the face of an international ultimatum, Khomeini recounted that there was "a bill presented in the Majles that would almost enslave Iran [to a foreign power]. All members of the Majles were quiet. They didn't know what to do. It is written in a foreign magazine that a cleric rose and, while his hands were shaking, came behind the podium and said, 'If we are going to be destroyed, then why should we destroy ourselves?' He then voted no. Others, too, dared to vote no and reject the ultimatum."[138] Piece by piece, Khomeini was introducing a narrative in which the clergy were in the lead. He constructed an Islam in which the Prophet Mohammad, regardless of his prophethood, was a prudent statesman.

Khomeini's discourse and examples reveal that before the revolution, he furtively envisaged clerical control over the future regime. For instance, he claimed that the Prophet astutely shared the enormous captured spoils with the infidels in order to soften them.[139] However, Khomeini's most immediate priority was to remove the Shah, which first required a united religious authority. Although Khomeini radically expanded the public role of Islam to include governing, he and his Islamist–nationalist followers could not initiate, sustain, or succeed in political activism if opposed by the clerics. Consequently, their constitutionalist approach and cautious deployment of religion aimed to increase the cost of inaction for the clergy—and it was successful in doing so. Khomeini's political leadership against the Shah unified the clergy despite their reluctance and concomitantly helped establish his own religious authority.

THREE

The "Islamic" Revolution

AYATOLLAH KHOMEINI'S agility and skill in deploying narratives that were targeted to the political needs of the moment allowed him to chart an unlikely path from outcast to ruler. By the late 1970s, his authoritative messages from Najaf had penetrated the Iranian clergy, the middle class, the elites, and even the army. The clerical establishment reluctantly united behind his political leadership as it did in the June 1963 uprising, compelled by the momentum of the revolution to join the opposition to preserve their legitimacy—but hoping in the process to dilute Khomeini's authority. During this period, Khomeini's careful distance from the concept of *Velayat-e Faqih* allowed space for the unified clergy to establish a strong alliance with the nationalists. This alliance was critical to effectively projecting a constitutionalist, anti-communist image for the protests, a necessary condition to weaken U.S. leverage and undermine the regime's cohesion. Contrary to conventional wisdom, the United States and Iran's Islamists were not hostile toward each other during the revolution. In fact, they even established amicable relations during this time. Taking advantage of U.S. president Jimmy Carter's human rights platform, the Islamist–nationalist alliance put forward a democratic religious narrative that made it possible to delink the monarchy from Washington, thereby enabling transfer of state control to a military-nationalist coalition that soon evolved into a nationalist–Islamist coalition and eventually an Islamist government. This chapter traces each step in this complex evolution of messages and relationships, demonstrating Khomeini's facility in swaying allies and enemies alike to achieve his ultimate objective.

As discontent with the Shah spread throughout the country, he feared Khomeini would instigate another uprising, similar to that of June 1963. The Shah decided to preempt Khomeini by discrediting him—both as a cleric and as a patriot. At a Rastakhiz Party congressional session in January 1978, the minister of information, Daryoush Homayoun, passed a sealed envelope bearing the logo of the Ministry of Court to a correspondent from the daily newspaper *Ettelaat*. Inside was an article titled "Iran and the Red and Black Colonialism." Although controversy over the piece's actual author remains to this day, there is little doubt that the royal court was behind it, hoping to drive a wedge between Khomeini and the rest of the clergy.

The article cast Khomeini as a reactionary and a corrupt foreign agent. In a detailed narrative, it claimed that the Shah's White Revolution and land reforms had ended the communists' appeal among the peasants and angered the British-linked big landowners. It expressed admiration for the clergy who had supposedly recognized the compatibility of the Shah's White Revolution with Islamic egalitarian principles, as evidenced by the fact that they had not declared the distributed lands *haram* (forbidden by Islamic law) and had allowed the peasants to keep their new properties. In response, the losers—namely the Red and Black reactionary forces (the communists and the pro-British landowners, respectively)—had looked for and "easily found" a cleric, an "adventurous," "ambitious," "non-believer" linked to "colonial centers," who would serve their purposes. The article claimed that Khomeini had turned to politics (and instigated the June 1963 uprising) after he failed theologically to achieve a position as a senior cleric and stressed that the uprising would endure as a reminder for "millions of Iranian Muslims" of how the country's colonial enemies (presumably Britain and Soviet Russia) could assume any shape, including one shrouded in "the clergy's sacred and respected garb."[1]

The article's publication sparked precisely what the Shah intended to prevent. Khomeini grabbed the opportunity to bring the ongoing anti-Shah communist and nationalist protests into spectacular mass Islamist rallies, in five cycles of forty-day Shi'a commemoration for the killed protesters. Instead of isolating him, it brought the reluctant clerics behind him, as their silence might be viewed as collaboration with the Shah against not only Khomeini but Islam itself. Khomeini's supporters made sure that the ayatollahs understood these options.

The morning after the article's publication, militant seminarians shut down schools and marched to the top ayatollahs' homes, one by one. According to SAVAK reports, Grand Ayatollah Mohammad Reza Golpayegani addressed the crowd and condemned the article, denying that the marjas had collaborated or would ever collaborate with the monarchy. Speaking into a microphone, he told the fiery seminarians that copies of all his protest letters against the Shah's policies were available at the telegraph house. He said, "Just before you came, I was writing a letter to [the Tehran-based] Ayatollah [Ahmad] Khansari, since I personally have no connection to the regime, to prevent these acts."[2] He approved the cancellation of classes and promised more measures to protect the clergy's unity and legitimacy.

The protesters clashed with security forces before marching on to Ayatollah Shariatmadari's house. Of all the grand ayatollahs, Shariatmadari arguably had the closest ties with the Shah and the most animosity toward Khomeini behind the scenes. Yet even he had to strongly denounce the *Ettelaat* article: "We will act, even though they don't listen to us. This [article] will work against them, because people all know him [Khomeini]. However, you remain calm and united. The fact that you came here demonstrates that you trust us. Therefore let us talk to other gentlemen [ayatollahs] to figure out what to do."[3]

The next stop was Grand Ayatollah Shahab al-Din Mar'ashi-Najafi's home. He, too, claimed he had already taken appropriate measures by writing letters to other clerics to urge them to react. Mar'ashi-Najafi stressed that Khomeini's great stature would not be diminished by such offensive acts.[4] Other senior clerics strongly condemned the *Ettelaat* article as an affront against all of them. As one ayatollah claimed, this piece was in fact less insulting to Khomeini than to other clerics, who were sullied by the admiration it expressed for them.[5] The Shah's attempt to gain religious legitimacy by associating the senior clerics with the monarchy undermined the clerics' credibility. Thus, they quickly distanced themselves from the state and demonstrated their dismay at the provocation, but in the process were put in the position of defending someone they had long considered politically ambitious.

The following week, the Shah sent an emissary to meet with Shariatmadari in Qom. Shariatmadari was neither a quietist nor a strong opponent of the monarchy. He had good relations with both the Shah and the nationalists and advocated that the constitutional monarch reign, not rule. With a sample of Persian and non-Persian media articles in hand, Senator Assadollah Mousavi delivered the Shah's message to the ayatollah: "See how many times Khomeini has insulted me and my father. Now if we respond once, what is all of this noise about?" The monarchy had been surprised by Shariatmadari's unusually harsh denunciation of the regime. While still condemning the killings of protesters by security forces and threatening that he had the power to "shut down the whole of Iran overnight," Shariatmadari stressed to Mousavi that those intelligence agents who tapped his phone could testify to his efforts to calm the situation.[6] In such an emotionally charged climate, he claimed, he had no choice but to do something—and issuing pro-Khomeini statements was the least he could do.

In this private meeting, Shariatmadari distanced himself from Khomeini and warned that the government was only giving him further publicity by mentioning his name. But in public, Shariatmadari had to take a different stance. As a SAVAK informant in Qom reported during the crisis, an ambulance from Shariatmadari's Saham Hospital drove throughout the city "pretending to be in charge of carrying the injured [protesters]."[7] This furnishes another piece of evidence for the senior clerics' strategic calculations to present a united front against the Shah, despite their disapproval of Khomeini's political activism. Six senior clerics wrote a letter to Ayatollah Khansari in Tehran to express "unhappiness" with the havoc in Qom. The mild letter criticized the state, not for being behind the article but for not carefully monitoring the press. It regretted the security establishment's disproportionate use of force and asked Khansari to take the "necessary steps" to prevent these events from happening again.[8] But the letter did not specify what those steps should be, and it was tellingly short of an explicit request to make any direct contact with the government.

According to SAVAK's interception, Khomeini's sympathizers relentlessly made threatening phone calls to the silent clerics demanding that they speak out against the Shah's action in their lectures and sermons.[9] As the pressure increased, the clerics' reactions and international media coverage of the events heightened. Radical seminarians portrayed the ongoing situation as an attack against Islam, shut down classes, staged demonstrations in Qom, and set government buildings on fire. In the clash with security forces, a few of the protesters in Qom were killed or injured. Commemorating the fortieth day of the Qom killings led to more deadly protests, and thus more Shi'a commemorations resulting in additional deaths. With each iteration of this vicious cycle of protests and violence, Khomeini's religious narrative was reproduced and presented as the authoritative voice of Islam and the aspirations of the nation. At the same time, the military began to disintegrate as more and more soldiers responded to Khomeini's call to desert the army.

On August 19, 1978, arsonists blockaded the exits and set fire to the Cinema Rex in the southern city of Abadan, taking about four hundred lives, and soon the country was aflame. Although the culprit was never proven, the opposition and SAVAK blamed each other for this tragedy. Khomeini accused the Shah of planning to commit similar atrocities in other cities to derail the revolutionary movement.[10]

With the arrival of the holy month of Ramadan and the associated increase in the cost of the crackdown, Khomeini ratcheted up his anti-regime tone, reviving his June 1963 strategy. His Islamist followers and nationalist allies turned the Eid-e Fitr celebration at the end of Ramadan on September 5, 1978, into the biggest of the anti-Shah demonstrations. Local and international reporters took advantage of the Shah's newly promised liberal climate to cover what they claimed to be a "three-million-person demonstration" on the hills of Tehran's Gheytariyeh area.[11] As the movement gained momentum, other prominent clerics, including Shariatmadari, called on millions of supporters throughout the country to revolt against a dictatorship—although Shariatmadari continued to oppose Khomeini's revolutionary agenda, pressing instead for a constitutional monarchy. But even Marxist oppositionists felt compelled by the tide of public sentiment to rally under the banner of their "reactionary" religious rivals. The French philosopher Michel Foucault observed firsthand the spectacular discipline, unity, and resoluteness of the protesters in the following statement: "I thought that the collective will was like God, like the soul, something one would never encounter. I don't know whether you agree with me, but we met in Tehran and throughout Iran, the collective will of a people."[12]

The regime's declaration of martial law failed to prevent further demonstrations. The Black Friday massacre in which the army killed approximately ninety protesters in Jaleh Square on September 8, 1978, made it clear that the Shah and his newly appointed National Reconciliation government under Prime Minister Jafar Sharif-Emami were unable to control the radical opposition. The Shah put pressure on the Iraqi government under the 1975 Algerian Agreement to silence or expel Khomeini. He rebuked his ministers, security chiefs, and advisers by remarking, "How many times should I say shut this voice up?" Iranian security officials traveled to Baghdad to provide specific information about Khomeini's activities that violated the mutual friendship treaty between the countries. Iran's Foreign Minister Amir Khosrow Afshar met with his Iraqi counterpart during the annual meeting of the United Nations General Assembly in New York and conveyed the Shah's message that Khomeini had to be silenced.[13]

The Ba'ath Party in Iraq feared Khomeini's increasing authority and influence among its Shi'a population as well. Iraq's security chief and Karbala's governor went to Khomeini's house to warn him not to continue his subversive activities from Najaf. Khomeini responded with a jab carefully targeting ethnic, anti-imperialist sensitivities—and devoid of religion: "What happened to your Arab zeal that you have turned into the [Persian] Shah's servant? He himself is a U.S. servant."[14] Iraqi security forces eventually surrounded his home and barred all visitors. In the days that followed, other Ba'athist officials from Najaf pressured Khomeini to end his classes. But he was not one of those apolitical clerics whose religion was limited to the mosque, he said. He would leave Iraq.

Going to Paris: "Internationalizing the Iran Question"

Khomeini was granted an exit visa from Iraq and an entry visa from Kuwait, but at the border he was barred from entering the sheikhdom. Once Kuwaiti officials recognized the dissident cleric, they did not even allow him to go directly to the airport to fly to another country with a sizable Muslim population. Adamant against returning to Najaf and staying silent, Khomeini looked to countries such as Syria, Bahrain, India, Pakistan, and Algeria. But his U.S.-educated and nationalist aide, Ebrahim Yazdi, had a more strategic plan: Europe. By moving to a liberal environment with advanced communication tools, Khomeini could become the center of the world's attention and thereby "internationalize the Iran question."[15] But where in Europe? Yazdi warned against moving to the United Kingdom because of century-old conspiracy theories regarding clerical ties with the British colonial empire. Nor should the ayatollah go to Germany. Even though Iranian citizens needed no visa to enter, it would not provide the same level of communication as the third option: France. The future foreign minister and one of the first devoured children of the looming revolution, Yazdi reportedly encouraged Khomeini to go to Paris: "Considering the deeply rooted freedom-seeking traditions in France, its politically free and progressive atmosphere, and the high-speed communication tools ... Paris should be a suitable location or perhaps the most suitable location."[16]

Although the move would strengthen the opposition's international posture, Yazdi was concerned that it would weaken the Islamic foundation of the movement. It was inconceivable for a Shi'a grand ayatollah to reside in a former colonial power, a morally and politically corrupt Western environment that was allied with the Shah: "What will be the reaction of the [Iranian] people? What will be the reaction of the reactionary clerics? How will the [Iranian] regime take advantage of this?"[17] Indeed, Khomeini initially hesitated. The cost of moving to Europe could be losing his already-controversial marja'iyyah position, perhaps even becoming irrelevant in the Shi'a world. But the Iraqis' mistreatment of Khomeini, particularly after he was sent back by Kuwaiti border officials, led him to fear similar experiences in other Muslim-majority countries. After conferring with his son, Ahmad, he accepted the French option. He issued a statement justifying this journey to the land of the infidels: "Now that I can no longer be at the Commander of the Faithful [Imam Ali]'s side [by his shrine in Najaf], since I don't see the Islamic countries' atmosphere as suitable to serve you, I am flying to France. What matters is executing the divine duty. The place has no significance to me."[18]

Najaf's traditional clerics viciously denigrated him for becoming a tool of "Westernized" activists desperate for a prominent cleric to mobilize the masses for them. Khomeini's daughter-in-law, Fatemeh Tabatabaei, later described in her memoir that they accused Khomeini of putting his political ambition above his clerical duties: "In an atmosphere in which [even] familiarity with a foreign language or listening to a foreign radio was inappropriate for a cleric and against religion and tradition, a marja's trip to France was absolutely unacceptable ... Some were saying that now it became clear that marja'iyyah had no meaning to him. Otherwise, they wondered how an established religious figure could go from Najaf to France, when his peers preferred to breathe in Najaf and die there? Some others were saying that being buried in Najaf's 'land of Islam' was worth being quiet."[19] Local people approached Khomeini's wife to remind the ayatollah that a single prayer at Imam Ali's shrine was "superior to all worldly affairs."[20] Khomeini's daughter-in-law was told that revolutionary Islam was "intellectual words that Shariati and other Westernized individuals have put in your brain" to slowly take away the people's religion. She questioned that logic by saying that Imam Hossein also left Mecca and the Prophet's grave to fight in Karbala: "Was Imam Hossein influenced by intellectuals, too?"[21]

Appropriating Liberal Democratic Narratives

Tehran and Baghdad both welcomed Khomeini's unorthodox decision to relocate to the suburb of Neauphle-le-Château, near Paris. Foreign Minister Afshar claimed credit for performing the "biggest service" to the Shah by pressuring his Iraqi counterpart to expel Khomeini. The Iraqis even offered to pay for Khomeini and his entourage's first-class tickets.[22] Khomeini politely rejected the offer, but Iraqi security forces accompanied him and his group all the way to Paris.[23] Yazdi ensured that as few clerics as possible came along to reduce the suspicion of the French authorities at the airport, a move viewed by some clerics as the beginning of Yazdi's unforgivable tactics to drive a wedge between them and Khomeini.

On October 6, 1978, the group entered Paris without incident but was soon visited by the French president's representatives and told to be silent. The Élysée officials claimed to not have been aware of Khomeini's travel plans, but now that he had entered the country, he was not to speak to any journalists, deliver political speeches, or conduct any political activity against the Shah. Khomeini's sarcastic response swiftly took a liberal turn: in the absence of France's much-boasted freedom of speech, what was the difference between France and Iraq?[24] In a letter to his wife, Khomeini's son, Ahmad, lamented that his father left his "marja'iyyah garb" in Najaf only to find himself surrounded by one hundred fifty French police officers.[25] Khomeini had no choice but to promise the French officials that he would not be "provocative," and he vaguely stressed that he would only follow his "religious" obligations.[26] Suddenly, it seemed that he and his advisers were losing the gamble of coming to Europe. This is what the monarchy had predicted when it facilitated Khomeini's transition to Paris. The ayatollah would be uprooted from his Islamic soil and wither in "infidelistan."

The Islamist–nationalist opposition, however, quickly mounted a multi-pronged effort to lift the French ban on Khomeini. Pro-Khomeini and nationalist *bazaaris* sent massive bouquets of flowers to the French embassy in Tehran, met with the ambassador and other diplomats to thank them for hosting their religious leader, and warned against not respecting "Iranians' desire [for freedom and human rights], which is the very French desire."[27] Unlike other international airlines, the Air France office in Tehran was reportedly not set on fire in return for its hospitality to the "dear guest" residing in Neauphle-le-Château.[28] But perhaps the most effective move belonged to Sadegh Ghotbzadeh, Khomeini's nationalist, flamboyant, French-speaking aide and future victim. He knew a close friend of the French president who happened to be the editor-in-chief of *Le Figaro*. Ghotbzadeh offered the right-wing paper an exclusive interview with Khomeini and hoped that the editor-in-chief would use his special relations with President Valéry Giscard d'Estaing to gain permission to publish it.[29] This would practically break the restriction on interviewing Khomeini and allow other media outlets to feature the emerging leader of the revolution.

The strategy worked. *Le Figaro*'s piece ended the ban and thus broke the dam. Soon after, the leftist *Le Monde* conducted an interview with Khomeini, and subsequently journalists from all over the world flooded to France. In the course of one hundred eighteen days, the media conducted approximately two hundred interviews with Khomeini.[30] In Najaf, Khomeini's aide had had to translate his statements and then beg "this newspaper and that newspaper" to publish them; in France, it was the reporters who were crawling over each other to access the ayatollah.[31] Additionally, political emissaries, academics, policymakers, and students from across the globe met with Khomeini to discuss the future government he had in mind.

Having left his prominent position in Najaf, Khomeini now put himself in the hands of the Western-educated Iranian activists who were promoting him as the unifying and peaceful face of their movement. They briefed and prepared the reclusive seminarian for interviews with reporters from all corners of the world. Yazdi noticed that although Khomeini was not familiar with the global village, he was smart enough to listen and adjust quickly. But Khomeini would sometimes make statements, particularly about women, that were not politically correct in Europe or among his middle-class supporters in Iran.[32] Fearful of a costly gaffe and public backlash, his aides created a committee to manage his image and coach him so that he would not deviate from his narrative. They required reporters to submit their questions in advance to ensure Khomeini's responses were proper and coherent. They sat him under an apple tree, showcased his simple lifestyle (as opposed to the Shah's luxurious palaces), and translated a consistently democratic, human rights–friendly message. They created a Gandhi-like figure and perhaps more: a holy and anti-communist man with little interest in power or even knowledge of politics. And the international media by and large bought their story. Khomeini soon became the internationally recognized leader of the opposition to the Shah, although internally, many—including Shariatmadari, the secular wing of the nationalists, and the leftists—did not desire his leadership.

The Shah watched in disbelief; he later singled out Yazdi and Ghotbzadeh for bringing Khomeini to the world's attention and turning international public opinion against him.[33] Just as sending Khomeini to Najaf did not result in other clerics overshadowing him, the Shah's strategy to uproot him from the Muslim world and let him be forgotten in France did not go according to plan. Khomeini was adept at quickly adjusting his discourse and his alliances to new environments. As the ailing Shah acknowledged in his last interview with David Frost in Panama, expelling Khomeini from Iraq was a "mistake," although he said he could not have prevented the ayatollah's move to France anyway.[34] The success of Khomeini's stay in France was so enormous that years later many clerics, including Khomeini's son, tried to minimize Yazdi's role and claim credit for that fateful decision.

Absent from Khomeini's messages from Paris were clericalism and anti-Americanism. In fact, he often took a conciliatory tone toward the United States, initially avoiding the topic of the "Islamic government" that he envisioned for Iran. For instance, in his first interview with the American PBS television channel, he did not mention Islam but promised good relations with the United States.[35] Statements and interviews by Khomeini, nationalist leaders, and others suggested that the agreed-upon plan was that the necktie bureaucrats would run the country in the capital and the turbaned clergy would supervise from their mosques and seminaries in Qom. Asked if he intended to head the future state, Khomeini said time and again, "Not myself. Neither my age, nor my position and status, nor my own will and desire is suitable for this. If the opportunity comes up, we will choose among those who are familiar with government-related Islamic concepts and thoughts."[36] On another occasion, he stated, "I will not lead the government but lead the people to choose the government."[37]

Khomeini altogether dismissed any prominent political position for the clergy in the future. When asked if the clerics' role would follow the 1906 constitution—specifically to ensure that the laws were not against the Qur- an—his response seemed positive: "Like in the past, the supervision of the Islamic clerics over the Majles will be confirmed." When pressed, he pressed back: "I have never said that the clerics will take over the government. The clerics' job is something else."[38] But he immediately followed with a critical line: "Supervision of the laws is, of course, their responsibility."[39] He never clarified what he meant by "supervision," let alone articulated what kind of legal–political system he had in mind. When asked by an Austrian reporter about the implementation of *shari'a*, Khomeini responded that it would re- quire many preconditions to make sure those laws were implemented justly. Yet, he added, only then would "it . . . be revealed that Islamic laws are much less violent than any other laws."[40] His discussion of the meaning of Islamic government was often ambiguous but seemingly anti-authoritarian: "If, God willing, we can implement the Islamic government . . . then it will become clear what governance is . . . then it becomes clear what the conditions for a ruler are; otherwise . . . he will be automatically dismissed."[41]

Gradually, the term "Islamic republic" entered his vocabulary, which was a reflection of his engagement with the nationalists. He deconstructed and explained the term in the following statement: "Its republic [aspect], as you all know, is popular votes. Its Islam is Islamic law."[42] On another occasion, when reporters inquired what he meant by an Islamic republic, he replied, "The same republic that you have here in the West."[43] In fact, he claimed to show the world what constituted a real democracy. To the young French girls and boys who came to visit him in the suburb of Paris, he said, "We want to implement Islam, or at least its government . . . so you understand the mean- ing of democracy the way it is."[44]

At this stage there was still no reference to *Velayat-e Faqih*, which would specify a cleric on top and *shari'a* as *the*, rather than *a*, source of lawmaking. But even when using his most ambiguous tone, Khomeini never questioned that the people would be the source of sovereignty: "The government of the Islamic Republic that we have in mind is inspired by the tradition of the Prophet (pbuh [peace be upon him]) and Imam Ali (pbuh), and the form of the government will be decided by the people's votes."[45] His explanation of the Islamic government was consistently focused on how Islam had practical and problem-solving laws for any situation. When it came time to put these dreams and promises into practice in Tehran, however, elite rivalries would breed authoritarian interpretations of Islam well beyond what even Khomeini himself might have secretly wished for. But in the meantime, his powerful message from Paris continued to polarize the political landscape, mobilize the population, weaken the cohesion of the military and political elites, and undermine U.S. support for the Shah. Khomeini was becoming the religious symbol of Iran's quest for freedom.

Challenging Khomeini's Monopoly Over the Use of Religion

Aware that the clerical establishment did not share Khomeini's religious and political views, the Shah turned again to religious authorities in Najaf and Qom, attempting to exploit his ties with top ayatollahs to challenge Khomeini's monopoly over the use of religion. He initiated various gestures that signaled his willingness to reestablish the clerics' institutional access to the state and the government's respect for religious traditions. In November 1978, Queen Farah visited Khomeini's quietist rival, Grand Ayatollah Khoei, in Najaf. Iranian state-controlled media reported that in the meeting, Khoei prayed for the monarch, took off his own agate ring from his finger, and sent it to the Shah as a gift of blessing.[46] Additionally, pictures of Farah in a full black chador praying at Imam Ali's shrine were widely circulated back in Iran. The monarchy also consulted closely with Shariatmadari in Qom. But these senior theologians, who had millions of followers, refused to publicly ally with the Shah by denouncing Khomeini's "Islamic" movement. As news of the Shah's overtures toward the clergy circulated, Khomeini sharply warned that any cleric who negotiated with the corrupt and Westernized Shah was betraying Islam, thus further polarizing the environment. The clerics' tacit support of and private advice to the Shah—for which they paid dearly after the revolution—was not sufficient to bring religious legitimacy to the monarchy and demobilize the masses. Rather, the Shah's efforts were perceived as acts of desperation, and they only encouraged the opposition both in Iran and abroad. Once again, the regime's tactics failed to undermine Khomeini's religious authority over a potent political movement engulfing the country—no credible voice questioned his religious and political message. The Shah had no authority to win this war of narratives, and those clerics who might have had that power feared being seen as collaborators if they spoke out against Khomeini.

Nevertheless, the Shah continued this fight in uncharted religious territory—and he continued to lose. He strove to furnish the government with a religious façade. He deliberately appointed figures with ties to the "moderate" clergy to head key institutions, including SAVAK. Prime Minister Sharif-Emami changed the royal calendar back to the Islamic calendar, dissolved the Rastakhiz Party, increased government employees' salaries, respected the freedom of the press, released religious political prisoners, shut down casinos and other "un-Islamic" centers, and banned sexually explicit movies. Sharif-Emami ordered General Abbas Gharabaghi, the newly appointed minister of the interior, to select "bearded" province and city governors—a sign of religiosity, particularly for Qom and Mashhad.[47] But these concessions only projected the Shah's weakness and further enabled the opposition. For example, Montazeri and Rafsanjani joined the secret Revolutionary Council after they were released from prison and helped organize the clergy and the opposition in the country.

Ironically, although these measures intended to delink the moderate opposition from Khomeini's radical supporters, they ultimately served as a bridge for military and political elites to defect. Now the heads of security forces and other military officers could visit opposition figures, many of whom had recently been released by the Shah, in their homes. Instead of co-opting the opposition figures, these negotiations softened the military elites, who expected similar privileges in the new regime. Vice Minister of War General Hassan Toufanian told a Pentagon envoy that the senior officers were "no longer the same men. They can't be trusted."[48] Following his release from prison, Montazeri was given a passport to visit Khomeini in France. On the eve of his trip, the new (and last) chief of SAVAK, Lieutenant General Nasser Moghaddam, visited Montazeri. After expressing respect for the clergy and claiming he, too, had once been a seminarian, Moghaddam had important messages to be conveyed to Khomeini: First, be aware of the communists. Past experiences reveal that they can penetrate the "sacred uprising" before backstabbing the movement, the general warned. Second, ask the striking oil industry workers to at least produce fuel for domestic consumption in this cold winter; otherwise, people will become pessimistic about the clergy and the revolution.[49] Pleasantly surprised by Moghaddam's soft gesture, Khomeini immediately ordered the oil workers to provide fuel for their compatriots. Many of the Shah's elites believed that the shared fear of the communists would keep them indispensable to the state regardless of the incumbent. Moghaddam would soon pay the ultimate price in Khomeini's Revolutionary Court.

Perhaps the Shah himself, more than anyone else, contributed to the disintegration of the regime's elites. While releasing many prominent political prisoners, he dismissed and imprisoned several loyal members of his own inner circle, including Amir-Abbas Hoveyda, who had served as prime minister for thirteen years. These measures sent a signal to other loyalists that they, too, could be the next scapegoats to save the regime. Some, such as Tehran's Military Governor General Gholam-Ali Oveissi, resigned and fled the country. Others contemplated working with religious and nationalist figures.

In this climate, the ailing Shah became even more indecisive and confused. It was later revealed that he had cancer. Some of his hawkish generals urged him to act, but he vacillated. He feared a bloodbath that would further alienate his domestic and international supporters. He told his military commanders that he intended to implement political reforms and thus leave a stable country for his young son.[50] Limited crackdowns, which killed dozens of protesters, only enraged the public and further expanded the demonstrations. So did his appeasing overture at the height of the crisis—"I heard the voice of your revolution"—in which he promised to reign and not to rule. He looked to the United States for support but received mixed messages. Astonishingly, the United States became a mediator between the Shah's military elites and the Islamist–nationalist coalition.

Delinking the United States and the Shah

In Washington, the White House was initially too preoccupied with the Egypt–Israel peace talks at Camp David (1977–78) to grasp the sudden turmoil in Iran, a country that President Carter had recently called an "island of stability." From Franklin D. Roosevelt's alliance with Saudi Arabia to Richard Nixon's twin-pillars policy and later the Carter Doctrine, every U.S. president after World War II prioritized efforts to effectively counter Soviet control over oil in the Persian Gulf. In sharp contrast to today's widespread fear that regime change in the Middle East may lead to an extreme Islamist government, U.S. concern at the time was that the Marxists' robust organizational networks would overwhelm the clerics. Communists and other leftist groups had long penetrated the region, including Iranian society, the army, and the intelligentsia.

As the revolution's fire spread throughout Iran, Khomeini's American-educated advisers and nationalist allies briefed him on the two key schools of thought in Washington. Carter's national security adviser, Zbigniew Brzezinski, feared that if the Shah were ousted, the communists would rapidly take control of state institutions and eradicate the "unorganized" militant clerics and liberal nationalists, turning Iran into a Soviet satellite. By contrast, the U.S. State Department had adopted a more optimistic view: in a deeply religious society, Khomeini and his allies would swiftly overrun the communists. No one seemed concerned about the rise of a staunchly anti-American religious autocracy. Some officials thought a future Islamic republic could resemble republics with strong armies such as Turkey or—with some religion added to the mix—a dictatorship such as Saudi Arabia. The world had yet to see a new form of state such as what the Islamic Republic would become.

Iran's nationalist opposition figures were in close contact with U.S. diplomats, intelligence analysts, and veteran Iran experts. They carefully presented a narrative to exploit the disagreement within Washington and convince members of the Carter administration that the Shah was not indispensable to U.S. strategic interests. They made a case that the opposition shared both the United States' anti-Soviet interests and its democratic values. Their promises ranged from keeping America's high-tech weapons and guaranteeing the safety of American military advisers to ensuring the rights of religious minorities, particularly those within the Jewish community. Washington might also have hoped that the next government would be more flexible on oil prices than the monarch was.

This position—approved by Khomeini and put forward by the nationalists—was credible enough that even veteran Iran experts ultimately fell for it. Richard Cottam, a former U.S. Central Intelligence Agency (CIA) analyst and longtime friend of Iran's nationalists, met Khomeini in Paris in December 1978. He shared the concerns of American officials, including Brzezinski, who believed that the Soviets were eager to see the Shah overthrown. Khomeini was aware that the Shah, too, was warning the United States and its allies that if he were deposed, the country would fall into the hands of the communists. The ayatollah decidedly postured himself against communist and Marxist ideologies and assured Cottam that Iran would never join the Communist bloc. He went further to claim that, in fact, Moscow was "even fearful of the Islamic call because of the [Muslim-populated] Caucasus."[51] In this way, Khomeini argued that an Islamic Iran could prove a more potent bulwark against the Soviets than was the secular Shah's Iran.

Furthermore, the Shah's balancing act to improve relations with Iran's northern communist neighbor and modify his pro-U.S. image came to be used against him. In a letter to the *Washington Post*, Cottam questioned the monarch's anti-communist credentials: "Iranian relations with the Soviet Union and Eastern Europe are excellent. Communist trade officials and Eastern European regimes in fact are even more obsequious in dealing with Iran than is the U.S. ambassador . . . Indeed, the Shah, even in the throes of this crisis, receives delegations of Soviet and Chinese leaders who are competing for his favors—hardly the behavior one would expect from an anti-communist bulwark."[52]

In various interviews and public speeches, Khomeini claimed that communism was a politically and economically bankrupt system not to be emulated in Iran. He often shared his favorite story about Stalin: at the Tehran Conference with Franklin D. Roosevelt and Winston Churchill during World War II, the Soviet leader brought his own cow to ensure the safety of his milk. According to Khomeini, this showed the depth of Stalin's paranoia, isolation, and dictatorial spirit.[53] During the occupation of Iran by the Allies, Khomeini saw Soviet soldiers begging and stopping cars on the road. He recalled, "When [passengers] would give [a Soviet soldier] a single cigarette, he would get so excited that he would whistle while putting his hand behind his back. Communism is just a game to play with the people."[54] Later, he and his followers would appropriate the leftists' "game" and adopt an anti-imperialist ideology to consolidate their position. But, for the time being, his unmistakable anti-communist posture was key to reassuring Washington.

Khomeini shrewdly addressed the fear of a Red East in the Cold War era while positioning his Islam in line with the liberal spirit of the West. Ten months before the victory of the revolution, he told *Le Monde*, "We will not work with Marxists even for the overthrowing of the Shah. I have always told my followers not to do this. We oppose their viewpoints . . . But in the society that we are planning to build, Marxists will be free to express their views."[55] As the movement gained momentum, so did his emphasis on the nonviolent nature of the revolution. He promised that—as in all legitimate and popular states—there would be "complete freedom" and respect for other minorities.[56] This was a particularly important point, because by January 1979, the future of religious minorities had become one of Washington's concerns.

The U.S. embassy estimated that ten thousand of the eighty thousand Iranian Jews had already fled the country. Seeking to alleviate this new concern of Washington's, Yazdi assured "the American Jews not to worry about the Jewish future in Iran."[57]

Thanks to nationalist allies such as Yazdi, Khomeini learned that he could further undermine Western support of the Shah by protesting that the monarch was against free elections and human rights, both of which would be ensured in the Islamic government.[58] He repeatedly extended responsibility for "all of the Shah's crimes" to the monarch's external backers in an effort to undermine the Shah–U.S. alliance, intensifying liberal–conservative tensions in Western capitals over support of the monarchy. This strategy to assuage concern that Khomeini was a man from seventh-century Islam was evidently effective, as demonstrated by the following assessment from the State Department's Middle East expert Philip Stoddard: "We would do a disservice to Khomeini to consider him simply as a symbol of segregated education and an opponent to women's rights. He also has not all that great an interest in foreign policy. He doesn't care that much about oil to Israel."[59] U.S. officials believed that Khomeini would simply revert to his religious role once his nationalist allies took over the government.

The U.S. embassy in Tehran, embarrassed at having been caught off guard by the expanding uprisings, quickly contacted noncommunist opposition figures such as Khomeini's associate, Ayatollah Mohammad Beheshti, and the nationalist leader of the Freedom Movement, Mehdi Bazargan. Impressed by their moderate, democratic, and anti-communist credentials, Ambassador William Sullivan sent a cable titled "Thinking the Unthinkable" to Washington on November 9, 1978. He stated that Iran's stability depended on accommodation between two key institutions: the religious hierarchy and the army. He advised the Carter administration to think beyond the Shah and connect the military with the religious opposition.[60] Another confidential cable from the U.S. embassy in Tehran in January 1979 summarized Cottam's recent meeting in Paris: "Khomeini did state that he was not interested in mullahs taking over government and left impression that present success of movement was God-ordained and inevitable. Cottam was struck by how little Khomeini's ego appeared to be involved in movement and by absence of deference patterns among those around Khomeini. Cottam notes that this is extremely unusual and probably reflects egalitarian dominance of Islamic socialist ideology expounded by Ali Shariati, which is dominant intellectual current in Khomeini movement."[61] These recently declassified and open-source materials suggest that Khomeini and his nationalist associates effectively adjusted their narratives to the anti-communist, pro-democracy positions of American officials and the U.S. and European public.

The U.S. intelligence community had all the right materials to analyze Khomeini's plan, but perhaps not the right tools. A confidential memorandum from the CIA's National Foreign Assessment Center on January 19, 1979, examined Khomeini's speeches and writings, expressing concerns over his earlier work:

According to a pamphlet "Islamic Government" alleged to be written by Khomeini, The Islamic Republic will have a strong executive. Citing Islamic history and doctrine, the pamphlet argues that a strong executive is essential to prevent the decay of society. It also claims that there is no need for a clear separation of church and state. The Islamic clergy and ulama should be actively involved in decision-making. We cannot verify the authenticity of "Islamic Government." Its text is compatible with other works by Khomeini, but his aides denied it represents his current thinking.[62]

The memo went on to stress that the Islamic Republic would have good relations with the United States if Washington came to terms with the new government. The CIA noted that Khomeini had stated, "There is an absolute disagreement between Marxism and Islam" and "The USSR is culpable for preventing contacts with the Shi'ites in the Soviet Union."

As I will discuss in chapter 5, U.S. officials made a similar mistake once Khomeini replaced his anti-communist discourse with anti-Americanism. They linked Khomeini's political views to his religious beliefs and rhetoric. Tellingly, American officials and analysts concluded later that they did not sufficiently understand the religious foundations of Iranian politics. Years later when the CIA hired Robert Jervis to study the American intelligence failure in the Iranian Revolution, the Columbia University political scientist pointed to Western secular bias as one of the explanations:

Much of the opposition was based on religion and it is difficult for most people living in a secular culture to empathize with and fully understand religious beliefs—especially when the religion is foreign to them. Modern analysts tend to downplay the importance of religion and to give credence to other explanations for behavior. Moreover, Shi'ism is an unusual religion, being a variant of Islam and therefore presenting a double challenge to understanding.[63]

But in fact, these analyses failed to unearth the *strategic calculations* behind the Islamists' religious narratives and instead took them at face value. Like everyone else, the CIA viewed Khomeini's stated theology as a cause shaping his politics rather than a crafted tool that advanced his politics as well.

Aware of its effectiveness, Khomeini's discourse toward the United States and its allies remained cordial and conciliatory until well after the regime transition. Subsequent to the fateful Guadeloupe Conference (January 4 through 7, 1979), during which Western powers discussed post-Shah Iran, Khomeini thanked France's President Valéry Giscard d'Estaing for "arguing against Carter's support of the Shah." As the United States was pushing for a new nationalist-military government in Tehran, he pressed the French president to "advise" Carter to stop supporting the Shah and to prevent a coup d'état, which would allow a stable and functioning Iran to "sell oil to the West or wherever there is a customer."[64] In response to a question by ABC-TV about the future of Iran's relationship with the United States, Khomeini proposed a quid pro quo: "As long as the regime is not completely gone and we cannot consolidate the Islamic government the way we want, we cannot talk about relations with the U.S. in a clear way. However, it is likely that if the U.S. has good relations with Iran [after the Shah], Iran will have good relations with it as well."[65] A recently declassified cable reveals that in fact Carter shared the same message with his Western allies in Guadeloupe: "Events in Iran evolve in a direction that will permit it to be stable, friendly to the West, a continuing source of major oil imports for Western countries, free of outside domination, and internally progressive."[66]

These Islamic–democratic narratives coming out of the Iranian opposition not only undermined the linkage between the Shah and the United States but also increased tensions within Washington between the State Department and the White House. Ambassador Sullivan eventually came to believe that a government led by Khomeini would move toward Washington, while the National Security Council (NSC) and the Pentagon continued to fear a communist takeover.[67] Despite President Carter's order, State Department officials kept leaking to the press critical information that further undermined the Shah and the army's will to crack down. As Gary Sick, Iran specialist on the White House NSC, noted, Carter's anger and repeated orders against leaking the government's internal debates on Iran did not change the situation.[68] The opposition was aware of the effectiveness of its strategy and that the State Department's view was slowly gaining an upper hand in Washington. Instead of encouraging the Shah to crack down, the United States pushed him to reach out to the opposition.

The Shah began a desperate competition with Khomeini over the "moderate" nationalists. As the Shah negotiated with respected secular nationalists such as Gholam-Hossein Sedighi and Karim Sanjabi, Khomeini unremittingly worked with Mehdi Bazargan, who had a religious bent, to form the Revolutionary Council. All of these leaders were disciples of Mohammad Mossaddeq, for whom neither the Shah nor Khomeini had much respect. The Shah had fled Mossaddeq's oil nationalization movement only to return with a CIA-backed coup in 1953. Khomeini's fellow cleric Ayatollah Kashani initially backed Mossaddeq in the movement, only to switch sides after conflicts between the two. But both the Shah and Khomeini understood the nationalists' prominent position among Iranian elites and liberal-minded Western officials.

The Shah's lack of legitimacy hurt his belated outreach to the nationalist opposition. Both Khomeini and the nationalists discredited as a sell-out anyone who entered into negotiations with the Shah. Nevertheless, the Shah made one final attempt to break the Islamist–nationalist alliance by appointing Shahpour Bakhtiar, a prominent figure from the National Front, as prime minister. Bakhtiar was a veteran opposition figure whose father had been killed by the Shah's father. He agreed to be prime minister and loyal to the constitutional monarchy provided that the Shah transferred his authority to a Regency Council and went on "vacation" indefinitely. But as a result of this move, Bakhtiar was subsequently expelled from the National Front and lost much of his credibility with the opposition.

Meanwhile, Washington tasked Ambassador Sullivan to "inform [the Shah] that the United States government felt it was in his best interests and in Iran's for him to leave the country."[69] On January 4, 1979, the very same day Bakhtiar began his tenure, General Robert E. Huyser, deputy commander in chief of U.S. forces in Europe, was dispatched to Iran. Huyser's stated mission was to preserve the integrity of the Iranian military and transfer its loyalty to the legitimate civilian government, but the mission evolved along with the situation. Huyser was there to prevent a possible move against Bakhtiar's government, but in effect he and Sullivan became American middlemen between the military and Khomeini. It was only a matter of time before the state smoothly fell: from the Shah to the National Front's Bakhtiar, to its religious offshoot the Freedom Movement and—as we will see in the next chapter—eventually into the Islamists' hands.

A cable from Ambassador Sullivan to Washington just days before he and General Huyser met with the Shah on January 12 points to this evolving debate within the Carter administration: "General Huyser has already asked Secretary [of Defense] Brown to ask President to reconsider in view of urgent appeals from Iranian military that we arrange relationship between them and Khomeini."[70] Sullivan, too, was pressuring the White House to move beyond Bakhtiar and "structure a *modus vivendi* between the military and the religious, in order to preempt the [communist] Tudeh."[71] He knew that the clerics were not united behind Khomeini. In fact, he informed Washington that moderate religious leaders were concerned that the Shah was leaving the country, because they were afraid of being blackmailed by leftists who could access classified documents about the clergy's ties to the monarchy. He, too, feared the leftists would take over and blackmail the clerics, many of whom were on the monarchy's payroll. So Sullivan impatiently pressed Carter to reach out directly to Khomeini. Both he and Huyser prepared the army for what seemed to be an inevitable power transition to a "moderate" government with which the United States could maintain good relations to prevent a communist takeover.[72] Huyser unequivocally advised the army to protect key installations instead of ordering any deployment in the streets: "If the mob wants to burn and destroy Tehran, let them do it."[73]

Various accounts from the Shah and his generals suggest that Huyser's unusual visit angered and lowered the morale of the Iranian army. In his own memoir published in September 1980, the Shah quoted his air force commander, General Amir Hossein Rabi'i, as saying to the "judges" before his summary execution, "General Huyser threw the Shah out of the country like a dead mouse."[74] The Shah claimed that in his meeting with Sullivan and Huyser, the ambassador said his departure "was no longer a matter of days . . . but of hours, and looked meaningfully at his watch."[75] Ambassador Sullivan recommended that President Carter offer the Shah asylum so that the United States could "gain some credit with the ayatollah for making the Shah's orderly departure feasible."[76] Meanwhile, General Huyser asked the Shah's last chief of staff, General Gharabaghi,[77] for a meeting with Bazargan, which—according to the Shah—may have prevented a military coup against Khomeini.[78]

As nationalist leader and Khomeini-appointed provisional prime minister, Bazargan pointed out years later, the opposition believed that the United States would never let its long-time loyal ally fall, nor would it ever recognize a new revolutionary government. He asserted that as late as two months before the revolution, American officials could not even entertain the idea of the Shah temporarily leaving the country. In various meetings at the embassy in Tehran, U.S. officials and representatives reacted "angrily" to any proposal that included the departure of the Shah and warned that a military coup would follow.[79] In October 1978, Bazargan warned Khomeini in Paris that he should tone down his revolutionary approach because the United States would not compromise its interests in Iran by removing the Shah. "The world of diplomacy and the international arena are not the seminaries of Najaf and Qom," he wrote.[80] But in December 1978, Bazargan himself encountered a different climate at the U.S. embassy in Tehran. He noted, "In a secret meeting that Mr. [Ayatollah] Mousavi Ardebili and I had with the [U.S.] ambassador, we saw that they were ready for an agreement in principle to have a national referendum on changing the constitution from a constitutional monarchy to an Islamic republic. Our only difference was who should execute the referendum: the Bakhtiar [the new prime minister] government or us."[81]

While Khomeini pressured Bakhtiar and the army to grant him permission to return to Iran, he sent a secret message to Carter through Yazdi. According to U.S. documents, it was the "first first-person" message that Khomeini conveyed to Washington:

The activities and words of Bakhtiar and the present leaders of the army are not only harmful for Iranians but also are very harmful for the American government, especially the future of the Americans (Yazdi: that means the Americans in Iran). Those activities may force me to issue new orders in Iran. It is advisable that you recommend to the army (Yazdi: the army as a whole, not just the leadership; We draw a distinction between the two) not to follow Bakhtiar and to cease these activities. The continuation of these activities by Bakhtiar and the army leadership may bring a great disaster. If Bakhtiar and the present army leadership stop intervening in the affairs (Yazdi: of Iranians), we will quiet down the people and this will not create harm for the Americans. These kinds of activities and behavior (Yazdi: by Bakhtiar and the army leadership) will not bring calm or stability to the region. The nation will listen to me and, through my command and implementation of my plan, stability will come. When I announce the Provisional

Government, you will see that many of the points which are vague will disappear (Yazdi: Khomeini means areas which are fuzzy to the USG) and you will see that we are not repeat we are not in any particular animosity with the Americans, and you will see the Islamic Republic, which is based on Islamic philosophy and laws, is nothing but a humanitarian one which will benefit the cause of peace and tranquility for all mankind. Closing down the airports and preventing me from going back to Iran will disturb the stability.[82]

Khomeini's aide also appealed to divine common ground with the United States to further stress anti-communism: "The Russian government is atheistic and anti-religion. We will definitely find it more difficult to have a deep understanding with the Russians . . . You are Christians and believe in God and they don't. We feel it easier to be closer to you than to the Russians."[83]

To counter the Bakhtiar government, Khomeini created the Islamic Revolutionary Council with secret members. However, Shariatmadari opposed the council, arguing that it would lead to more violence.[84] Unaware of Khomeini's negotiations with U.S. representatives in Paris, he pushed for a gradual transition of power through existing legal channels to preserve the constitutional nature of the government. This would have hindered Khomeini's budding leadership and the Islamists' control over the state.

Bakhtiar declared martial law, which Khomeini urged people to disobey, threatening to declare jihad and bring the masses out if the "illegal" prime minister did not resign. On January 27, 1979, Bakhtiar wrote an informal letter to Khomeini requesting a meeting in Paris within forty-eight hours. In the letter, he introduced himself not as the prime minister but as a fellow revolutionary activist who needed guidance from the spiritual leader. Understanding that this was a symbolic tactic to divisively penetrate Khomeini's opposition narrative, the ayatollah proposed one precondition: resign and repent before getting your ticket. Bakhtiar's letter not only failed to divide the opposition, it further undermined his credibility with the royal military elites, who feared that he, too, was furtively seeking a deal with the opposition. Later in exile, Bakhtiar defended his humiliating overture by stating that he had no other option but appeasement to demobilize the masses: "Let's be honest, Khomeini had turned forty million [the population of Iran] into donkeys [fools], many of whom are still donkeys. What else could I have done? . . . This man had turned everybody, from Sanjabi [head of the National Front] to the neighborhood's sweeper into a donkey. Perhaps there were only two hundred to three hundred individuals who knew what was going on, but they had no courage to speak up."[85]

En Route to Tehran

As Khomeini planned to leave Paris for Tehran after fourteen years in exile, the fear of an imminent military coup remained. Islamist clerics and nationalists were negotiating with the army generals directly or through the U.S. embassy in Tehran to abandon the Shah and stop shooting the protesters. According to U.S. estimates, one thousand soldiers were deserting the army every day. Khomeini was aware that the bulk of the army was not willing to fight for the fleeing Shah. In his words, "all the violence comes down to a few commanders who will inevitably fail."[86]

The announcement of his plan to return to Iran prompted Bakhtiar to close Tehran's Mehrabad Airport. Desperate to buy time, Bakhtiar urged him to wait for three weeks until he could "calm down" the army, lest there be a coup. Khomeini quietly agreed not to confront Bakhtiar upon his arrival. Washington hoped this would lead to a pact between a moderate government and the army under the auspices of the United States. So did Bakhtiar himself, who told Ambassador Sullivan that Khomeini "should be drowned in mullahs" upon his arrival in Qom.[87] "This might make him more reasonable or at least less involved in political affairs," he added. Once again, Khomeini's adversary predicted that the majority of the clerics—who did not share his radical views and political ambitions—would marginalize him. But he managed to salvage his odd position within the clergy by adopting a strategy that divided the elites and galvanized the population.

Khomeini's allies and disciples chartered a 747 Air France jet and boarded one hundred eighty-nine passengers, including prominent figures returning home after years of living in exile and journalists from all the major international networks and publications. The latter group was included partly to reduce the likelihood that a much-rumored threat of downing the plane was realized. The nationalists—who had previously surrounded Khomeini in exile and effectively portrayed him as a saintly, exalted, and peace-loving charismatic leader—now accompanied him to Tehran, where his fellow

Islamist clerics had already begun institutionalizing their role in the new regime.

Upon landing in Tehran in February 1979, Khomeini was reportedly greeted by millions of people in the flower-strewn streets of Tehran. He went straight to the Behesht-e Zahra cemetery to pay homage to the martyrs of the movement and then delivered a strongly worded speech promising to "appoint a government" and "slap this [Bakhtiar] government on the mouth." As soon as his audience clapped, his clerical disciples rose up and directed the audience to shout "Allah Akbar" or "God Is Great." Little by little, "Islamic" gestures were being imposed on the masses. Then Khomeini reached out to the army: "Mr. General, don't you want to be independent? Do you want to be a servant? I advise you to join the people. Say what the nation says. Say we want to be independent. The army should not be under the U.S. and foreign advisers. We say this for your own sake. *You* say this for your own sake too . . . Don't think that if you give up [supporting the Shah] we will hang you."[88] He was aware of the possibility of a military coup and his allies' ongoing negotiations with the army, SAVAK, and other elements loyal to the Shah behind the scenes. After assuring the army of Islamic mercy, he was taken to his temporary residence at Refah, an Islamic elementary school for girls in southern Tehran.

Two days after his arrival in Tehran, Khomeini met with the Revolutionary Council and appointed the interim government led by Bazargan and other nationalist figures. In his "order" to Bazargan, ceremoniously delivered and read by Rafsanjani at Refah School, Khomeini obliged state employees, the army, and all citizens to obey the new "Islamic government" and not the Shah-appointed Prime Minister Bakhtiar. Nevertheless, the fear of a military coup remained high.

Earlier, Khomeini had issued a fatwa to obligate soldiers to desert the army and join the masses. The Islamist–nationalist opposition then shrewdly reached out to the Homafaran, an underclass group within the air force consisting of twelve thousand military technicians trained to maintain advanced U.S.-made aircrafts, weapons, and equipment that was perhaps the least loyal due to its deep grievances and dissatisfaction with the Shah over limited prospects for promotion and other benefits in the otherwise much-privileged Imperial Air Force.[89] Opposition leaders believed that the promise of equality and dignity under an Islamist–nationalist political system would appeal to them. Per the suggestion of Ayatollah Taleqani, the spiritual leader of both the nationalists and the Marxist-Islamist Mojahedin-e Khalq Organization (MKO), about eight hundred Homafars met with Khomeini on February 8. The daily newspaper *Kayhan* published a picture of the uniformed officers, unidentifiable from behind, meeting their new leader with a headline that read, "Air Force Pledged Allegiance to Imam Khomeini."[90]

The meeting was a tremendous symbolic victory for the revolution that led to the disintegration of the air force and the rest of the army. That same day, the Shah's Imperial Guard attacked the Homafaran's base in Dushan Tappeh, Tehran. Newly resurfaced leftist guerilla groups, including Fadaiyan-e Khalq Organization (FKO) and MKO, along with many protesters came to defeat the last remaining backers of the exiled Shah. With the monarch gone, the army—pressured by the United States to negotiate with the new government and promised by the nationalists and Islamists to maintain its position and privileges within the system—ultimately announced its neutrality, and thus Bakhtiar's government fell on February 11. Gharabaghi and Bakhtiar, who went into hiding separately before fleeing to Paris, later accused each other of betraying the monarchy by secretly negotiating with the opposition to secure their position after the regime transition.[91]

On February 16, the military commanders, some of whom had trusted Khomeini's earlier assurances, paid the ultimate price. They were arrested, taken to the rooftop of Khomeini's initial residence, Refah School, and executed after summary trials. Khomeini gave his old disciple, Sadegh Khalkhali, a special mandate based on "Islamic law" to decapitate the army. Khalkhali invoked Quranic terms and accused the Shah's loyalists of "seeding corruption on earth" and "declaring war on God." He was adamant that the public treasury (*beytol mal*) should not be used on due process for men who were "lower than animals." In an interview with the BBC, Khalkhali later stressed that Khomeini had urged him to resist the nationalists' pressure and to execute the Shah's loyalists swiftly and mercilessly.[92]

The bloody pictures of Iran's top and internationally renowned officials, naked and executed, became the first images of Khomeini's Islamic Revolution. Until a few days earlier, U.S. officials had been urging the same military commanders to work with the new regime to ensure the army's cohesion and an orderly transition. Now they were waking up every morning to news of new executions. The U.S. embassy's official mandate, however, was to ensure good relations with the new government in Tehran, despite the fact that Khomeini was purging the army.

The debate over the fate of the army, however, soon shifted from removing all senior officers to dissolving the entire institution. Communist groups were pressing for a complete dissolution of the "imperialist" army. Bazargan noticed how the leftists' narrative was radicalizing the Islamists: the communists "were the first group whose slogans were to dissolve the army and claiming that this army is imperialistic, and this slogan later became a model for others [Islamists]."[93] Khomeini advised the "extremist youth" to put aside their expectations and be patient until the army became loyal.[94] The nationalists, who were critical of the summary executions, strongly resisted and argued that the country needed the army to defend the nation against external and internal enemies.

Khomeini ultimately decided to keep—but "Islamicize"—the army. Future Supreme Leader Ali Khamenei and future president Hassan Rouhani were among the clerics who took up this mission. Mid-ranking "religious" army officers replaced senior military commanders. Similarly, the Islamists and leftists clashed with the nationalist government over purging the rest of the state apparatus. The nationalist Provisional Government removed the ministers, governors, and ambassadors but kept the rest of the *ancien régime* intact. However, as Prime Minister Bazargan put it, the leftists and Islamists radicalized the climate, arguing that no one, not even the janitors or the servants of the old system, should stay.[95]

With the Shah's departure, the Islamist–nationalist coalition remained in communication with the United States to ensure a smooth transition from the monarchy to the Islamic government. Khomeini maintained a friendly tone toward the United States and promised normal ties with Washington provided that the White House prevented the army from carrying out a coup. The Islamists' "moderate" approach and alliance with the nationalists prevented any opposition from the clerical establishment and proved to be critical for the transition of power. In a book that Bazargan published later, he stated that Khomeini's treatise on *Velayat-e Faqih* was largely perceived only as a jurisprudential debate about the general principles of governance. Perhaps an exceptional case was the nationalists' reaction to one of Khomeini's speeches on July 27, 1978, in which he left no doubt about the clergy's ownership of the movement: "Iran's recent sacred movement, which has been one hundred percent Islamic since its inception on the 15th of Khordad [the uprising after his arrest on June 5, 1963], was founded only by the capable hand of the clergy with the backing of the great Islamic nation of Iran. And it is and will be under the leadership of the clergy without relying on any front or individual or group."[96] Bazargan's Freedom Movement immediately sent a letter to Khomeini and inquired about this message.[97] Khomeini quickly brushed it aside and responded by assuring the nationalists that his statement was in fact for their own protection and only a reaction to those who had accused the nationalists of being "un-Islamic." He appealed to them to continue their unity and support in removing the Shah. As discussed earlier, many nationalists and even American officials were initially content with the adjective "Islamic," since it implicitly excluded the powerful communist opposition groups from the future government.

Bazargan believed that Khomeini's order to him to head the interim government was about replacing a dictatorship with popular sovereignty. Absent from it was any mention of founding a new political order, spreading and implementing Islamic law, exporting the revolution, fighting Western imperialism, or helping the world's downtrodden.[98] However, Bazargan's Islamist rivals argue now that the ayatollah was simply concealing his true intentions and using him to deceive the United States and remove the Shah. "Bazargan was Imam [Khomeini]'s biggest trick to outfox America. He [Khomeini] employed a force that the U.S. would not consider dangerous," declared IRGC commander Mohsen Rezaei three decades later.[99]

Khomeini's disciple Akbar Hashemi Rafsanjani acknowledges that the affinity Bazargan and other nationalist figures had with Bakhtiar and his cabinet was crucial in negotiations between the revolutionaries and the state elites in those critical days as Khomeini was returning from exile. As Rafsanjani, too, asserts, Khomeini's discursive adjustment and alliance with the nationalists were essential in ensuring the smooth regime transition: "Against the nature of a stubborn revolutionary, Imam [Khomeini] maintained the connection with and accepted these [nationalist] elements. The Imam both deceived the regime to some extent and made the National Front hopeful and prevented it from possible troublemaking. Otherwise, it is possible that the revolution, assuming it was victorious, would have been more costly and we would have witnessed more bombings, mass killings, and violence."[100] Writing years after purging all nationalist rivals, Rafsanjani points out that these "appropriate" mediators were chosen to negotiate and neutralize the key officials of the *ancien régime*. Well positioned domestically and well versed in Western society and politics, the nationalists were critical to delinking the Shah from his international backers, his army, and the middle class, and thus engineering a smooth transition. The militant clergy made perfect use of the "moderates" for the regime transition before dealing with them in the consolidation phase.

Nevertheless, Rafsanjani's comments should be viewed as self-serving in the sense that they implied Khomeini was determined to have total clerical control over the state. As the next two chapters argue, other factors, including pressures from Khomeini's clerical disciples such as Rafsanjani himself, as well as the threat of the leftist groups, shaped the way in which the doctrine of *Velayat-e Faqih* was implemented in the first few months after the revolution.

FOUR

Institutionalizing *Velayat-e Faqih*

DESPITE THE STUNNING VICTORY of the revolution and the seemingly orderly transition of power, Iran's political landscape remained uncertain. In February 1979, Ayatollah Khomeini had become a divine idol-smasher whose face people imagined they saw on the surface of the moon at night. He had ended two and a half thousand years of unjust monarchy and terminated hundreds of years of foreign intervention. Yet he and his Islamist followers vied over the direction of the new republic with three other well-established groups: the orthodox clergy, the nationalists, and the leftists. In the face of this competition, Khomeini and his disciples advocated a direct—not supervisory—role for the clergy. Scholarship is divided about Khomeini's objective in establishing *Velayat-e Faqih* after bringing down the Shah. Pointing to the Islamic Republic's constitution, many observers argue that Khomeini was determined to establish clerical rule based on his lectures in Najaf. Others refer to his earlier approval of the draft constitution, which did not include *Velayat-e Faqih*, as evidence that he had initially abandoned the idea. This chapter argues that, regardless of Khomeini's true intention, the political climate after the fall of the monarchy was instrumental in prompting him, and more importantly his Islamist followers, to press for institutionalizing *Velayat-e Faqih* alongside a republican political structure.

The situation was complex. Notwithstanding Khomeini's massive popularity, the clerical establishment had never embraced his political agenda, as senior clerics continued to view Islamism as a threat to the mosque's independence from the state. Although many ayatollahs had come to approve the uprising against the Shah and favored the Bazargan government for its religiosity and respect for Qom's independence, the majority remained opposed to any clerical involvement in the new government. The fact that Qom's marjas did not go to Tehran to welcome Khomeini and acknowledge his leadership worried the Islamists. It is important to stress that—paradoxically—the "Islamic" Revolution did not have roots in the traditional clerical establishment but rather in modern urban institutions, universities, and secular intellectual circles. Furthermore, because Khomeini's power stemmed from his near monopoly over the use of religion, he was particularly vulnerable to the clergy's quietism or criticism. If the clerical establishment did not publicly endorse Khomeini's religious authority, it could potentially undermine his political leadership as well.

On the secular front, once the Shah was removed, well-organized leftist groups came out from prison, the underground, and exile to quickly change the political landscape. The leftists wished to topple both the Islamists and their nationalist allies as being reactionary and bourgeois agents of U.S. imperialism, respectively. Conversely, the Islamists felt an urgent imperative to dominate their secular rivals to avoid a clerically backed nationalist takeover or a leftist second revolution. In the first scenario, the nationalists would forge ties with moderate clerics such as Ayatollah Shariatmadari to marginalize Khomeini and his militant followers. In the second scenario, powerful leftist organizations would bring down the Islamist–nationalist government and create a communist regime similar to that of neighboring Afghanistan. The establishment of *Velayat-e Faqih* (discussed below) was instrumental in disarming the first threat; the second threat (examined in the following chapter) provoked an ideology of anti-Americanism and, subsequently, the hostage crisis.

Statizing the Sacred and Sacralizing the State

Following his arrival in Iran, Khomeini appointed Mehdi Bazargan to complete the transition to an Islamic republic through a national referendum and a new constitution. The appointment was "based on the Revolutionary Council's recommendation and according to the religious right and the legal right" the Iranian people bestowed upon the movement's leadership through their demonstrations.[1] Khomeini's vague statement could have been a reference to either his *Velayat-e Faqih* doctrine or the general supervisory role of the jurists to which many Shi'a clerics ascribed, particularly in the absence of a legal custodian. Bazargan and other nationalists assumed the second reading with no contingency plan for the first. Hours after his appointment as prime minister of the Provisional Government, he appeared on television, thanked the army for surrendering to the nation's will, and praised General Gharabaghi for meeting with him to pledge cooperation. He asked the protesters to respect the security forces and protect military installations against mobs; otherwise, he presaged, chaos would bring calamities worse than before. Meanwhile, Qom's most senior clerics, including Ayatollahs Golpayegani, Mar'ashi-Najafi, and Shariatmadari, issued statements commending the army, offering congratulations on the victory of the revolution, and backing the "Islamic" Provisional Government without explicitly acknowledging Khomeini's leadership.[2] For the nationalists and the clerical establishment, the revolution was over. The dictator was gone, the army had retreated to its base, and the world had recognized the new Iran. It was time for protesters to go home, for militant clerics and leftist students to return to their seminaries and schools, and for all to leave the polity to the religious nationalist democratic technocrats.

But neither the Islamists nor the leftists would accept this arrangement. For the former, the revolution was not over; for the latter, it had not yet begun. The nationalists were gradually replacing the monarchy as both groups' enemy. The interim government was increasingly seen as weak and an impediment to the militant clergy, who sought to capture the state before the leftists took over. Both Islamists and leftists remained concerned that a U.S.-backed military coup or a U.S.-supported nationalist-military alliance would remove them altogether.

A week after the Shah's regime fell and three days after the inauguration of the interim government, a surprising entity emerged: the clerically founded Islamic Republican Party (IRP). Despite Khomeini's repeated opposition, his disciples—such as Mohammad Beheshti, Akbar Hashemi Rafsanjani, Ali Khamenei, Abdulkarim Mousavi Ardebili, Mohammad Javad Bahonar, and a few laymen, including Hassan Ayat, Mohammad Ali Rajai, and Mir-Hossein Mousavi—established the IRP. Modeled after the Soviet Union's Communist Party, the IRP aspired to recruit members of the future government.[3] Bahonar, a cofounder, claimed that two million members registered for the party within one hundred days.[4] While in exile, Khomeini had strongly disagreed with the notion of a political party founded by clerics, arguing that it would inexorably invite political and religious rivalry.[5] He contended that the clergy should not take center stage in the political scene or become partisans. Prominent militant clerics, such as Seyyed Hassan Taheri-Khoramabadi, Mohammad Mousavi Khoeiniha (the future mentor of the students who occupied the U.S. embassy), and Beheshti, met with Khomeini in Najaf and later in Paris seeking to convince him otherwise. But Khomeini was not swayed until he arrived in Tehran. There he witnessed the serious ideological threats that various groups, particularly radical leftists such as the Fadaiyan-e Khalq Organization (FKO), posed to his new regime. These groups were recruiting new members and growing exponentially, predicting the collapse of the nationalists' "liberal bourgeoisie" and the Islamists' "reactionary forces." So Khomeini eventually allowed his followers to form a political party, although he prevented his son, Ahmad, from joining. The IRP's motto was "One community, one religion, one order, one leader."[6] A constant theme of its official newspaper, *Jomhuri Islami* (Islamic Republic), was denouncing the "pseudo-clerics" along with Westernized and Easternized (Marxist) groups who were not in line with the Imam. Connecting its vast network of offices to mosques and other religious institutions across the country, the IRP aspired to control the clerical establishment, shape religious narratives, and create a formidable wave of clericalism.

Learning from the communist and Marxist groups, the IRP distributed bulletins and leaflets to government offices, the army, revolutionary committees, universities, and factories. It mobilized and recruited clerics for new government positions; for instance, official Friday prayers were now held and led by appointed clerics in every town, who had to coordinate their sermons with the official IRP line. The party also worked with other clerical assemblies to create and control new institutions, such as the Revolutionary Courts, Revolutionary Guard (IRGC), and Komiteh—which paralleled the judiciary, the army, and the police, respectively. In contrast, Bazargan's interim government consisted entirely of technocratic laymen with religious affinities. While he controlled the official state institutions, the IRP was forming a parallel state. In late February, Khomeini appointed Ayatollah Mohammad Reza Mahdavi-Kani to head the Komiteh, and the IRGC came under the control of Ayatollah Abolghasem Lahouti and later, Rafsanjani and Khamenei. To monopolize the legitimate use of force, the IRP needed to first multiply it.

But the IRP's activities did not go unanswered, for Shariatmadari's followers founded the Muslim People's Republican Party in February 1979. Shariatmadari pointed out that the new "party" was created to forestall "the danger of a one-party dictatorship."[7] He and Iraq-based Ayatollah Khoei were considered the two most established sources of emulation in the Shi'a world. Shariatmadari had achieved his marja'iyyah years before Khomeini did. Thanks to his immense popularity, particularly among the *bazaaris* and middle-class professionals, the new entity soon opened offices in various parts of the country. Shariatmadari would not easily cede to Khomeini's monopolization of religion, and Bazargan could rely on him and other clergy to balance the Islamists. Once again, Khomeini and his followers had to overcome the clerical establishment's hostility or quietism toward their political objectives.

Four weeks after the formation of the Provisional Government, Khomeini departed Tehran and, as he had promised in Paris, returned to Qom, the city he had been forced to leave more than a decade earlier. Shariatmadari welcomed Khomeini's return, emphasizing that the two could now "sit down, talk and solve the problems together."[8] Qom's clerics still refused to recognize Khomeini's ultimate religious and political authority. Khomeini himself was cautious to not fracture the clergy and consequently lose his grip on the state. He was afraid of a clerical boycott of the new government. Accordingly, upon arrival in Qom, he made a series of statements for his clerical audience that signaled a rapid turn to *shari'a*. This move—which contradicted his previous statements in Paris—would make it costly for the ayatollahs to oppose him and his *shari'a*-implementing Islamic government, while compelling junior clerics to join the state. He promised a ministry separate from the government dedicated to "enjoining good and forbidding wrong"—two purifying Islamic requisites in the Quran.[9] He attacked clerics who opposed implementing Islamic laws on the grounds that certain theological preconditions did not exist, warning that seminaries throughout the country needed to wake up and not act as passively as they did in the past.

In a meeting the following week with Qom's seminarians, Khomeini said that all ministries should be Islamic and that women must veil themselves. Soon the Komiteh began enforcing the hejab for women in government offices and on the streets. Khomeini's statement about veils provoked unexpected mass protests on March 8, International Women's Day. He quickly

softened his position by warning against the harassment of women, Ayatollah Taleqani stressed that there would be no compulsory veiling, and the
Provisional Government denied reports that unveiled women would be fired.[10]
The IRP accused the media of exaggerating the controversy and, ironically,
ordered the Komiteh to arrest anyone harassing unveiled women![11] However,
the move to implement *shari'a* and pressure dissident clerics quietly continued. Following the Provisional Government's ban on the production of alcoholic beverages, the Komiteh and the IRGC arrested not only producers but
also consumers of alcoholic drinks and lashed them in public.[12] In another
move to box in the orthodox clergy, Khomeini banned broadcasting music,
except specific revolutionary songs, from the state-controlled media.[13]

As the Islamists were "Islamicizing" and sacralizing the state, they
launched a parallel campaign to statize the mosque, eventually institutionalizing their efforts to stifle dissident clerics in the Special Court for the Clergy
(SCC).[14] Once the SCC was established, opposing the Islamic state could lead
to the loss of religious credibility or, worse, religious credentials themselves.
Iran's Shi'a clerical establishment's long independence from the state was
about to end. Apolitical clergy were pressured to cooperate, but dissident
clerics were intimidated, prosecuted, and even executed. Tehran's notorious
chief justice, Ayatollah Mohammad Mohammadi Gilani, pressed Khomeini
to "issue the order to purge and cleanse the clergy,"[15] which had been Khomeini's goal dating back to the Borujerdi era (as discussed in chapter 2). In
prison, seminarians-turned-security agents interrogated dissident clerics,
including Ayatollah Reza Sadr, who opposed the Islamist government and
Velayat-e Faqih. The agents demanded to know how he could resist a government that was implementing God's laws: "Did you not see women have
veiled, bars have been shut down, and record stores distribute religious
cassettes?"[16] Ayatollah Sadr acknowledged in his memoir that he remained
silent and tried to change the subject. The media reported daily on the de-
frocking and even imprisonment of "pseudo-clerics" linked to the previous
regime.[17] In a veiled threat, the minister of information, propaganda, and
endowments revealed how SAVAK had co-opted senior clerics against Khomeini.[18] Khomeini frequently pointed to their past "shortcomings" and
pressured seminarians to support the government in implementing Islamic
laws.[19] The IRGC, the Komiteh, the IRP, and the SCC launched a colossal campaign to break the independence of mosques throughout the country and
bring them under state control. The IRP accessed SAVAK's documents and

blackmailed clerics with close ties to the monarchy. According to Rafsan-jani, many of those following Khomeini during the revolution and regime transition did so not out of genuine belief but rather because they were "practicing *taqiyya*."[20] In other words, their position was a rational decision as opposed to a sincere display of loyalty. Remarkably, Khomeini and his disciples were receptive to this response and even took steps to create a climate that induced *taqiyya*.

However, some clerics, such as Shariatmadari and Taleqani, resisted Khomeini's parallel state. Echoing Bazargan, Shariatmadari strongly opposed the brutalities of the IRGC, the Komiteh, and the Revolutionary Courts, as well as the involvement of clerics in government. In his relentless public statements and interviews, he claimed that such violence was not Islamic, urged all forces to work with the Provisional Government, called for a stalwart army against the IRGC, and opposed relegating the judicial power of a *faqih* to low-ranking clerical judges.[21] His party criticized the mushrooming growth of self-claimed ayatollahs and pointed out that no marja had sovereignty in political matters.[22] Sadeq Khalkhali—a mid-ranking cleric who had become known as the "hanging judge" for his brutal sentences—initiated an unsuccessful attack against Shariatmadari, which resulted in angry reactions from even quietist grand ayatollahs and the closure of seminaries throughout the country.[23] The IRP quickly dissociated itself from these efforts and Khalkhali denied any offense against the grand ayatollah.[24] Shariatmadari continued to pose a serious threat to Khomeini's authority.

In March 1979, Ayatollah Taleqani—a longtime political prisoner under the Shah, Tehran's first Friday prayer leader, and the pious mentor of many nationalist and Islamist–Marxist groups—protested the arbitrary activities of the Komiteh and the IRGC. His sons were detained for their ties to the Marxist-Islamist MKO, although they were released shortly thereafter upon intense political pressure by the interim government and the public. Outraged by their mistreatment, Taleqani's office announced that, in protest against the activities of unaccountable groups whose illegal detention centers violated the rights of the people all "in the name of Islam and Muslims," his offices throughout the country were closing and he was leaving Tehran.[25] Taleqa-ni's dissidence sent shock waves throughout the country with the potential to inflict enormous damage on the new regime's religious legitimacy. Although he did not seem to harbor political ambitions, in the eyes of many respected veteran political activists, he was no less popular than Khomeini.

Khomeini's son, Ahmad, mediated and brought Taleqani back to Tehran, and Taleqani then visited Khomeini to put an end to widespread rumors that the two had fallen out. In that meeting, Khomeini urged the Komiteh to purge its "arbitrary" elements, but he strongly praised them for protecting "the people's lives and properties."[26] The incident did not abate the extra-judicial activities of the Komiteh and the IRGC. Six months later, Taleqani died of a heart attack, and with that, a potential challenge to Khomeini's authority vanished. Until his death, Taleqani had remained contemptuous of what he called the instrumental use of the Quran for political ends, which was a clear reference to Islamism.[27]

The IRGC and Komiteh collaborated with local militant clerics to remove newly appointed governors, detain law enforcement officials, and arrest leftist activists.[28] As rivalries among the Komiteh, IRGC, FKO, and MKO increased, separatist ethnic groups engaged in a bloody conflict with the central government, and Bazargan's appeals to these groups for solidarity with the Provisional Government fell on deaf ears.[29] Ironically, the nationalists remained the Left's primary enemy because of their perceived ties to the United States. The outcome of these external pressures on the Provisional Government was a further shift in the balance of power within the government toward the Islamist militant clerics.

Bazargan repeatedly threatened to resign over continued interference by the IRP and its militias in the interim government. In the end, a compromise was reached: the Revolutionary Council and the Provisional Government practically—although not nominally—merged, with Bazargan effectively agreeing to allow the Islamist clergy to shadow the executive branch. In July 1979, Khamenei and Bahonar became deputies of the Ministries of Defense and Education, respectively, while Rafsanjani and Mahdavi-Kani took deputyships of the Ministry of the Interior. Bazargan hoped that this measure would bring the IRGC and the Komiteh under government control and that assuming executive positions would induce the clerics to weaken the parallel state in favor of the state.[30] He held weekly meetings with Khomeini in Qom in an effort to restrain the Islamist clergy, whom he accused of taking over the government against Khomeini's will. But the IRGC and the Komiteh continued their extralegal and extrajudicial activities, while the gates to the last stronghold of laymen, the executive branch, opened to the Islamists.

Khomeini moved swiftly to legalize and protect the new regime against his subversive opponents. Disagreements over the nature of the regime quickly arose. Khomeini insisted on the "Islamic Republic," while Bazargan favored the "Democratic Islamic Republic." But Khomeini argued that adding an adjective would demean Islam's already comprehensive platform. Meanwhile, senior Shi'a clerics in Iran and even Iraq privately warned Khomeini against calling the new republic "Islamic." Some considered any government in the absence of the Hidden Imam "un-Islamic," while others worried Islam would be blamed for any shortcomings.[31]

Confident of his popular support, Khomeini resisted, declaring, "The Islamic Republic. Not one word more, not one word less." Bazargan had little choice but to capitulate. He held the referendum on March 30 and 31, 1979, less than two months after the fall of the Shah. Khomeini appealed to people from all social strata and religious denominations to vote in favor of the Islamic Republic.[32] His old tactic of carefully polarizing the climate forced Shariatmadari and some others who had opposed the single-option format of the referendum to support it.[33] Shariatmadari emphasized that according to Islam, sovereignty belonged to the people and no single group had any special privilege to rule.[34] Cautiously backing the referendum and yet worried about Khomeini's authoritarian mission, he stressed that the Islamic government simply meant individual liberty.

The Islamists played down any differences among the clerics on the nature of the next government. Instead, they attacked the leftists—who opposed the referendum—by appropriating leftist rhetoric. Nationalists were apprehensive as Khomeini began to adopt anti-American language. This served to strengthen his constituency's cohesion, as the left wing of the IRP and many of his followers shared the communists' anti-Americanism. He used the leftists' own accusation against them: "Do not listen to the deviants. They are American stooges in the form of leftism."[35] The anti-American narrative that would isolate the Islamic Republic for decades was about to become an integral part of post-revolutionary Iran.

On polling day, there were only two types of ballots: "Yes," written in big green letters, and "No," written in big red letters. The voting arrangements violated the ballot's secrecy, as voters had to choose between the preprinted green "Yes" and red "No" ballots in public. Following massive campaigns through the media and mosques, 98 percent (more than twenty million) were reported to have voted in favor of the Islamic Republic. Despite this astonishing result, Khomeini seemed utterly surprised that about 141,000 individuals were against the Islamic government. "There have been some irregularities, otherwise everybody's vote must be with the Islamic Republic," he said.[36]

With the referendum's impressive electoral show behind them, the postrevolutionary players went on to battle for the main prize: the constitution of the state. Inspired by French law, the nationalists prepared a constitutional draft, which received the general approval of Khomeini and other senior ayatollahs. Absent from the draft was *Velayat-e Faqih*, and yet Khomeini was initially content to submit it directly to a national referendum. The draft included the creation of the Guardian Council, which consisted of a number of sources of emulation to supervise the compatibility of laws with *shari'a*; however, unlike the 1906 constitution, Islamic jurists were in the minority with no veto power over civil jurists. In other words, the Islamic Republic's draft constitution reduced the power of the clergy, yet Khomeini still approved it. As scholar Ali Rahnema argues, perhaps Khomeini put his vision aside "for the sake of rapidly installing the state organs and institutions of the revolution."[37] This was also evident in Khomeini's careful distinction between the "transitional" nature of the Islamic Republic and the ideal Islamic government.

Nevertheless, Khomeini pushed to ensure that all laws were "Islamic" while claiming that the clerics should remain outside the government. In a meeting with members of the newly established Revolutionary Guard, he spoke of the importance of *feqh* (jurisprudence): "We didn't want an Islamic republic in form . . . its content must be Islamic, too . . . its people claim they are Muslim, but in some places it has been seen that they are not observant."[38] In Paris, his emphasis when discussing the Islamic republic had been on the noun; in Tehran, it was on the adjective: "When we say an Islamic government must have Islamic content, it means that wherever you go, in any ministry, in any office, on any street, in any *bazaar*, at any university, and in any school that you go to, you must see Islam and Islamic laws there!"[39] Although Khomeini argued that the referendum left no doubt that people wanted Islam and the clergy,[40] he and clerical members of the Revolutionary Council and the IRP continued to stress that no cleric would assume any political position.[41] *Velayat-e Faqih* would be a general supervisory concept, embodied in institutions such as the Revolutionary Council[42] or Revolutionary Courts,[43] particularly in the absence of a constitution and legally elected government.

Despite Khomeini's pressure for a quick referendum, the nationalist interim government argued that, as promised, an elected Constitutional Assem-

bly had to examine the draft before a referendum. With Taleqani's mediation, a much smaller Constitutional Assembly of Experts was agreed upon,
with seventy-five "expert" members instead of several hundred ordinary
representatives. Rafsanjani's warning to the nationalists that the election
could bring ossified clerics into the assembly went unheeded; Bazargan
would later regret this strategic error. Had he pursued the initial plan and
put the nationalists' constitution to a direct vote, the IRP would have faced
the daunting task of finding another legal–institutional mechanism to
consolidate clerical control. He was confident of the popularity and the
indispensability of his government to the survival of the new regime.

Khomeini and the militant clerics turned this dilemma into a political opportunity to institutionalize clerical control over the state. With the coun-
trywide eruption of separatist movements and the call against clerical
involvement in politics intensifying, Khomeini and his followers suddenly
began a campaign to institutionalize the Guardianship of the Jurist in the
constitution. As the draft constitution appeared in the media for public
debates, IRP members challenged its provisions. In two separate articles,
Ayatollah Montazeri left no doubt that the clergy would be involved in
government affairs; the difference between the two articles reflected the
rapidly evolving political climate. In the first article on June 23, he argued
that ideally, the president should be a *mujtahid* (a high-ranking jurist who
has the authority to interpret the holy scriptures—one level below a *marja*).[44]
However, in the second piece he authored on July 10, Montazeri stressed
that the president *must* either himself be a *faqih* (a *mujtahid*, if not a *marja*) or
be appointed by one.[45] The Islamists were now calling on Khomeini to assume an official political leadership position.

What had happened in the time between the two articles was mounting
opposition to the government from ethnic groups, leftists, and religious authorities. Ethnic unrest and leftist guerrilla attacks in Gonbad-e Kavus, Kurdistan, Khuzestan, and Baluchestan were engulfing the country. Khomeini
and his followers perceived the nationalist Provisional Government's handling
of these crises as weak, and they increasingly feared a communist takeover.
Blaming the army and the nationalists for not maintaining order, the Islamists
expanded the power of the paramilitary Komiteh and the Revolutionary
Guard to brutally suppress rebel groups. Even the pro-Khomeini Homafaran
that had helped break the Shah's army a few months earlier was on strike in
protest of continued discrimination against it within the air force.[46]

The radicalization of politics, including assassinations of Khomeini's followers such as Ayatollah Morteza Motahari by armed Marxist–Islamist groups, prompted Khomeini to conclude that it was the result of his tolerance and the interim government's weakness.[47] He expressed regret that he had not been more "revolutionary": "Every day that is passing in this revolution, I realize more that the nation acted in a revolutionary manner and we [the leaders] did not . . . From the beginning we had to [create] a government that was revolutionary and young . . . We didn't have such a person at the time . . . It was a mistake . . . now we should compensate by being revolutionary."[48] In the run-up to the elections for the Constitutional Assembly, his clear criticism of the nationalists signaled a further tilt in favor of the Islamists.

In this climate, senior religious authorities, particularly Shariatmadari, became more vocal in their protest against the Islamists' political use of Islam and clerical involvement in the government. In a move reminiscent of Khomeini's civil disobedience tactic under the Shah, Shariatmadari wrote public letters to other ayatollahs denouncing the Islamists' "anti-Islamic" violence against the clergy, the army, and ordinary citizens. He criticized the Revolutionary Courts' harsh sentences against the remnants of the Shah's regime, pressed for a national amnesty, demanded freedom of the press, and tried to intervene in the settlement of the civil war in Kurdistan.[49] In an implicit reference to Khomeini, Shariatmadari contended that no marja should accept any state position.[50] He opposed the second referendum for the constitution, and his party threatened to seek help from marjas against the new constitution.[51] Given his position as a marja, Shariatmadari's disapproval could not be ignored.

In response, Khomeini labeled all those who opposed the referendum to establish an Islamic state as either communists or uninformed about Islam.[52] However, he was careful not to confront Shariatmadari directly and publicly before consolidating his regime. In an effort to demonstrate unity within the clergy, Khomeini met with his three counterparts (Golpayegani, Mar'ashi-Najafi, and Shariatmadari) often at a "neutral" place, such as Golpayegani's house, to deliberate "critical issues" facing the nation. The state-controlled media purposely showed pictures of the four marjas together without details of the meetings.[53] As I discuss in the following chapter, it would take the hostage crisis and the Iran–Iraq War to completely eliminate the clerical threat to the Islamists. In the meantime, Khomeini and the IRP relentlessly pressured quietist clerics to endorse *Velayat-e Faqih* by linking it to the implementation of God's laws. Islamist figures were cautious to downplay any disagreement among the four marjas and claim unanimous clerical support for the Islamic Republic and *Velayat-e Faqih*.

In the run-up to the Constitutional Assembly elections, the IRP initiated a nation-wide campaign to portray itself as Khomeini's party (although Khomeini claimed he was above partisan politics) and undermine rival candidates, from the Left to the nationalists to the moderate clerics. Its members reportedly committed far-reaching electoral fraud to open the Constitutional Assembly to a flood of fellow militant Islamist clergy and their sympathizers. Election rigging was condemned by a wide range of groups, including religious figures and associations, but the charges fell on deaf ears.[54] Consequently, the IRP dominated the forum, 80 percent of whose members (fifty-five out of seventy-five) were clerics, although pro-Shariatmadari and nationalist candidates won a considerable number of seats. This was a turning point that would establish a political system based on Khomeini's vision of *Velayat-e Faqih*. With such an impressive majority on the assembly—despite the electoral irregularities that produced it—the Islamists had summoned a wave of power that even Khomeini could not resist.

Enter *Velayat-e Faqih*

In his inaugural message to the Constitutional Assembly, which was again delivered by Rafsanjani, Khomeini was now unprecedentedly unambiguous about the central role of the clergy in the legislature and judiciary. He pointed out that, since the majority of the people voted for an Islamic republic and not simply a republic, the laws must be "one hundred percent according to Islam. And even if one provision is against Islamic laws, it will constitute a violation of the republic and the vast majority of the people's votes." He demarcated the limits of the lay members of the assembly and stated, "Identifying what is according to or in violation of Islamic laws is exclusively in the hands of respected *'ezam* [jurists], some of whom are, thank God, in the [Constitutional] Assembly. And since this is a niche issue, if other respected representatives interfere in *ijtihad* [the academic qualification to interpret the holy scriptures] and extract Islamic laws from the Book and Sunna [the Prophet's and the Imams' traditions], they will be interfering in others' expertise without having the necessary qualification and expertise." Then he warned: "With utmost emphasis, I recommend that if some of the representatives are inclined toward Western or Eastern schools [of thought] or other deviant thoughts, they should not bring their proclivities to the constitution of the Islamic Republic. They should separate their deviant path from this constitution, because the expediency and virtue of our nation is in distancing itself from these schools, which even in their own environment are considered bankrupt and declining." He asked the clergy in the assembly to resist and publicize any pressure from the media and intellectuals to shape any constitutional provision "against Islam."[55]

After Rafsanjani finished reading Khomeini's message, Prime Minister Bazargan went to the podium and uttered the kind of statement Khomeini had just warned against: "In the submitted proposal [the draft constitution], the principles of freedom, the right to criticize, national sovereignty, and majority vote are not gifts from the West, nor an imitation or imposition of outsiders, nor an inheritance of the deposed monarchy, but . . . are in accordance with the Quran."[56] The battle line was clear, but the battlefield was chaotic. Backed by Ayatollahs Shariatmadari, Taleqani, and others, the nationalists were pushing for a secular constitution to preserve the former political order sans the monarchy and its dictatorial, anti-religious rule. Khomeini, on the other hand, now sought a new order that he and his militant associates could control. He invoked what he called a *shari'a*-based state, whose judiciary and legislature had to be under clerical control. The IRP was even more exclusive than Khomeini: it sought to bring the entire state apparatus, including the executive branch, under the total control of the militant clergy while Khomeini was still alive. In the absence of Khomeini's power and charisma, the militant clerics feared the nationalist and leftist blocs would quickly marginalize them. Invoking the vague yet powerful concept of *shari'a* could effectively disarm Khomeini's opponents and brand them as anti-Islamic. The challenge was how to present and tailor *shari'a* to meet the looming threats.

The debate began. By the third session, IRP members of the constitutional body had laid out their plan: a marja must be above all three branches of government. Instead of discussing Bazargan's proposed draft, which had been previously approved by Khomeini himself, they presented Khomeini's earlier work on *Velayat-e Faqih*. Only two days earlier, Taleqani, also an assembly member, died. Having warned against despotism with a religious façade, Taleqani was widely known to be unhappy with the assembly's proceedings and the militant clergy's quest for power. Meanwhile, Shariatmadari and several other prominent clerical figures remained opposed to *Velayat-e Faqih* for transferring the power that God reserved for the infallible Prophet and Imams to fallible, turbaned men.[57] The orthodox and moderate senior clerics understood that they could now become Khomeini's subjects under an Islamist regime. However, IRP offices across the country advertised the wide range of opportunities and duties that the new Islamic state was creating for clerics. Many low- and mid-ranking clerics realized the enormous power that *Velayat-e Faqih* could bestow upon them in a system under which any jurist's will could instantly become law. The following statement by a clerical deputy captures this notion: "I have a 17-year-old son who can drive well, but he does not have a driving license [because the minimum driving age in Iran is eighteen]. I told him to drive the car and take me from a place to another. He said, 'Sir, with the current law, wouldn't it be illegal if I drove you somewhere?' If we really incorporate *Velayat-e Faqih* into the law and keep the Guardianship of the Jurist in mind, then people have to obey orders."[58]

The Islamists in the assembly argued that people had risen up against the Shah because they wanted an Islamic state. Hojjat al-Islam Javad Fatehi pointed out that government and guardianship came from God, who delegated it to the Prophet, then to the Imams, and finally to the jurists.[59] Hassan Ayat, one of the few lay founding members of the IRP, claimed that he had come to the assembly with the single mission of including *Velayat-e Faqih* in the constitution. He made an extreme case to dismiss the original draft constitution: "What is important for the president is to be Muslim; being of Iranian origin is a secondary matter . . . According to the draft constitution, if [the First Imam] Ali ibn Abi Taleb (pbuh) were alive, he could not become the president of Iran since he was neither originally from Iran nor a naturalized Iranian. However, the former Shah could, since he was both Iranian and apparently Muslim according to his [birth] certificate."[60] The IRP spoke of four thousand "proposals" that were submitted to the constitutional body and sent long petitions to the assembly claiming that even people in remote areas were insisting on including *Velayat-e Faqih* in the constitution.[61] Otherwise, the Islamic Republic, which 98 percent of the voters had approved, would be a misnomer.

Outnumbered nationalist representatives such as Ezzatollah Sahabi tried to argue within the religious framework by pointing out that the infallible Imams gave their power to the people, not to clerics:

> On his deathbed, Ali (pbuh) advises the people . . . that managing society and [establishing] order and systems in society is up to them . . . These were the bases of this [draft] constitution, which by no means contradict the Guardianship of the Jurist. The Guardianship of the Jurist is not equal to the jurist's necessary involvement in and supervision of executing politics or distributing political power . . . The person who is in charge of society's political affairs, and governs and oversees political power needs to have much higher qualifications [than those of a jurist].[62]

Similarly, Rahmatollah Maraghe'i, a pro-Shariatmadari nationalist, stressed that he did not oppose the sovereignty of Islam if that was what *Velayat-e Faqih* meant. However, he opposed the notion that "a special social class should monopolize Islam for itself."[63] Islam came precisely to end these special privileges and establish equality among people regardless of status and background. By reinterpreting *Velayat-e Faqih*, Sahabi, Maraghe'i, and their minority allies unsuccessfully struggled to keep it within the realm of general Islamic laws, external to—but compatible with—the draft constitution.

Outside the assembly, the armed struggle with various ethnic and political groups was escalating. Some members of the assembly and their families had already been assassinated in these bloody conflicts, or later would be. Meanwhile, the media, trade unions, and university campuses were scenes of the fiercest ideological battles between the leftists and the Islamists. The nationalists feared the former much more than the latter, and their deputies came under enormous pressures to maintain ties with the Islamists.

In the assembly's fifth meeting, Montazeri (the assembly's chair), who was later designated as Khomeini's successor before his subsequent removal, set the record straight:

> The gentlemen should be assured that we will never pass a constitution that is not based on *Velayat-e Faqih* and whose laws are not entirely according to the Book and the Tradition [of the Prophet] . . . the Iranian nation elected the gentlemen and the *ulama* [senior clerics] since it concluded that the *ulama* are experts in Islamic issues. Therefore, it becomes clear that the Iranian nation wants Islam.

Even if somebody says this constitution is *akhoundi*, yes we are *akhounds* [a pejorative word for cleric], so let it be *akhoundi*. But we want it to be a hundred percent Islamic and based on *Velayat-e Faqih*."[64]

Three decades later, Montazeri would regret his role during these days and apologize to the Iranian nation for the authoritarian system he inadvertently helped establish.

In the fifteenth session, Montazeri and his powerful deputy Beheshti sealed the fate of the state through Article 5: "During the Occultation of the Lord of the Age [the Hidden Imam], may God hasten his renewed manifestation, the Guardianship [*Velayat-e Amr*] and Leadership [*Imamat*] of the nation [*ummah*] in the Islamic Republic of Iran devolve upon the just and pious jurist who is acquainted with the circumstances of his age; courageous, resourceful, and possessed of administrative ability; and recognized and accepted as leader by the majority of the people."[65] Yet many deputies remained uncertain about the meaning and consequences of this article; they continued to view *Velayat-e Faqih* as a supervisory position. Of the sixty-five members present in that session, fifty-three voted in favor, eight voted against, and four abstained.[66]

But the battle was far from over. The assembly clashed over the source of sovereignty: God or the people. Some nationalists, including Maraghe'i and even Khomeini's associate and future president, Abolhassan Banisadr, argued that the assembly had no right to give away national sovereignty and the fate of the people once and forever to jurists. Their opponents, on the other hand, argued that "absolute sovereignty," which came from God, should not be delegated to the nation but rather to those who understood God's law. Fierce clashes over the source of legitimacy eventually led to the approval of vague and contradictory provisions, such as Article 4, which recognized the principle of popular sovereignty. *The tension between Articles 4 and 5 created dual sovereignty, laying the groundwork for a potential crack in the system. Iran's factional politics in the next four decades would revolve around these Islamist and republican principles.*

The conflict over the source of sovereignty led to a debate regarding the separation of powers and various branches of government. The IRP feared a reproduction of the 1906 constitution, under which a clerical body established to monitor the Islamic nature of the laws was functionally ineffective. Therefore, proponents of *Velayat-e Faqih* sought to institutionalize it into every article of the constitution. To that end, they submitted all branches of government to oversight by the Guardian Jurist. Many deputies pushed to reserve the presidency for a jurist. When they lost that battle—perhaps due to Khomeini's objection—they ensured that the president's power was under direct control of the jurists. Additionally, the twelve-member Guardian Council was created to guarantee that all laws the Majles intended to pass were in accordance with their reading of Islamic law. Only the Guardian Council's six clerical members could decide if a law was Islamic. Without their endorsement, Majles-approved bills would have no legal status. In other words, the Majles was not a legislative body but rather a *consulting* one, or an "institution for planning" as Khomeini had originally foreseen.[67] Parliament was viewed as a Western and "un-Islamic" institution that could give an impression of deficiency in *shari'a*. Ironically, the Guardian Council would come to be filled by some of Khomeini's traditional rivals, whose preoccupation with Islamic law often clashed with the pragmatic demands of day-to-day governance. As I discuss later in the book, Khomeini would ultimately elevate *Velayat-e Faqih* to Absolute *Velayat-e Faqih* to further consolidate his supreme religious authority over senior clerics within and outside the regime.

Velayat-e Faqih now penetrated the entire constitution. Nationalist members of the assembly suddenly realized how the constitution was shaping up as they found the stumbling block of *Velayat-e Faqih* in every single article. They were subject to vicious attacks by the Islamist media, exacerbated by the radicalized environment following the seizure of the U.S. embassy on November 4, 1979. Islamist followers of Khomeini carefully translated and published materials that would implicate, intimidate, and thus stifle the nationalists, Shariatmadari, and others who opposed the inclusion of *Velayat-e Faqih* in the constitution.

Feeling frustrated, manipulated, and powerless, the nationalists demanded to know the clergy's endgame. Seyyed Ahmad Nourbakhsh, a member of the assembly, summarized their aggravation in this allegory, which he shared on the floor:

> They told an elementary school boy: "Write A!" He refused. They insisted. He said, "I will not write it." Finally they asked him, "Why don't you write it?" He said, "If I write A, then will come B, then C, and then D." Now we have accepted *Velayat-e Faqih*, but it is not clear what kind of system is going to be implemented. Let us finally discuss the overall political system that is going to dominate our country. We cannot continue this step-by-step approach. First, we need to understand the po-

litical system we want to govern the country—we need to understand what it is, and then we can discuss these articles one by one. Otherwise, we are going to be stuck in every article.[68]

The endgame was suddenly clear. The final product was a written document that unified religious and political authorities headed by Khomeini himself. The man who until recently had been confined to a small seminary in Najaf was now both the supreme jurist and the supreme commander in chief: he appointed heads of the armed forces and Guardian Council jurists, and oversaw all branches of the government along with the state-controlled media. Moreover, his clerical representatives, or mini-Guardian Jurists, would be deployed in every government office, from the ministries of foreign affairs, agriculture, and finance to the army, the IRGC, and the media. Yet still no one understood the depth and breadth of this clerical control over the state. As Bazargan bitterly declared later, *Velayat-e Faqih* entered the constitution "secretly and namelessly" and "practically replaced the national sovereignty."[69]

Ironically, this constitutional triumph posed a new threat to the Islamist clerics. They feared that if the army, the nationalists, or the radical left did not take over through a coup, elections, or a second revolution, their newly created political system could fall into the hands of their old enemy. The traditional clerics, including Shariatmadari, who were more learned than the politically active clerics, could still challenge their authority—or worse, take over the state after Khomeini's death. With the blessing of Khomeini, the Islamists would soon designate Montazeri as his successor to ensure that none of Qom's grand ayatollahs would inherit the throne.

Outside the assembly, opposition groups finally began to grasp what was happening, too. Though many had criticized the original draft constitution for giving too much power to the president,[70] they later realized that something worse had been adopted: clerical sovereignty instead of popular sovereignty. The FKO and the MKO understood that with Article 5, the entire state apparatus, including the presidency and the Majles, came under the direct control of the Islamist clerics. In this system, the Guardian Jurist would have "custody" of forty million people who were treated as "infants," the FKO warned.[71]

Many clerics, and above all Shariatmadari, intensified their opposition to Khomeini's supreme control of both the mosque and the state. Perhaps they had seen it coming since Borujerdi's death. Shariatmadari's criticism of

Velayat-e Faqih was best summarized in his supported party's weekly paper, *Moslem People*: "All powers are put at the disposal of one person who is not responsible to anyone, while all responsibility is entrusted to those who lack power compatible with their responsibilities."[72] He boycotted the referendum for the constitution. The ensuing clashes between his followers and the Islamists' militias in Qom, during which his bodyguard was killed, quickly spread to his home region of Azerbaijan. His immense popularity among ten million fellow Azerbaijanis—compounded by discontent among other ethnic groups like the Kurds, Baluchis, Arabs, and Turkmens, who together constituted around 50 percent of the Iranian population—threatened both the Islamists' power and the state's territorial integrity. In Tabriz, where Azerbaijani demonstrators had played a critical role in bringing down the Shah a year earlier, Shariatmadari's followers poured into the streets again, seized the state-controlled radio-TV station, took over the governor's office, and threatened to march to Qom.[73]

The Islamists called for the dissolution of the pro-Shariatmadari Muslim People's Republican Party, and IRGC forces attacked its headquarters in Tabriz. Against the background of the U.S. hostage crisis, Khomeini labeled Shariatmadari's followers "American spies" and "enemies of Islam" and called for their punishment.[74] The Revolutionary Court swiftly executed eleven protesters. At a Friday prayer session in Qom, in front of hundreds of his followers, Shariatmadari wept and compared Khomeini to the monarch: "Under the Shah I was not free to speak and they came to my house and killed a student. Under this government I am still not free to speak and they come to my house and kill a guard."[75] Prime Minister Bazargan's attempt to mediate between two ayatollahs he had long known became instead an effort to press Shariatmadari to help protect the country's territorial integrity. Shariatmadari urged his die-hard followers not to challenge the central government and the parallel state. Khomeini then put him under de facto house arrest. Several senior clerics privately and publicly protested the harsh treatment of the very source of emulation that had helped save Khomeini's life by recognizing him as a source of emulation sixteen years earlier. These efforts were unsuccessful. The Guardian Jurist's control over the mosque was now nearly complete.

The vicissitudes of the emerging political and religious challenges to Khomeini's authority precipitated doctrinal measures that laid the foundation for a lasting political order. The diminishing threat from the United States and the army to the new Islamist–nationalist ruling regime heightened the inter- and intra-elite rivalries after the 1979 revolution. To co-opt the orthodox clergy and marginalize the nationalists (in the government) and the leftists, the Islamists increasingly invoked self-serving readings of Shi'a jurisprudence, culminating in a return to Khomeini's doctrine of *Velayat-e Faqih*. This move resulted in the creation of an Islamist-controlled parallel state, led by the Guardian Jurist and armed with the extralegal and extrajudicial tools of the Guardian Council and the IRGC. This divine *nezam* ("system") was specially designed to contain a variety of threats emanating from the traditional clerical establishment, nationalists, leftists, and state intuitions such as the army and the popularly elected president.

It would be reductively misleading to label the Islamists' sudden turn to *shari'a* as a long-calculated, deceptive move without accounting for all the political contingencies that opened space for one option while closing possibilities for another. It is these contingencies that color an ally as a rival and a rival's ideology as an asset to acquire. In hindsight, both actors and scholars tend to disproportionately refer to what they describe as Khomeini's consistent deception instead of examining the possibility of his unforeseen reactions to diverging and changing threat perceptions under uncertainty.

Many analysts and political actors, including Rafsanjani himself, claim Khomeini planned all along to establish a clerically controlled state by using, and then discarding, the nationalists once he consolidated his position. According to Rafsanjani, there was an unwritten agreement that the clergy would stay in the Majles and give the executive branch initially to the non-clerics. Since the leftists were not trusted, Khomeini then asked Bazargan and other veteran nationalists to form a cabinet. In his diaries, Rafsanjani insists that Khomeini did not want a "genuine" revolutionary organization to take over the executive branch; rather, he wanted a group of professionals who could smoothly run the country until his trusted men gained experience to take over that branch, too.[76] However, Bazargan believed the ayatollah's radical turn from "Islamic revolution" to "revolutionary Islam" was not premeditated, but a reaction to the unpredictable events on the ground. Empirical evidence presented in this and the next chapter partially validates this assertion. Neither Bazargan nor any other group posed a fixed, predictable challenge to the Islamists from the outset. Rather, an aggregate threat emanated not from each group per se but from their alignments in a rapidly changing political context.

However, there is some validity in Rafsanjani's convenient contention as well. Khomeini preferred that the technocrats run the administration, particularly because he was not confident that the clerics and their young, passionate followers could manage a country in chaos. But this does not mean that Khomeini, unlike his disciples, envisioned total control of the entire state. He favored the technocrats over the clergy to be the face of the state in the executive branch and responsible for its shortcomings. He reserved the judiciary and the Majles for the clergy. However, his disciples worried that should Khomeini die, they would be purged from the polity. Therefore, they sought a gradual and total control of the state apparatus while Khomeini was still alive. The formation of the IRP is a case in point that demonstrates the disagreement between Khomeini and his politically ambitious followers, who instrumentally used the radical political climate to monopolize power. The Islamist clerics were not unified under the leadership of Khomeini. Time and time again, they contested his decrees and negotiated with him until they reached a compromise in their favor, particularly against the nationalists. In this struggle for power, they strategically contributed to the polarization of the political climate by unleashing their followers against the militant Left. They continued to push not only for an Islamist government but for a state under total clerical control.

FIVE

The Hostage Crisis

The Untold Account of the Communist Threat

SOON AFTER its establishment in February 1979, the new Islamic Republic found itself in a political—and ultimately armed—struggle with growing leftist groups throughout the country, from the mountains of Kurdistan in the west to the forests of the Caspian Sea provinces in the north to the deserts of Baluchestan in the south. The sudden victory of the Iranian Revolution had challenged these groups' class-based Marxist theories, which predicted a bloody revolt led by the armed proletariat against the bourgeoisie and its reactionary allies. How could the latter two, namely the nationalists and their Islamist allies, carry out such a movement against a capitalist state backed by the United States, and bring about a smooth regime transition from the Pahlavi monarchy to the Islamic Republic? Inspired by the 1917 Russian Revolution, the leftist groups construed nationalist Prime Minister Bazargan and even Ayatollah Khomeini as Iran's "Kerensky." The Islamic Revolution was an interim step that only presaged the "real" revolution to come. But who would play the parts analogous to those of Lenin and the Bolsheviks? The fall of the monarchy, their thinking went, was only a political transition at the very top that did not constitute an authentic revolution to transform the state. The Shah was gone, but the rest of the state apparatus—including the political, economic, and military institutions— remained intact and tied to the international capitalist system. The old state institutions had to be dissolved altogether and replaced by classless, mass-based, anti-imperialist, and revolutionary organizations and councils. In short, the Left was pushing for a state-building project from scratch. But it grossly underestimated the Islamists' ideological flexibility and organizational capability to stay in power.

The Islamists' thinking mirrored that of the leftists. As they strove to institutionalize clerical control of the state, the Islamists emphasized an anti-American discourse designed to garner the Left's intellectual and mass support. But to outbid the Left on anti-imperialism required credibility, which the Islamists lacked in the early days of the revolution. Not only were the clerics allied with the U.S.-friendly nationalist Provisional Government, but they preserved ties with the Western bloc and U.S.-backed institutions, such as the army. Moreover, they, too, were working closely with U.S. officials before, during, and after the revolution, as described in the previous chapters.

In this climate, radical action against the United States—which came in the form of the seizure of the American embassy by "Muslim Students Following the Imam's [Khomeini's] Line"—would, some Islamists believed, help establish their anti-imperialist credibility among the intelligentsia, students, and labor forces. Khomeini shrewdly called it the "second revolution," to be followed by a "cultural revolution," which would shut down the center of leftist activism in universities across the country. Thus, although Marxist groups deployed their anti-American narrative masterfully, the Islamists outbid them, and the Left's doubling down after the seizure of the embassy only contributed to prolonging the crisis and institutionalizing anti-Americanism. The Left was so concerned about the pro-U.S. "deep state" (the alliance of the remnants of the Shah's regime, the nationalists, and the orthodox and liberal clerics) that by the time it woke up, it was facing an Islamist parallel state that, unlike its predecessor, was capable of liquidating the opposition altogether.

This chapter offers a revisionist account of the hostage crisis, arguing that the embassy takeover was not a product of Khomeini's preconceived and predictable Islamist ideology nor an inevitable measure to protect the revolution against the plotting United States. The ayatollah's rising antagonism toward the United States had little to do with the latter's backing of the Shah or exploitation of Iran's resources, as is often asserted.[1] The conventional wisdom is challenged by evidence of an overlooked factor found in scores of primary materials, many of them recently released. This evidence demonstrates that on the eve of the hostage crisis, the Islamists were in fact seeking to maintain normal relations with the United States. They were preoccupied instead with a far more immediate domestic threat to their power from the communist Left. To be sure, the reluctant decision of the Carter administration to allow the deposed monarch into the United States increased anti-American anxieties in Iran. But American officials privately and consistently assured Iranian leaders that Washington had accepted the Islamic Revolution and had no intention of investing any longer in the dying Shah.

Instead, these new sources show that as the Islamists moved from opposition to incumbent, their threat perceptions shifted. Few had expected the Iranian leftists to capitalize so successfully on the popular animosity toward the United States once the Shah was ousted. Universities, labor unions, and factories—which had played a critical role in bringing down the Shah—were now hotbeds of both anti-clericalism and anti-liberalism in response to the Islamist-nationalist coalition's associations with the United States. As political factions clamored for power, anti-Americanism became a commodity to be appropriated for political gain. Leftist and Islamist factions instrumentally deployed anti-Americanism to outbid one another's anti-imperialist credibility. This chain of strategic interactions culminated in the Islamists' seizure of the U.S. embassy on November 4, 1979. The embassy occupation effectively undermined the Left's cohesion, prevented the radical Islamists from defecting to the Marxist camp, and further united the loose coalition of radical and conservative Islamists behind Khomeini. An account that includes the leftists' activism and the Americans' and the Islamists' silent attempts to work with each other—two facets of this period that are underappreciated in existing studies—helps to correct common misunderstandings of the Islamists' threat perceptions in 1979, thereby changing the entire story of the hostage crisis.

The empirical literature on this critical event largely infers the Islamists' intentions from their observed behavior, with at least two consequences: (1) it underestimates the Islamists' perceived threat from the Left, and (2) it overestimates the Islamists' perceived threat from the United States and the nationalists. Scholars have principally focused on Islamist, nationalist, and American interests while downplaying, if not ignoring, the cardinal role of the Marxist-communist groups in shaping the anti-American narrative in Iran. This is perhaps partly because the Islamists would not acknowledge their intellectual debt to, and their appropriation of, the Left's anti-American rhetoric as a means to achieve a strategic edge in their political competition. Rather, they masked their drive for power under potent rhetoric of Islamism and anti-Americanism, making it difficult for observers to detect their political concerns. Additionally, scholarship tends to overlook the leftists' important roles in the lead-up to the crisis, perhaps because they had no official position within the revolutionary government and therefore did not constitute the "political elite." Conventional accounts thus fail to consider the ways in which leftists tapped into their vast network and exploited bottom-up pressures against the new Islamist government. To my knowledge, no one, from the hostage takers and the hostages to U.S. policymakers and academics, has accounted for the Islamists' outbidding competition with the Marxists as a contributing factor to the seizure of the embassy.

Ignoring this important dimension has led many observers to reduce the growing anti-Americanism and eventual seizure of the embassy to a reaction to American threats or the incompatibility of Western and Islamic values. They posit that the hostage crisis was a response to the Shah's admission to the United States because it reminded many Iranians of the 1953 CIA coup and that by taking American diplomats hostage, the Islamists ensured the 1953 scenario would not be repeated.[2] The hostages themselves pointed to the Shah's entry into the United States as the explanation provided to them by the radical students throughout their captivity.[3] However, recently declassified documents reveal that Khomeini did not consider the United States an immediate danger to the revolution, particularly after he brutally decapitated Iran's American-trained army without any significant reaction from Washington.

Various U.S. policymakers correctly surmised that the takeover was a deliberate attempt by the Islamists to unify the nation and divert the people's attention from other internal crises.[4] But they either ignored the radicalizing role of the leftists or were oblivious to its significance and argued that Khomeini used the embassy takeover to sideline the U.S.-friendly nationalists. Some scholars did note the vicious rivalry between the Islamists and the leftists—and even the influence of the latter over the former—but they failed to link their outbidding competition to the hostage crisis. Barry Rubin identifies anti-Americanism as an ideological "agreement" between the Islamists and the leftists.[5] To Stephanie Cronin, the Left's "influence, in both organizational and ideological terms, on the evolution of Islamist trends, including on Khomeini himself has been profound."[6] Ali Mirsepassi posits that Islamists "unabashedly appropriated large portions of leftist discourse for their own purposes."[7] Others acknowledge the "confusion" among the leftists as an outcome of the crisis. They argue that the Islamists used the takeover and the ensuing U.S. threats toward Iran to unite the masses behind them, which "took the thunder away from the Left."[8] What these scholars view as an outcome of the event, namely the Islamists' ideological victory over the leftists, should in fact be seen as a *primary cause* of the hostage crisis.

Surprisingly, a few Iranian Islamists and even the hostage takers have recently admitted that the anti-American statements and actions by Khomeini and his followers were directly aimed at disarming the leftists. Prominent reformist and former supporter of the hostage takers Emadeddin Baghi points out in passing that the seizure of the embassy broke the leftists' monopoly over anti-imperialism.[9] Without elaborating further, Baghi even acknowledges that the operation was "in fact about outbidding the Marxists."[10] Yet the role of the Left remains surprisingly underexamined in his rather lengthy analysis of the hostage crisis. Ebrahim Asgharzadeh, who claims to be the mastermind of the seizure, underlines the "seriousness" of the leftist threat and the prevalence of anti-American sentiments in Iranian society. He concedes that in the absence of the Muslim students' takeover, "more violent groups" would have certainly seized the embassy.[11] Similarly, the hostage takers' English-speaking spokesperson, Masoumeh Ebtekar, acknowledges that the rivalry with the Left "might have been one of the factors" in the students' decision to "take the initiative" and occupy the U.S. embassy.[12]

At the same time, these activists are careful to make a distinction between their competition with, and their intellectual debt to, the Left. Ebtekar underscores that the radical students were by no means "influenced by the leftist trends, because they had their own intellect and organization."[13] Likewise, the hostage takers' cleric mentor, Mohammad Mousavi Khoeiniha, strongly denies that the Left played any ideological or organizational role in the occupation of the embassy.[14] Four decades later, the hostage takers are still proud and firm that the Islamists, not the Marxists, raided the U.S. embassy. As Khoeiniha boasted later, one of the "benefits" and "blessings" of this embassy seizure was the "cohesion" it brought the nation.[15] He claimed that it ended the enmity and divisive activities of the "armed students" throughout the country.

Despite these occasional statements on their competition with the Left, the hostage takers overwhelmingly remain adamant that the occupation was a reaction to the Shah's admission to the United States. But even this explanation indirectly points to the Islamists' fear of internal consequences of U.S. president Jimmy Carter's decision: namely, the potential collapse of the Provisional Government and takeover by the Left. Asgharzadeh now claims that the Islamist students had good relations with Bazargan throughout his tenure as the provisional prime minister; their frustration was that he was too weak to stand against immediate threats to the revolution both internal and external.[16] Similarly, another leading hostage taker, Abbas Abdi, argues that Bazargan fell because his moderate path did not match the post-revolutionary radical climate.[17] This is not to deny the rivalry between the Islamists and the nationalists; the Islamists feared that the nationalists might become strong enough to take over the regime in the long term. But the more immediate security threat faced by both was potential chaos and overthrow by the Left. Thus, the Islamists had to manage two different threats: the nationalists within the state apparatus and the leftists without. Consequently, the hostage takers' statements can also be interpreted as follows: radical Islamists, in an act of fratricide, brought down the nationalists before others (including the leftists) could. They predicted that the Provisional Government would collapse as a consequence of the embassy takeover.[18]

The embassy occupation effectively undermined the Left's cohesion and united the loose coalition of radical and conservative Islamists behind Khomeini, but it brought unintended consequences the Islamists never anticipated. A symbolic move meant to last only a few days—enough to undermine leftist rivals—ultimately entrapped all actors for a fifteen-month struggle that would estrange Iran and the United States for decades to come.

Washington and the Post-Revolutionary Factional Politics

Communications between the Islamists and the United States remained in place after the monarchy was abolished in February 1979. Khomeini's nationalist allies and clerical disciples met frequently with American representatives. Ebrahim Yazdi (Khomeini's nationalist aide) and a cleric named Mahdavi Kermani[19] saved General Philip C. Gast, the highest U.S. military official in Tehran, and dozens of his staff from armed groups and personally delivered them to the American embassy on the eve of the Iranian Revolution's victory.[20] Ayatollahs Beheshti, Ardebili, and Taleqani, as well as Yazdi and other clerical and nationalist figures, were all "embassy contacts" until the hostage crisis.[21] Carter later recalled the positive signals he continued to receive from the new Islamist-nationalist government after the revolution: "From roughly March until through October of '79 we had increasingly good relationships with Iran, even including [Ruhollah] Khomeini, who was sending emissaries over to talk directly to [Secretary of State] Vance and say, 'You support the revolution, don't try to overthrow our government,' and 'We want to increase trade,' and so forth. And they were quite friendly. In fact, they made some beautiful speeches about the importance of repairing relations with the United States."[22] Throughout this period, the United States used every opportunity to improve relations with the new Iranian government. Charles Nass, the deputy ambassador and chargé d'affaires in Tehran, planned to go to Qom and meet with Khomeini to reassure him that Washington had no intention of working with any opposition group. His trip never happened, but according to a State Department cable, he told Yazdi that "we accept the Iranian Revolution and that we do not intend to attempt in any way to reverse its course. I pointed out that we are approached almost every day by a variety of individuals who do not wish the revolution or the PGOI [Provisional Government of Iran] well, seeking our help, and that our answer is always 'no.' "[23] As a confidence-building measure, U.S. officials gradually began sharing intelligence with Iran.[24] In October 1979—a year before Iraq invaded Iran—the CIA informed Tehran of Saddam Hussein's intentions and offered further intelligence collaboration against Baghdad.[25] To be sure, U.S. diplomats in Tehran had no illusions about their lack of popularity in that revolutionary country. Acknowledging a "latent anti-Americanism," which various actors were adopting, Ambassador Sullivan warned that U.S. ambitions had to be tailored to realities and that Washington had to "adopt a low profile."[26] Nevertheless, the broad assumption was, as Sullivan told Carter, "The long-term strategic interests of Iran dictate that Iran will wish to maintain decent relations with the United States. The military hardware Iran has bought from the United States will need to be serviced if the armed forces are to be revived. There are the seeds of a new relationship there. But they are going to have to be nurtured very slowly."[27]

Viewing Iran as a black box with systemic insecurity in the Cold War led many U.S. policymakers to underestimate the immediate factional competition and the leftists' threat to the new government, although—ironically—U.S. intelligence predicted that the leftist influence, particularly among ethnic minorities, was only growing after the revolution.[28] Various assessments in Washington pointed out that Marxist groups, predominantly Tudeh and the Fadaiyan-e Khalq Organization (FKO), had ties with the Kurdish, Azeri, Turkmen, and other ethnic minorities throughout the country. Others within the State Department stressed "a very uncertain immediate future for Iran," in which the nationalist government could "disappear without a trace" due to the activities of the leftists.[29] Ambassador Sullivan described the leftist student organizations as one of Iran's three "real institutions of power" along with the clergy and the army.[30]

However, American officials, like Iranian nationalists, believed these challenges would serve to intensify the Islamist-nationalist alliance and its dependence on Washington. Both Iranian nationalists and American officials believed Khomeini and his followers needed them to stay in power. The nationalists were the technocrats who could manage the country and serve as the link with the army and the United States. A relationship with Washington could provide a buffer against interference by the Soviet Union. U.S. leaders perceived Khomeini as a figure whose periodic anti-American rhetoric was intended for the masses, a nonconfrontational assessment based not only on his limited engagement with the United States during the revolutionary period, but perhaps also on his previous message to the Kennedy administration proposing cooperation against the USSR (as described in chapter 2) and other classified reports from various American agencies. It is important to note that Khomeini's prerevolutionary statements against the United States were not confrontational, but rather expressed a collective sense of victimhood that implicitly offered Washington an opportunity to remedy its past mistake of backing a dictator. Many U.S. officials viewed him as xenophobic, but not inherently anti-American.

After the revolution, American officials continued to believe Khomeini and his "trusted" nationalist advisers were "struggling to protect Iran and the U.S. against a conservative majority." A cable from Tehran to Washington accurately described the first brief takeover of the embassy on February 14, 1979, by the FKO as an attempt to capitalize on massive anti-American sentiments among ordinary Iranians: "The attack was an example of the leftist strategy to continue to pose problems for Khomeini and [Prime Minister] Bazargan without openly challenging the stated goals of the Islamic government. The [FKO] Chariks appear to have gambled that the attack on the embassy would not provoke a crackdown by Islamic militia groups since such a move would be tantamount to defending 'American Imperialism.'"[31] In fact, the Provisional Government removed the FKO members and apologized to the United States. However, the Left expanded its campaign against the Islamist-nationalist alliance by portraying it as a U.S. stooge.

In this climate, both U.S. and Iranian officials understood that their communication should continue but remain quiet, lest it provoke dangerous anti-American sentiments. Beheshti, the powerful chairman of the Revolutionary Council, head of the judiciary, and secretary general of the Islamic Republican Party, told U.S. officials privately that more changes in American policy, including cutting off the last ties with the remnants of the Shah's regime, could help reduce anti-Americanism in Iran and improve the two countries' relations quickly.[32] The following anecdote recounted by embassy official John Limbert a few days before his capture underlines the internal dynamic and the U.S. dilemma:

> On October 26, 1979—nine days before the "Moslem Student Followers of the Imam's Line" seized the American embassy—I accompanied a visiting State Department official to Friday prayers at Tehran University. We heard a sermon from Ayatollah Montazeri [chair of the Constitutional Assembly] in which he barely mentioned the United States and made no mention of the deposed Shah, who had recently arrived in the United States for medical treatment. After the sermon and the prayers there was a pep rally in which someone chanted slogans and the fist-waving crowd repeated them. Our visitor, whose Persian was not strong, asked me, "What should we do?" I responded, "Think about it. There are two of us. There are over a million of them. You know the answer." The first slogans were innocuous enough: "The Kurds are our brothers!" and "Unity will bring us victory." Then I heard, "Marg bar seh mofsedin, Sadat o Karter o Begin!" (Death to the three corruptors, Sadat, Carter and Begin). The visitor asked, "Isn't there something in there about Carter?" I told him, "Yes there is, and you know what to do. Carter will understand and God will forgive us." As we screamed for our president's death, we were accompanied by our escort from the Foreign Ministry, who joined the chorus of denunciation with great enthusiasm. His face turned red and his eyes bulged as he shouted. A few minutes later the ceremony ended, and he asked us, "Please do me the honor of being my guest for lunch this afternoon."[33]

A day earlier, Ayatollah Montazeri had met with the same U.S. officials and expressed "great admiration" for Carter as a Christian believer and human rights supporter. He stressed that the two nations shared similar values.[34]

If U.S. officials understood the domestic functions of "Death to America," surely they would tolerate a few days of a hostage crisis, too, if that was the price to pay to maintain strategic relations. Despite their appreciation of the

Islamists' instrumentally adopted anti-American rhetoric, U.S. officials did not fully grasp the boiling context that produced such a discursive strategy. Perhaps even the Islamists themselves did not initially expect to act on their slogans.

The Leftist Threat

Iran's Communist Party was one of the first in Asia, even older than the Chinese Communist Party. The leftist tradition constituted a main pillar of Iran's modern political history and intellectual dissidence. The Left was initially composed of a dozen competing groups, which multiplied after the revolution into about eighty organizations and continued to branch and spread at an increasing rate.[35]

Foreign observers noted Khomeini's inability to control the armed guerilla groups and consequently the possibility of collapse of the army and the prevailing political order.[36] Thousands of youngsters had acquired up to one hundred thousand guns from defenseless army bases and were joining the Left, despite Khomeini's plea to disarm and come under the Islamic banner.[37] Similarly, workers who had obeyed Khomeini's order to strike against the Shah were now leaning to the left. In those critical days of the revolution, Iran experts such as Ervand Abrahamian predicted that the Left could soon control the labor force: "It is likely that the religious groups will soon begin to lose their hold over the labor movement. The Left will then have an easy entry into an arena that includes more than two-and-a-half million wage earners and forms the single largest middle class in contemporary Iran."[38]

The Islamists were aware of such a danger. They had long competed with the Left in universities, underground, in prisons, and abroad to forge a powerful opposition movement against the Shah. In the immediate aftermath of the revolution, the Islamists held political debates on TV with leftist leaders to demonstrate the latter's ideological "bankruptcy" before arresting and bringing them back on TV to make forced confessions about their betrayal of the country.[39] These public recantations, which continued throughout the 1980s, reveal the depth of the Islamists' fear of the Left's ideological popularity. Islamist militant forces cracked down on the mushrooming leftist organizations, demonstrations, and media that appeared after the fall of the Shah. Nonetheless, more and more students, laborers, and autonomy-

and independence-seeking ethnic groups were joining the Left. The most prominent leftist organizations included the pro-Soviet Tudeh, the Marxist FKO, and the Marxist-Islamist MKO.[40] Starting as offshoots of Tudeh and the National Front, both the FKO and MKO had decades of armed struggle and ideological exercise under their belts.

What was particularly worrisome to the Islamists was the Afghan communists' ascendance to power in April 1978 through a coup, despite their marginal status in society. Later, in December 1979, Soviet forces invaded Afghanistan to protect the communist government in Kabul. Iran's leftists were far more deeply rooted in society, ethnic groups, labor forces, and the army. Iran also shared 1,250 miles of border with the USSR. U.S. intelligence sources noted that the Left, including Tudeh, were "strongly represented in northwest Iran and [were] assisting in the reconstitution of the Azerbaijan Democratic Party and the Kurdish Democratic Party, which [sought] autonomy for their areas."[41] These activities were reminiscent of the communist republics that the Soviet Union had set up in Iran's occupied Azerbaijan and Kurdish provinces during World War II.

The Left aimed to exploit the growing rift between Khomeini's Islamists and the nationalists in the Islamists' favor. They believed Khomeini would protect the revolution in the short term before "forces of history" could bring him down, too; this, in turn, would allow them to carry out the socialist revolution.[42] They also calculated that they could not challenge Khomeini, whose enormous charisma and power as a unifying leader had brought the masses out to topple the Shah. Instead, driving a wedge between the two factions could facilitate the downfall of both. The Islamists would serve as a bridge in transferring the revolution from the nationalists to the Marxists.

In addition to deploying their anti-capitalist, anti-American ideology to undermine the alliance between the Islamists and nationalists, the leftists used it to exacerbate tensions within the loose coalition of Islamists. The radical left wing of the Islamists had more affinity and competition with the communist Left, while the conservative right-wing Islamists were closer to the nationalists. Ideological overlaps among competing Marxists and Islamists on the entire political spectrum in post-revolutionary Iran rendered detection of factional identities on the margins difficult and defection a common phenomenon. The porous borders between political factions only worsened Khomeini's shaky standing. Pro-Khomeini activists and sympathizers who leaned left were particularly at risk of succumbing to Islamist-leftist groups before ending up in the leftist camp. Many Islamist students eventually joined armed leftist organizations. Among them were the children of the most senior clerics within the Islamist government. For instance, the leftist sons of Ayatollah Ahmad Jannati, Ayatollah Mohammad Mohammadi-Gilani, and Ayatollah Gholamreza Hassani were ultimately killed by Islamist forces.

The Left's divisive strategy became effective particularly as the Provisional Government struggled to impose law and order in the post-revolutionary country. The newly established IRP cautiously welcomed and contributed to the decline of Bazargan's power. With the IRP's parallel organizations, particularly the IRGC and the Komiteh, shadowing and purging the army and other state institutions, the nationalists struggled to remain a viable political force. But the IRP was particularly fearful of the communists. While the former was securing more power within the state, the latter seemed to be winning the streets. Despite internal divisions, the leftists' networks and constituencies grew, thanks to decades of ideological and organizational work. They carried out large demonstrations and rallies in Tehran and other major cities, bringing out hundreds of thousands of marchers. It is estimated that between five hundred thousand and a million supporters participated in the 1979 Labor Day demonstration in Tehran.[43] According to U.S. intelligence reports, the FKO's rallies at its birthplace, the University of Tehran, alone attracted between 50,000 and 150,000 supporters.[44] Taking advantage of the new freedom in the immediate wake of the revolution, the leftists overwhelmed the fragile civil society by distributing previously underground bulletins and secret pamphlets as legal newspapers. The Left's papers, including the FKO's *Kar*, reportedly had a weekly readership of one to three hundred thousand.[45]

The most dominant theme in their publications and statements was anti-Americanism. Mere days after the victory of the revolution, the FKO sent an open letter to Khomeini warning that the revolution had not ended. In fact, the letter continued, the struggle against American imperialism and its local forces had only just begun. The letter acknowledged Khomeini's "critical" role in the movement but also expressed concerns that "reactionary" Islamists had attacked the leftists' newly launched newspapers, gatherings, and offices while monopolizing power in the name of religion.[46] The Moscow-backed Tudeh demanded that Bazargan expel U.S. advisers and contractors, end Iran's membership in the anti-communist Central Treaty Organization (CENTO),[47] cease purchasing weapons from the United States, deny U.S. companies any share of Iran's oil exports, pull Iranian troops back from Oman, and support the secular leftist Palestinians. All leftist organizations were pushing for the nationalization of banks, factories, and other industries.

Khomeini's previous strategy—adopting a moderate discourse and forging an alliance with the nationalists to ensure a peaceful political transition without intervention by the army or the United States—was not effective in the increasingly uncertain post-revolutionary era. The regime's initial transition had been relatively nonviolent, but now, after the revolution, the government faced real security challenges.

Not even one hundred days after Khomeini's arrival in Tehran, unexpected violence erupted; assassinations of his devotees by smaller armed Marxist-Islamist groups began. Khomeini's rhetoric against the United States became more radical at this time, but the intended audience seemed more internal than external. In a meeting with students from the University of Tehran's School of Law, Khomeini identified the United States as the "real" foe and cannily tied this enemy to the leftists.[48] In the following month of June, Khomeini's rhetoric grew more impatient as student unrest continued. In a meeting with another group of Islamist students, he said, "Gentlemen! Are you waiting for a few communists [to] come and dominate the university? Are you less than them? . . . They need to be slapped on the mouth, gentlemen! You are more. Your *hujjat* [proof of evidence] is stronger; their treason is evident. It needs to be said. Get together. Convey the issues. If you see a dean or a teacher who is a communist, kick them out of the university."[49]

But as IRGC commander and police chief Ismail Ahmadi-Moghaddam—then a young Islamist and new seminarian—bitterly recalled later, the leftists were popular and winning the discursive battle in society:

From Esfand 58 [February/March 1979], the Monafeghin ["hypocrites"—a derogatory term for the MKO] and the leftists were turning every crossroad in Tehran into a forum for debate and discussion. And so often the Hezbollahis [Islamists] did not have the power in terms of logic to beat them. Until Mehr 58 [September/ October 1979] when the universities opened, they would gather at high schools, and often the Hezbollahis were the losers in this field, because [the leftists] were prepared and these people [the Islamists] could not present the right [ideological] response to successfully end the debate.[50]

Baghi, an Islamist activist at the time, has pointed out that the leftists' recruitment success prompted Khomeini to match his rival's anti-American rhetoric:

> Before the revolution, the Leader had several negotiations with the Americans in Paris. But at the beginning of the revolution, the leftist current, meaning the Marxists, influenced the [internal] political atmosphere, which was very critical in radicalizing the foreign policy atmosphere. They [the leftists] were in the minority, but they were potent in spreading movements and political propaganda. With their terms and slogans, they mesmerized the youth and students, and the Leader had to promote more radical slogans to disarm them. The hostage crisis itself was in fact about outbidding the Marxists.[51]

Ongoing military operations against the Kurdish separatists added more fuel to the leftists' narratives. Marxist groups accused the Iranian army of using the same anti-insurgency tactics as its old U.S. patron did against the Vietnamese.[52] They published chilling pictures of the executions of the Kurds to demonstrate the brutality of the central government in Kurdistan.[53] As the leftists warned against the return of American imperialism, Khomeini and his Islamist supporters could less and less afford a neutral, or even a mildly negative, tone toward Washington. Their alliance with Bazargan had become a liability in their confrontation with the Left.

Every day, the Provisional Government was the target of ruthless attacks for its "deep" ideological and political dependence on the United States. Unlike other leftist groups, Tudeh had to mind Soviet interests in Iran as well as its own agenda and help improve relations between Moscow and the new regime in Tehran. Its main objective was to ensure that the Soviet Union's southern neighbor entirely cut all American ties. Tudeh pressed Bazargan to cancel military contracts with U.S. companies such as Bell Helicopter; otherwise, the country would have to pay for spare parts and bring back American military advisers.[54] Its newspaper, *Mardom*, argued against the Bushehr nuclear power plant as "completely illogical," since Iran was sitting on the second-largest gas reserves in the world.[55] Ironically, it would be Tudeh's patron, the Russians, who would come to complete the project decades later. Tudeh sought to close ranks with the Khomeinists while pushing the nationalists out of the way and attacked other leftist groups for not backing Khomeini against the nationalists. In order to delink the Islamists from the nationalists, Tudeh strongly backed the referendum for the Islamic Republic under Khomeini's leadership as a progressive and united front against "imperialism."[56] It claimed to be the first political party that supported the referendum and complained that state-controlled television under the nationalists was attacking the Kremlin instead of covering Tudeh's support.[57]

Tudeh made explicit efforts to reconcile Islam and Marxism while criticizing the nationalists who followed in U.S. footsteps and pointed to the "danger of Marxism" and "Godless communists." It provided a revolutionary reading of Islam, claiming that Islam had ended the caste-based system established by the Sassanid Persian empire (224–651 A.D.) and brought about a new civilization on earth. Tudeh further praised the rise of Shi'a Islam as an important movement in countering the Sunni Arab domination of Iran. Fiercely attacking other leftist groups for not following Khomeini, it stressed that religion was not an opiate of the masses and invited observant Shi'ites to join the organization.[58] Communism and Shi'a Islam were not contradictory, it proffered; they were quite compatible and shared a common enemy in the United States. Nothing seemed to change Tudeh's pro-Khomeini and anti-Bazargan stance. Even when it reported that "suspicious elements" had attacked its offices in various cities[59] and several of its members had been arrested and executed,[60] Tudeh was careful not to blame the IRGC and the Komiteh, claiming instead that the Shah's SAVAK was now a part of those organizations.[61] It expressed concerns that remnants of the old regime were now infiltrating the revolutionary organizations that shadowed the state. Tudeh blamed the U.S. embassy for suspending the Revolutionary Courts that were rooting out anti-revolutionaries.[62] Throughout this period, as Mohsen Milani points out, the Islamists shrewdly "tolerated the Tudeh's activity because it kept the left divided and solidified their position" against the Provisional Government.[63]

Even when they lost the Constitutional Assembly election to the Islamists, the leftists continued their attacks on the nationalist interim government. They blamed their failure on the electoral engineering of the Islamists, the IRGC, and the low level of "mass consciousness,"[64] but they still saw the nationalists as their main enemy because they kept the state under imperialist control. Throughout this phase, the Left continued to view the Islamists as a less organized and less formidable enemy, attacking them primarily for allying with Bazargan. Until his downfall, they relentlessly pushed Bazargan to prove that his government was independent and that the deep pro-imperialist state had been eradicated. Tudeh asked why the government refused to release information on which countries bought oil from Iran. Considering how much of Iran's oil resources had been "looted" in the past, people deserved to know, Tudeh's daily *Mardom* wrote.[65] The paper further asked why Bazargan's government had not established diplomatic relations with the Democratic Republic of Yemen or Cuba, or expanded ties with other socialist countries such as Algeria, Libya, or Syria.[66] A few weeks later, Tudeh expressed its approval that Cuban, Libyan, and Yemeni delegations had visited Tehran and praised Khomeini for breaking relations with Egypt after the Camp David Accords.[67]

Provocation Competition

The Left stepped up its anti-American provocations when the United States nominated Walter Cutler as its next ambassador to Iran in April 1979. Referencing Cutler's previous "roles" in plotting against revolutionaries in Vietnam and Zaire, Tudeh accused him of preparing a coup against the Islamic Republic,[68] drawing on the history of CIA coups against Iran's Mosaddegh and Chile's Salvador Allende. U.S. officials assured Iranian leaders that Cutler was going to Tehran to renormalize ties. Cutler made all the arrangements, chose his team, and even shipped his personal items, but before departing was suddenly ordered to abort his trip.[69] Anti-American sentiments had reached a new level in May 1979 when the U.S. Senate condemned the execution of an Iranian-Jewish entrepreneur, Habib Elghanian, by the notorious judge, Khalkhali.

Although a Senate resolution expressed concerns over human rights violations in Iran, it had respectfully welcomed Khomeini's measures to establish the rule of law. But the leftists pressured the Provisional Government to protest American interference in Iran's internal affairs and Khomeini, too, demanded to know why Iran needed a relationship with the United States in the first place. The Provisional Government, which had initially consented to Cutler's nomination, was forced to oppose his appointment. All competing political groups, including the nationalists, invited their supporters to rally against the United States. The leftists, however, went the furthest by organizing nationwide anti-American demonstrations and attacking the interim government because it had promised only to "reconsider" relations with the United States. Tudeh claimed that the interim government's delay in canceling contracts and treaties with the United States had emboldened Washington to interfere in Iran's internal affairs.[70] Quoting Khomeini's new anti-American statements, *Mardom* published poems to praise him, with references to the Prophet Mohammad and Islamic prayers.[71]

From this point on, the frequency and intensity of anti-American rallies only grew. Nevertheless, both the nationalists and the Islamist militant clerics struggled quietly to maintain ties with Washington without further provoking anti-American sentiments. Bazargan revealed later that Khomeini had instructed him to maintain normal ties with the United States but warned, "You need to prepare public opinion in order to continue relations under these limitations."[72] But the Left insisted on publicizing every communication Tehran had with Washington and blaming it on the nationalists. After Agence France-Presse (AFP) quoted anonymous sources in Tehran stating that forty American military technicians had arrived in Iran, Abbas Amir-Entezam, the prime minister's spokesperson, pointed out that the government intended to continue its military ties with the United States so long as Washington was interested in friendly relations with the Islamic Republic, which "they themselves have repeatedly stated, too."[73] He denied reports that Iran was planning to resell its F-14 fighter jets and Phoenix missiles.[74] But the Left pushed to get rid of advanced U.S. weapons beyond what the Shah's last prime minister, Shahpour Bakhtiar, had already canceled before his downfall. Prime Minister Bazargan argued that Iran could not throw out forty billion dollars' worth of Western weapons and that not every contract the Shah had signed served the interests of the imperialists; many of them were for the well-being of the country and served to improve "the technical, economic, military, and defensive levels of the nation."[75] The FKO published "highly classified" documents from the office of the prime minister that revealed that the interim government had approved deals to maintain military and logistical contracts with the United States in order to meet the needs of the army, particularly the air force.[76] Even the names of U.S. military advisers who had allegedly arrived in Tehran were published.[77] The FKO demanded that the government identify even a single contract with the imperialists that favored Iran. Why did Iran need these sophisticated, expensive, high-maintenance weapons? A state with a large population can defend itself against imperialists with "the most basic weapons," as Vietnam did. The organization continued, "Instead of justifying it, Mr. Bazargan needs to say explicitly that he is preserving these contracts to deepen the country's dependence on the imperialists ... People would like to know what the American advisers are doing in Iran, and what the group-by-group return of CIA spies and U.S. advisers is for, and based on what kind of a deal."[78] Through the FKO's vast network within the state, every minor step, including the army's measures to improve its image, was leaked, broadcast, and denounced during that relatively censorship-free phase.[79]

Every concession the Provisional Government made to the Left was followed by more radical demands. When the interim government announced that Iran was leaving CENTO, Tudeh demanded an end to the bilateral military accord with the United States as well, claiming the accord was "worse" than CENTO, as it gave the United States the "right" to invade Iran and end the revolution.[80] The only reason such a scenario had not yet occurred, Tudeh explained, was the Soviet Union's warning to the United States—a year earlier in November 1978—not to interfere in Iran's internal affairs during the critical revolutionary months.[81] Tudeh asserted that the United States was changing its posture, implementing an old plan to establish a fifth fleet in the Persian Gulf and the Indian Ocean,[82] and deploying a special Delta Force with 110,000 American troops in the region.[83] The longer the interim government delayed canceling the bilateral military treaty, the more aggressive the United States would become.

With the reopening of the schools in the fall of 1979,[84] all actors anticipated a showdown. Institutions of higher education were the center of the anti-Shah movements. Now the Left aimed to use this network to bring down the nationalists and eventually their Islamist allies. With the religious masses behind Khomeini, the leftists believed that students, workers, and the intelligentsia comprised the bulk of their supporters.[85] The Islamists were aware of this dynamic, too, and feared a new uprising under an anti-imperialist banner.

Admitting the Shah

Early in the fall of 1979, the United States informed the Provisional Government that it had decided to admit the Shah for medical treatment. Iranian officials warned of the serious consequences of this decision, but the State Department assured them that the dying Shah had no political future. Tehran requested to send its own doctors to examine the Shah to ensure that he had terminal cancer, but the State Department rejected the request.[86] Fearing public backlash, Iranian officials asked the United States to send the Shah to Europe for medical treatment—or at least to Texas, since New York City was viewed by Iranians as "a center of Rockefeller and Zionist influence and this would compound the problem."[87] U.S. officials told their Iranian counterparts that although they could not keep the Shah's arrival secret, they would emphasize to him that he should "avoid any political activity." They repeated that the Shah was out of the picture and they were "anxious to work together in every way possible to build a new relationship with Iran."[88]

Throughout this period, Iran's state-owned media continued to cover routine stories about U.S.-Iran relations with occasional anti-American and anti-Soviet headlines. For instance, as late as September 1979, *Ettelaat* reported the U.S. embassy's six-month delay in issuing visas to the thousands of Iranians who apparently applied every day.[89] When the Shah arrived in the United States on October 22, the IRP, the Provisional Government, and their media outlets covered the news mildly. The government's spokesperson announced that the United States had admitted the Shah for humanitarian reasons and that Iran had received assurances that he would not engage in any political activities during his stay. Barry Rosen, the embassy's press attaché, noticed, "The [Iranian] press outrage was less explosive than we had anticipated. Reaction was *relatively* controlled."[90] State-owned newspapers ran small headlines about the Shah's entry into the United States for medical treatment,[91] and they reported that Iranian officials warned the United States against the Shah's political activities.[92] Interestingly, the IRP's official newspaper, *Jomhuri Islami*, covered the event only as a short news story on page eight. The front page quoted then-deputy minister of defense and future supreme leader Ali Khamenei stating, "Our confrontation today is not only with America."[93] Khamenei warned against "reducing" the revolution's internal and external enemies to the United States. Khomeini's own first reaction was, "What will happen to our money?"[94] He was concerned about the billions of dollars the Shah had allegedly taken to the United States.

However, the Left immediately jumped on this opportunity to attack the nationalists and galvanize fears of U.S. interference against the revolution. The news became the main topic of all leftist media and forums. Tudeh alleged that the Shah had turned his hospital into a political campaign headquarters, coordinating with his allies in the region and inciting unrest in

Iran.[95] The leftists organized rallies and promoted chants of "Death to America" throughout the country; this slogan, originating first and foremost from the communists, would only *later* become a symbol of the Iranian Revolution. Thanks to their effective tactics, leftist students in particular gained further leverage against the Islamists on campuses. They were now mobilizing restlessly to seize the opportunity, rally the population around anti-Americanism, and take over the state from the streets.

Khomeini matched the leftists' tone by speaking of an imminent American plot, and the IRP decided to outbid them by organizing a mass demonstration in front of the U.S. embassy on November 1. According to a State Department cable, the embassy appealed to the Ministry of Foreign Affairs and the Tehran police to provide security for what it estimated to be a one-million-participant march on that day.[96] The IRP rerouted the demonstration in an attempt to avoid attacks against the building and American diplomats. In response, Tudeh, the FKO, the MKO, and other leftists planned for a showdown with the government. They called for a massive anti-American demonstration on November 4, choosing the date to coincide with Student Day, which commemorated students who had been killed by the Shah's forces a year earlier. The leftists provocatively publicized the news that Bazargan and Yazdi had met with U.S. national security adviser Zbigniew Brzezinski in Algeria a few days earlier after the Shah had entered the United States. They accused the nationalists of collaborating with Washington to undermine the revolution.

Despite the nationalists' claim that they had not acted against his wishes, Khomeini hesitated to back them publicly, and he remained quiet. Although he had been critical of external powers in his earlier writings and statements, he had not had an "anti-imperialist" tone. Sensing that the tide was shifting, he now had to ratchet up his rhetoric and become unprecedentedly confrontational toward Washington. Echoing the leftists, Khomeini suddenly denounced Iran's military ties with the United States and urged the "rotten brains that love America and the West" to be purged. However, his words were not enough to establish an anti-American credibility for his Islamist camp. His discursive shift required empirical credibility.

It was in this context that Khomeini's radical followers, the left wing of the Islamists who had the most contact and rivalry with the Left, decided to demonstrate who was truly anti-American. They chose an act that would constitute unmistakable proof: on November 4, a group of Islamist students, apparently without Khomeini's knowledge, climbed the United States embassy walls, overwhelmed the security forces, and took sixty-six Americans hostage. The internal and international ramifications of what would become known as the hostage crisis would surpass all expectations. Soon, new terms appeared throughout the Islamic Republic. The Muslim Students Following the Imam's Line, as the group strategically called itself, occupied the embassy and stole the anti-American torch from the patently anti-imperialist—and now stunned—Left.

The Takeover

Preparations for taking over the U.S. embassy had begun before the Shah was admitted to the United States. About four hundred students linked to the militant cleric Khoeiniha, himself a student of Khomeini and close associate of Khomeini's son, Ahmad, meticulously planned and implemented the assault. They secretly acquired the equipment and materials with which to bind and blindfold the hostages and methodically created a brand—Muslim Students Following the Imam's Line—to distinguish themselves from their leftist rivals.[97] They feared their plan would fail either because of the Provisional Government's intervention or because it would be hijacked by one of the better-organized leftist groups, particularly the FKO. Islamist and leftist students were already competing in occupying hotels and other government- or foreign-owned buildings throughout the country.[98] According to Ebtekar, one of the hostage takers and their translator, a leftist group was working on the "same strategy" to take over the embassy and "there was a general consensus that something had to be done."[99] But the Islamist students' main concern was that their action might be "undermined, blocked, or destroyed" by their Marxist rivals.[100] Despite their anti-Bazargan rhetoric, they feared the leftists more than other rivals because, as Ebtekar acknowledged, "they [Marxists], not the nationalists or other religious groups, did all they could to obstruct us."[101] It is therefore not surprising that Khomeini's followers were determined to preempt their rivals.

The student leaders printed pictures of Khomeini to neutralize the Islamist paramilitary Komiteh security guards and carried identity cards to prevent the Left from infiltrating their group. They called themselves "Muslim Students" to be distinct not only from the atheist FKO but also the Tudeh communists who claimed to be following Khomeini's anti-imperialism. Additionally, the "Following the Imam's Line" description would distinguish them from the Marxist-Islamist MKO. With the exception of the primary organizers, the students were apparently unaware of the plan until November 4.[102] On the morning of the attack, Islamist student leader Mohsen Mirdamadi gathered his followers and informed them of the plot. They initially expressed shock and questioned the prudence of such an act, citing concerns over how Khomeini would react, what the Provisional Government would do, and whether the Komiteh would stop them, since it had recently clashed with the communists who had assaulted the embassy. In response, Mirdamadi—who two decades later would become an unlikely proponent of democracy and better relations with the United States—gave them a provocative analysis of recent American moves against Iran. He argued that the United States was preparing to interfere in Iran's internal affairs, reverse the Islamic Revolution, and restore the old order. He assured them that although Khomeini was "not aware" of their plan, they had "information" that he would not object to what was supposed to be a "one- or two-day" occupation.[103] He also stressed that Bazargan's weak government would collapse as a result of the takeover. Students were then divided according to their university affiliations to capture key buildings within the embassy compound. They swiftly overcame the passive security guards outside, neutralized the U.S. Marines inside, and seized the facility. Shortly thereafter, they contacted the state-controlled radio to announce the news. In a statement they had prepared in advance of the occupation, they claimed that the embassy takeover was a reaction to the anti-revolutionary plots by "the world-devouring America," and, more specifically, to Carter's decision to grant asylum to the Shah.[104]

As news of the embassy occupation spread, Bazargan angrily called Mohammad Reza Mahdavi-Kani, a militant cleric in charge of the Komiteh whose armed men were protecting the embassy, asking, "Who are these who entered the embassy? Aren't you responsible for protecting the security [of the embassy]?" Although Komiteh forces had previously removed the FKO members from the embassy, this time they did not act, because they noticed that the perpetrators were their own Islamist allies. Baffled and concerned, Mahdavi-Kani's first action was to contact Khomeini's son, Ahmad. His conversation with Ahmad clearly suggested that there had been coordination with Khomeini's office, if not Khomeini himself, before the takeover. In his memoir, Mahdavi-Kani recalls three decades later that he anxiously asked Ahmad who was behind it, what their objective was, and who was going to be held accountable for it. Ahmad tried to calm him down. He "kept laughing and saying, 'It's not a big deal' and in the end said, 'If the Imam [Khomeini] is happy, do you still have any issue [with this incident]?' I said no. If the Imam has ordered this, then no problem. But . . . why did we have to learn about it after it happened?"[105] Mahdavi-Kani concluded that Ahmad's reaction revealed that "this act had been coordinated. But I do not know if they [the students] committed it and then asked for permission or if they received permission beforehand. I do not know these things, but *maybe it was beforehand after all.*"[106]

Despite strong circumstantial evidence, there continues to be uncertainty as to whether Khomeini himself was aware of the plan to occupy the embassy. According to Yazdi, Khomeini immediately urged him to expel the students from the embassy. However, it is possible that Khomeini had prior knowledge of the plot, but preferred to deflect accountability for and maintain plausible deniability of his involvement. In any event, Khomeini soon blessed the seizure of what his followers called the "Nest of Spies," sent his son to the embassy, and exhorted the Islamist students to stay there. Although he was careful not to call for an end to diplomatic ties with the United States, Khomeini branded the United States the "Great Satan" and the takeover the "Second Revolution," one that was "bigger than the First Revolution," thus stealing the Left's Leninist terminology.

The immediate fruits of the occupation of the embassy were greater than Khomeini could have expected. With one blow, both the interim government and the Left were weakened and would eventually be entirely eliminated. Although Khomeini had rejected Bazargan's previous resignation attempts, he accepted it this time without hesitation and called for a complete purge of all imperialist elements of the government.[107] Bazargan stressed repeatedly that he had submitted this final resignation to Khomeini just before the hostage crisis,[108] adamantly refuting the Islamist students' boasts to the leftists, claiming credit for his fall. Although some of Khomeini's close disciples—such as Khamenei, Rafsanjani, and Beheshti—were apparently unaware of or even opposed to the action of the radical students, they soon came on board and tried to use the event to further eliminate their rivals. Meetings between U.S. officials and the Iranian militant clergy suddenly stopped; Khomeini refused to meet with former U.S. attorney general Ramsey Clark or other emissaries, nor would any other Islamist dare to have public or private communication with American officials. Secret messages that

European or other interlocutors conveyed to Tehran largely remained un-answered. When the Swedish ambassador to Tehran carried a secret pro-posal from the United States to Beheshti, the powerful cleric helplessly and vaguely kept referring to "the social facts of Iran" that prevented the hos-tages from being released.[109]

The occupation of the U.S. embassy certainly created an external enemy for the Islamist state, but it weakened its more immediate internal adversary. It provided a whole new arsenal for Khomeini and his followers as they pushed all rivals aside. Khomeini's faction benefited enormously, despite the international condemnation and isolation that resulted from the hos-tage crisis. The Islamists had the leverage to shape the elected and ap-pointed bodies and thus effectively institutionalize *Velayat-e Faqih* in those critical days of debating the constitution in the assembly. They labeled dis-sidents and opponents of *Velayat-e Faqih* as American spies, silencing and in-timidating their opponents, including the nationalists and the dissident moderate clerics, in the run-up to the first presidential and Majles elections. So the embassy seizure continued, and its golden treasure—classified documents—was about to be unearthed. These documents would be used to blackmail or eliminate any remaining opposition.

The Ideological Disarmament of the Left

In this political coup, the Left went mute as the Islamist students gained the upper hand. Those who had criticized Khomeini for being reactionary and supporting the Westernized interim government now struggled to attack him. Islamist students published pictures of blindfolded American hostages with a quote from Khomeini—"Others Talk, We Act"[110]—clearly a jab at the leftists. Within days of the takeover, Khomeini turned the tables and sarcas-tically asked the leftist groups, particularly the formidable FKO, "My ears did not hear that they supported [the occupation of the embassy]. If they are not pro-American, why didn't they support [this act]?"[111]

The instant and utter confusion the event created among the nationalists and even some right-wing Islamists cannot be overstated. But for the left-ists, the result was nothing short of an identity crisis. Viewing it as a natural reaction of angry people against a looming U.S. plot, they initially extended their strongest support to Khomeini. A week later, however, the FKO came to a different conclusion: "In our 14th of Aban (November 5th) statement analyzing the seizure of the American embassy, we committed a serious mistake. What we considered a self-motivated move by the masses was in fact an act that a segment of the clergy committed in order to ... strengthen its domination over the [nationalist] liberals and among the masses."[112] In a lengthy analysis, the FKO argued that the Islamists originally used the nationalist technocrats as their executive arm to compensate for their own lack of managerial skill in running an inherited capitalist state. However, the article continued, the ensuing economic, social, and political crises alarmed the Islamists, who decided to create "a controlled anti-imperialist wave" to regain their mass popularity and remove the nationalists.[113]

In another analysis a few months later, the FKO acknowledged Khomeini's successful appropriation of anti-Americanism to compensate for his diminishing popularity:

> Except for a few pockets of the Left, almost all forces backed the seizure of the embassy one way or another. A new movement based on the struggle against imperialism was born. The authority of the faction following "The Imam's Line" and particularly that of Khomeini himself, which had been partially lost during the war in Kurdistan, was renewed and strengthened with Ayatollah Khomeini's Aban 26 [November 17] message. Khomeini said that he wanted all people to shift their pens and machine guns toward the Great Satan, that is, America. And in practice, to some extent this happened as well. Millions of people marched in front of the American spying base several times a week and chanted against American imperialism.[114]

But by then, the discovery of Khomeini's strategy to undermine the Left's cohesion came too late to be of use. Disagreements and confusion over the nature of the Islamic Republic had already divided the leftists. The FKO eventually split into "majority" and "minority" factions. The hostage takers snubbed the MKO's and Tudeh's prominent leaders, refusing to meet and grant them "the prestige of entering the embassy grounds."[115] The Islamists permanently hijacked popular anti-American sentiments; other groups were no longer allowed to hold anti-imperialist rallies. The Komiteh attacked and arrested non-Islamist anti-American students and workers who demonstrated at the U.S. embassy in Tehran or consulates throughout the country, ironically accusing them of being American stooges.[116]

As the crisis continued, an increasing number of leftist organizations and groups broke ranks and joined Khomeini's anti-American expedition. His success in absorbing a wide range of key constituencies and undermining the cohesion of the Left cannot be overstated. Peasants, workers, and labor unions from major industrial complexes to small local factories sent telegrams or joined anti-American demonstrations to express support for Khomeini's anti-imperialist undertaking. Prominent writers, poets, and artists such as Siavash Kasrai, Amir Hushang Ebtehaj (Sayeh), Mahmoud Etemadzadeh (Beh Azin), Amir-Hossein Aryanpour, and Ahmad Shamlu sent open letters to Khomeini and the Islamist students praising the occupation of the embassy and inviting other intellectuals to join. Many were longtime leftist figures and communist sympathizers. Others were independent members of the intelligentsia, some of whom became anti-American at this focal point to make up for their "un-Islamic" past and association with the monarchy.

But Khomeini did not want the situation to get out of hand. Demands arose for further measures, such as confiscating the assets of the rich and other capitalist agents of Western imperialism. Anti-Moscow leftists and some competing Islamists planned to occupy the Soviet embassy in Tehran. Soviet officials had supported Khomeini since his return from Paris and warned the United States several times not to interfere in Iran's internal affairs. So Khomeini stepped in and issued a statement calling on the people to prevent the "CIA agents" from occupying the Soviet or any other embassy.[117]

Doubling Down on Anti-Americanism

As the FKO was losing the anti-American bidding to the Islamists, it doubled down on both the Islamists and the remaining liberals to prolong the crisis in hopes of winning this war of narratives. Fearing that the crisis would end within a few weeks, it questioned the Islamists' anti-imperialist credibility by maintaining that they protected certain class interests and thus remained a tool of the United States:

Why doesn't the ruling [Islamist] party, after the occupation of the U.S. embassy, take a step to cut all economic, political, military, and cultural ties with American imperialism? Why are they trying to contain the masses? Why are they afraid of the masses' anti-imperialist move? Why are they stopping at occupying the embassy and exchanging a few spies with the Shah, who is [practically] long dead for the people, and not paying attention to completely cutting off all relations with American imperialism? The answer to all these questions is hidden in the class-based nature of the reactionaries.[118]

The FKO attacked the state-controlled TV for showing "positive" programs about American women who converted to Islam or for allegedly backing Senator Ted Kennedy against Jimmy Carter in the 1980 primaries. There are no good or bad imperialists, the FKO argued; "an imperialist is an imperialist, whether it is headed by Carter or Kennedy or anyone else."[119]

Although the nationalists had resigned from the Provisional Government, they were still members of the powerful Revolutionary Council and were planning to run for the upcoming presidential and Majles elections. Therefore, they remained a political menace to the communist Left, and they believed that Khomeini's fear of communism would force him to keep them as a vital ally. The leftists strove to discourage his anti-communism: "Today Ayatollah Khomeini needs to realize the truth: that these agents [nationalists] exploited his fear of the communist revolutionaries and other revolutionary forces to ensure his support."[120]

Soon after seizing the embassy, the Muslims Students Following the Imam's Line began to collect and put together the shredded documents they discovered. They gradually and selectively published these classified documents to discredit the nationalists as American agents, even though several clerics were involved in negotiations with U.S. representatives as well. The Left pushed to eliminate the nationalists too, understanding that the nationalists had both the governing expertise and the international linkage to run the state. Relying on the documents seized at the embassy that showed that Bazargan and Yazdi had been in communication with U.S. officials, the FKO asked the Islamists why these foreign agents still held positions within the Revolutionary Council or other state institutions.[121] They claimed that the Revolutionary Council, which had become the de facto government after the collapse of the Provisional Government, was essentially the same as the Bazargan cabinet under a different name. The council consisted of the nationalists and Khomeini's clerical disciples, many of whom had had routine meetings with American diplomats before the hostage crisis. FKO's *Kar* reprinted a document from the embassy revealing that Bazargan's spokesman, Amir-Entezam, had privately accused the radicals of derailing

U.S.–Iran relations. According to the document, Amir-Entezam told his American interlocutors, "We thought it would not take more than a few months to resolve our issues [with the United States], but these people continue to interfere."[122] The documents gave further credence to the leftists' claim that the nationalists were conspiring against the new regime and planning to bring the United States back.

When the United States stopped buying oil from and selling wheat to Iran, which was one of its first responses to the hostage crisis, the FKO portrayed it as a move to empower the nationalists.[123] It further argued that the clerics' policies had mostly been at the service of liberal capitalists who were the "main base of the imperialism after the revolution."[124] The FKO attempted to exploit the gap between the radical left wing of the Islamist IRP, involved in the embassy seizure, and the more moderate right.[125]

Tudeh also fanned the flame but remained pro-Khomeini to the end. It strongly supported the seizure of the "Center of Conspiracy Against the Iranian Revolution," condemned Bazargan's meeting with Brzezinski, and urged the Islamists not to release the hostages before the United States extradited the Shah to Iran.[126] Tudeh increasingly emerged as the Kremlin's bridge to the Islamist IRP, and it strongly backed Khomeini's new anti-American stance. Unlike the FKO and MKO, Tudeh sent flowers to the hostage takers at the embassy, published front-page photos of burning American flags, and practically became Khomeini's mouthpiece for his anti-American statements.[127]

As the student hostage takers published pictures of the embassy's spying devices and documents, Khomeini publicly banned all members of the Revolutionary Council from negotiating with U.S. officials. After finally canceling the bilateral military treaty, the Revolutionary Council cut off oil exports to the United States as well, but stopped short of severing diplomatic ties with Washington despite mounting pressure from the Left. Beheshti, known for his communication with high-ranking U.S. officials until a few days earlier, struggled to defend this decision. He said the issue had been discussed as "a possibility" but cautioned against any reactive measure.[128] For five months, until April 7, 1980, the Islamists resisted breaking diplomatic relations with the United States. Even then, it was Carter who took the initiative to sever diplomatic ties with Iran before launching the ill-fated Operation Eagle Claw in an effort to rescue the hostages.

Washington's Take

In Washington, the Carter administration was confounded to see the U.S. embassy in the hands of Khomeini's followers even as the Leader's disciples and allies were in communication with senior American officials. The White House viewed the seizure as an ideological gambit and "entirely a function of Iranian internal politics," according to Gary Sick, a National Security Council staffer at the time.[129] For the Carter administration, it was merely a showdown between the Islamists and the nationalists. American officials hoped to see a quick resolution after factional scores between these two groups were settled. As the crisis dragged on with no end in sight, the White House struggled to comprehend the course of events. Neither the president nor his cabinet appears to have understood the anti-leftist dimension of Khomeini's instrumental deployment of anti-Americanism. The eternal realist Brzezinski, who was previously dismissive of any role for religious figures in post-revolutionary Iran, now recommended threatening to bomb the holy city of Qom. Carter on the other hand, himself a religious person, viewed Khomeini positively as a man of belief, albeit an irrational one: "It's almost impossible to deal with a crazy man, except that he does have religious beliefs . . . I believe that's our ultimate hope for a successful resolution of this problem."[130] Carter invited theologians, clerics, Islamic studies scholars, and Muslim politicians to help him fathom Khomeini's mentality and to make a *shari'a* case to convince him to free the hostages. But as the CIA noted, Carter's use of Islam was doomed to fail because Khomeini himself was "the ultimate interpreter of Islamic law."[131] In fact, Khomeini used Christianity to discredit Carter and even the pope. He told the Vatican mediators, "If Jesus Christ were here today, he would call Carter to account and deliver us from the clutches of this enemy of humanity."[132] Khomeini advised the pope to follow in his footsteps and rise up against oppression: "He should proclaim to all Christendom the crimes that Carter has committed and reveal his true identity to the world, just as we did with Muhammad Reza [Shah]."[133] To add insult to injury, the Iranian embassy in Washington published the text of Khomeini's message to the pope in a paid advertisement in the *New York Times* on November 18, 1979.

While exploring every possible political and religious contact with Iranian officials, Washington ended military assistance to Iran and later, on

November 14, froze Iranian assets. Carter ordered the Justice Department to take action against fifty thousand Iranian students and eighty thousand other Iranian citizens who were in the United States on visas. At a time when the Islamists were cracking down on dissident youth back at home, the administration believed that this would be a "clear, firm . . . punitive step against Iran."[134] Thousands were rounded up and deported to Iran, while heavy restrictions were imposed on issuing new visas for Iranian nationals. When these actions failed to force the release of the hostages, Carter resorted to a military attempt to rescue the captive diplomats on April 24, 1980. But Operation Eagle Claw was unsuccessful; mechanical failures during a desert storm resulted in a helicopter colliding with a C-130 transport aircraft, killing eight American servicemen. The remaining Delta Force commandos escaped the scene, leaving behind their equipment, documents, and the burned bodies of the dead. These confrontational measures gave more credibility to Khomeini's anti-American rhetoric at the expense of the Left. The Islamists proved that they were much more capable of humiliating the United States than any other competing group.

While the United States struggled to make sense of the events in Iran, the FKO torpedoed every effort by the remaining nationalist figures and the Revolutionary Council to resolve the crisis and release the hostages. The Carter administration's decision to ask the dying Shah to leave the United States did not lessen the Left's anti-American propaganda. The new nationalist foreign minister, Sadegh Ghotbzadeh; Beheshti; and others sought to end the crisis after the Shah left the United States, claiming that they had turned the monarch into a persona non grata all over the world. Indeed, at one point the Shah sat on a plane in Panama for hours before finally his old friend, Egypt's President Anwar Sadat, invited him to Cairo. But the FKO's *Kar* undermined the credibility of these statements, provoking more fear and uncertainty: "The U.S. imperialists, the government of Panama, the Revolutionary Council, and Ghotbzadeh's foreign ministry are trying to gain the release of the hostages . . . in exchange for a few hours delay of the [Shah's] flight in Panama."[135] In these analyses, the Shah was not a homeless, cancer-stricken man but still the U.S. gendarme in the region, going to Egypt with the mission of mobilizing anti-revolutionary forces for his return to Tehran.[136]

Tudeh and the FKO relentlessly pushed the Revolutionary Council to put the hostages on trial.[137] But Khomeini's clerical disciples and Revolutionary Council members, Beheshti, Montazeri, and Khamenei, all downplayed the need for a trial. They were cautious not to be pushed around too much or to make the Great Satan too angry. Montazeri stated, "If the hostages have not committed any wrongdoing, they will only attend the trials as witnesses."[138] Similarly, Khamenei called the hostages petty agents who were "manipulated by the U.S. government."[139]

The Electoral Politics of Anti-Americanism

This factional war of narratives turned anti-Americanism into an essential component of every political and policy issue, including most immediately the referendum in December 1979 for the constitution that would place the clergy at the top of the state. In the previous referendum for the Islamic Republic in March 1979, there was no reference to the United States. But now in the context of the hostage crisis, the Islamists employed anti-Americanism to mobilize the masses against their opponents, particularly the leftists. State-controlled media and mosques all over the country encouraged people to vote, calling boycotters American stooges.

The leftists' response was to try appropriating some of the Islamists' narratives, including even *Velayat-e Faqih*. Although the FKO had initially opposed the constitutional draft as institutionalizing clerical despotism, it adjusted its position later by reinterpreting the proposal as an anti-American document. *Kar* stated, "Even most of those who voted yes to the constitution share the boycotters' view and seek the materialization of anti-imperialist, democratic goals."[140] Yet again, the FKO called on "communists and other enlightened progressive forces" to remain aware of the nationalists' and the liberal clergy's plots to wait for the eventual decline of the inept Islamist clergy before they bring the United States back in.[141] Ayatollah Shariatmadari and Maraghe'i, two opponents of *Velayat-e Faqih*, were among the first targets of the Left. In other words, the FKO rejected the new constitution not only because of its clerical control but also because it would allow liberals, capitalists, and pro-imperialists to remain a part of the political process.[142]

After the constitutional referendum, all actors geared up for the presidential and Majles elections on January 25 and March 14, 1980, respectively. Despite earlier opposition to the constitution, both the FKO and MKO decided to participate in the presidential election. They asked the working class and its supporters "not to leave the masses alone" but rather to enlighten them against the liberal candidates.[143] The election was another opportunity in which to "kick the U.S. imperialists out."[144] Despite continuing conflicts with the nationalists, Khomeini was careful not to be distracted from his main target. After appropriating their anti-Americanism, he moved to bar the original anti-Americanists—the leftists—from running for any office. The FKO had thrown its support behind the MKO's candidate, Masoud Rajavi. These two powerful organized forces could launch an impressive campaign throughout the country. Khomeini addressed the threat with a simple solution. Putting— or rather, keeping—his turban on, he issued a one-liner he called a fatwa: "Anyone who did not cast a positive vote for the constitution of the Islamic Republic is not qualified to become president."[145] Having silenced every powerful clerical or political voice that could question the credibility, legality, and applicability of this fatwa, the Islamists laid the groundwork to permanently exclude both the FKO and MKO from any role in the government.

These organizations responded by portraying Rajavi's disqualification as an indication that Khomeini was leaning back toward the United States.[146] If Khomeini was anti-imperialist, as he had shown "in practice," why wasn't he eliminating liberals such as Bazargan and Ghotbzadeh?[147] Why could anticlerical elements become presidential candidates while anti-imperialist candidates could not?[148] Nevertheless, these groups were cautious to not attack Khomeini personally just yet. He was the powerful charismatic leader who had recently acquired anti-American credentials, too. His heart attack compelled them to issue statements to wish him a quick recovery but also warn again that the pro-American elements were waiting for his death to fully take over.[149]

During the presidential campaign, the nationalist candidate Admiral Ahmad Madani became the Left's target. *Kar* published classified documents revealing that the Iranian navy continued close ties with the U.S. Navy even after the November 4 attack on the embassy and despite the official anti-American rhetoric of the Iranian army.[150] In the following issue, *Kar* ran a sarcastic headline mocking the nationalist officials' struggle to maintain ties with the United States in such a climate: "On Azar 3 [November 24], Admiral Madani orders the navy to be on alert 'against the U.S. invasion,' and on Azar 21 [December 12] requests missile parts [from the United States] 'against the U.S. invasion'!"[151] When Abolhassan Banisadr, a nationalist-Islamist aide to Khomeini, won the presidential election after defeating the IRP's and other candidates (to be discussed in the following chapter), he became Tudeh's new enemy. They attacked his equal treatment of the United States and USSR: "Mr. Banisadr says, 'I equally consider both superpowers, America and Russia, as Iran's main enemies.' It looks like he does not know what 'main enemy' means. The main enemies are the dominance-seeking forces now controlling our homeland, meaning that American imperialism has become our main imperialism, particularly since the Mordad 28 [August 19, 1953] coup."[152]

The FKO expanded its relentless anti-imperialist bidding beyond the United States and demanded an end to Iran's economic and political ties with Japan, Britain, France, and Germany, claiming that all of these countries were taking part in international imperialism. It complained that Iran had brought back the same European defense industry advisers who had served under the Shah.[153] It attacked the Islamic Republic for extending billions of dollars' worth of contracts to British and French auto industry assembly lines in Iran.[154] President Banisadr was clearly struggling to justify his foreign policy when he said, "I don't want to replace superpowers with Europe and Japan. I want to bring the European nations out of the superpowers' domination."[155] His statement brought ridicule and further pressure from the Left to cancel all contracts and treaties with imperialist powers.

Kar published documents signed by Revolutionary Council members to allocate money for the anti-Soviet forces in Afghanistan. This was further "proof" that behind the seizure of the U.S. embassy, the Islamic Republic remained in alignment with the United States.[156] Khamenei was even accused of helping to reinstall U.S. spying stations.[157] After U.S. Operation Eagle Claw failed to rescue the hostages in April 1980, the Left accused the army of collaborating with U.S. operatives, allowing them to enter Iran's territories, and destroying what documents remained in the crashed helicopters.[158]

But while the embassy occupation continued, the leftists' ideological power diminished, and the Islamists became ever more emboldened to remove them. The Islamists prevented the Left from winning the first parliamentary elections in March and May 1980. In the first round, MKO and IRP candidates won about 906,480 and 1,617,422 votes in provinces, respectively. Yet the MKO could not secure a single seat while the IRP won more than half the ninety-six seats filled in the first round.[159] The IRP's and IRGC's massive voter fraud and electoral engineering prompted even Khomeini's brother to question the elections' outcome.[160] But Tudeh used its small but sophisticated organization and propaganda expertise to attack anti-Khomeini leftists and silence the

IRP's moderate clerical and nationalist rivals.[161] Iran scholar Sepehr Zabih argues that Tudeh was "instrumental in ensuring the victory of the candidates of the Islamic Republic Party in close to 35 percent of the districts where a run-off was held."[162] Despite the Left's potent presence in Iran's political scene as revealed by these figures, the cost of suppressing it was declining in the aftermath of the hostage crisis.

Ending the Crisis

Although leftist accusations would contribute to prolonging the hostage crisis, deepening Iran–U.S. animosity for decades, they no longer posed a serious threat to the Islamists or affected the internal balance of power. The battle between the Left and the Islamists had moved onto other ground; despite the critical ideological usurpation accomplished by the seizure of the embassy with resulting damage to the Left, the universities remained in turmoil. In the spring of 1980, the Revolutionary Council issued an ultimatum that political groups close their offices and leave university campuses. Soon after, security forces brutally cracked down on leftist students. Radical Islamist students began to seize campuses throughout the country and shut down classes. The Cultural Revolution, as it became known, lasted for two years, during which time university professors, students, and curricula perceived to be anti-Islamic were purged, depriving the Left of a critical forum to spread its message and recruit new members.

In the ensuing violence between leftists and Islamists, the leftists lost thousands but the Islamist faction was nearly decapitated. In the bombings of the IRP's headquarters and subsequent assassinations in 1981, nearly one hundred of the most senior Islamist leaders, including Beheshti; President Mohammad Ali Rajai; and Prime Minister Mohammad Javad Bahonar, were killed. Many more clerics, officials, judges, and IRGC members were targeted in suicide bombings and other leftist operations during these years. The Left paid a dear price for its activities, too. The MKO alone announced that close to eight thousand of its members were killed by security forces in this reign of terror.[163]

After stealing the leftists' message, removing their university lifeline, and gradually liquidating them, Khomeini moved to end the hostage crisis. With the parliamentary elections in March and May 1980 complete, Khomeini referred resolution of the crisis to the new, IRP-dominated legislative body—not to the lay president. The Shah's death on July 27 and his lonely burial in Egypt removed a major obstacle to releasing the hostages, as the Islamists were no longer trapped into insisting on his extradition. Two days after his death, one hundred eighty-five members of the U.S. Congress sent a respectfully crafted letter to the Majles requesting release of the hostages. The Majles' cautiously positive response concerned the FKO. The only way to prevent the crisis from ending was to insist that the hostages be put on trial. But with Saddam Hussein's invasion of Iran on September 22, 1980, the revolutionary government needed to resolve one issue to be able to focus on another.

Khomeini set forth Iran's conditions for ending the hostage crisis, making it clear that the government wanted to end the conflict, even precipitously. The conditions included releasing Iran's frozen assets, promising no further legal claims against Iran, guaranteeing no interference in Iran's internal affairs, and returning all of the Shah's assets. Contrary to the Islamists' public claims at the time, these demands did not impose any major concessions on the United States. There was no longer any mention of putting the hostages on trial. The assets whose release he demanded had been frozen *after* the seizure of the embassy. The legal claims were related to the hostage crisis. The question then posed by the Left and the nationalists was, what had Iran gained from seizing the U.S. embassy except international isolation? It was more evident than ever that the whole crisis had factional roots. The FKO reiterated that the Islamists had used the hostage crisis to "fool" the masses; now that they had consolidated their position, they were restless to resolve the issue.[164] But it would take several more months of negotiations, the removal of nationalist intermediaries, and the assurance of Carter's defeat by Ronald Reagan.

Although the hostages were finally freed on January 21, 1981, a few minutes into Reagan's presidency, the incident and its aftereffects would continue to bring sanctions and international isolation upon the country in the years and decades to come. However, as one of the hostage takers unequivocally summed it up decades later, the occupation of the embassy was instrumental in changing the internal balance of power, consolidating the Islamists, and defeating their formidable leftist rivals:

Seizing the Nest eradicated many internal problems. There were the issues of Kurdistan, Gonbad, Khuzestan, and the danger of disintegration that was threatening Iran. There were questions that the communists were promoting ruthlessly, but were lies—that this [Islamic] government that has come to power is [pro-]American. Since the Shah was [pro-]American, the people were awfully anti-American. No one liked America. We were saying we were anti-American. The communists were saying, "No, you are American." You can almost say that the occupation of the embassy disarmed the communists tremendously in this respect and established heavy security in Iran. One of the main positive consequences of the seizure of the embassy was that it created such intense security that it derailed the Monafeghin's [the MKO's and the FKO's] and Tudeh's plans. These groups were forced to support [us] and the label of "American" lost its credibility. But now from a political perspective, I think our confrontation with the U.S. was not prudent.[165]

Without resorting to anti-Americanism and occupying the U.S. embassy, the Islamists might not have consolidated their power in the aftermath of the revolution. Although bringing about massive—even tragic—political and economic costs that undermined Iran's national security for decades, it empowered the Islamists and helped them capture the weakened state. Their factional interests trumped the state's interests and determined their ideological turn. As I will discuss in the second half of the book, the radical Islamists who occupied the American embassy would paradoxically go on to become the most outspoken proponents of democracy, liberalization, and engagement with the United States two decades later. With declining anti-imperialist sentiments in the Islamic Republic of Iran, their anti-American outbidding of the Marxists would be replaced by a new pro-American outbidding of the conservative establishment. Capitalizing on shifting popular sentiments, they would struggle to defend their occupation of the embassy in Tehran while strongly pressing for its reopening. Both anti-Americanism and pro-Americanism were endogenous to elite competition in Iran rather than the fixed elements of political factions.

SIX

Religion and Elite Competition in the Iran–Iraq War

ON SEPTEMBER 22, 1980, Saddam Hussein initiated what became one of the longest wars of the twentieth century. Intending to take advantage of the political and military chaos in post-revolutionary Iran to claim a quick victory reminiscent of the Six-Day War, his troops instead faced fierce resistance in Iran; they were expelled from Iranian territories nineteen months later. Iran's Islamist forces then brought the war into Iraqi territories for another six years. The war of attrition finally ended in August 1988, leaving both countries devastated.

Throughout the conflict, Iranian leaders often boasted about the latitude religion provided them in conducting the war. Saddam Hussein himself eventually took a sharp Islamic turn to counter his theocratic adversary.[1] But despite the Iranians' intensely religious language—which permeated war rooms, negotiating tables, battlefields, and streets—the actual role of religion in the war remains underexplored. Foreign observers, reporters, politicians, and even some academics described Tehran's conduct as irrational and ideological, with many claiming Iran's primary goal was to export its Islamic revolution and expand its apocalyptic Shi'a identity.[2] Many scholars, on the other hand, have focused on the pragmatism of Iranian clerical rulers in pursuing the war, ignoring their systematic use of religious narratives.[3] These rationalists reduce religious narratives to their utility for public consumption, or they point to the fading of Tehran's ideological foreign policy and the rise of pragmatism as a result of a partial socialization of the revolutionary state in the international system.[4] Others have examined how religion materially or ideationally constituted the Iranian and Iraqi regimes' threat perceptions.[5] But none have yet offered a systematic analysis of the (changing) religious doctrines over the course of the conflict.

The causal linkage between Iran's factional politics and the war remains understudied as well. Thanks to the 2003 U.S.-led occupation of Iraq and seizure of documents from within Saddam Hussein's inner circles, we now have a better understanding of the decision-making process on the Iraqi side.[6] But on the Iranian side, many unanswered questions remain about internal debates and threat perceptions during each stage of the conflict: the resistance phase after the Iraqi invasion, the offensive phase after Iraqi forces were evicted from Iranian territories in 1982, and finally, the attrition phase up until the acceptance of the ceasefire in 1988.

This chapter examines the factional causes and ideational consequences of the Iran–Iraq War, focusing on how Iranian elites developed and deployed religious narratives in response to internal and external threat perceptions. It explores their use of religion, including manipulating existing narratives, altering old theologies, and crafting new doctrines. I contend that the existing literature has largely underestimated the threats Islamists perceived from domestic groups and from each other and that a critical driving force behind Iran's prosecution of the war was domestic politics. The evolving rivalry between the IRP and the IRGC in one camp and the nationalists and the army in the other at the beginning of the war eventually penetrated into the heart of the Islamist camp between the IRP and the IRGC.

I argue that Iran's Islamists welcomed the Iraqi invasion not simply as an opportunity to export the revolution, but rather as a chance to deflect the threat from the army, expand the IRGC, and undermine their internal rivals. But the calculations were complex; if the army and the nationalist-leaning president succeeded in defeating the Iraqi army, their popularity and authority might eclipse that of the Islamists, who could lose their grip on power in Tehran. The IRGC commanders are nowadays openly gleeful with the army's initial failures, calling those defeats "divine" measures. Framing their offensive operations as part of the liberation of Palestinians and defense of the Shi'a Lebanese, the Islamists later constructed an anti-Israeli narrative and established the Quds Force to expand the war into Iraq while secretly acquiring weapons and spare parts from Israeli sources.

By the mid-1980s, the IRP had liquidated the leftists, eradicated the nationalists, and subdued the regular army with the IRGC's help. World powers were arming Saddam Hussein to assemble a formidable force against Iran, and the IRP began looking for an exit strategy. The IRGC objected, fearing it would be dissolved if not victorious in the war, an ironic twist since both the IRP and the IRGC were concerned early on that a victory by the Iranian army could cause their demise. But by the end of the war, the IRP was alarmed by the increasingly expanding and politicized IRGC. The external threat of an Iraqi military victory and the internal threat of IRGC political dominance prompted the IRP to devise a multipronged military, political, and ideological strategy to end the war.

In this chapter, I process trace the evolution of the war and the corresponding religious narratives chronologically to analyze the inner Islamist-nationalist and army-IRGC rivalries, dividing the conflict into three phases: from Iraq's invasion to the liberation of Khorramshahr (1980–1982); from the invasion of Iraq through the Iran–Contra affair (1982–1986); and from the period after Iran–Contra until the ceasefire (1986–1988).

Phase I: Resistance and the Islamist-Nationalist Rivalry

Iran's Political Landscape Before the Iraqi Invasion

The campaign for president of the new Islamic Republic began a mere three months after the dramatic seizure of the U.S. embassy and collapse of the interim government, and two months after the new constitution was approved. The judiciary and legislature were under total control of the Islamist clergy, but Khomeini insisted that the president must be a lay politician—albeit one who was "religious" and loyal to his cause. The Islamists remained quiet for the time being, but started preparing for a looming battle ahead.

The IRP decided to field Hassan Habibi, a lay candidate who had helped prepare the initial draft of the constitution that was ultimately put aside in the Constitutional Assembly. The nationalists did not officially nominate or unite behind any candidate. Despite the IRP's massive campaign, the winner of the January 1980 presidential election was Abolhassan Banisadr, a French-educated nationalist-Islamist candidate with close ties to Khomeini.

Although he ran an independent campaign, it was rumored that he was Khomeini's candidate. He also enjoyed the support of the Marxist-Islamist Mojahedin (MKO), whose leader, Masoud Rajavi, was barred from running by Khomeini. Banisadr's landslide support (76 percent of the vote) was followed by that of Admiral Ahmad Madani (15.8 percent), a nationalist candidate who ran as an independent. The IRP had to face a dismal result of only 4.8 percent. Fear of losing the Majles to the nationalists forced the militant clerics to act, lest Banisadr become the nexus of a new alliance between the nationalists and the Left.

A week after Banisadr's victory and less than two months before the Majles elections, five top militant clerics (Rafsanjani, Beheshti, Khamenei Ardebili, and Mohammad Javad Bahonar) wrote a blunt letter to Khomeini, who had been transferred from Qom to a hospital in Tehran due to heart failure. Disregarding his fragile condition, the letter was a warning to Khomeini that put the responsibility of losing the revolution squarely on his shoulders:

> It would have been better if there were no necessity to write about these issues under these conditions, but unfortunately, after discussions and debates, we concluded that not warning you is a sin and warning you is a duty, and therefore, against our will and feelings and according to reason and responsibility. We summarily bring the following points to His Excellency's attention.[7]

Claiming that they had "accepted the most dangerous responsibilities" both before and after his return to Iran and pointing to the establishment of the IRP as a major victory in protecting the Islamic Revolution, they complained that despite its success in the Constitutional Assembly election and the constitution-writing process that followed, Khomeini was not sufficiently supporting the party anymore. Anticipating the upcoming parliamentary elections, they warned that the Majles might fall into the hands of those who had "surrendered" to the president and would not "protect Islam against the possible deviations of the executors." They blamed close relatives and associates of Khomeini for spreading rumors that he was "angry" at the IRP and siding with President Banisadr. They protested that their efforts to ensure the "Islamic content of the revolution" were being portrayed as "power seeking (which we all hate from the bottom of our hearts) . . . At least we [wish] to be assured that you yourself have faith in their [the nationalists'] qualifications and are optimistic about its consequences." They shrewdly ended the letter with Khomeini's nightmare: "To sum up, signs of the repetition of the Constitutional [Movement]'s history are seen. Despite their differences, the Easternized and Westernized modernists [*motejaddedin*] have joined forces to push Islam out of the revolution."[8] The five clerics specifically warned that the IRP's cohesion was in danger, as many Islamists were joining the leftists or the nationalists.

This letter lays bare the conflict between Khomeini and his disciples at the time. Contrary to the conventional wisdom that they were one homogenous camp, it is evident that Khomeini did not entirely share his lieutenants' extreme opposition to the nationalists. It also signifies the depth of the militant clergy's concern about losing power. They put enormous pressure on Khomeini to sever his limited support of the nationalists and nationalist-leaning Islamists. Two months later, the first Majles election was held, and the IRP ran a vicious campaign across the country. Capitalizing on Khomeini's solid support for an Islamist legislative body, they used state-controlled radio and television, mobilized the Friday prayer imams in urban and rural areas, redrew the boundaries of districts, and selectively applied and interpreted election laws.[9] The results were satisfactory, with the IRP winning more than half of the ninety-six seats in the first round. Despite several reports of irregularities and complaints by Banisadr and other nationalists, Khomeini blessed the election results.

Once the IRP dominated the Majles, it used its majority control to reject the credentials of some of the elected deputies from other parties on the pretext of election irregularities. Several other nationalist deputies were eventually removed or stifled as a result of the much-publicized U.S. embassy documents. Nevertheless, a number of prominent nationalists such as Bazargan and Yazdi entered the chamber. Within days, Rafsanjani became the speaker, a position he then held for a decade before eventually ascending to the presidency. His fellow IRP deputies and clerical allies immediately changed the name of the Majles from the National Consultative Majles to the Islamic Consultative Majles. Because 98 percent of the people had voted for the Islamic Republic, they argued, every institution had to bear that brand and be 100 percent Islamic.

With Banisadr as president, the conflict between the nationalists and the Islamists was drastically exacerbated because unlike Bazargan, he was not reluctant to challenge the militant clergy. However, the Islamists were institutionally more consolidated than the lay president. Banisadr fiercely resisted the IRP-dominated Majles's attempts to shape his cabinet, but in the end, he had no choice but to accept Mohammad Ali Rajai as his prime minister. Rajai, a lay member of the IRP, then clashed with the president over the choice of ministers. Increasingly paralyzed and turned into a ceremonial president, Banisadr sarcastically wondered why Rafsanjani and Beheshti themselves were not taking over the office of the president. "It has been 18 months [since the 1979 revolution] that they began controlling the country," he wrote in his newspaper *Enghelab-e Islami* [The Islamic Revolution].[10]

Clerical representatives were also penetrating ministries, state-controlled media, and all branches of the army. In response to Banisadr's emerging ties with army commanders and the police, the IRP purged the IRGC of his sympathizers.[11] Lacking legal and institutional support, Banisadr adopted a nationalistic tone and strove to forge an alliance with the army, which he claimed had qualitatively changed from the Shah's era. This "new" army had in fact neutralized several coup attempts against the Islamist government. But the clerics wanted a more "Islamicized" and loyal army.

The Nuzhih plot in July 1980 intensified the frenzied climate. Collaborating with Shahpour Bakhtiar (the Shah's last prime minister) and the Iraqi government, several hundred army officers, including dozens of pilots, allegedly planned to bomb Khomeini's home, Qom seminaries, IRGC and Komiteh bases, and the Revolutionary Courts before other forces would join them to carry out the coup.[12] Although disrupted before it could be carried out, the unsuccessful attempt further weakened Banisadr and the army. To the dismay of both, the IRP and its IRGC and Komiteh were often credited for neutralizing coups even when the army officers themselves had reportedly prevented a plot.[13] Against this backdrop of fierce infighting came reports that the Iraqi army was amassing on Iran's borders.

Responding to Invasion

On September 17, 1980, Saddam Hussein appeared on television to publicly tear apart the Algiers Accord, which he had signed in 1975 with the now-deposed Shah; five days later, Iraqi air and ground forces invaded Iran. The Iraqi army crossed Iranian borders and advanced toward oil-rich and other strategic areas without any serious resistance from Iran's recently purged military forces. Iran's Islamist leaders perceived the Iraqi invasion through the lens of factional politics. In his first meeting after the war began, Khomeini greeted senior officials with a "happy face," claiming that Iran's eventual victory would lead to the "complete consolidation of the regime" against all its internal opponents.[14] Pointing to the quick deployment of the air force, he stated that it was evident that the army was loyal and no longer a threat since it had "completely converted to the revolution."[15]

As the army struggled to organize its forces, Khomeini and his disciples projected a fanatical image to challenge the international order and signal steadfastness. They constructed a religious narrative to make sense of the war for both Iranians and outsiders. For a revolution whose mission was to perfect mankind, war could be viewed as a natural next step toward remaking the entire world. The same divine message that created their movement—that toppled the Shah and the fifth-mightiest army in the world—had now established a state that would challenge the unjust international system.

But this would not be the last battle. Khomeini stressed, "the Quran has not said 'war, war until the victory,' but 'war, war, until the removal of *fitna* [sedition] from the world' and even more."[16] He warned that hardship would follow, saying, "This movement is not about your belly . . . If the entire world closes itself to us . . . we would prefer [international isolation] to the open doors of the looting countries."[17] Therefore, economic and social difficulties were the expected price for the nobler goal of preserving the dignity of the Islamic nation: "We want to protect our dignity and we want to protect our dear Islam, which has everything; it has independence, freedom, and dignity. We want to protect it. We want to protect the Quran. It is worth it if we all die for it . . . We have to prepare for wars and we are powerful."[18] To Khomeini, "peace between Islam and *kufr* [heresy] has no meaning." Pragmatic concepts such as "compromise" and "expediency" (*maslahat*) had no place in Prophet Mohammad's lexicon, he now said. The early Muslims had found themselves in various wars, through which they prevailed and dominated Arabia and much of the world. Like the Prophet's state, the Islamic Republic would not compromise with bullying powers and their puppets. Just as the Prophet's followers had "defeated" the Roman and Persian empires, the Islamic Revolution would challenge corrupt powers.

In the first Friday prayer after the war started, Ali Khamenei claimed that "Islam and the Islamic Revolution were looking for a playing field."[19] However, the uneven playing field was interpreted as a sign of righteousness and thus divine power. According to Khomeini, in the early days of Islam, sixty Muslims ambushed and defeated sixty thousand Romans because "in war, numbers don't mean anything. What counts is the power of human thought, the same power that relied on God in the early Islamic era and defeated many armies."[20] Now, with the additional power of technology, victory might be imminent. Khomeini stated that the prophets worked hard to spread their messages. Prophet Mohammad had to "wait months before a messenger could get his message to the rest of Arabia. Now through radio you could spread your message within hours."[21] The objective of the war was not only to resist the Iraqis; as Rafsanjani pointed out, "it is not enough for us to say that we are not defeated, because we have to show that the revolution is very strong and that the mandate of the revolution is a victory in this war and to open the road for the idea of the revolution to expand."[22] In other words, the war was a "shortcut" to export the revolution. The message was clear: Iran was ready to endure a long war.

In an attempt to undermine the enemy's cohesion, Khomeini called on Iraqis to "rise, crush this criminal party, send Saddam to hell and establish an Islamic, humane government with the help of the [Iraqi] nation."[23] He encouraged Iraqi soldiers to leave the frontlines and warned, "A war against Iran is a war against Islam, against the Quran, against God's Prophet, and this is a cardinal sin that God will not forgive."[24] Khomeini stated, "Even if Jesus, who brought the dead back to life, comes, he cannot bring this dead man [Saddam Hussein] back to life."[25] Thousands of Shi'a Iraqis reportedly defected to Iran or deserted from the army, thus risking mutilations and death sentences.[26]

Using this narrative, Iran mobilized fearless volunteer forces, successfully signaling resolve and projecting the image of an irrational nation ready to wage war endlessly. A senior Iraqi army officer told a *Washington Post* reporter at the outset of the conflict, "Those Revolutionary Guards simply do not know when to stop. They are crazy. They are determined to become martyrs."[27] As the Iraqis pushed to capture the strategic port of Khorramshahr and one of the world's biggest oil refineries in Abadan, the *Washington Post* reported:

Western diplomats here believe that Iraq could sustain such a war for six months to a year. Iran would seem less prepared for such an effort except for the stubbornness and fanaticism of its revolutionary leaders—a factor that makes any true assessment of their real staying power hard to measure.[28]

By the second week of the war, it became clear that Hussein, despite his early military advancement, had miscalculated the long-term strength of his army against the Iranians' tenacity in the battlefield. The *Washington Post* reported:

> For Iraq, with all its illusions of greatness in the region and the Arab world, the stakes are much higher in this war than they are for Iran. Iraq has gambled on a victory which would give it the power it has long craved in the region and, as one Western diplomat in the Persian Gulf said recently, "If the Iraqis don't win, they lose. If the Iranians don't lose, they win."[29]

Despite the imminent loss of Khorramshahr and the siege of Abadan, Iran rejected Hussein's conditional offer to end the war and called instead on Iraqis to overthrow him. Khorramshahr had achieved symbolic status from the early days of conflict; Iranian navy commandos, the IRGC, and local forces defending the city renamed it *khoonin shahr*, or the city of blood. Khomeini prevented his militant leftist rivals from defending Khorramshahr, and instead urged the local people to resist the overwhelming Iraqi troops: "It is up to you Muslims and revolutionary people of Abadan and Khorramshahr to be completely prepared—now more than any other time—to defend Islam and the Quran and to be prepared to attack the army of the faithless and the oppressors."[30]

Israeli Support of the Islamist State

Behind their extravagant narratives, Iranian leaders were quite practical from the earliest days of the war about the need to acquire weapons and spare parts for the army's American equipment. But the Carter administration could not resume ties with Iran's army while American diplomats were still hostages. In this climate, the most unlikely country, Israel, stepped in. Fearing what Saddam Hussein might do upon defeating Iran, Israel's prime minister, Menachem Begin, quickly began an operation to provide critical spare parts and mortars to the Iranian army. Six days after the Iraqi invasion, Israel's defense minister, Mordechai Zipori, said his country was ready to supply Iran with artillery shells, sea-to-sea missiles, and other weapons if Iran demonstrated a "serious turning point" toward the Jewish State.[31] In the following weeks and months, other top Israeli officials applied pressure on the White House to not oppose their shipping of arms and spare parts to Iran. On October 23, 1980, only a month after the invasion, Israel shipped 250 F-4 tires to Iran.[32] The United States occasionally tried to limit, interrupt, and even suspend Israel's military assistance to Iran. But the flow of weapons never stopped and ultimately culminated in the Iran–Contra affair. According to former CIA analyst Bruce Riedel,

> Israel was the only consistent source of spare parts for the Iranian air force's U.S.-built jets throughout the war. Israeli leaders, notably Yitzhak Rabin and Shimon Peres, brought considerable pressure to bear on Washington, and the Iran-Contra affair was in many ways their idea. American diplomats and spies abroad were told to turn a blind eye to Israeli arms deals with Tehran.[33]

This direct military link with the Iranian Islamists' ideological archenemy was necessary to defend the state's territorial integrity against the advancing Iraqis. But they kept it a secret to protect the sanctimonious image—or perhaps more accurately, ensure the survival—of their regime.

Competition Within: Who Will Fight? Who Will Rule?

Below the surface of the Iraqi threat, an existential battle among Iranian political factions continued to roil. Although the war reduced the likelihood of a coup by the army against the regime, the Islamists worried that if the Iraqis were defeated outright, the army and the increasingly nationalist President Banisadr would become too powerful at the expense of the militant clergy. Khomeini's old age and poor health exacerbated the IRP's and IRGC's sense of uncertainty, and this dynamic further heightened when he appointed Banisadr as acting commander in chief of the armed forces to better coordinate war planning.

Ali Shamkhani—then a young IRGC commander who would rise to national security adviser in 2013—admitted three decades later that the Islamists feared Banisadr was planning to win the war as a means to "conquer" Tehran. Similarly, Mohsen Rezaei, chief commander of the IRGC during the conflict, stressed that if Banisadr had won the war, no one could have removed him from power.[34] Another IRGC chief commander, Mohammad Ali Jafari, has also acknowledged that a victory by the army could have become a threat to the revolution.[35] From their perspective, it was important that the army protected the state from Iraqi forces but not be seen as triumphant; the IRP and the IRGC viewed the Iraqi army as the nation's external enemy and the Iranian army as their internal "opponent."[36] The 10,000-member IRGC could be no match for Iran's once-Imperial Army of 400,000 with advanced American equipment.[37]

The army, however, was at its lowest point. Most of its senior commanders had fled the country or been purged after the monarchy's collapse. Pressures by the leftists and Islamists to dissolve the army and create a "classless," "monotheistic" military had debilitated its hierarchy. Fearing reprisals, many officers would arrive at work with no uniform or star. The promotion system was now based on ideological commitment. Moreover, an early policy of the new government allowing officers to transfer to any city or other state agency had bled the army of its engineering and medical professionals.[38] Leftist and Islamist groups had looted many of the military bases during the revolutionary chaos. The new government had reduced compulsory military service for men from twenty-four to twelve months and recalled all military attachés from Iranian embassies worldwide. With the dissolution of the army's intelligence division in 1979, its deep network of informants in Iraq had been lost. Additionally, Saddam Hussein was now receiving unprecedented assessments of the army from a number of Iranian officers in exile.[39] The revolution and the hostage crisis had also deprived the army of its main supplier, the United States. The army could not even properly deploy its arsenals due to the lack of spare parts. Ironically, the Iraqi invasion saved the army from further structural deterioration under the Islamists.

According to Banisadr, many of the army's commanders confided in him their determination to defend their country knowing that they could later be executed for opposing the revolution. The mutual distrust and animosity between the IRGC and the army cannot be overstated: a few months earlier, IRGC members had been involved in arresting, interrogating, and executing senior army commanders; now the remaining forces of this humiliated institution feared control by these repressive revolutionaries half their age and lacking military training. IRGC commanders pointed to the army's reliance on secular ideology and the classic method as the reason for Iraq's early success. But their later descriptions of the army's early failures as "divine fate"—which eventually paved the way for their involvement—may be a more telling representation of their concern.[40]

Despite these concerns, the IRGC's central command left the early fighting largely to the army, as it was occupied with defending the regime against its internal leftist enemies.[41] But local IRGC offices in the western provinces had begun engaging with Iraqi forces in border skirmishes even before the war started and were frustrated by the lack of support and attention from Tehran.[42] As the internal conflict eventually subsided and the war with Iraq spread, the IRGC expanded and its involvement grew. According to Shamkhani, each battle proved to be a "boxing ring" that further advanced and institutionalized the organization.[43] The IRGC went from street fighting with leftists to guerrilla warfare in Kurdistan to an all-out war with Iraq; it needed to assert its efficacy against this new enemy to solidify itself as a viable military force. "We had a rival in the war. We were looking for ways to prove our identity," Shamkhani later said in reference to the army. The war gave IRGC commanders a chance to demonstrate their military effectiveness and solidify their political position. Khamenei, then a member of the Supreme Defense Council, took two young IRGC members to a war meeting chaired by President Banisadr. After the senior commanders of the army reported the latest developments on the front line, Khamenei asked the reluctant president to allow the IRGC commanders to share their plans. Little by little, these young forces became decision makers at top military levels.

The IRP and the IRGC initiated a media campaign, relentlessly accusing the army and Banisadr of not conducting the war effectively, rushing to compromise, and intending to terminate the war prematurely for internal gain. Banisadr in turn accused the Islamists of plotting to dissolve the army and worrying about the political implications of a quick victory. "Tehran is the center of all conspiracies," he declared.[44] In his daily newspaper column, he wrote: "I fear the internal enemies more than the external enemies."[45] Banisadr announced that he would not appear on television until the state-run medium ended its "psychological war" against him.[46] In the meantime, he was pleased that people had "turned their backs" on television and were reading his newspaper *Enghelab-e Islami* instead, as evidenced by the skyrocketing circulation rate of from "30,000 to 200,000 to 320,000."[47] Banisadr noted that in any corner of the world, when there is an attack, all factions unite behind their leaders; he cited Winston Churchill, Joseph Stalin, and Gamal Abdel

Nasser. In Iran, he argued, opposing factions backstabbed their leaders and undermined their army. He angrily rebuked his rivals for not listening to his earlier warnings to resolve the hostage crisis quickly, lamenting that this had led to Saddam Hussein's attack and the electoral loss of moderate U.S. president Jimmy Carter to the hawkish Ronald Reagan.[48]

Banisadr summarized the post-revolutionary era as "two years of intimidation, labeling, imprisoning, killing, and monopolizing power."[49] He began to move to the left to compensate for his lack of organized constituencies. He questioned the Cultural Revolution and the closure of universities and claimed that the Islamists were planning to dissolve the army. In so doing, Banisadr brought himself more and more at odds with Khomeini. Yet Khomeini continued, although more cautiously now, to back Banisadr and his conduct of the war—he was adamantly against any radical action against the first elected president of the Islamic Republic. But this continued approval in the face of ceaseless efforts by the Islamists to discredit the lay president further aggravated his disciples' impatient struggle for the executive branch. Time and again, these Khomeini followers warned him that Banisadr was both hijacking the revolution and losing the war.

On February 14, 1981, a year after the initial warning letter written with his fellow clerics, Rafsanjani sent another blunt missive to Khomeini. Attaching the previous letter, he began by asking Khomeini to read it first, implying that they had predicted the ongoing "predicament" a year earlier. He noted that because he felt "constrained" in private meetings with Khomeini, he had decided to put down his concerns on paper to prevent giving the impression that this was about personal and factional rivalries with "liberals" like Banisadr. He criticized Khomeini for replacing his "revolutionary" language with a vague and impartial approach to resolving internal conflicts. Rafsanjani claimed that the Islamists were simply implementing Khomeini's political jurisprudence, which included cracking down on liberal newspapers, removing corrupt and irreligious people from government offices, and preventing music and unveiled women on the radio and television. He asked Khomeini to tell them frankly to back off if this was his true intention but added, "We do not believe it is right to leave the ground to the rival and . . . will remain on the scene to protect the Islamic line of the revolution and will not fear problems, opposition, and accusations. We have faith in His Excellency's qualified leadership, but we find it hard to tolerate the vagueness of the Leader's opinion, unless you say this vagueness is prudent."[50]

Rafsanjani questioned Khomeini's judgment for not taking a side when the militant clergy opposed Banisadr by asking, "What will people think? How will history judge this later?" He claimed that although Khomeini had previously downplayed the importance of the presidency as a "political position with not much power," that office was now undermining the entire Islamic state and revolutionary organizations. He warned that the status quo was affecting the newly started Iran–Iraq War and the army by putting "expertise" above Islamic faith. He repeated his old complaint that Khomeini was not providing sufficient support for the IRP; he was concerned that Khomeini would die before the clergy consolidated its power, writing, "Many people, too, are confused why the determined and frank Imam is not explicit about these fateful issues? God forbid! If you are not around one day and this confusion remains, what will happen?"

Militant clerics and their Islamist followers were accusing Banisadr of trying to compromise with Saddam Hussein and thereby end the war without a victory,[51] de-Islamizing the air force,[52] and possibly even conspiring with nonrevolutionary colonels to assassinate religious-revolutionary pilots.[53] Pressured to not accept international mediation to end the war, Banisadr understood the grave consequences of taking a moderate position. When UN secretary general Kurt Waldheim informed him of a Security Council meeting on the conflict, the Iranian president rejected the invitation to send his foreign minister to the special session.[54] But his efforts to cultivate support from the IRGC and moderate clerics did not change the balance of power in his favor. Despite Khomeini's insistence, various mediations between him and the clergy did not mend the rift, either. In one of the meetings about Banisadr, Khomeini angrily accused Rafsanjani, Beheshti, and Khamenei of dividing the polity and creating conflict: "Aren't you afraid of God? . . . Why don't you think about the people?" Rafsanjani aggressively responded and then cried, "Why do we have to be ashamed? It is Banisadr who speaks against us and our reputation, and you never utter a word."[55]

Rafsanjani's diaries and communication with Khomeini's son Ahmad, the conduit between the IRP and the Leader, further reveal the internal conflict between Khomeini and the militant clergy. These clerical disciples were often the driving force—sometimes even against Khomeini's will—behind the relentless push toward an "Islamic" government, including capturing the executive branch and thus the entire state apparatus: "Mr. Ahmad wanted to understand what we were eventually going to do with Mr. Banisadr. I said if he is content to be the president within the limits of the constitution and does not abuse the presidential position against legal organizations, we can tolerate him. Our general policy is to move toward Islam, and anyone who has Islamic qualifications can work with us."[56] Rafsanjani framed this rivalry in terms of *feqhi* (jurisprudential) Islam, which the "liberals" didn't believe in: "They don't believe in this *feqh* and in an Islamic government, we see no way except implementing this *feqh* (with more work and a lively *ijtihad*) . . . In reality, this is the Imam's will and we have become the shield [protecting Khomeini against Banisadr]."[57] Thus, Rafsanjani tried to entrap Khomeini with his own narrative by arguing that he could not wish for an Islamic government and yet put the nationalists in charge of the presidency. In practice, it would not work unless the author of the *Islamic Government* gave the entire government over to the clergy. It was all or nothing.

Banisadr's increasing reliance on the nationalists and leftists combined with his blunt, populist statements only vindicated the Islamists' earlier warnings. As a result, Khomeini's approval of Banisadr gradually diminished. Rafsanjani and his fellow clerics separately, incessantly, and ultimately successfully put pressure on Khomeini until the end: "Mr. Beheshti gave a description of his meeting with the Imam, and Mr. Khamenei, too, explained in the Majles about his own meeting [with the Imam]. Based on all these reports, it seems that the Imam has become attentive to the danger of the liberals and their influence in the army and is contemplating a solution."[58] Even minor respect for the president could anger not just clerics such as Rafsanjani but his wife, Effat Mar'ashi, as well: "I was very tired when I got home at night. Effat was very upset that again there was an admiration of Banisadr in the Imam's speech and was saying that Martyr Motahari's wife is upset, too. I explained that this was not an important admiration. But there is a view that even this much is still too much under the current conditions."[59]

These clerics disagreed with Khomeini's reluctance to accept a cleric president from the beginning; now they hoped for an opportunity to replace Banisadr. In his diary, Rafsanjani discussed a meeting he had with some sympathizers: "They talked about the mistake in not preserving the presidency for the clergy, which led to Banisadr's presidency, and they showed a copy of a letter that they had written to the Imam before the presidential election warning against forbidding the clergy's candidacy. They had mentioned my name and Mr. Khamenei and Mr. Rabbani-Shirazi for the presidency. It is an interesting letter. Today, this warning has become manifest and has materialized."[60]

In the end, Khomeini gave a critical speech that paved the way for Banisadr's impeachment. A note by Rafsanjani about Khomeini's speech—in which he called for a "new revolution"—is perhaps more revealing of the behind-the-scenes activities than the speech itself. He wrote, "It was so destructive against those who oppose the Imam that many did not believe it would be aired. He humiliated and weakened the liberals, particularly Banisadr and the [nationalist] Freedom Movement. He called them *fozool* (obtrusive) and said 'you cannot do a damn thing,' and he called the Majles' decisions *gheire ghabele khadshe* [untouchable]. He clearly strengthened the clergy, the Imam's Line, and the IRGC. God protect him."[61] Soon the IRGC and other revolutionary organizations prepared to follow up on Khomeini's green light.[62] "Liberal" newspapers, including Banisadr's *Enghelab-e Islami*, were quickly suspended for disturbing the public at the time of the war. Thugs attacked Khomeini's former right-hand man in Paris, Ebrahim Yazdi, as well as other nationalist figures.

Then, on June 10, 1981, Khomeini issued a short order informing the army's joint chief of staff that he had removed Banisadr from the position of commander in chief. Khomeini himself assumed that position, but the story did not end there. The Majles planned to remove Banisadr from the presidency because Khomeini, Rafsanjani, and others knew that he would not "surrender to the law" and be a submissive president. Indeed, Banisadr promised to fight back. Pro-Banisadr demonstrations were quickly put down by the IRGC and Komiteh forces, leading to many deaths, or as Rafsanjani put it, "wastes."[63] The media did not cover Banisadr's reactions and protests. His supporters in the Majles were beaten by the IRGC inside the parliament's building and attacked outside by thugs.[64] Even prominent nationalist figures such as Mehdi Bazargan, Khomeini's first appointed prime minister, came under increasing pressure. Rafsanjani claimed that they went to him for help: "They expected that the Imam would say something or that I [Rafsanjani] would endorse them."[65] Instead, Rafsanjani advised them to take a strong position against "anti-revolutionaries." Not only were the nationalists who once helped lead the revolution removed from the government and other state institutions, they now had to appeal to the militant clerics for protection from "social pressure" (in Rafsanjani's words), or psychological and physical attacks by revolutionary thugs.

Khamenei, who was on the front lines of the Iran–Iraq War at the time, was summoned by Khomeini to Tehran to implement fundamental changes to the army's command structure.[66] Khamenei had previously complained about his lack of legal power over the army and resigned from it. Now he accompanied a few trusted top commanders of the divisions and air bases to see Khomeini, a sign that the army was siding with the clergy, not Banisadr.[67]

On June 14, Banisadr disappeared and later resurfaced in France along with the head of the MKO, Rajavi, who had been his ally since the presidential election. Within days, waves of terror engulfed Iran. Beheshti, along with other top members of the IRP, was killed in a single bombing of their party's headquarters reportedly carried out by the MKO. Khamenei escaped the attack only because he had already been severely injured when a bomb went off in his microphone a few days earlier, compliments of a different leftist-Islamist group called Furqan. Rafsanjani survived, too, because he had left the IRP meeting before the explosion to visit Khamenei in the hospital.[68]

Capturing the Presidency

After Banisadr's impeachment, Rafsanjani pushed again for a cleric president: "It was decided that [IRP co-founder and prime minister] Rajai should become a candidate for president. I had suggested that the administration stay [with Rajai as prime minister] and Mr. Khamenei become president. The Imam did not view this as expedient and believed that it was better [for the president] not to be a cleric." Rafsanjani cautiously complained, "That is why we did not have a cleric president in the past either."[69] Prime Minister Rajai became president but picked Bahonar, a mid-ranking cleric, as the prime minister, a move the Majles overwhelmingly approved. Less than a month later, both were killed at the office of the prime minister in a bombing that was reportedly carried out by the MKO.

The time had finally come to install a cleric in the presidential office. Rafsanjani and others mobilized their resources to convince Khomeini to allow Khamenei to run. At the IRP's central council, "again it was decided to persuade the Imam to agree on a cleric president. Because we have no other candidate among non-clerics who has natural votes . . . most friends disagree with the Imam and say a cleric president is better. I talked to Mr. Ahmad [Khomeini's son] to talk to the Imam."[70] The next day, September 10, 1981, Ahmad informed Rafsanjani that the Imam had agreed "in principle."[71] Moments later, Rafsanjani, Khamenei, and Ahmad met with Khomeini to discuss the details. Khomeini told them that he had agreed out of "desperation" and that no other person had popular votes.[72] That same day, Rafsanjani's wife visited and approved of her family's new house, right next to Khomeini's.[73] The militant clerics and Khomeini were closing their gap not only politically but also geographically. The following day, Rafsanjani "convinced" Khamenei to accept the presidency, as the electoral outcome was already obvious.[74] Within four weeks, elections were held and Khamenei effortlessly defeated his lightweight rivals. "It was exciting," Rafsanjani said of the inauguration ceremony at Khomeini's residence.[75] This political victory coincided with a sharp reduction in daily assassinations of IRP and IRGC members, after months of summary executions of hundreds of members of militant leftist organizations.[76]

"Back to the War"

With Banisadr's removal, the army lost its last protector and suffered more purges. Junior officers with "religious" credentials were promoted to cooperate with the IRGC. But neither force was prepared to obey the other. Unwilling to be reduced to the status of the army's volunteer forces, the IRGC conducted its own reconnaissance missions and war planning, expecting the army to provide firepower for its daring forces as they carried out nightly surprise attacks against the Iraqis. The IRGC was contemptuous of the army's classic "Western" doctrines and operations, and the army was equally disdainful of the IRGC's guerrilla tactics in a conventional war. Defiance and lack of coordination led to many casualties and bitterness between the two. But after a year of scattered operations, the IRGC and the army jointly developed plans to expel Iraqi forces from Iranian territories, including Khorramshahr, which had fallen on November 10, 1980, after resisting the Iraqis for thirty-four days.

Their efforts began on September 27, 1981, with Operation Samen-ol-A'emmeh (Operation Eighth Imam), aimed at ending the siege of Abadan. For the first time, the commanders of both forces were involved in planning and conducting the operation. The army provided air and artillery support, while its Division 77 Khorasan joined IRGC soldiers in attacking Iraqi defense obstacles at midnight. In his opening remarks delivered at parliament the next morning, Rafsanjani announced the details of the operation and "clarified" that the attack demonstrated that Banisadr had prevented the army from acting,[77] although in reality, the planning of this operation had started while Banisadr was president.

Nevertheless, the IRGC was concerned that the army would receive all credit for future victories. To give the IRGC more weight going forward, the Islamist government further reshuffled army officers, marginalizing those who had been appointed by Banisadr. It promoted Colonel Ali Sayad-Shirazi to commander of the joint chiefs of staff specifically to increase the army's "coordination" with the IRGC.[78] As a major, Sayad-Shirazi had led joint operations with the IRGC in Kurdistan before Banisadr dismissed him for incompetence. Per Rafsanjani's suggestion, Khomeini brought him back and reinstalled him in the army as a colonel. This was part of a reorganizational strategy to provide more training and equipment to IRGC members and share more responsibility in command and control.[79] While the IRGC continued to boast that it was an ideological force, it was furtively opting for military training. In order to better compete with and control the American-trained army, the IRGC realized it first needed to learn from the army's expertise.

Staging the Battle of Karbala

Operation Samen-ol-A'emmeh was followed by Operation Tariq al-Quds (Operation Road to Jerusalem), designed to break the Iraqis' defense line in northern and southern Khuzestan, and liberate the city of Bostan. It was in Operation Tariq al-Quds that young volunteer forces were first used to walk over Iraqi landmines. These waves of martyrs induced panic among the fleeing Iraqi forces. The IRGC consistently blamed the army's "secular" ideology for its earlier failure in the battlefield, because it was "impossible" to fight with nationalism as a motivation.[80] They needed to reconstruct the "scene of Karbala" to mobilize their forces for the battlefield.[81] Such religious mobilization involved a greater role for the IRGC.

For a Shi'a population that had mourned Imam Hossein's martyrdom for centuries and damned those soldiers who betrayed him in the battle of

Karbala, the war with the Iraqis (many of whom were inconveniently Shi'a, too) was constructed as a divine test. Responsibility for creating such a scene was partly bestowed upon Sadegh Ahangaran, a twenty-six-year-old native of Khuzestan, whose powerful voice at communal prayers had already brought him recognition. On the eve of Operation Tariq al-Quds, a fellow IRGC member—believing Ahangaran would serve better if he used his voice to motivate the soldiers—prevented him from going to the front line by taking his gun and reportedly dying in that battle.[82]

Invoking the bloody tragedy of Karbala and linking it to Imam Khomeini, Ahangaran helped engender an "imagined community" of Imam Hossein's era. Later, Ahangaran accompanied a group of Arab tribes to Tehran and performed his first religious song, or *noheh*, to commemorate the martyrs of "Khuzestan's Karbala" in front of Khomeini—an event orchestrated by the IRGC to counter Saddam Hussein's claim that the Arab minority had no loyalty to Khomeini.[83] Himself a preacher, Khomeini realized Ahangaran was an asset in mobilizing the country, and transcending nationalism and tribalism. He banned Ahangaran from any singing activities unrelated to war,[84] and from that point on, Ahangaran became the cornerstone of every operation, before which he would perform to prepare the IRGC and volunteer forces for battle. Iraq's state-controlled radio sarcastically called him "Khomeini's Nightingale." The content of his songs often reflected the politics of the war. When Khomeini and the IRGC commanders realized that the war was going to be long, Ahangaran was commissioned to write new *nohehs*, including "Seeing Karbala Entails Many Adventures,"[85] to elicit more patience and sacrifice among the population as well as the IRGC and volunteer paramilitary Basij forces. Mixing local tribal and Arabic rhythms with simple but meaningful concepts, Ahangaran's potent *nohehs* particularly appealed to traditional, religious, and poor urban and rural teenagers and their families. The strategic deployment of *nohehs* was essential in motivating foot soldiers sent to the front lines, but material incentives were provided, too, as the government established various institutions, such as the Martyr Foundation, to offer financial assistance and special privileges to the IRGC, the Basij forces, and their families.

Thanks to these steps, the number of IRGC members suddenly skyrocketed. With the conscripts joining the army, the Islamists decided that the IRGC would receive the volunteer forces instead; this helped increase the size of the IRGC from early on. According to Rezaei, after Operation Tariq al-Quds, the army could no longer refer dismissively to the "elements of the IRGC" but would rather recognize these fighters as the "divisions of the IRGC."[86] An ide-ological force that had only light weapons in the first forty days of the war and then mortars for the first year, the IRGC was now seeking to acquire heavy weapons. Colonel Sayad-Shirazi had no choice but to further open the army's arsenals and schools for IRGC members to enter artillery training.

As the IRGC played a bigger role in the battlefield, it became concerned with domestic punishment and political reactions to its activities. Before the next Operation Fath ol-Mobin (Operation Undeniable Victory) in March 1982, Commander Rezaei flew to Tehran to ask Khomeini to seek advice from God on the success of the operation by randomly opening the Quran. This practice, generally called *estekhareh* (bibliomancy) in the Islamic tradition, could boost the troops' morale and reduce disagreements about the operation within and between the IRGC and the army. Additionally, Khomeini's posi-tive interpretation of God's words to carry out an operation could shield the commanders against any accountability should the operation fail. There were concerns over a lack of trained forces and equipment in a difficult ter-rain. Himself a master of religious deployment, Khomeini told Rezaei that he and his army counterparts had to make "rational calculations" for such an important operation. Once they made a decision, of course they could always open the Quran to see what it said, Khomeini advised his soldier. However, they had to act rationally regardless of the result of the *estekhareh*.[87]

While the operation began, rumors circulated that Saddam Hussein might be overthrown by an imminent military coup. However, the question for Teh-ran was not only about ending the Iraqi occupation but about shaping Iraq's future. The Iraqis still held the important port of Khorramshahr, but in Iran, a debate over the next stage of war had begun. Khomeini opposed continuing the war into Iraq after recapturing Khorramshahr, counter to the desires of the IRGC, Rafsanjani, and other Islamists. The IRGC had already begun push-ing for an offensive operation inside Iraq and the militant clergy was enter-taining the possibility of creating an Iraqi government in exile. Khomeini's son, Ahmad, met with Rafsanjani to convey his father's opposition to both prospective adventures: no offensive operation inside Iraq and no creation of the Supreme Council for the Islamic Revolution in Iraq (SCIRI) in Iran.[88]

In another meeting after Operation Fath ol-Mobin, about two months before liberating Khorramshahr, Khomeini again opposed entering Iraq's territory. The following day, Rafsanjani and military commanders visited Khomeini again to report on their recent victories and "divine aids" on the battleground, but the latter remained unconvinced.[89] Despite this, both the IRGC and the Islamist clergy skillfully pushed back. According to Rezaei, the IRGC initially sought to move toward the Iraqi port of Basra even before liberating Khorramshahr, which would have preempted domestic and international pressure against an offensive operation in Iraq, since the Iraqis would still be holding Iran's territories.[90] This reveals how determined the young and ambitious IRGC was to ensure that the war continued after recapturing Khorramshahr. But Rezaei cited lack of sufficient manpower and resources (and perhaps Khomeini's opposition) for not pushing into Iraq first, fearing that a failed attack on Basra would weaken their forces and compromise the liberation of Khorramshahr.

While Iranian forces were circling Khorramshahr, a new movement began in Muslim-majority countries to end the war. Intermediaries shuttled between Tehran and Baghdad. Iran had opposed terminating the war as long as its territories were under Iraqi occupation. But if Iraqi troops withdrew to international borders, Tehran would have difficulty justifying its opposition to end the conflict, a prospect that concerned the IRGC.[91] To legitimize the next operations inside Iraq, Iran's Islamist leadership gradually reframed the war and presented a new narrative: the battle was no longer about defending the nation against Iraq but about a broader liberation of fellow Muslim Palestinians from Israel. In this context, the operation to recapture Khorramshahr was a prelude, and thus named Beit ol-Moqaddas ("Jerusalem" in Arabic).

Liberation of Khorramshahr

On April 30, 1982, at 12:30 A.M., Rezaei and Colonel Sayad-Shirazi stood side by side at the central command—located in Ahvaz's former golf club—with communication devices in hand to simultaneously order their respective forces to launch Operation Beit ol-Moqaddas. First, Rezaei and then Sayad-Shirazi uttered the Quranically-inspired secret code: "In the Name of God, the Conqueror of the Tyrants, Oh, Ali." Then Ayatollahs Mohammad Sadoughi and Ali Meshkini, also present at the golf club, sent their religious blessings to the troops before the battle began. In addition to natural obstacles, such as the Karun River, Karkheh River, Hawizeh Marshes, and Arvand River (Shatt al-Arab), Khorramshahr's 6,000-square-kilometer operation area contained land mines, barbed wire, water canals, and other defensive obstacles. It was no secret that Iran was readying itself for the final liberation of this critical port. Iranian forces were prepared for massive casualties as they pushed the panicking Iraqis first inside Khorramshahr and eventually to the other side of the international borders. Three weeks later, on May 24, 1982, the army, the IRGC, and volunteer forces ended Khorramshahr's nineteen-month occupation. Upon entering the city, they placed the Iranian flag on the Grand Mosque and commemorated Khorramshahr's legendary IRGC commander, Mohammad Jahanara, who had died earlier in a plane crash, with what became an epic song: "O Mammad, you were not to see, the city has been liberated, the blood of your companions bore fruit." A conflict between the IRGC and the army over exactly who liberated the city quickly emerged, but Khomeini instantly declared, "God freed Khorramshahr," attributing all the calculations and planning for the operation to divine intervention. According to military officers, it was a calculated statement to manage the conflict between the IRGC and the army over which force could claim credit for such a historic victory.[92]

Phase II: Aggression and Consolidation of the Islamists

The enormous success of Operation Beit ol-Moqaddas, which included capturing twenty thousand Iraqi soldiers, was a turning point in the war with significant implications for the larger dynamics of the region. As Baghdad seemed to be the losing party, Syria deepened its ties with Iran and shut off the Iraqi pipeline to the Mediterranean Sea. The Persian Gulf Arab monarchies reportedly offered Iran war reparations after Saddam Hussein desperately proposed peace. In Tehran, the fateful decision of whether or not to launch an offensive operation into Iraq was about to be made. The isolated nationalists,[93] the army,[94] and even clerics like Ayatollah Montazeri advised Khomeini to end the conflict while Iran had the upper hand and its main military objectives were achieved. Montazeri suggested the Iraqi Shi'ites could be armed against Saddam Hussein instead of sending Iranian fighters— although according to him, the IRGC opposed any option that would undermine its growing involvement.[95] The IRGC, Rafsanjani, and other militant clerics, on the other hand, made a case to Khomeini that within a few months, they could overthrow the Ba'ath Party in Iraq and replace it with a friendly Shi'a government. It was very likely, they believed, that upon entering Iraq, the Shi'a opposition forces would rise up and overthrow Saddam Hussein.

At a minimum, Iran could cut off the nearby oil-rich port of Basra, Iraq's second-largest city, from Baghdad and thus landlock the country by disconnecting it from the Persian Gulf. Iran could then negotiate peace under more favorable conditions. Otherwise, they argued, Saddam Hussein would rebuild his army and attack Iran once again. Paradoxically, Khomeini's position was that the war should continue along the borders, but Iran should not enter Iraq. Perhaps he, too, viewed the war as beneficial but feared the consequences of entering Iraqi territories.[96] He warned that the Iraqis would fight harder on their own land and Iran would lose its strong religious affinities with the Iraqis, who might now see it as an aggressor. But the IRGC argued that Iran could not continue the war without substantively entering Iraq; Iranian forces could enter in sparsely populated areas of Iraq, the pro-war camp proposed. In the end, Khomeini was persuaded.[97]

Various scholars remain puzzled as to why Iran decided to continue the war after the liberation of Khorramshahr. The proposed settlements would have ended hostilities in Iran's favor, allowing the Islamist regime to reallocate its resources and further consolidate itself domestically. But a closer look at the internal political landscape in 1982 reveals the challenges the Islamists continued to face. With the decline of the external Iraqi threat, internal threats to the Islamists could rise again. Even though much of the opposition, particularly the armed leftist groups, had been liquidated by this time, the IRGC and the militant clerical government sensed the potential for serious political challenges in a postwar era from the nationalists, their moderate clerical allies, and the reorganized army. Popular nationalist figures like Bazargan were still in the Majles and allied with the non-Islamist clergy. Although Bazargan's cabinet fell after the hostage crisis, he had won more votes than leading Islamists such as Khamenei and Rafsanjani in the 1980 parliamentary elections, and Banisadr's 75 percent of the vote against the IRP's 4.8 percent in the presidential election had not been forgotten. Peace could necessitate more political openness, and Iran's mounting social and economic problems would no longer be justifiable in the name of war.

Numerous statements from the Islamists during the first years of the war demonstrate that they viewed the bloody conflict principally through a factional lens. From early on, Rafsanjani pointed out the domestic dimension of the war and its "good fruit"—namely, that it would allow the regime to deal with internal conflicts against "anti-revolutionaries."[98] He stressed that the regime's opponents had thought that the army would be an obstacle to the revolution; instead, it was serving the revolution by fighting an external enemy. A few weeks before recapturing Khorramshahr, Rafsanjani emphasized that the war was "politically beneficial."[99] Foreign Minister Ali Akbar Velayati pointed out that it would have been impossible to remove Banisadr and other internal enemies if the war had not occurred.[100] During this period, the Revolutionary Court accused Sadegh Ghotbzadeh, Khomeini's aide in Paris, of subversive activities and sentenced him to death. One by one, other nationalists and non-Islamist figures were marginalized in this post-revolutionary wartime chaos, including Khomeini's formidable rival and moderate cleric, Grand Ayatollah Shariatmadari—who had strongly opposed clerical rule. Shariatmadari was accused of collaborating with the United States to carry out a coup and bomb Khomeini's house, and in an unprecedented move in Shi'a history, he was removed from his top jurisprudential position as one of the few sources of emulation in the Shi'a world. The parallel state confiscated his vast endowments and foundations, and the frail cleric was forced to "confess" and plead for mercy before television cameras. As Rafsanjani cheerfully proclaimed, with the removal of Shariatmadari, "so was lost the hope of the moderates" who were seeking an end to the war.[101] But the truth might have been just the opposite. Shariatmadari was not removed so that the "divine" war could go on; rather, the war had to continue to enable the removal of religious and political opponents such as Shariatmadari, who could be a fearsome threat to the Islamists, especially in the absence of Khomeini. Shariatmadari's humiliation and ouster completed the Islamists' monopoly over the use of religion.

Detour to Israel

The international community, which was largely passive in response to the Iraqi invasion, now feared the spread of Islamism and put pressure on Iran to end the war. Meanwhile, Saddam Hussein announced that the two Muslim sides should not fight, but join forces against Israel. His words placed Iranian leaders in the difficult position of attempting to justify attacks against another Muslim nation. In this climate, Iran adopted a newly intensified anti-Israeli discourse, claiming that the army and the IRGC were ready to enter a war with Israel and putting forward a new condition for accepting a ceasefire with Iraq. Rafsanjani said, "Since we have no borders with Israel, [the Iraqis] have to give us a path through Iraq so we can send our forces quickly to Syria. This is one of our important conditions, since after the end of the war with Iraq, we see the battleground in Israel."[102] President Khamenei, Speaker Rafsanjani, and Prime Minister Mir-Hossein Mousavi asked the Muslim world to join Iran in creating "an International Islamic Quds [Jerusalem] Army."[103] Foreign Minister Velayati announced, "The complete elimination of the Zionist regime is one of the most important strategic goals of the Islamic Revolution."[104]

Rafsanjani claimed that Iran could use the same "cheap" techniques it had successfully employed against Iraq to fight Israel, predicting an "eight- to fifteen-day" war, since Israel was smaller than Iraq in both size and population. He said that there would be no need for sophisticated weaponry because inexpensive and small weapons would be equally, if not more, effective.[105] Adding to the anti-Zionist atmosphere, Montazeri stated, "The most natural path to Quds [Jerusalem] goes through [the Iraqi city of] Karbala." He anticipated that "Muslims will support this war [as] it gets us inside Iraq in order to reach Quds."[106] However, privately, Montazeri wrote to Khomeini asking why he did not agree to end the war now that Arab countries were prepared to compensate Iran. But the pro-war camp quickly dismissed Montazeri as being greedy and having "smelled dollars" (a reference to the Arab proposals to pay war reparations). Even the army commanders spoke in favor of the war. The minister of defense said, "It is unavoidable for Islam's soldiers to enter Iraqi soil," since that would be the superpowers' nightmare.[107] Sayad-Shirazi proclaimed that Iran was "ahead of all countries" in its ability to confront Israel militarily. He promised that after Iraq, Iran would take "more fundamental measures to liberate Quds."[108]

Many Muslim-majority nations viewed the Iran–Iraq War as primarily benefiting Israel, with the Arab states particularly skeptical. But Rafsanjani stressed to these countries, "We are the most important center to destroy Israel."[109] The state-controlled media reminded the Arabs, "Iran is the most determined ally of the Arabs in their struggle against Zionism."[110] Ayatollah Mohammad Bagher Hakim, a prominent Iraqi Shi'a cleric who would soon head SCIRI in exile in Tehran, praised Iran's "completely Islamic" goals in the war and blessed Iran's entrance into Iraqi territories.[111] Iranian leaders bragged about their pragmatism and "open hands" in conducting the war. Referring to the religious justifications employed to support the war, Rafsanjani asserted, "There is nobody under this sky who could fight with this much freedom. The U.S. has to satisfy NATO. We don't. Independence cannot be higher than this."[112] He promised that Iran would turn the United States into an unclean "menstrual stain."

The deliberate appearance of this narrative coincided with the Israeli invasion of Lebanon on June 6, 1982, which prompted the IRGC and the army to send limited forces into Lebanon. For a while, it seemed that Iran might be trapped in its own anti-Israeli rhetoric. But Khomeini resisted pressures to open a new war front, insisting on prioritizing war with Iraq over initiating an adventurous conflict with Israel. In a public statement, he called the Israeli invasion of Lebanon a U.S.-backed diversionary war to prevent Iran from defeating Iraq.[113] In a meeting with Rafsanjani and President Khamenei, he said, "The Arabs will not enter a serious battle with Israel. Additional battles will only disrupt the war front with Iraq and cause us not to succeed there, either."[114] He pointed out that Iran wanted to "save" Jerusalem; however, this was not possible without "saving" Iraq first, hence the emergence of the motto "The road to Jerusalem goes through Iraq." Khomeini then reprimanded the IRGC and the army, and ordered them to return recently dispatched forces to Iran instantly, limiting their operations in Lebanon to training local groups to fight Israel. Evidently, the Islamic narratives and symbolic gestures did not trap the elites or prevent them from pursuing their strategic interests. Iran was careful not to enter a war with Israel.

Operation Ramadan

On July 13, 1982, Iran launched its first offensive, Operation Ramadan, into southern Iraq. Shi'a-inspired ideology informed the operation's plan; Iran's strategy was to link its Islamic Revolution to Basra, despite the fact that, in the contingency plans under the Shah, Baghdad was a militarily, geographically, and politically better option than targeting Basra and its marshland.[115] For the revolutionary Iranian state, Basra's Shi'a population made the port much more desirable than the Sunni-dominated capital, as from there a Shi'a blaze could reach the rest of Iraq and empower the local Islamists whom Saddam Hussein had successfully put down a few years earlier.[116] But by the morning of July 14, Rafsanjani received reports from IRGC forces that they had failed to achieve most of their objectives. The following day, Khomeini's son visited Rafsanjani to complain that his father's message had not created "the appropriate wave" among the Iraqi Shi'ites.[117] It suddenly seemed that the euphoria of Khorramshahr and God-given victories was over. There was no serious uprising inside Iraq. Instead, Iran suffered heavy casualties, relying on volunteers whose martyrdom was intended to induce fear in the Iraqis.

Iran's invasion of Iraq, however, alarmed the United States. The National Intelligence Council (NIC) warned that Iran's ideology was now threatening U.S. interests in the Persian Gulf. In a memo to the NSC dated July 20, 1982, a week after Operation Ramadan, the NIC cautioned that there was no guarantee that the Iraqi Shi'ites would "remain in their thousand-plus year passive, largely apolitical state."[118] The memo pointed out that the IRP was targeting the holy cities of Karbala and Najaf to arouse "the Shi'a populations of Bahrain, Kuwait, and other Gulf states and the replacement of these regimes with ones more compatible with Teheran. More broadly, it appears to seek dominance over the Persian Gulf region." The area contained "35 percent of the non-communist world's [oil] production capacity," loss of which could result in economic damage "comparable to the Great Depression of the 1930s in the U.S." The memo warned that if the United States did not back Iraq against Iran, all Middle Eastern states, including "moderate" and "radical" regimes, might be replaced by other fundamentalist Shi'a and Sunni governments. The NIC memo was unequivocal about the ideological, rather than the simply military, nature of Iran's threat. The United States began to rapidly supply Iraq with intelligence on the movement of Iranian forces. In 1983, the U.S. State Department launched Operation Staunch to stop the flow of weapons to Iran. Concomitantly, Washington and its allies strengthened economic ties with Baghdad and exported dual-use items and other materials that could be used for chemical weapons against Iranian soldiers.

Within the IRGC, discontent over the management of the war arose swiftly after the initial defeats. A number of Guardsmen accused Rezaei of lying to Khomeini in promising a quick victory in the "next operation" after each failure. The misinformation had led Khomeini to make statements that undermined his own credibility. For instance, in refuting Saddam Hussein's claim that more than four thousand Iranian soldiers had been killed in one of the operations, Khomeini (relying on the IRGC's report) claimed that Iran did not have four thousand soldiers in that area let alone lose that many. But subsequently, several commanders who were involved in that operation personally met and informed Montazeri of the accuracy of that defeat. Montazeri then left Qom for Tehran to alert Khomeini in person against deception by military commanders, since the dishonesty had "very badly undermined the morale" of the IRGC members. He feared that Khomeini's loss of credibility could be devastating to the war-torn country that relied heavily on its Leader's charisma, his Islamist ideology, and the ultimate sacrifices of his soldiers.[119]

More critically, some Islamist factions accused the IRGC of shaping the war according to its own internal interests, claiming that promises of a quick victory for Khomeini were intended to shift more resources to a particular institutional factional base. They argued that instead of focusing on the war, Rezaei and his allies in the IRGC were lobbying to empower certain religious figures and undermine others, such as Montazeri. Although Khomeini agreed with Montazeri that he had been duped on specific issues, he listened to Khamenei and Rafsanjani in the end and kept Rezaei in charge. In a speech, Khomeini warned agitators still deeply loyal to him that if they did not stop undermining their commanders, he would "consider exposing them as the opponents of Islam."[120] Heartbroken by this ultimate threat, many of these rank-and-file members left the IRGC or volunteered and died on the front line. Khomeini's invocation of religion minimized dissent within the IRGC.

Even as Tehran intensified its anti-American and anti-Israeli language in framing the war, it doubled its efforts to obtain weapons through both of these states. Fearful that Iraq might prevail, Prime Minister Shimon Peres pressed the Reagan administration to sell anti-tank TOW and surface-to-air Hawk missiles and other weapons that Iran badly needed. This would maintain the balance of power that Israel was eager to strike between Iran and the U.S.- and Soviet-supplied Iraqi forces. Iran might also be able to facilitate the release of American hostages being held in Lebanon. On May 25, 1986, Reagan's envoy and former national security adviser Robert McFarlane arrived at Tehran's Mehrabad airport with a Bible signed by the U.S. president. On the way, McFarlane had stopped in Tel Aviv to unload five hundred eight TOW missiles to replace the missiles Israel had already sent to Iran. They also picked up Prime Minister Peres's adviser, Amiram Nir, and several other members of the team, along with a kosher cake and a Colt handgun to be presented to their Iranian counterparts.[121] They were also carrying weapons and Hawk spare parts that Iranians urgently needed to use against the Iraqi air force.

The secret engagement soon leaked to the media. The Iran–Contra affair, or Irangate, as it became known, haunted the rest of Reagan's presidency.[122]

But for the Iranians, the crisis was not only political but—perhaps more importantly—ideological. It created an identity crisis among fierce supporters of the Islamist government, including those fighting and dying for a supposedly Islamic, anti-American, and anti-Zionist cause with what turned out to be American and Israeli equipment. The scandal would plague Iranian leaders for months, years, and even decades to come. While the U.S. government was compelled to reveal the extent of the deal, the Iranian officials were forced to cover it up. In the first Friday prayer after the scandal broke, Rafsanjani turned the tables on the United States by claiming that Washington was using its hostages as a "tool to correct its previous mistakes [and] to get close to the Islamic Republic of Iran, and this is a sign of their defeat and our victory."[123] He denied the existence of any deal to trade arms for hostages. But uproar among members of the parliament and other elites forced Khomeini himself to intervene and silence them by warning against any "anti-Islamic" act.

Phase III: Attrition and the Militant Clergy–IRGC Conflict

In the aftermath of the scandal, Iran was on its own again. Reagan faced an unprecedented credibility problem in the Middle East and back home, leaving the NSC to explore ways to boost security ties with the Persian Gulf Arab states and consider "what more can be done to help" the Iraqis.[124] At the same time, the Soviet Union and European countries increased their weaponry exports to Iraq. With increasing sanctions and nosediving oil prices, the Iranian government had difficulty acquiring even basic equipment for its soldiers. Iran's ally, Libya, halted the shipment of Scud missiles due to pressure from fellow Arab countries. Iranian troops were working with old, scarce, inferior equipment with no prospects for replacement or even spare parts. A sense of loneliness, isolation, trepidation, and mutual distrust permeated both the IRGC and the political establishment.

At this point, the Iranian leadership began to admit the harsh truth, and Rafsanjani bitterly acknowledged the cost of the once-celebrated isolation of Iran: "Our military forces need to know that in this world [the foreign powers] have released dogs . . . no one [helps us] get our rights."[125] Talk of divine miracles and exporting the revolution ebbed, in contrast to the early years of the war, when Iranian society was flooded with stories of God-sent miracles that helped poorly equipped Iranian soldiers defeat the well-equipped

Iraqis. The army was increasingly unwilling to fight if it had to humiliatingly submit to what it considered incompetent IRGC commanders. After all, it had completed its mission back in 1982 following the expulsion of the enemy from Iran's territory; since then, it had been forced to fight a hopeless war for the IRGC and the clergy. Nationalism, previously despised by the Islamist regime, was gradually employed alongside religious rhetoric in efforts to mobilize volunteers to go to the front lines. State-controlled television and radio began to occasionally air a pre-revolutionary nationalist anthem, which had been banned earlier. Iran was further than ever from its final and much-promised victory. Khomeini's prestige was particularly at stake, as he had encouraged hundreds of thousands of young volunteers to welcome martyrdom for a divine victory that would unquestionably arrive even if it took "twenty years." Now, he privately reprimanded the IRGC commanders for not fulfilling their promises.

Meanwhile, the conflict between the IRGC and the army reached a new level. As the IRGC's manpower increased, so, too, did its demands for resources and power. But now, even the submissive Colonel Sayad-Shirazi had had enough. In a meeting at Khomeini's office, he complained that the IRGC demanded to be fully in charge of the war on the grounds that, thanks to the Basiji volunteers, its forces were now seven times bigger than the army's.[126] Khomeini responded by appointing Rafsanjani as, effectively, the commander of the war. Rafsanjani helped the IRGC to expand its military capabilities and develop into a more classic military organization, particularly after Operation Kheibar (February and March 1984), in which Iraq used chemical weapons against Iranian forces for the first time—a practice that became more systematic and effective (Iraq's widespread use of chemical weapons was met with international silence, if not tacit approval). More encouragingly, the IRGC demonstrated its ability to use small boats to enter the Hawizeh Marshes and capture the oil-rich Majnoon Islands. After this assault, the IRGC moved to create its own naval and air forces and thus became more independent of the army.

But in acknowledgment of reality, Rafsanjani—backed by other top officials in Tehran—began pressing for a new, undeclared strategy of "war, war, until a victory." This was a clear departure from Khomeini's "war, war, until the [final] victory" approach and put the political leadership at odds with the IRGC commanders, creating a mutual suspicion that would persist for the next three decades. The IRGC quietly accused the "system" in Tehran of conspiring to prove that the war was unsustainable and inconclusive;[127] commanders were suspicious above all that Rafsanjani would convince Khomeini to prematurely end the war. They feared that anything less than a complete victory could damage its prestige and jeopardize its survival in the post-war, post-Khomeini environment.

The Islamist clergy, on the other hand, had already eliminated all of its enemies, established itself, and dominated the state, thanks in part to the continuance of the war after 1982. Ending the war now, ideally with a small but face-saving victory, would best support its future. In fact, the clerically dominated government was becoming concerned about the IRGC's growing political influence, viewing it as a potential rival.[128] Government officials learned that the IRGC secretly used a significant portion of its swelling war budgets to amass properties and bureaucratic positions in Tehran and other major cities.[129] Several senior clerics warned of a coup by the IRGC.[130]

Under these circumstances, Rafsanjani concluded that he should secure a settlement with Saddam Hussein, while Khomeini was alive, arguing that "final victory" was not possible because the world was determined to prevent it. To do that, however, he first needed to demonstrate that the IRGC— regardless of its will—did not have the capability to win the war. He began by pressuring the IRGC and the army to carry out another major operation, which the IRGC commanders had conditioned on receiving more weaponry. With full knowledge that their requests were unrealistic and that both international and internal sentiments were further turning against the war, Rafsanjani pressed the IRGC to act, saying it was their religious duty to do so.

Operations Karbala 4 and 5

On December 25, 1986, Operation Karbala 4 began with the aim of completing the occupation of the strategic al-Faw Peninsula and moving toward Basra. Iranian forces learned quickly and painfully that the Iraqis were fully aware of and prepared to counter the offensive, having multiple sources of information. Ten days earlier, the *Washington Post* reported that the CIA had stepped up its collaboration with Iraq by "establishing a direct, top-secret Washington-Baghdad link to provide the Iraqis with better and more timely satellite information."[131] At the same time, the Soviet Union further shifted away from Iran and toward Iraq in reaction to the secret dealings of Iran and the United

States.[132] Tehran–Moscow relations had been deteriorating since the liquidation of the Tudeh Party in 1983. Iran–Contra sources told Rafsanjani that Soviet military advisers were on the ground helping the Iraqis against Iran,[133] a rare case of two Cold War superpowers working with the same regional country against another. In addition, the MKO and a host of European and Persian Gulf Arab countries were shoring up the Iraqis' intelligence, defense, and economic capabilities. Even the Israelis seemed to no longer be interested in propping the Iranians up against the Iraqis.[134] Up to twelve thousand Iranian soldiers died in the three-day operation. The enormous human loss and swift failure prompted Rafsanjani to call Khamenei and advise him against praising the operation at Tehran's Friday prayer sermon.

But within days, Rafsanjani pushed for another operation. On January 7, 1986, he secretly traveled to Ahvaz to discuss and lead Operation Karbala 5. His meeting with the division commanders to finalize details of the operation devolved into a soul-searching performance that revealed their fear of domestic punishment. During a blame game two decades later over the failures of the war, both the IRGC and Rafsanjani published the transcripts of this secret meeting. In the meeting, Rafsanjani acknowledged that Operation Karbala 4's failure had crushed not just the forces but also the people's spirits. However, he added that there was no option but to fight and win, and nowhere else to go but toward Basra. "If we don't come out as a winner in this war, it will be a major loss for the revolution," Rafsanjani warned.[135] Frightened of the consequences of a looming defeat for the IRGC, Jafari, then a commander (later to become chief commander) of the Guard, resorted to religion. He asked Rafsanjani to clarify the distinction between *tavakkol* (trust in God) and *tadbir* (rational management). The operation needed tremendous amounts of fire support now that the enemy had established insurmountable defenses, the element of surprise was probably void, and the moonlight made the troops easy targets for the Iraqis. All odds were against them and yet they were willing to rely on God to compensate for these basic deficiencies, Jafari said. Rafsanjani perhaps perceived Jafari's narrative as a shield against accountability for failure. He snapped and corrected Jafari's religious beliefs:

> No, this is not what *tavvakol* means at all. You are obliged to do *tadbir* and remove any ambiguous point [in the operation]. We don't have such a [divine instruction] meaning. God does not allow us to do such *tavakkol*. You see! There is a big

difference. Currently, you are doing *tavakkol* on the principle of war under conditions that Russia, America, England, France are all supporting Iraq and yet we are still fighting. This is *tavakkol*. But we need to properly plan for our war. The point is that the IRGC or the IRGC members are the only force that stands up and says "We need to fight" and if someone from a corner says, for example, 'let's go for a ceasefire,' or whatever, it is only the IRGC that will create a massive uproar. We have put together all of our strength and we have the best conditions. If you cannot conduct this operation, then you should go to the Imam [Khomeini] and say "we cannot fight." In other words, take a manly step, all of you sign that it is not possible to fight with Iraq. The Imam will sit, we will sit, think, see . . . We have a revolution, people. We caused trouble for the people; we cannot just continue like this.[136]

Implying that only the IRGC wanted the war, he gave them two options: carry out Operation Karbala 5, or acknowledge the lack of capability and end the war. Jafari responded that now it was Rafsanjani who was "pushing" them into a corner to pursue the war without meeting their needs.[137] Rafsanjani admitted that he, too, understood the tragic consequences of a ceasefire: "I am with you. I, too, believe that there is no way but to win [the war]. If we seek to end the war without victory, we have been defeated, meaning we don't know what to say to the people. It has been five years that we have been talking about Saddam's fall. The Imam says, we say, you say 'Saddam's fall.' And in these five years since the liberation of Khorramshahr, we have given all these martyrs, we have caused all these ruins. If all of a sudden we give up, the revolution's foundation in the world will falter."[138]

The blame game was well underway before the operation even started. No one was ready to accept responsibility for the operation's outcome. Rafsanjani accused the IRGC of not planning properly, while the IRGC accused Rafsanjani of not providing the requested equipment. Rafsanjani asked Commander Safavi to testify that the IRGC had promised victory: "That night . . . in the bathroom, I asked if you had faith in this. You said 'I have faith.'"[139] Safavi responded, "Yes, we have faith that this is the best area [to fight]. Everybody agrees. This is the right area, but the conditions to fight should be provided."[140]

In the hours before dawn, when the operation was scheduled to begin, there was still no decision to launch it. Commanders warned that the longer they waited, the more casualties they would suffer in the approaching daylight. Others argued the delay might lead to discovery of the operation; they hoped the Iraqis would not expect another operation so soon after the failed Karbala 4 offensive. But an army colonel present at the meeting assured everyone that with the Iraqis' advanced equipment, the element of surprise no longer existed. Meanwhile, another IRGC commander, Shamkhani, warned that their 120-millimeter mortar ammunition was not enough for even the first stage of the operation to break the enemy's line. As usual, the army was ordered to "lend" some of its equipment to the IRGC, though the army was concerned that the IRGC would not return the borrowed items in a timely manner. Eventually, Rafsanjani and Rezaei retired to a different room to consult further, and they decided to move forward with the operation.

Lasting nearly two months, the assault left heavy casualties on both sides, but more so for Iran. In previous operations, it had taken the Iraqis two or three days to deploy chemical weapons; in Operation Karbala 5, they were used on the first day. Nevertheless, Iranian troops managed to reach the outskirts of Basra, but were eventually forced to retreat after Iraq's counterattacks and massive bombardments. During this time, Iraq intensified its strategic bombing of Iranian cities; Iran could retaliate only with its much more limited arsenal of missiles. Meanwhile, the tanker war between Iran and Iraq expanded to the Persian Gulf monarchies, with the IRGC using small boats and mines to attack oil tankers. In response, the U.S. and Soviet navies escorted Kuwaiti ships to protect them from Iranian attacks, leading to a direct naval confrontation in which the United States assaulted Iran's warships and offshore oil platforms.

The United States also pressured the United Nations to impose an international arms embargo on Iran. The attempt failed to bring consensus in the UN Security Council (UNSC), perhaps partly due to the Reagan administration's own lack of credibility after the Iran–Contra affair.[141] In July 1987, however, the UNSC unanimously passed Resolution 598, calling on both parties to end hostilities immediately and withdraw to international borders. Although Iraq agreed to the resolution, Iran neither accepted nor rejected the UN measure. Tehran tasked its diplomats in New York, including the future foreign minister, Javad Zarif, with implementing a delaying strategy. Iran asked the UN secretary general to "clarify" various points of Resolution 598 and prepare an implementation proposal.[142] Several months later, the United States pushed for a new measure, including the use of force to end the war, and the United Nations pressed Iran to accept or reject the resolution. Zarif found the word "tantamount" in the dictionary on a late Sunday night. The next day, he presented a letter to the UNSC meeting on the war, arguing that Iran's acceptance of the implementation proposal was tantamount to accepting the resolution. According to later comments by Zarif, the letter further delayed UN actions against Iran and provided more time to settle the disagreement over the future of the war back in Tehran.

The Endgame

As it became clear that there would be no total victory over Saddam Hussein—a formidable enemy with determined international backers—the political leadership now needed an elite consensus to end the war. A quarter of a century later, the internal confrontation that emerged among Khomeini's disciples, along with the resulting discussion about what happened in the last stage of the war, shed light on how the ceasefire came about. In the final months of the Iran–Iraq War, Rafsanjani asked the commanders of the army and the IRGC to prepare a list of what was needed to conquer Baghdad, which they provided. Rafsanjani then sought an assessment from Prime Minister Mousavi, who stated that the country could not financially meet those demands. Rafsanjani attached to that a letter from the minister of culture and Islamic guidance, Mohammad Khatami, stating that people were no longer volunteering to go to the front lines. He took the entire folder to Khomeini, who only then realized that the state was on the verge of bankruptcy and could not even continue the war, let alone win it. In a letter to Khomeini, IRGC commander Rezaei pointed out that there would be no victory in the next five years, but if they could get the equipment they needed—including twenty-five hundred tanks, three thousand artillery weapons, three hundred fighter jets, and three hundred helicopters, and expand the IRGC by a factor of seven and the army by a factor of two and a half—it would be possible to go on the offense against Iraq. But there was still an additional condition that would be necessary to win the war: "Of course, we have to kick the U.S. out of the Persian Gulf as well. Otherwise, we will not succeed." Khomeini wondered how the state could meet those demands and also expel the United States from the Persian Gulf, adding that Rezaei's claim to be willing to continue the war regardless of resources was "nothing more than a slogan."[143]

A 2011 correspondence between Rafsanjani and Rezaei is particularly revealing. In this letter, Rafsanjani defended his actions to end the war, saying that Iran had reached a point where it could not even buy shoelaces for its troops. He denied setting the stage to end the war and claimed to simply have asked how the IRGC commanders envisioned Iran's eventual victory. "You keep talking with the Imam [Khomeini] about an Ashura-style [Karbalaesque] war. What is your plan? . . . Do we have money? We have five to six billion dollars in oil revenue, which is enough for our basic needs and that is it. We have to provide for the living of our people as well. If the people behind the front lines have no bread and water, they will not support [the war]."[144]

According to Rafsanjani, when Rezaei specified what the IRGC needed, Rafsanjani replied, "Instead of telling me . . . write your demands to the Imam so that he knows what you want. If we can, we will provide, and if we cannot, we have to follow whatever decision he makes. This is not right, as people are dying and the war of attrition continues."[145]

In response, Rezaei denied he had written a letter to Khomeini to end the war and claimed he had provided a list specifying what the IRGC would need to *win*. Rezaei stressed that the IRGC could continue—although not win—the war, but ultimately it was "the politicians" who met with Khomeini and decided to bring the war to a conclusion.[146]

In the final months of the war, Iraq evicted Iranian troops from its territories thanks to better training, better equipment, and the effective use of chemical weapons. Meanwhile, the IRGC made plans to secure more control over the central government as a means to acquire the most logistical support for the war. While its commanders were attending a seminar in Kermanshah to discuss plans to run for parliamentary elections in April 1988, the Iraqis swiftly liberated the al-Faw Peninsula, which they had lost to Iran, and marched forward to reoccupy Khorramshahr. Upon hearing the news, the IRGC chief commander initially dismissed it, assuring Rafsanjani that Faw would never fall unless Iraq deployed nuclear weapons. But hours later, the truth was confirmed and panic permeated both the battlefield and Tehran. Khomeini angrily warned of a "forever humiliated and dead IRGC" and requested that the commanders responsible for the latest defeats be put on trial and executed.[147] Rafsanjani claims that he convinced Khomeini not to hand these well-intentioned revolutionaries to the notorious judge Sadeq Khalkhali. Rahim Safavi and Ahmad Vahidi, who later became chief commander of the IRGC and minister of defense, respectively, were among the accused.

In the end, an accidental attack by the U.S. Navy triggered the conflict's end. On July 3, 1988, the USS *Vincennes* shot down a civilian Iranian airliner, killing all two hundred ninety of its passengers and crew. Iranian leaders claimed this was an intentional act and a warning signal by Washington that the United States was moving toward a direct confrontation. Two weeks later, Iran announced its willingness to accept UNSC Resolution 598 with no preconditions. Tehran sent Foreign Minister Velayati to New York with the mission of returning with a ceasefire agreement. On July 20, Khomeini announced that he had drunk the "cup of poison" and accepted the humiliating ceasefire.[148]

Iranian officials argued that they had important information that led to the decision; both Khomeini and Rafsanjani said that for reasons "we cannot tell for now," accepting the ceasefire was in the interest of the state and the revolution.[149] They never revealed what prompted the sudden decision to end the conflict. However, information that emerged later from the inner circles of the establishment demonstrates a fear of domestic punishment, which these statements were designed to manage. Top clerical and military officials were concerned about how religious and political elites, not to mention the people, would receive the news. Rafsanjani later disclosed that in one of the final private meetings prior to publicly accepting the ceasefire, Khomeini stated that they had repeatedly said that they would stand and continue the war until the last breath and the last drop of their blood, even if the war lasted for twenty years. Khomeini was concerned that he would lose his massive support.[150] The clerical leadership discussed what measures it could take to mitigate domestic reaction. According to Rafsanjani, Khomeini may have proposed to resign as Supreme Leader: "He first said a point, which we did not accept."[151] Similarly, Khomeini rejected Rafsanjani's rather absurd suggestion that he (Rafsanjani) would unilaterally end the war, and then Khomeini could imprison him for supposedly acting on his own.

Ultimately, Khomeini took responsibility for the decision. The Islamist government quickly found a parallel religious precedent to explain its decision to the people and the world. Khamenei referred to the Treaty of Hudaybiyyah (628 A.D.) that Prophet Mohammad signed with his enemies, and said that the benefits and "blessings" the agreement brought to Muslims were more valuable than all the wars they had fought. Ironically, until a few days before the acceptance of the UN resolution, Iranian commentators were arguing that the analogy of this treaty did not apply to the war. The government consistently brushed it aside as well, but once it was deemed useful, it was employed to rescue the regime.

Until August 20, 1988, when the conflict officially ended, factional politics remained a consistent driving force behind Iran's conduct of the war. Camouflaged in ideological terms, these inter- and intra-elite rivalries manifested the political actors' changing threat perceptions. As the actors' positions within the system changed, their threat perceptions—and consequently their use of religious narratives—shifted, too. The Islamists' goal of capturing the state required continuing and expanding the war, invoking a culture of martyrdom, and capitalizing on anti-Israeli sentiments. Once the militant clerics had complete control over all branches of the government, it was more advantageous (in fact, imperative) for them to end the conflict, and so they convinced both Khomeini and the IRGC to accept a ceasefire with the Iraqi Ba'ath regime. Religion remained an important enabling tool for these competing elites throughout these machinations.

SEVEN

The Metamorphosis of Islamism After the War

THE EXPERIENCE of the "Jurisprudential Government," or *Hokoumat-e Feqahati*, in the first decade after the Islamic Revolution—particularly during the Iran–Iraq War—raised unanswered questions, posed critical challenges, and in the process transformed the ideology of the state. The use of strong religious language in the course of the war only increased the enormous ideologically vested interest of the Islamic Republic in the outcome of the conflict. A complete victory against Saddam Hussein was cast as inevitable and imminent, since God was unquestionably on Iran's side. The same God who surprisingly and quickly ousted the mighty, secular, wicked Shah (who had enjoyed the backing of world powers) would also remove the mighty, secular, and wicked leader of Iraq who was armed to the teeth by both the West and the East. The militant clergy initially used the war to consolidate its control over the executive branch and the army; its hegemony, however, turned the conflict into an ideological test for the Islamist government and its *Velayat-e Faqih*. A doctrine founded as the basis of a state specifically devoted to the implementation of what it claimed to be *shari'a* underwent a fundamental transformation. The state was no longer the means to implement *shari'a*. Instead, it was an end in itself. The war and the broader experience of governance led to the institutionalization of *maslahat* (expediency or pragmatism) and the construction of Absolute *Velayat-e Faqih*.

The imperatives of the otherwise much-despised "Western" state system dictated the construction and deployment of these religious doctrines. It could not, however, secure a victory in the war. The humiliating ceasefire after boundless ideological gymnastics posed a credibility crisis for Ayatollah Khomeini and his *Velayat-e Faqih*. His initiatives following the war—most notably a proselytizing delegation he sent to the Kremlin and a controversial fatwa against the British author, Salman Rushdie—should be seen in this context. Just as Khomeini's political leadership in the June 1963 uprising brought reluctant clerics behind him, establishing his marja'iyyah, the Kremlin delegation and fatwa against Rushdie were political moves intended to reassert his religious authority. They were demonstrations of ideational consistency as well as a show of force designed to heal a bruised ideology. Rather than Islamicizing the state—the stated objective of the Khomeini-led Islamists—he continued to statize Islam, culminating in Absolute *Velayat-e Faqih*, to better protect the state from the clergy. The "upgraded" *Velayat-e Faqih* in fact degraded religious qualifications for the Guardian Jurist. A mid-level jurist could now take the position that was, according to Khomeini's Najaf lectures, exclusively reserved for a marja. This would ensure that one of his mid-ranking disciples succeeded him instead of another grand ayatollah in Qom. If *Velayat-e Faqih* intended to achieve religious authority to capture the state, Absolute *Velayat-e Faqih* would guarantee that no religious authority could challenge the "Islamic" state as it was established.

Jurisprudential Pragmatism

From 1980 until 1982, when the Iran–Iraq War was progressing in Iran's favor, the Islamist state continued to claim that it would mobilize all of its resources to create the perfect man and "elevate humans from animal to angel status." Even oil was "a means for transcending human culture," as President Khamenei put it.[1] For Prime Minister Mousavi, sports were "a means for human, religious, and cultural transcendence."[2] The dominant view was that Islamic jurisprudence was ready and had all the necessary tools to resolve domestic and international problems in every field.

However, as the Islamic Republic matured and found itself locked in a war of attrition with Iraq, the realities on the ground challenged the effectiveness of Islamism and Islamic law. If the law were divine, why then did economic crises persist? Why did the prices of basic goods continue to rise? Why were lashings, mutilations, executions, and stonings unable to solve Iran's social problems? How could the banking system remain intact even though Islamic law forbade usury, a sin Khomeini had called "worse than committing adultery with one's own aunt or sister seventy times"?[3] Khomeini had inevitably sanctioned the interest-based banking system; otherwise, the country's financial system would have collapsed. Countless such cases led many to doubt the capacity of traditional Islamic jurisprudence to function in the modern world. But Khomeini and his disciples were determined to prove that Islam "works." In the case of usury, they ordered "Islamicized" banks to pay their clients *sood* (profit) instead of *bahreh* (interest). They stated that the *sood* was not forbidden because it was part of the profit the bank had shared after using the client's money.[4] However, this was only a change in terminology, since the *sood* happened to have a fixed rate, too, which was even much higher than the *bahreh*.

The clerical leadership's initial justification for the government's pragmatism was to argue that although Islamic law was complete, "specialized" research in the field was not. Rafsanjani argued that there should be more study of the writings of classic Shi'a scholars. He insisted that there were "miracles" in Shi'a jurisprudence; in some cases, one sentence of Shi'a jurisprudence could resolve the most complicated and longstanding debates occurring at the world's major universities.[5] However, that miraculous sentence needed to be found and decoded according to the context of the era. At first, Iranian Islamists claimed that everything they needed to run an Islamic state was explicit and complete. Now they needed to conduct research to find and interpret the text according to the present context.

Nevertheless, the more convincing explanation for Iran's massive domestic problems was that the country was at war. The conflict was prolonged precisely because Iran was working within the framework of Islamic law, which placed restrictions on its conduct, the government argued. For example, Iran could not buy weapons from its ideological enemies or retaliate against Saddam Hussein's use of chemical weapons or bombing of Iranian cities, because such actions would be un-Islamic. However, some of these principles were replaced by another imperative: the necessity of the survival of the Islamic state. During the course of the war, the government was forced to compromise many of its stated ideals. It acquired weapons from its American and Israeli enemies and found a religious justification for bombing Iraqi cities during the "War of the Cities" (in the mid-1980s). Iranian officials also threatened to close the Strait of Hormuz and destabilize the Arab monarchies. For each of these actions, they boasted to have a religious justification as well.[6]

These discursive adjustments often troubled not only the orthodox clergy but even the conservative right-wing Islamists in charge of interpreting *shari'a*. During the course of the Iran–Iraq War, the increasing problems of the state often brought literalist interpreters face-to-face with the radical left wing of the Islamists who controlled the executive and legislative branches at the time. As I will explain in the following chapter, this was as much a conflict between the two Islamist groups as it was a manifestation of the tension between the interests of the war-torn state and the divine provisions of Islamic law. The Majles, led by the Islamist Left, was concerned with daily politics, while the Guardian Council, controlled by the right, feared any breach of Islamic law and the long-term consequences for its own relevance. Time and time again, Khomeini interfered to end the tension according to the interests of the (parallel)state. His increasing pragmatism was eventually institutionalized in several forms, including the creation of the Expediency Discernment Council of the System in February 1988. In that final year of the war, he tasked the Expediency Council with settling differences between the Majles and the Guardian Council. This move effectively limited the power of the Guardian Council's jurists over the state. The left welcomed this measure, seeing the Expediency Council as a powerful institution that could "open the hands of the government" to continue resisting the religious authority of the Guardian Council after Khomeini died.[7] But the unhappy traditionalists among the conservative right perceived this as a temporary measure to be weakened or dissolved once the Iran–Iraq War ended.

Frustrated by the continuing complaints of the traditional clergy and bickering between the two political factions, Khomeini issued what may be his single most revealing and consequential statement. On January 8, 1988, he unequivocally asserted that preserving the Islamic state superseded *all* other ordinances:

> The state, which constitutes a part of Prophet Mohammad's *Velayat-e-Motlaqeh* [Absolute Rule], is one of the primary ordinances of Islam and has precedence over all the secondary ordinances, and even prayer, fasting, and pilgrimage . . . The

state is empowered to unilaterally revoke any *Shari'a* agreement that it has con-cluded with the people when that agreement is contrary to the best interests (*ma-saleh*) of the country and Islam. It can prevent any matter—be it devotional or non-devotional—when it contravenes the best interests of Islam for the duration that it is so.[8]

In his treatise, *Islamic Government*, Khomeini had argued that the state was simply a means to implement *shari'a*. Now, as a practitioner of statecraft and after experiencing a devastating war, he had to officially reverse this order. The state was no longer a means to the divine goal of implementing *shari'a* but rather an ultimate "divine" goal itself. In the end, Khomeini officially chose a fundamentally secular path and put politics above Islam and Islamic law.[9] This decree, which eventually morphed into what he called Absolute *Velayat-e Faqih* in the revised constitution, diminished any challenge that re-ligious authorities could pose to the state.

At this point, the right realized that it could lose its jurisprudential edge against the more populist left. Many conservatives opposed or tried to lessen the significance of Khomeini's statement regarding the paramount impor-tance of protecting the Islamic state. For instance, conservative cleric and then-ceremonial president Khamenei publicly downplayed the nov-elty of Khomeini's latest declaration. But the founder of the Islamic Re-public rebuked and embarrassed Khamenei by asserting, "He clearly didn't understand the ruling."[10] Khomeini stated that the Supreme Leader was not a mere executor of the divine laws, as Khamenei suggested, but rather was equipped with the same status and authority as the Prophet himself to abolish certain aspects of *shari'a* and replace them with new rulings.

Ironically, many of those right-wing theologians and politicians concerned about the consequences of concentrating so much power in the hands of one individual became the main proponents of the doctrine's update a decade later, when they found themselves in a position to enjoy the mighty institu-tion of *Velayat-e Faqih*. Khamenei himself is a case in point. Despite his earlier objection to Khomeini's statement on the unlimited power of the Guardian Jurist, Khamenei would go on in 2010 to issue his own religious decree stressing that *Velayat-e Faqih* is a "branch" of the Prophet's *Velayat* (Guard-ianship).[11] In the aftermath of the 2009 Green Movement, he claimed that the Guardian Jurist (himself) was the leader of the world's Muslims, and that *all*

Muslims, including the most senior jurists, were required to obey his political orders.[12]

These doctrinal changes decisively cleared obstacles to the effective functioning of the state, but they did not help Iran win the war. Many, including Khomeini's own devout followers, began to doubt his credibility, his consistency, and the efficacy of his Islam, particularly after the conflict. Nationalist figures criticized him for ignoring their warnings about the hostage crisis, continuing the war after liberating Khorramshahr, isolating the country internationally, destroying its resources, and sacrificing the youth. Perhaps more devastating was the impact on Khomeini's authority in Qom. His old rivals quietly accused him of manipulating religion for political ends, undermining the stature and independence of the clergy, and weakening the Iranian people's religiosity as a result of the failure of his *Velayat-e Faqih*. In this challenging post-Iran–Contra and postwar environment, he needed what sociologist Ahmad Ashraf called an antidote[13] for the cup of poison that he drank to end the war.

Converting the Superpower: Khomeini's Letter to Gorbachev

On January 4, 1989, Khomeini's emissaries arrived in Moscow for an important meeting with Soviet president Mikhail Gorbachev. They were carrying a highly classified letter with instructions to not only hand-deliver it, but also to read it word for word to the atheist leader. Gorbachev, who perhaps expected a message containing strategic signals on economic, political, and military cooperation between the two neighbors, politely and patiently listened for sixty-five minutes to what turned out to be an invitation to embrace Islam.[14]

In the letter, Khomeini praised Gorbachev for his "courage" and "initiative in dealing with the realities in the world," but added that his reforms were only reactions to solving immediate internal problems. Gorbachev's pragmatic adjustments, ironically reminiscent of Khomeini's own, would not salvage Marxism: "In theory, you may have not turned your back on certain aspects of Marxism—and may continue to profess your heartfelt loyalty to it in interviews—but you know that, in practice, the reality is not so."[15] He also cautioned Gorbachev against looking for the cure in the equally doomed materialist capitalist world: "The main problem confronting your country is not one of private ownership, freedom and economy; your problem is the absence of true faith in God, the very problem that has dragged, or will drag, the West to vulgarism and an impasse."

The solution was Islam, "the religion that has made Iranians as firm as a mountain against superpowers." It would similarly release the Soviet Union from all of its problems, not the least of which was the costly occupation of Afghanistan. After a few citations from the Quran, Khomeini made numerous references to "peripatetic philosophers, al-Farabi and Avicenna," "the Eshraqi theosophy of Sohrevardi," and the "Transcendental philosophy of Molla Sadra." Of course, there were many more hidden resources in the Islamic civilization, as the former Islamic philosophy and mysticism seminary professor pointed out: "I won't tire you further by mentioning the works of mystics, in particular Mohiuddin ibn al-Arabi. [But] If you wish to make yourself acquainted with the doctrines of this celebrated mystic, send a number of your brilliant scholars, who are well-versed in this field, to Qom so that, by reliance on God, they may, after a couple of years, glimpse the depth of the delicate stages of gnosis, which will be impossible for them to acquire without making such a journey."

Khomeini ended the letter with a show of confidence: "In conclusion, I declare outright that the Islamic Republic of Iran, as the greatest and most powerful base of the Islamic world, can easily fill the vacuum of religious faith in your society." However, given Tehran's improving relations with Moscow, he was not going to take it personally if Gorbachev was not interested: "In any case, our country, as in the past, honors good neighborliness and bilateral relations."

By sending a warning note to a superpower to follow his religion, Khomeini effectively put himself in the position of his own success model, the Prophet Mohammad. After negotiating the peace Treaty of Hudaybiyyah, conquering his enemies, and eventually establishing his Islamic state in the Arabian Peninsula, Prophet Mohammad—some historians[16] have claimed—sent envoys to the Byzantine, Persian, and Ethiopian emperors. He invited them to accept God's message or vanish. Khomeini was demonstrating confidence to his audience in Iran and the larger Muslim world. Contrary to appearances, the Islamic Republic was neither defeated militarily nor contained ideologically. Rather it was well-established, consolidated, and gearing up for further advancement.

Interestingly, the bulk of the letter intentionally discussed not Quranic verses or Islamic jurisprudence but rather Islamic philosophy and mysticism, both of which were taboo subjects in many Islamic seminaries. What Khomeini presented in essence was that not just Islam but *his own brand* of Islam—inspired by Islamic theology, philosophy, and mysticism coming out of a decade of praxis—was superior to not only orthodox Shi'a theology but also what was once his most challenging ideological rival: Marxism. There was a time when Khomeini's struggle with the Marxists nearly cost him his regime. Now, that powerful ideology was only at the "world's political history museum," his envoys bluntly enunciated to its main patron in the Kremlin.

Iran's state-controlled media aired the story for weeks. Not all groups in the traditional clerical establishment remained silent or welcomed the letter. A Qom-based group called "The Protectors of Jerusalem" protested Khomeini's references to Islamic philosophy and mysticism in an open letter:

> Your Holiness . . . you have not referred Mr. Gorbachev to the truth of the holy Qur'an, but have asked him to read [the works of] the condemned heretic Avicenna, the Sunni pantheist and arch-mystic Ibn al-Arabi, the works of Sohravardi who was executed by the Muslims for his ideological deviations, and the writing of Mollah Sadra, who was exiled to the village of Kahak near Qom because of his intellectual deviations . . . Your Holiness's lectures at the Feizieh School of theology were cancelled for exactly the same reason . . . In view of all this, we fail to understand why you refer the gentleman to deviant philosophers and mystics for the study of Islam. Are there not sufficient reasons in the Qur'an to prove the existence of God and to explain the principles and precepts of religion? Does it mean that leaders of Islam are unable to explain the truth of the Qur'an without resorting to philosophy and mysticism?[17]

Khomeini's wrath against such a challenge would come soon, but first, he needed another antidote for his cup of poison.

The Rushdie Affair

In September 1988, British-Indian author Salman Rushdie published *The Satanic Verses*, a novel that many Muslims viewed as offensive toward the Prophet Mohammad. The book was immediately banned in many Muslim-majority countries and led to violent demonstrations. In Iran, however, a reaction did not come for several months; the war-ravaged, isolated state needed international help for economic reconstruction. But as the anti-Rushdie demonstrations spread outside Iran, Khomeini finally issued a fatwa on February 14, 1989, obligating all Muslims to kill Rushdie: "I inform the proud Muslim people of the world that the author of the *Satanic Verses* book, which is against Islam, the Prophet, and the Koran, and all those involved in its publication who are aware of its content, are sentenced to death."[18]

With one short but powerful religious decree, the dying leader rekindled his old uncompromising stature. While the international media portrayed Khomeini as fanatic and irrational, his action effectively brought the scattered anti-Rushdie opposition in the Muslim world under his brand in a move reminiscent of the June 1963 uprising and the 1979 hostage crisis. The Rushdie affair would restore his internal and external credibility in religious and political circles. Massive demonstrations broke out in Qom, Tehran, and the rest of the country in response to his call. The 15 Khordad Foundation (named after the 1963 June uprising), established to protect the families of martyrs and the impoverished, allocated three million dollars to anyone who carried out Khomeini's edict to assassinate Rushdie. Once again, the ayatollah resorted to action to back his Islamist, anti-imperialist narrative; although a latecomer in reacting to the book, he swiftly monopolized the anti-Rushdie international crisis.

But his disciples managing the day-to-day affairs of the state dreaded the long-term repercussions of the fatwa. Underestimating Khomeini's resolve, Khamenei offered a way out for Rushdie at a Friday prayer: "[He] may repent and say, 'I made a blunder,' and apologize to Muslims and the Imam [Khomeini]. Then it is possible that the people may pardon him."[19] Fearing a repetition of the hostage crisis, he warned against any extremist act: "I will issue the order right now as a government official, as a Friday prayer leader and as a Muslim scholar: Don't go near the embassies. If you don't like British or American policies, the way to express grievances is not like some who go over embassy walls in an uncontrolled manner."[20] Concurrently, many Muslim scholars challenged[21] Khomeini's fatwa on religious bases, particularly after Rushdie issued an apology and said he regretted offending his fellow Muslims.[22]

But the euphoric hope that moderation might prevail in postwar Iran evaporated within twenty-four hours with Khomeini's angry reaction: "Even if Salman Rushdie repents and becomes the most pious man of his time, it is incumbent on every Muslim to employ everything he's got, his life and wealth, to send him to hell."[23] Then, to stop the growing religious and political doubts inside and outside Iran regarding his edict, he used his old tactic of associating his opponents with the United States. He blamed the "imperialist mass media" for "falsely alleging that if the author repented, his execution would be lifted . . . This is denied, 100 percent."[24] Khamenei, Rafsanjani, and other pragmatic officials who had wished to contain the international uproar immediately dropped their previous statements and backed Khomeini's hardline position. Although various clerics and religious nationalist figures objected to the fatwa on theological or political grounds, Khomeini soon silenced them.

A few days later, he issued one of his strongest statements against his recent clerical and nationalist critics. Addressing seminarians at all levels, Khomeini warned them against "pseudo-clerics" who dared to declare his political project and the experience of *Velayat-e Faqih* a failure. He noted that the same clerics who used to promote the separation of religion and politics, defend the Shah for being Shi'a, call him the "Shadow of God," and cooperate with the monarchy to break the revolutionaries' strikes and boycotts were now questioning the achievements of the first decade of the Islamic Republic and dividing the clerical establishment. He pointed out that he had made the "slogan of overthrowing the Shah" a reality and demonstrated "Death to America" through the occupation of the U.S. embassy. Although he acknowledged that he often had to change "methods and tactics," he stressed that "not even for a second" did he ever regret his actions during the Iran–Iraq War. It was a war of good against evil, motivated primarily by duty and not by outcome, which awakened Muslims and popularized Islam in all continents, he stated.

Khomeini claimed that the imperialists were using these pseudo-religious-nationalist figures to sow doubt in the society, particularly among the war veterans and families of the martyrs. He asserted that the Rushdie affair revealed that it was not "our mistakes" that brought calamities to the country, but rather the Western and Eastern powers determined to root out Islam and the clergy every day through new methods. Striving to restore his theological consistency and political credibility, Khomeini maintained that his fatwa, like his actions during the war and the hostage crisis, demonstrated that Islam was a dynamic religion.[25]

Khomeini then attacked his most formidable enemies in traditional and orthodox seminaries, the "snakes" that he feared would emerge after his death:

> The old father of yours has suffered more from stupid reactionary mullahs than anyone else. When theology meant no interference in politics, stupidity became a virtue. If a clergyman was able, and aware of what was going on [in the world around him], they searched for a plot behind it. You were considered more pious if you walked in a clumsy way. Learning foreign languages was blasphemy; philosophy and mysticism were considered to be sin and infidelity. In the Feizieh, my young son Mostafa drank water from a jar. Since I was teaching philosophy, my son was considered to be religiously impure, so they washed the jar to purify it afterwards. Had this trend continued, I have no doubt the clergy and seminaries would have trodden the same path as the Christian Church did in the Middle Ages.[26]

His son, Ahmad, proclaimed that Khomeini's biggest achievement was his triumph over the orthodox clergy: "Was his greatest art to set up the Islamic Republic? No. What made him the Imam and led to the historic and victorious Islamic movement was the fact that he fought the backward, stupid, pretentious, reactionary clergy . . . He fought them with theology, mysticism and jurisprudence, philosophy, art, and poetry."[27]

Khomeini's statement reveals that even at the height of his power, the clergy remained his primary nemesis. He would soon further cripple the traditional clerical establishment, preventing them from inheriting his state.

Constitutional Revisions

As Khomeini neared the end of his life, his regime had managed most of the security threats from other states and internal opponents. Saddam Hussein was already signaling his readiness to return to the 1975 Algiers Agreement with Iran, while he was secretly preparing for the invasion of Kuwait. The Persian Gulf Arab countries would coexist with the Islamic Republic, provided that the latter respected their internal affairs. Above all, the United States had not recovered from the loss of Iran and sought new avenues to reengage its strategic partner in the region. The biggest threat to Khomeini's state-building project remained his fellow grand ayatollahs, most of whom had not supported the revolution or shared his theological and political ideas. Moreover, some of his ostracized followers, including his protégé and once-designated successor Montazeri, were back in Qom. An effective figure in establishing *Velayat-e Faqih*, Montazeri joined other isolated but highly learned clerics after he criticized human rights violations. With Khomeini absent, a system ruled by a top jurist could fall to or at least be challenged by a non-Islamist grand ayatollah. It was time to structurally protect the regime from the "ossified" clergy, as Khomeini would derisively label his old adversaries.

In April 1989, two months before his death, the ailing Khomeini appointed a council to amend the constitution based on "ten years of tangible and practical experience in running the country." Headed by President Khamenei, the Assembly for the Reappraisal of the Constitution was tasked with "centralizing" the political system within two months. Although Khomeini died before the assembly completed its work, the essential amendments were rapidly adopted according to his wishes and those of his disciples. Article 109 removed marja'iyyah as a requirement for assuming leadership of the Islamic Republic and replaced it with *ijtihad*. This important downgrade in religious credentials from the ultimate model (marja) to a senior jurist (mujtahid) was then compensated for by the addition of the adjective "Absolute" to *Velayat-e Faqih*. It would give the supreme authority on all religious, political, and social matters to the Leader. The Supreme Leader would be more powerful than before against the clerical establishment in Qom and yet potentially weaker against the president. The position of prime minister was abolished and Article 113 elevated the president from a ceremonial figure to the "highest state official of the country after" the Supreme Leader. Furthermore, the Leader would "determine the general policies of the System of the Islamic Republic after consulting with the Expediency Discernment Council of the System." Additionally, one *mujtahid* chief justice appointed by the Supreme Leader for five years replaced the five-member High Court. As Mehdi Moslem points out, "the main goal was to provide more autonomy for the judicial institution and disengage it from the influence of the opposing high-ranking *ulama*, who could overrule decisions from the judicial system."[28] To give an additional religious appearance to the system, the parliament's adjective was officially changed in the constitution from "national" to "Islamic." Yet, following the American system, a Supreme National Security Council headed by the president was formed.

Khomeini's Death

The prospect of Khomeini's death shaped Iran's post-revolutionary politics long before it actually occurred. The Islamists' rush to dispatch their internal nationalist and leftist opponents, their premature designation and then removal of Montazeri as successor, and their extension of and eventual end to the Iran–Iraq War were all driven at least partly by the constant fear of the old man's imminent death. Khomeini's first heart problem arose less than a year after the revolution, prompting Rafsanjani and the other clerics to write their famous letter to the ailing Leader rebuking his support of Banisadr and warning him of its consequences for the revolution after his death. Following his heart surgery, Khomeini stayed in Tehran and was monitored by doctors at a small hospital built next to his house in the city's Jamaran neighborhood. Physicians monitored his heart twenty-four hours a day through a special sensor Khomeini carried in his pocket.[29] They also installed emergency buttons throughout the house for Khomeini to activate in case of another heart attack. According to his medical team, these measures saved him from death on at least two occasions. In the first incident, his doctors rushed into his bedroom at 2 A.M. when they saw abnormal heart signals on their monitoring devices; Khomeini's wife, Khadijeh Saqafi, was reportedly still in the room and had to hide under the blanket to avoid being seen by strange men.[30] The second time, Khomeini was in the bathroom when he suffered a major heart attack. He pushed the emergency button before losing all signs of life for a few minutes. Thanks to his doctor's use of cardiopulmonary resuscitation (CPR), Khomeini resumed breathing. This incident, which took place in March 1986, may have pushed Rafsanjani as the commander of the war to intentionally and prematurely carry out the disastrous Operations Karbala 4 and 5, which factored into the war's end as discussed in the previous chapter. Political uncertainties in a post-Khomeini era would certainly have intensified elite competition and complicated wartime decisions.

In the end, Khomeini was diagnosed with a rare and aggressive form of stomach cancer. Doctors did not reveal the details of the diagnosis to Khomeini himself, except that it was a "dangerous" illness. However, Ahmad and the heads of the executive, legislative, and judicial branches of the government were all aware of the dire situation. They first avoided chemotherapy because of its side effects with regard to hair loss and instead approved surgery as a more appropriate option. They did not wish Khomeini's charismatic image to be eroded. However, two operations could not stop the spread of the cancer. Within two weeks, it had metastasized to all parts of his body. They then agreed to authorize the chemotherapy option, but Khomeini suffered a serious heart attack the second time doctors injected the drugs into his body.[31] The founding father of the Islamic Republic was pronounced dead on June 3, 1989.

Ahmad Khomeini, together with the heads of the three branches of the state (Rafsanjani, Khamenei, and Ardebili), decided to resolve the succession issue prior to announcing the news. They secretly summoned all members of the Assembly of Experts to Tehran by the next morning. Fearing Saddam Hussein's reinvasion of Iran, Rafsanjani also ordered the IRGC's commander in chief to put his forces on high alert. At the Assembly of Experts meeting, the majority of the clerical members agreed that there was no comparable marja with strong political credentials who could replace Khomeini and concluded that a council of leadership was not desirable either. So the choices were narrowed to mid-ranking clerics in senior political positions. Shrewdly guiding the conversation toward his preferred choice, Rafsanjani claimed that Khomeini had once pointed to Khamenei as an acceptable successor. Ahmad Khomeini and Ardebili jumped in to provide similar anecdotes. But Khomeini's supposed recommendation was contrary to the constitution, whose ongoing revisions had yet to be approved by a national referendum. Additionally, Khamenei was not even a *mujtahid*, let alone a marja. The solution was to meet halfway: remove the marja'iyyah requirement from the constitution (which was already under way in the Assembly for the Reappraisal of the Constitution) and at the same time inflate Khamenei's credentials to the minimum *mujtahid*. Several clerics objected to the second provision. As the group was pondering Khamenei's low religious qualification for this job, Rafsanjani warned that his right-hand man, Hassan Rouhani (who later became Iran's president in 2013), had just informed him that Iraqi forces were on high alert, implying that Saddam Hussein was anticipating chaos in Iran after Khomeini's death and perhaps planning to reinvade the country. Then, instead of asking for secret ballots, he ordered those who were in favor of Khamenei's selection to rise. Khamenei thus received sixty votes out of seventy-four and was selected as the Supreme Leader. Rafsanjani claimed later that the "news" about the Iraqi army was particularly helpful in concluding the debate over succession quickly.[32]

As it was revealed years later, Khamenei was initially chosen as the "temporary" Leader since it was irrefutably against the constitution. Once the new constitution, which removed the marja'iyyah condition, was adopted a few days later, the Assembly quietly convened to vote once more. Again, several members protested against naming Khamenei as a *mujtahid* but ultimately consented due to the political "necessities" of preserving the Islamic government. In return, as Ayatollah Ahmad Azari-Qomi pointed out later shortly before his death, "we insisted that His Excellency [Khamenei] does not enter the forbidden area of fatwa."[33] Azari-Qomi, himself a hardline advocate of Absolute *Velayat-e Faqih* and an initial backer of the new leader, later declared that Khamenei's leadership was illegal under both the old and new constitutions.[34] He was neither a marja (a qualification according to the old constitution) nor a *mujtahid* (a qualification according to the revised constitution).

Dissident theologian Mohsen Kadivar has long argued that by no means was Khamenei a *mujtahid* before Khomeini's death.[35] A *mujtahid* does not need to follow a marja. But, according to Kadivar, Khamenei had always acknowledged Khomeini and in some cases even Montazeri as his own sources of emulation. No marja had ever certified his *ijtihad*. In public statements, Khomeini had referred to Khamenei as someone "familiar" with *feqh* and nothing more. Yet Khomeini agreed to reduce the theological qualifications to prevent any of the marjas, none of whom he trusted, to inherit his prized position of supreme authority. Khomeini's successors further tailored the political/ theological ratio of the position and used his tool of the "expediency" and interests of the Islamic state borrowed from Sunni jurisprudence to groom Khamenei. This was a sharp departure from what Khomeini had articulated in his concept of *Velayat-e Faqih*, both before and after the establishment of the Islamic Republic. Once again, *Velayat-e Faqih* followed politics as opposed to the other way around.

Azari-Qomi, Ardebili, Ahmad Khomeini, and Rafsanjani would soon modify or even regret these anecdotes and procedures that led to Khamenei's selection. But for now, it was the Islamist left that viewed the succession as an internal coup. Otherwise, the transition was spectacularly smooth and welcomed by the world. International media and leaders expressed content with the triumph of the "moderate" conservative right over the radical left, which was largely associated with the memory of the hostage crisis and ideological excesses of the 1980s.[36] Much of the world expected that with the death of Khomeini's charisma, Rafsanjani's pragmatism would prevail and Iran could finally become a "rational" actor again.

Khamenei's low religious credentials were obvious enough that he himself initially argued against his own selection at the Assembly of Experts meeting. In his first statement after assuming Supreme Leadership, Khamenei pointed out that Khomeini "was that first who had no second, and the distance between him and the likes of me is deep and unbridgeable."[37] Rafsanjani, who was even now editing Khamenei's statements, began a relentless campaign to legitimize the succession. One by one, top ayatollahs in Qom were pressured to back Khamenei's selection. Addressing him still as "Hojjat al-Islam" instead of "Ayatollah," they largely endorsed him on the assumption that Khamenei would understand the limits of his religious authority and defer theological issues to them. But this posed a theological and consequently political challenge to the Absolute Guardian Jurist. With Khomeini gone, the senior clerics, if not co-opted, could still question the legitimacy of the state's policies. It could even challenge Khomeini's old rulings, since in Shi'a theology, a marja's death required followers to switch to a new source of emulation. But Rafsanjani and his right-wing allies rapidly unearthed the unknown Ayatollah Mohammad Ali Araki and promoted him as a marja in Qom after he agreed to sanction the followers of a dead marja to remain his *moqalled*, or followers.[38] The most pressing obstacle was Khomeini's previously designated successor—and now dissident—Ayatollah Montazeri. Rafsanjani offered a quid pro quo: Montazeri would endorse Khamenei's leadership and, in return, the state would promote his marja'iyyah after Khomeini.[39] But Montazeri's erudite scholarship had elevated him to the verge of an undisputed marja and he needed no state validation. Indeed, Rafsanjani acknowledged that it was impossible to block his emerging marja'iyyah. Montazeri eventually agreed to issue an endorsement yet reminded Khamenei of the importance of "consulting" with grand ayatollahs when it came to "fateful" religious issues. Tellingly, Khamenei prohibited Montazeri's letter from being aired on national television. He privately stated to Rafsanjani that his decision came after he received "complaining" phone calls to his office and consulted the Quran on this issue.[40]

Like the rest of the world, both Khamenei and Rafsanjani were aware that a mere hojjat al-Islam had replaced a grand ayatollah, an Imam, the Leader of the Revolution, and the Guide of the Muslim World. The regime needed to initiate a massive process of what Max Weber called routinization of charisma. Khamenei's pictures precipitously appeared in government offices and public places, and Khomeini's alleged designation of Khamenei emerged on billboards and walls throughout the country. Various officials stressed that Khamenei had always been an ayatollah but that his humility never allowed him to assume this title. Additionally, Rafsanjani claimed that many Muslims outside Iran requested the term "Leader of the Revolution" to be used for Khamenei because they wanted to be part of the revolution.[41] However, Khamenei himself understood his theological, and thus political, constraints. In fact, he confided to Rafsanjani that his life was getting "monotonous" and he needed to "diversify daily plans."[42] Khamenei would often go to Rafsanjani's office to coordinate policies with him; Rafsanjani repeatedly pointed out in his memoir that the two had a "mutual understanding on all issues."[43] This was a radical transformation compared to the hierarchical gap that had previously existed during the Khomeini era between him and the rest of the statesmen. Now the divine Guardian Jurist was on par with the earthly president.

Concurrently, the state itself went through a "rationalization" process. In an attempt to strengthen the legal-rational state, many of the shadow revolutionary institutions gradually merged into the official state. The Islamists had initially formed a parallel state to control and eventually absorb state institutions inherited from the Shah in 1979. After a decade of purging them and installing loyal functionaries, it was no longer threatening to improve bureaucratic efficiency by combining the revolutionary organizations with their state counterparts. The original "Islamic" state-building project of the Islamists did not replace, but partially penetrated the modern state that the Pahlavi monarchy established in the early twentieth century. The Komiteh, the police, the gendarmeries, and judicial police merged to establish the Law Enforcement Forces under the undeniable command of Komiteh and IRGC figures. Despite the army's objection, the Ministries of Defense and *Sepah* (the IRGC) merged, too. However, the two forces remained distinct, distant, and competitive. The rivalries and bitter memories of the revolution and the Iran–Iraq War eras ensured a gap between them. Moreover, Khamenei's weak position as the Supreme Leader would necessitate a separate IRGC outside the purview of the state. The Ministries of Construction Jihad and Agriculture initially went through a new bureaucratic demarcation and division of labor before they, too, eventually merged. However, the Revolutionary Courts as well as the Special Court for the Clergy remained in place to carry their sensitive mandates outside conventional judicial channels.

The revolutionary elites, particularly the IRGC and the Basij war veterans, had put their youth and inexperience behind. With years of fighting experience under their belt, they came to lead not only government agencies but also state-owned factories and industrial complexes. Many more took advantage of the special privileges the state granted them to enter universities in Iran or abroad. Capitalizing on a 50 percent quota that the Ministry of Higher Education provided for war veterans and other revolutionaries and their families, the IRGC members and Basijis flooded universities throughout the country.[44] At a time when only 10 percent of aspiring Iranian youth could get into college, this special privilege was highly valuable. It placed loyal veterans and their families in prestigious schools and competitive programs before (re)joining the government. This is not to mention others who received scholarships to go abroad to acquire graduate degrees before returning to become ministers, ambassadors, faculty members, and university presidents back in Iran. Additionally, new military institutions of higher education, such as the IRGC's University of Imam Hossein, were established following the army's model and that of other international academic institutions.

The IRGC itself began an internal overhaul to mirror the classic structure of more traditional armies. It had previously opposed the army's ranking system and boasted its own "classless" and "monotheistic" nature. But the IRGC members would soon also be ranked according to a set of criteria, including education and the number of months served on the front line. These new generals, colonels, and lieutenants were required to follow the army's procedures and be schooled in classic military doctrines. The army's schools had already provided technical training to IRGC and Komiteh members during the war. After the ceasefire, its specialized schools for top-level commanders had to admit them into advanced programs. As a result of these new academic credentials, Ali Shamkhani, once the IRGC commander in the province of Khuzestan, transferred to and headed the army's navy in 1989 and eventually the National Security Council in 2013. He trained at the army's College of Command and Control (DAFOOS) as well as other institutions

of higher education. Similarly, Esmail Ahmadi Moghaddam, another senior IRGC member, studied at DAFOOS before becoming the nation's police
chief in 2005.[45]

In the postwar era, the parallel state shrank before it expanded again a few
years later by Khamenei and his extrajudicial and security arms, namely the
Guardian Council and the IRGC, respectively. The disputed Guardian Jurist, overshadowed by both his predecessor Ayatollah Khomeini and his successor President Rafsanjani, would pursue policies and promote doctrines to
assume Khomeini's supreme religious authority.

EIGHT

The Factional Battle Over Khomeini's
Velayat-e Faqih

THE PREVIOUS CHAPTERS demonstrate how the Islamists strategically shaped and shifted ideologies and narratives in response to evolving factional, regime, and state-level political dynamics during the course of the revolution, the hostage crisis, and the war. The threats and opportunities they faced domestically and internationally required articulating—and institutionalizing—contradictory attributes of their religious discourses. As their position in the political system changed from opposition to incumbent and their adversaries moved from the Shah, the United States, and the army to the nationalists, the communists, and Saddam Hussein, a corresponding kaleidoscope of constitutionalist, revolutionary, Islamist, and anti-American doctrines appeared.

In this chapter, I explain how the Islamists split into conservative right and radical left factions after Ayatollah Khomeini's death in 1989, the discursive consequences of this split, and the battle over the legacy of Khomeini's doctrine of *Velayat-e Faqih*. The conservatives, led by the new Supreme Leader, Ayatollah Khamenei, and soon-to-be President Rafsanjani, marginalized the radical left in the aftermath of Khomeini's death. I argue that in the course of their intense rivalries, the Islamist conservatives leaned toward new liberal, pragmatic foreign and economic policies while domestically continuing on an authoritarian path. This dual approach, which had religious foundations, was meant to consolidate both the regime and the incumbent conservative faction within it. Anxious to return to the political arena, however, the radical Islamist left—headed by former hostage takers at the U.S. embassy in Tehran—reinvented itself a decade later as a reformist force. Astonishingly, it adopted a democratic platform and successfully challenged the right in the electoral process in 1997, resulting in the presidency of Mohammad Khatami (1997–2005). In response, the right moved further to the right and employed an increasingly anti-democratic interpretation of religion to eliminate the reformists and retake control with the election of Mahmoud Ahmadinejad in 2005.

In the midst of this battle, a highly nuanced pluralistic debate on the role of Islam in politics emerged. But theological "moderation," which became the backbone of the 1997 reforms and later the 2009 Green Movement, was adopted and promoted by an unlikely faction. The radical left, which had structured itself around modern religious thinkers and anti-American groups such as the former Muslim Students Following the Imam's Line, reconstructed its ideology and resorted to a more democratic view of politics as a means to challenge the Guardian Jurist's monopoly over the use of religion. By contrast, the conservative right, which was considered more moderate in its pragmatic foreign and economic policies even in the early years of the revolution, eventually evolved into an ultraconservative anti-American faction. Led by the Supreme Leader, a bloc composed of the Guardian Council, the IRGC, and co-opted religious circles that emerged in reaction to electoral defeats by the reformists in 1997 and the challenges posed by the Green Movement increasingly questioned the compatibility of Islam and democracy altogether. As a result, it granted ever greater religious and political authority to the Supreme Leader. The end result of this intra-elite competition was the confrontation of two religious doctrines: revolutionary political Islam versus reformist civil Islam.

Soon after the removal of the leftist communists and the nationalists in the early 1980s, Iran's Islamists split into two factions: the radical left and the conservative right.[1] The radical Islamist left consisted of younger revolutionaries and mid-level clerics who had had the most intense rivalry with the communists on university campuses in the early days of the revolution. They later dominated institutions such as the powerful office of the prime minister, the Majles, and Islamist student associations. The conservative right, on the other hand, which had a base in the bazaar and traditional religious networks, comprised more senior theologians and controlled the Guardian

Council as well as many other key appointed bodies. The two factions soon found themselves in a bitter battle over how to interpret and implement *feqh* (jurisprudence) in response to the challenges posed by social, political, and economic problems, which were compounded by the Iran–Iraq War. The left promoted *feqh-e pouya* ("dynamic jurisprudence") to make a case for government regulation of the economy, land reform, and higher taxes. The right backed *feqh-e sonnati* ("traditional jurisprudence") and thus promoted the private sector and less regulated foreign trade. The right criticized the left for pursuing "communist" Islam, while the left accused the right of being capitalists and backing "American" Islam.

By the mid 1980s, the two camps' differences became more evident and confrontational. The increasing gap between the rich and the poor was a case in point. The right criticized Prime Minister Mir-Hossein Mousavi's Eastern socialist distributive system, arguing that there was nothing Islamic about his economic policies, which they claimed had no jurisprudential basis. The Guardian Council, which monitored laws passed by the Majles to ensure their compliance with Islamic law, pointed to the class differences in the Prophet's "state" and argued that the "adjustment of wealth and filling the gap between the rich and the oppressed" was "Islamically incorrect."[2] These never-ending political and religious debates within and between the Majles and the Guardian Council paralyzed the state. For example, Prime Minister Mousavi complained in January 1985, "It is now two years since we sent up bills on taxation, land distribution, foreign trade, privatization and the limits of private sector, (and) nothing has been done about them."[3] By the late 1980s, these confrontations had reached a new level inside the ruling Islamic Republican Party (IRP). The IRP had been established in 1979 to consolidate the Islamists during the competition with the leftists and nationalists. Once all credible opposition groups had been eliminated, increasing intra-elite rivalries eventually prompted Khomeini to dissolve the IRP in 1987. Its associated Society of the Combatant Clergy, which had been established by Khomeini's followers two years before the revolution, split as well. The new offshoot was the Association of Militant Clerics, led by the radical Islamist-leftist followers of Khomeini, including the mentor of the U.S. embassy hostage takers, Mohammad Mousavi Khoeiniha. Khomeini's death and the new political structure, however, engendered new positions for both the right and the left.[4]

The Conservative Right: Pragmatic Economic and Foreign Policy and Authoritarian Domestic Politics

Within weeks of Khomeini's death, Speaker of the Majles Rafsanjani announced his candidacy for president, and he won the non-competitive election in July 1989. He declared the first decade to have been the era of establishing the Islamic Revolution, to be followed by the second decade of economic reconstruction.[5] Newly adopted constitutional amendments eliminated the position of prime minister, transferring its authority to the president.

The ascending right put aside its earlier reservations about Khomeini's pragmatic and absolutist interpretation of his *Velayat-e Faqih* doctrine and began to enjoy the powerful tools and nondemocratic institutions he left behind. Led by Khamenei and Rafsanjani, the ruling faction selectively pursued policies in keeping with its new dominant position within the state, adopting a more accommodating foreign policy and improving its relationship with the outside world. Rafsanjani and Khamenei worked together to shelve many of the revolutionary-oriented policies of the 1980s and create a team of technocrats to embark on a path of economic privatization and deregulation. They also pursued more effective interactions with international financial organizations such as the World Bank and the International Monetary Fund. Initially, many senior clerics warned against the state receiving loans from the infidels. However, the right's promotion of pragmatic foreign and economic policies was justified through Khomeini's ruling that, because these policies strengthened the Islamic state, they were ultimately Islamic acts. The confrontational, revisionist foreign policy of the 1980s was replaced by efforts to integrate Iran into the international order.[6] The Islamic Republic that had belittled Arab leaders as Western puppets began reaching out to these same leaders. Additionally, in 1989, Rafsanjani led an enormous delegation to the USSR to sign long-term military and economic contracts. The historic trip to the Soviet Union, which Iran had demonized for a decade as Godless and imperialistic, signaled that Tehran's next move would be to expand ties with Europe and eventually the United States. Indeed, Iran's relationships with European countries improved throughout the 1990s, and foreign companies were lured to Iran to invest and help repair the destruction of the Iran–Iraq War. This change in policy was also reflected in Iran's foreign policy choices. Iran continued to support the Palestinians and Lebanon's Hezbollah against Israel but remained quiet when Russia and China brutally suppressed fellow Muslims in Chechnya and Xinjiang.[7] After a limited adventure cultivating a potent Islamist network to "Lebanize" Central Asia and the Caucasus failed, Iran fostered new alliances in those regions, siding with Christian Armenia against the Shi'a Azeris in the Nagorno-Karabakh conflict. In Central Asia, Iran improved its relations with the region's secular governments instead of the Islamist opposition groups.[8]

The leadership explained the new foreign policy in religious terms, partly to counter those on the left who criticized the shift from a revisionist, revolutionary state to a typical status quo power. Developing the "Doctrine of the Islamic Umm al-Qura [one of the names of Mecca]," the right argued that the state first needed to be powerful and prosperous, and serve as a model for the Muslim world in order to successfully export the Islamic Revolution. To be sure, this movement toward "moderation" in economic and foreign arenas was not repeated in the autocratic domestic political scene.[9] An increasingly authoritarian reading of *Velayat-e Faqih* was propagated to compensate for Khamenei's lack of religious credentials and charisma. For the right, the combination of pragmatic foreign and economic policy and authoritarian domestic policy was designed to consolidate the regime and the faction within it internationally and internally.

Purging the Left and (Re)Turning to Anti-Americanism

Almost immediately after Khomeini's death, Khamenei and Rafsanjani initiated the most fundamental purge and state overhaul since the early days of the revolution. They removed the Islamist left from the Majles, judiciary, government administration, and other key entities through a combination of electoral and nonelectoral means. Ayatollah Ardebili (the head of the judiciary) and Ahmad Khomeini were among the first casualties. Khamenei accepted Ardebili's resignation and in return granted him state patronage to establish Mofid University in Qom. Ahmad Khomeini's fate was more precarious, as he suddenly found himself isolated from the polity. His numerous complaints to Rafsanjani and Khamenei about being excluded from their weekly meetings suggests that he had expected to be treated on par with the Leader and the president in a decision-making triangle.[10] Once the gatekeeper of the most powerful man in the country, he became marginalized, depressed, and ill until his sudden death in 1995 at the age of fifty.

Other prominent members of the Islamist left were excluded as well. Despite Ahmad Khomeini's heavy lobbying, Ali Akbar Mohtashami, a founder of Hezbollah in Lebanon, was forced out of the government and started a dissident magazine, *Bayan* ("Expression"). Similarly, Ahmad Khomeini's pressure to appoint Mohammad Mousavi Khoeiniha—the mentor of the U.S. embassy hostage takers—to be in charge of the judiciary was rejected by both Khamenei and Rafsanjani.[11] Khoeiniha and his protégés who held high positions within the government were all purged. Khoeiniha turned down an offer for what he considered to be an inconsequential position in Khamenei's office, but in the end agreed to join Rafsanjani's newly established Center for Strategic Studies, bringing along his old associates from the hostage crisis era.[12] As I will discuss later in this chapter, this initially marginal center would go on to become an intellectual powerhouse for the radical Islamists to reinvent and return to power as reformists.

Despite their common antipathy for the Islamist left, Rafsanjani and Khamenei held different positions within the system and, consequently, different preferences. Khamenei moved from being a weak president (1981–1989) overshadowed by Ayatollah Khomeini to a weak Supreme Leader overshadowed by President Rafsanjani in 1989. Lacking both Khomeini's charisma and religious credentials, Supreme Leader Khamenei increasingly turned to anti-Americanism and relied on IRGC support to claim marja'iyyah, garner legitimacy, and consolidate his appointed position. This led to a split within the conservatives: the traditional right versus the modern right.

While both Rafsanjani and Khamenei were considered pragmatic on foreign policy-related issues throughout the 1980s, following Khomeini's death, they gradually diverged regarding relations with the United States. Unlike Rafsanjani, who was presiding over a war-weary state and needed to deliver goods to the public, Khamenei was responsible for protecting the revolution against any deviation from Khomeini's path. Anti-Americanism had been the cornerstone of the first decade of the revolution, even though Rafsanjani's and Khamenei's views had been on the less ideological end of the spectrum. As the left accused the right of embarking on de-Khomeinization, Khamenei employed a powerful anti-American tone to shield himself and his conservative right faction against these charges. Just as the Islamist left had appropriated the anti-American torch from the leftist communists a decade earlier to consolidate its position after the revolution, Khamenei would now steal anti-Americanism from his radical rivals, the former hostage takers, to weather the storm during the transition to succeed Khomeini.

It was only two months after his succession and in the midst of secret negotiations between Rafsanjani and U.S. president George H. W. Bush over the hostages in Lebanon that Khamenei took his first robust stance against Washington. The Bush administration was in search of a new regional order in the aftermath of the 1990 Persian Gulf War, including the possibility of a different approach toward post-Khomeini Iran. In his inaugural address, Bush stated that if Iran helped release the hostages, then "good will begets good will." Later, he stated in an interview, "We don't have to be hostile with Iran for the rest of our lives. We've had a good relationship with them in the past, they are of strategic importance . . . They would be welcome back into the family of law-abiding, non-terrorist-sponsoring nations."[13] In response, Khamenei declared, "Next to the usurper regime ruling over occupied Palestine, you [American leaders] are the most cursed government in the eyes of the Iranian people. No one in the Islamic Republic will hold talks with you."[14] But at the same time, Rafsanjani cautiously commissioned his envoys and intermediaries to explore various channels to Washington.

On April 26, 1990, an editorial in the Iranian state-run newspaper *Ettelaat* spoke of the unspeakable: the potential for direct negotiations with the United States. A decade after the hostage crisis broke diplomatic ties between Tehran and Washington, Ataollah Mohajerani, a lay columnist and parliamentarian deputy to Rafsanjani, proposed that it was time to have a dialogue with the United States. The piece was a response to a statement by U.S. secretary of state James A. Baker that expressed a willingness to open a direct channel of communication with Tehran. With the blessing of Rafsanjani, the editorial pointed out that a cordial relationship with the United States would help strengthen the Islamic Republic in the aftermath of the devastating eight-year war with Saddam Hussein. Mohajerani concluded that the country was in a "special" situation and therefore "expediency" had to prevail over empty revolutionary slogans and "individual and factional interests."[15]

Conservatives reacted to this proposal with massive anti-American rallies, and Khamenei joined them, backing the crowd and condemning the gambit. He harshly denounced the piece, calling those who advocated direct talks with the United States "naïve or fearful"—a verbatim repetition of the pro-Soviet Tudeh Party's statements a decade earlier. But understanding that the article was in fact published with a nod from his ally President Rafsanjani (who had just helped tailor the long robe of leadership for him after the death of Khomeini), Khamenei was quick to send an open and personal letter to Mohajerani to thank him for his service, stating "I heard that some people had an impression that my statement today contained an intention to insult you . . . I apologize. I have known you, your honesty, and your pureness for ten years. You are still my good brother and at the worst, we will not follow your advice in 'Direct Negotiations.' "[16] Mohajerani, too, apologized and assured the Leader that he believed the time was not ripe for such a move, either. With this editorial, Rafsanjani was testing the waters— he had, in fact, privately urged Khamenei to "compensate" for what might be viewed as an offensive letter.[17] But he quickly reverted to the status quo in response to the public outcry, and the taboo against rapprochement with the United States remained in force.

Claiming Marja'iyyah and the Split of the Right

The 1989 constitutional amendment permitted a mid-ranking cleric such as Khamenei to become the Supreme Leader by removing the marja'iyyah condition. This legal alternation, however, had the potential effect of undermining the Guardian Jurist's monopoly over the use of religion. Even with the "Absolute" supplement to Velayat-e Faqih, religious and political institutions could contest his decrees. To the senior clergy's dismay, Khamenei would soon elevate his religious qualification from that of a disputed mujtahid to that of an undisputed marja. This theological status would grant him unassailable authority to interpret Velayat-e Faqih and thus control the polity. Unlike Khomeini, who ended his jurisprudence classes once in power, Khamenei would begin "teaching" after he became the Supreme Leader. His exclusive and high-level debates and classes of kharej, the equivalent of graduate courses, would be specifically designed and publicized to demonstrate his scholarship.[18]

In 1994, after Ayatollah Araki passed away, right-wing militant clerics controlling the Society of Seminary Teachers in Qom declared Khamenei a marja. The surprising move worried Khamenei's political rivals and many senior religious figures, such as Grand Ayatollah Montazeri. The dissident cleric and once-designated successor of Khomeini had reluctantly approved him as Supreme Leader five years earlier, cautioning him against entering the realm of religion. After privately expressing his objection, Montazeri finally publicly proclaimed in 1997 that Khamenei was by no means a marja, alleging that this move would "vulgarize" the supreme Shi'a institution. The IRGC forces viciously raided Montazeri's office, confiscated his scholarly works, occupied his home, and placed him under house arrest for several years. The parallel state called the man who helped institutionalize *Velayat-e Faqih* anti-*Velayat-e Faqih*. Montazeri's fate had a chilling effect on the clerical establishment in Qom.

As Khamenei turned further to the right, he perceived Rafsanjani's "liberal" economic and foreign policies as threats to the parallel state. The conservative Majles, along with the IRGC and other right-wing constituencies, blocked Rafsanjani's initiatives to improve relations with the United States and Europe, privatize the economy, and relax religious restrictions on youths and women. Rafsanjani's elected, executive position necessitated these steps, even if they were unsuccessful. Backed by technocrats, he understood the important role of elected bodies in resisting the ultimate authority of Khamenei and other appointed officials. This rivalry between God's representative on earth and the popular president stemmed from dual sovereignty, a contradictory concept built into the original constitution. As president, Khamenei had had to bitterly remain quiet when the charismatic Ayatollah Khomeini overrode him on key issues such as nominating the prime minister. But Rafsanjani and his successors would invoke this provision of popular sovereignty to seek grassroots legitimacy in an effort to gain leverage over the Supreme Leader, the IRGC, the Guardian Council, the judiciary, and other institutions that legitimized *Velayat-e Faqih* through divine laws.

However, Rafsanjani's constituency shrank after he failed to enact these economic, political, and social policies in his first term. The sharp decline in his votes from 15.5 million in 1989 to 10.5 million in 1993 signaled growing dissatisfaction with both him and the system. The tension between the Guardian Jurist and the president only increased during Rafsanjani's second term, eventually leading the conservative right camp to split into two factions: the traditional right behind Khamenei and the modern right allied with Rafsanjani. When the conservative Society of the Combatant Clergy refused to include some of Rafsanjani's cabinet members in its list of candidates for the fifth parliamentary elections, his technocratic team founded *Kargozaran-e*

Sazandegi-e Iran, or the Party of the Executives of the Construction of Iran. Then Khamenei publicly rebuffed Rafsanjani's attempt to change the constitution to allow him to run for a third term in 1997, intending instead to capture the presidency through the conservative speaker of the parliament, Ali Akbar Nategh-Nouri. As they saw the exit door from politics looming, Rafsanjani and his Kargozaran allies turned toward their old enemies on the left, who had been spending their time soul-searching in various religious, political, and intellectual centers and institutions.

The Radical Left: Toward a Democratic Civil Society

When the Islamist left was pushed out of power in the aftermath of Khomeini's death, it withdrew to various organizations where it could reinvent itself intellectually. Having participated in the eradication of major political parties following the revolution, these political actors knew well enough not to repeat their victims' mistake of becoming anti-systemic and either voluntarily leaving the political scene altogether (like the nationalist Freedom Movement) or becoming a militant opposition (like the communist Left). Instead, the left decided to modify its Islamist principles, seeking a more democratic interpretation of religion that would catapult it to power. To this end, it needed a platform that was Islamist enough to ensure its survival in the *Velayat-e Faqih* system but democratic enough to open the political process and capitalize on people's frustration.

Various topics emerged in the left's internal debates, mostly concerned with questions of political development, religious governance, theological methods, pluralism, civil society, and modernization. The Kiyan Circle, the Center for Strategic Studies, the *Salam* daily, and the intellectual circles around Montazeri were the playgrounds on which various ideas were entertained and eventually the launch pads for what became known as the reform movement in 1997.[19] Within these forums, former practitioners and independent scholars reexamined dominant revolutionary ideologies and religious ideas rooted in the 1960s, having seen the results of those ideas firsthand while they were in power. They employed Max Weber's typology of forms of authority to explain Khomeini's charisma and how it unintentionally opened the way for a secular polity after his death. Karl Popper's *Open Society and Its Enemies* and John Rawls's *Theory of Justice* helped them replace the ideological excessiveness, historicism, and essentialism that had shaped many radical activists and intellectuals in the past with the concepts of civil and political liberties, social justice, and religious pluralism.[20] They invited lecturers from around the world to give talks on the dependency paradigm, theories of revolution, conspiracy theories, authoritarianism, democratization, and state formation.[21] Armed with novel theological methods, they reexamined Islamic texts and claimed that Khomeini's *Velayat-e Faqih* was only *one* hypothesis, among many others, in the history of Shi'a political thought.[22] These new theories and methodologies helped address the many contradictions between the text and modern ideas, including the concept of human rights.[23] As I explain below, the left criticized the political establishment from three fronts: political, jurisprudential ("inner-religious"), and theological/philosophical ("outer-religious"). Its goal was to build a powerful religious and political platform to challenge the incumbent conservative right.

The Political Front

In the early 1990s, several left-wing politicians, including Saeed Hajjarian, an architect of the Islamic Republic's intelligence apparatus, joined the Center for Strategic Studies in Tehran. President Rafsanjani had created this center to keep his enemies close after removing them from their positions in the post-Khomeini era. There, they immersed themselves in the social science literature on revolution, war, religion, and other topics of research. Influenced by both the experiences of post-revolutionary Iran and the writings of social scientists (from Max Weber and Émile Durkheim to Charles Tilly), Hajjarian authored a series of articles in the mid-1990s on how the nation-state was essentially a "catalyst" for secularization.[24] Referring to Khomeini's decree that put the state above religion, Hajjarian described the first decade of the Islamic Republic as the secularizing era. His stated goal, however, was to take this process one step further and engineer a transition toward a more democratic society.

By examining Khomeini's jurisprudential and political legacies, Hajjarian traced the foundation of a modern nation-state and argued that earlier state-building attempts under the Pahlavi dynasty had created a "modernizing nation-state" but not a "modern nation-state."[25] According to Hajjarian, it was Khomeini who established the first "genuine" nation-state in Iran, a process reminiscent of state formation in Europe. As those states ultimately moved toward secularism and democracy, so would the Islamic Republic of Iran—or so he claimed. He commended Khomeini for taking a pragmatic route to protect the Islamic state, which he believed unintentionally paved the way for the separation of mosque and state. As evidence, he pointed to the numerous conflicts between the somewhat more pragmatic Majles and the Guardian Council, which had been created to ensure that all legislation abided by Islamic law. However, the Guardian Council's lack of flexibility had ultimately forced Khomeini to create a third body, the Expediency Council, to settle differences between the Majles and the Guardian Council according to the interests of the Islamic state. Having led a revolution to create an Islamic state to implement God's Law, in the end Khomeini had to reverse the means and end to ensure that state's survival. Praising Khomeini's "prudence," Hajjarian perceived the creation of the Expediency Council to be the ultimate example of "secularizing the sacred": "Accepting the concept of *maslahat* [expediency] as the most important tool to quickly secularize the sacred jurisprudence apparatus is another important innovation that the Imam [Khomeini] brought into Shi'a thought."[26]

Arguing that the Expediency Council was a vital institution where national interests were determined "with no [religious] limitation," Hajjarian pointed out that this body was in fact what "distinguishes the old from the modern thought" in Iran.[27] He then concluded that *Velayat-e Faqih* was the equivalent of the absolutist state in Europe, which eventually paved the way for the modern secular state in Western Europe in the nineteenth century.[28] He thus portrayed the secularization process as the inevitable result of the creation of an Islamic state:

> Essentially, the moment a religious apparatus moves toward creating a state, it will be imperative to make the necessary changes in its religious laws in order to adjust to the new conditions. [But] it will have to accept the consequences and have a strong digestion to swallow the bite called the "state." The secularization process is a catalyst that has made the digestion of the state in the institution of religion possible and, in turn, it will cause the digestion of religion in the institution of the state as well.[29]

Hajjarian argued that the more religion was involved with the state, the greater "capacity" it would have for tolerance. In its arduous struggle with governance, religion would be forced to adjust itself to the norms and rules of the day.[30] As the secularization process deepened, its democratic capacities would expand and the participation of elite groups who represented the interests of other strata would increase. The dialectic relationship between the state religion and the religious state would lead to a more democratic society.[31] It is worth noting that exactly at this time, these modernization and secularization theories were being questioned—and even rejected—in American and European academia.[32] But Hajjarian and other Iranian reformists found them useful for "understanding" and opening up the political process in Iran—efforts not limited to the Center for Strategic Studies.

The Jurisprudential ("Inner-Religious") Front

There had always been critics of Khomeini's theory of *Velayat-e Faqih* among traditional scholars, but the Islamist government often silenced them; criticism of *Velayat-e Faqih* was seen as reactionary and subversive, overshadowed by Khomeini's charisma and the revolutionary fervor of the 1980s. However, following the Iran–Iraq War and in the aftermath of Khomeini's death, many of his followers as well as students in religious circles—particularly those being marginalized—began to reinterpret *Velayat-e Faqih* from a purely jurisprudential perspective.

Montazeri and his seminarians were among those to revisit Islamic texts to deconstruct the foundations of *Velayat-e Faqih*. Montazeri himself was a main architect of *Velayat-e Faqih* after the revolution. His immaculate religious and political credentials led to his nomination in 1984 to succeed Khomeini as Supreme Leader. He was dismissed in 1989 after falling out of favor with Khomeini due to religious and political disagreements. He became a prominent religious dissident, and now a decade later, he and his students would shake the jurisprudential foundations of the establishment.

Khomeini had argued that during the Occultation, it was the jurists' divine duty to rule and implement Islamic law. Montazeri now stated that if there were other ways to implement Islamic law, provided that the "people want to implement it," then there was no need for a jurist to rule. Indeed, "in cases where God has not chosen a person or persons [i.e., a prophet or an Imam] for this [to rule], He has given this right to the people."[33] In other words, it was precisely during the Occultation that God gave the people the right to choose their leader. Therefore, the source of legitimacy was the "people's selection . . . and not God's appointment."[34]

Mohsen Kadivar, one of Montazeri's prominent and prolific students, published numerous books and articles to demonstrate that *Velayat-e Faqih* was not a requirement of religion but rather simply a *minor hypothesis* within Shi'a scholarship.[35] Kadivar's typologies of Shi'a scholars' opinions on the state stressed that Khomeini's doctrine of absolute rule of the jurist was, in fact, an anomaly. Kadivar quoted various verses from the Quran to make the case that there was no obligation to follow *Velayat-e Faqih*. Challenging Khomeini's crucial argument that the prophets' missions were to create a state and to rule, Kadivar made a clear distinction between prophethood and statesmanship. He referred to numerous cases in the Quran to point out that the two were neither "necessarily connected nor mutually exclusive."[36] There were prophets who ruled, but there were also prophets who coexisted with and did not challenge the ruler.

However, the first and most consequential blow to *Velayat-e Faqih* came not from theological dissidents but from a philosopher who had once been Khomeini's choice to "Islamicize" the universities during the Cultural Revolution: Abdolkarim Soroush.

The Theological/Philosophical ("Outer-Religious") Front

By distinguishing between "accidentals" and "essentials," Soroush criticized the notion of political Islam as an aberration, a new concept in the history of the faith.[37] In sharp contrast with Khomeini's theory of *Velayat-e Faqih*, Soroush argued that the prophets came to establish a "faithful-spirited community, not a legal-corporeal society."[38] Their mission was not governance but "augmenting justice, eradicating tyranny, crushing pharaonic arrogance, teaching the lesson of servitude to God, and preparing the conditions of a blissful end."[39] If the Prophet Mohammad created an Islamic state, it was secondary to his mission, and Muslims were not bound to follow it in the modern world. Governance was not a God-given mandate but a set of managing skills that required ever-changing scientific knowledge and should be open to constant critique. Soroush warned against religious essentialism, stating, "We can not have a religious water (or wine, for that matter) and an irreligious one. The same would apply to justice, government, science, philosophy, and so on."[40]

By distinguishing the nonreligious from the anti-religious, Soroush introduced his theory of secularism: "The story of secularism is the story of nonreligious reason; a reason which is neither religious nor antireligious. The veil that separates this reason from religion is none other than the metaphysical reason."[41] For him, secularism was necessary to keep religion clean from the polluting effects of government:

> Secularism rejects God-like pretensions because it does not consider government to be an extension of the divine power within human society. Management skills require merely human, not God-like powers. In the modern world, the government and the rulers are the most responsible agents. They are, by no means, embodiments of the truth. The subjects do not await their high-handed generosity but rather demand their rights and participate in political affairs.[42]

Soroush attacked the core assumption of Islamists: Islam is the solution. He argued that although Islam was complete, it was not comprehensive. Islamic knowledge should not be seen as a Walmart-like superstore holding all the tools human beings could ever need. He pointed out that religions lacked certain modern concepts, such as human rights, which were not necessarily against religion. Instead of being opposed, these concepts should be dealt with outside of religion and then introduced into it:

> It is the religious understanding that will have to adjust itself to democracy, not the other way around; justice, as a value, cannot be religious. It is religion that has to be just. Similarly, methods of limiting power are not derived from religion, although religion benefits from them.[43]

If there was no tolerance in Khomeini's *Velayat-e Faqih*, it was because religious principles and injunctions were limited to duties and did not include rights.[44] If there was no mention of human rights or freedom of speech in religion, it did not mean that religion could not accept these concepts. In fact, the compatibility of religion with human rights and democracy was both possible and desirable. In the modern world, a democratic society was the only fertile ground for religion:

Sober and willing—not fearful and compulsory—practice of religion is the hall-mark of a religious society. It is only from such a society that the religious government is born. Such religiosity guarantees both the religious and the democratic character of the government. Democracy needs not only sobriety and rationality but liberty and willing participation . . . The acknowledgment of such varieties of understanding and interpretation will, in turn, introduce flexibility and tolerance to the relationship of the ruling and the ruled, confirm rights for the subjects, and introduce restraints on the behavior of the rulers.[45]

Soroush argued that the prophets' messages were close to those of today's democracies. God's prophets

refused to consider themselves captains of history and culture or to impose their views in matters of faith. They were willing to see all nations as equally captivated and fascinated by Satan as well as by their own customs. They spoke the truth and exposed the falsehood in order to discharge their divine duties and attain bliss in the hereafter. They did not set out to survive or win or wipe out ignorance, inequity, and evil.[46]

Political Islam vs. Civil Islam

What these three interrelated leftist camps (political, jurisprudential, and theological) had in common was their efforts to alter the theological ideals established in the aftermath of the 1979 revolution. Their diagnosis was that religion had become obese, as Soroush put it. By slenderizing their understanding of religion, people could create a society that was moral, free, and prosperous.[47] While still acknowledging the public role of religion, this view shifted its focus from the state to society. Unlike the previous discourse (political Islam), which targeted the state and defined itself against the "West," the new discourse (civil Islam) concentrated on civil society, religious pluralism, and the "necessity" of secularism. The more this "project" was pursued, the "slimmer" and yet stronger the notion of religion would become. Accordingly, a more visible and pronounced religious state was not inevitably beneficial to people's religiosity. A religious government was a government run by religious people, not a government that followed a literal interpretation of the Holy Text. These controversial ideas, many of which emerged in independent intellectual circles, were critical to the left's ability to reinstate itself into Iranian politics.

These self-proclaimed reformists did not advocate a form of secularism that relegated Islam to the private sphere. They continued to ascribe a public role to religion or what sociologist José Casanova calls the "core definition of secularism," in which the "thesis of the differentiation of the religious and secular spheres" strives to emancipate "the secular spheres from religious institutions and norms."[48] However, the Iranian reformists entered the debate from the opposite end of the ideological spectrum: emancipating religion from secular institutions and norms. Their definition of secularization began as a process of walling off religious institutions from instrumental use by the state. As Ali-Reza Alavi-Tabar, a prominent reformist figure, wrote:

> The government has no right to determine the direction and content of religious research and teachings based on its political expediencies. Moreover, it cannot promote and propagate religious doctrines and execute religious rituals in a way to justify its legitimacy or guidelines and control them according to its interests and expediencies. Conversely, the independence of the institution of power has to be protected from the institution of religion. This means presence in religious institutions does not provide any special rights to play a role in the institution of power.[49]

And so a new form of Islam joined a very public battle against the reigning order as the establishment's political Islam (Islamism) was challenged by civil Islam, or what some scholars have denoted as "post-Islamism."[50]

Two critical conclusions can be drawn from this account. First, factional interests determined the emergence and adoption of this more democratic, secular perception of Islam. Second, contrary to the arguments of some scholars, this "cognitive" shift was not an accidental outcome of behavioral change,[51] nor was it a mere intellectual journey devoid of political goals. Rather, the cognitive shift resulted from a calculated plan and conscious learning process undertaken with the help of independent intellectuals.

Armed with a new platform of civil society, rule of law, and democracy, the former radical leftists reentered the political process as reformists. They deployed a powerful religious-democratic narrative that appealed to a wide

range of constituencies, from the secular strata of society to religious voters, from the youth and women who were dissatisfied with the Islamic codes
to demoralized revolutionaries and Islamists searching for what had gone
wrong in the previous two decades. The reformists cautiously embraced their
old rival Rafsanjani and enjoyed financial and logistical support from his
pragmatist allies, including the powerful mayor of Tehran, Gholam-Hussein
Karbaschi. In a landslide presidential election in June 1997, this coalition's
candidate, Mohammad Khatami, won 70 percent of the popular vote. Despite
massive support from the IRGC and other parallel-state institutions, Khamenei's candidate, Nategh-Nouri, earned only 25 percent of the vote. Rafsanjani
later revealed that he himself voted for Nategh-Nouri, even though his political machinery was behind Khatami.[52] Two years later, the reformists swept
the local councils, and then in 2000 they won the Majles. Once they dominated the elected bodies, they moved toward the appointed institutions. The
media that flourished in this new liberal environment targeted the IRGC, the
judiciary, and even the office of the Supreme Leader. The left no longer attacked the right for promoting "American Islam" but instead criticized their
disregard of human rights and democratic ideals. In an interview with CNN,
President Khatami even praised American democracy and implicitly referred
to the United States as the reformists' ideal model through which religion
could give birth to democracy:

> The American civilization is founded upon the vision, thinking, and manners of
> the Puritans. Certainly, others such as adventurers, those searching for gold, and
> even sea pirates, also arrived in the United States. But the American nation has
> never celebrated their arrival and never considered it to be the beginning of their
> civilization. The Puritans constituted a religious sect whose vision and character-
> istics, in addition to worshipping God, was in harmony with republicanism, de-
> mocracy, and freedom.[53]

Khatami compared the Iranian Revolution to the American Revolution to
point out that, like the latter, the goal of Khomeini's Islamic Revolution was
to bring independence and democracy to his country. This was a sharp departure from the anti-American, despotic, and Islamist readings of the revolution and the Quran that Khatami and his faction had promoted two decades
earlier.

The Emergence of the Neoconservatives

The defeated conservative right saw the reform movement as an existential threat and hardened its autocratic position in response. Convinced that the reformists' ultimate agenda was to remove him and his parallel state, Khamenei turned to the ultra-right to ensure that the reformists were expunged from the legislative and executive branches in 2004 and 2005, respectively. He used the appointed body of the Guardian Council to disqualify reformists from the elections and barred most of them from running for parliament. In the presidential election of 2005 and again in 2009, he employed these tools along with reportedly massive electoral fraud to bring about Mahmoud Ahmadinejad's victory at the ballot box.[54] It is in this context that a neoconservative movement, blessed by the nervous Supreme Leader, emerged in various religious and political circles to bolster his authoritarian turn. Khamenei, the moderate, mid-ranking, conservative cleric of the 1980s, reinvented himself as a marja with an ultraconservative agenda concocted in various right-wing theological centers during the reform era. Threatened by a democratic religious pluralist discourse, he had to deploy an equally powerful doctrine to make the case for the existence of the final reading of Islam, which only he possessed.

In the first years of the reform movement, the right tentatively was open to the idea of a "religious democracy," but the consecutive losses of the presidency, the local councils, and the Majles signaled a political avalanche comparable to the collapse of the Soviet Union in the aftermath of glasnost and perestroika. The portrayal of President Khatami as Iran's Gorbachev by supporters and commentators outside the country deepened the conservatives' anxiety. As I will discuss in the next chapter, the reformist media's attack against top conservative clerics and bodies underscored to the traditional right that the movement was an existential threat that had to be addressed. Fearing that Rafsanjani would betray them again by making a U-turn at the last minute to save Khamenei and his old conservative allies, a few reformist writers targeted him as well. In a series of articles, they implicated Rafsanjani and other top officials in the killings of Iranian dissidents during the prior decade.[55] This audacious move alienated Rafsanjani and other centrist allies from the reformist faction, which in turn further emboldened Khamenei and the IRGC to act. Their immediate response was to unleash security forces to crack down on the media and student movements, but the longer-term tactic was to create a neoconservative political faction based on an ultra-right theology. Again, the point of departure was *Velayat-e Faqih*.

As Iranian-French sociologist Farhad Khosrokhavar argues, "the unifying traits [of the neoconservatives] include their recognition of the absolute supremacy of the Guardian Jurist and their opposition to democracy, civil society, and religious pluralism. Some are imbued with the non-democratic, even anti-democratic, Western political thought."[56] The neoconservatives did not maintain Khomeini's ambiguity with regard to the issue of sources of sovereignty. Khomeini famously stated that the "Majles is the head of all affairs" while preserving enormous power for the Supreme Leader and other nonelected bodies. It was a delicate balance that his much less charismatic successor could not easily maintain. The conservative establishment, which had experienced serious blows during the electoral process in the late 1990s, could not afford Khomeini's double game. They needed to reformulate *Velayat-e Faqih* to inoculate it from the negative impact of the popular vote; hence the neoconservatives' increasing emphasis on the divine origin of *Velayat-e Faqih* and other nonelected bodies at the expense of democratically elected institutions.

One of the neoconservatives' first steps was to emphasize the notion of duty as opposed to individual rights. Ayatollah Sadeq Amoli Larijani, a top theologian in Qom who later became the head of the judiciary, argued:

> In the Islamic state, according to *Velayat-e Faqih*, the source of legitimacy for the system is the authenticity of duty and not the authenticity of the individual. Therefore, while all the pillars of the state, whatever their significance, are important for the efficiency of the system, they owe their legitimacy to their divine origins . . . As for those who say that in an Islamic government God has given to the people the right to choose their ruler, that they can do so and so with their votes, and that they may give the reins of power to anyone, these people are speaking from the liberal doctrine, and this is not in accord with the concept of *Velayat-e Faqih*.[57]

The neoconservatives revived and co-opted figures who had been isolated during Khomeini's reign. Traditional jurists such as Ayatollah Mohammad Taghi Mesbah-Yazdi had opposed Khomeini's revolutionary ideology in the 1970s. But Khamenei found some of these reactionary ideas beneficial to his quest for divine sources of legitimacy. Mesbah-Yazdi, also known to be Ahmadinejad's mentor, unequivocally rejected democracy and the will of the people as a source of legitimacy.[58]

Nondemocratic Western Ideology

The neoconservatives also had roots in nondemocratic Western thought, such as that of the Nazi philosopher Martin Heidegger. This non-native aspect provided them with additional ammunition to launch an attack on the reformists' liberal position, claiming that the reformists' views were caricatures of selected streams of Western thought. They denounced liberalism and secularism not only as essentially incompatible with Islam but as failed ideologies in Western political thought. To the neoconservatives, *Velayat-e Faqih* protected Islamic society from the wicked, dominating West. Unlike the left, which argued that separating the state from the mosque was not only desirable but necessary for the future of Islam in the modern world, the neoconservatives claimed that secularism was neither universal nor compatible with Islam. They accused the reformists of seeking to deprive Islam of its divine values and of limiting religion's role in the name of human rights and democracy.

Targeting Hajjarian and other reformists who claimed that Khomeini himself had opened the door to secularism by institutionalizing the notions of expediency and pragmatism, Hassan Rahimpour Azghadi, another neoconservative, argued, "Khomeini did not secularize Islam, but, on the contrary, he Islamized the 'century' by submitting to religious law that part of tradition (*urf*) that had escaped it in the past."[59] He argued in effect that according to the doctrine of *Velayat-e Faqih*, no social behavior could be autonomous from Islamic ends.

While for Hajjarian the first "authentic" state formation in Iran took shape through *Velayat-e Faqih*, Azghadi did not view the two concepts as comparable at all. He argued that the nation-state was constructed in the Western secular world, while *Velayat-e Faqih* was a divine concept that emerged to "religionize" all aspects of human life.[60] As Khosrokhavar argues, the neoconservatives

are "modernizing" religion in a regressive way because social reality and the concrete evolution of society in today's Iran are in the direction of secularization.

This regressive modernization is a hyper-traditionalization based on the extension of *shari'a* to every aspect of life, thus submitting to Islamic regulations those acts that traditional religion used to consider as being neutral.[61]

Although democracy inevitably entered the right's lexicon as well, it was reinterpreted not as a source of legitimacy but as being only "complementary" to the divinity of *Velayat-e Faqih*. With the help of the Guardian Council, the IRGC, and other right-wing institutions of the establishment, such as the Society of the Combatant Clergy, the neoconservatives took the local councils (2003), the Majles (2004), and the presidency (2005 and 2009) from the reformists' grasp. They also became more powerful within the conservative camp and in traditionally conservative bodies. Thus, while the left took *Velayat-e Faqih* in a more secular and democratic direction to challenge the status quo of domestic politics, the right used increasingly conservative readings of *Velayat-e Faqih* to not only keep the institutions whose members are appointed under its control, but also to bring the elected bodies under the supervision of the Guardian Council to limit the left's access to the ballot box. Once again, institutional and factional interests dictated the religious approach, but in this case toward further conservative politics.

In their quest for power, "Islamic" parties require theological latitude to better utilize political opportunities and enforce—or survive—state repression. During the last four decades, Islamist factions on the right and the left have modified, reversed, and even swapped their theological ideals according to their shifting threat perceptions. In doing so, both factions have distanced themselves from Khomeini's original vision of the Islamic government. One emphasizes the theocratic nature of the political system while the other stresses the importance of its republican institutions. Nonetheless, for both the right and the left, the point of departure was Khomeini's *Velayat-e Faqih*. The left took the notion of *Velayat-e Faqih* and baptized it in Western democratic literature to present a theory of a "democratic religious government." In contrast, the right, using the same concept, adopted nondemocratic Western thought and turned to the traditional right, framing *Velayat-e Faqih* as a divine, holy, and anti-Western concept that required absolute obedience.

NINE

Media, Religion, and the Green Movement

AS OUTLINED in the previous chapter, the diverging viewpoints on *Velayat-e Faqih* and the broader relationship between religion and politics that emerged in the late 1980s and early 1990s were initially debated primarily in the closed circles of academic and religious institutions. However, when Islamist leftist radicals reentered politics as reformists in the 1997 presidential election, they discussed universal norms and values such as religious pluralism and democracy more openly in the media, in contrast to the esoteric debates in the preceding era.

In this chapter, I examine how the reformists endeavored to bring those discussions—and, more importantly, their daily social and political implications—to debates in the public sphere in order to weaken the incumbent's cohesion, expand their own popular support, and further open the electoral process. I argue that the reformists intensified their discursive battle with the conservative establishment through the instrumental use of the media. It was one of the few critical tools that the reformist faction had at its disposal to challenge, expose, and compete with those who controlled the office of the Supreme Leader, the IRGC, and other appointed parallel-state institutions. The advent of new, electronic media later added a different dimension to this intra-religious confrontation, which became more direct, transparent, and radical. In the absence of viable political parties, the Iranian media became a decisive battleground for Iran's domestic tensions as the reformists and conservatives waged their political and religious wars. Many political activists entered the field of journalism instead of government institutions. Even those who did take up high official positions understood the importance of the media, founding their own news sites or newspapers. Their coverage and interpretation of internal politics and international stories were consistent with their factional interests. They continued criticizing the official authoritarian reading, if not the entire institution of *Velayat-e Faqih*, to mobilize mass support. Then they framed authoritarianism as a security threat that could induce the democracy-promoting United States to launch a military attack against Iran, which seemed plausible after the invasions of Afghanistan in 2001 and Iraq in 2003.

The conservative establishment, on the other hand, used a variety of methods, including strict censorship laws, massive crackdowns against journalists, filtering, cyberattacks, and misinformation campaigns to counter the media, stifle dissent, and control the narratives. Although typically one step behind the reformist media outlets, the parallel state showed enormous determination as well as the capability to catch up with new technology and adapt to the changing media landscape. In this war of religious and political narratives, both sides were calculating, goal-oriented, and interest-driven. Religious and secular ideas were simplified, framed, and introduced strategically to the public and elites, while political events, both international and domestic, were narrated selectively. Each side brought its reading of religion into the public sphere to articulate its political implications. Pursuing factional interests, however, each side tied its view of religion to the security of the state and regime, the independence of the nation, and the prosperity of society while accusing the other of undermining the foundations of the Islamic Revolution.

As this chapter illustrates, the reformists' political strategies and media tactics, while potent, carried inherent vulnerabilities that contributed to their undoing. Lacking central leadership, and therefore central control of the messaging, the opposition could not properly manage the strategic deployment of its narratives. As a result, they alienated allies (most prominently Rafsanjani) and demonstrated ideological inconsistencies within the movement—which opened themselves to criticism from within and without. When set against the parallel state—which had both near-absolute control over its messaging and the brutal capacity to shut down opposing voices and activities—they were unlikely to prevail. But the new media had opened

Pandora's box—the alternative narratives were now out and continue to play a role in Iranian consciousness.

Factional Politics and the Media War

The media provided the intellectual rendezvous platform for Iranian scholars, activists, and journalists to discuss a variety of topics from politics to society and culture. After the 1997 election, these thinkers and activists took advantage of the newly born liberal era to bring their political and religious struggles into a new battlefield, the press. Mohsen Sazegara, who had moved from cofounding the IRGC in 1979 to becoming a key establishing member of the Kiyan Circle in the early 1990s, opened the newspaper *Jame'a* (The Society), "Iran's First Civil Society Newspaper." Saeed Hajjarian, who made a similar journey from establishing Iran's intelligence service in the early 1980s to emerging as one of the main theoreticians of the reform movement in the 1990s at the Center for Strategic Studies, became managing editor of the *Sobh-e Emrouz* (This Morning) daily after the 1997 presidential election. These reformist publications introduced forbidden topics relating to interpretation of the Quran, the fallibility of the Supreme Leader, human rights, and the duty of believers to engage in civic action within the public sphere. They contested official narratives and engaged the public in fervent debates on daily politics. They also covered and interpreted international news and events through the lens of their ideology, which claimed to cut across the traditional religious/secular cleavage. Iran's frustrated youth welcomed this new perspective, which advocated integration with the rest of the world. The reformists understood that by addressing these issues and the people's decade-old grievances with the Islamic Republic—as well as exposing the political and economic corruption of the establishment—they would be able to maintain their bottom-up popular force and at the same time negotiate at the top with appointed figures and institutions, inspiring the motto, "pressure from below, bargain at the top," coined by Hajjarian. The key was to maintain a crucial balance of Islam and democracy. Reformist intellectuals had theorized this balance in their previous debates, but now it needed to be introduced to the public in a tangible way to secure grassroots support.

Khatami's victory ushered in a short but critical era of relative freedom in Iran's contemporary history. It allowed hundreds of newspapers to emerge, paving the way for thousands of young, ambitious journalists to launch their careers and go on to deeply shape their society throughout the decade to come. This media opening resulted in daily papers and weekly magazines with reportedly unprecedented circulations; publishing houses simply could not meet the overwhelming popular demand. Newsstands were filled with newspapers and long lines of buyers. Student organizations started their own publications on university campuses. Later, the advent of blogs opened a whole new arena in which youths could anonymously express themselves from the safety of their own homes. Many of these young people were noticed and subsequently hired as journalists in the reformist print and online media.[1] The wide variety of taboo topics covered by blogs, ranging from the authority of the Supreme Leader to homosexuality, signaled that their boldness and willingness to cross red lines could move from the virtual arena into the real world.

The conservatives' position worsened when reformists took control of other elected bodies, namely, the local councils and the Majles, in 1999 and 2000, respectively—in effect, adopting the strategy Rafsanjani had unsuccessfully attempted a few years earlier, leveraging the concept of dual sovereignty to capture the elected bodies as a prelude to challenging the parallel state. Drunk on a chain of landslide electoral victories, they promised their followers that the irreversible train of reform would soon bring about the "end of patriarchy," a code word for Khamenei's *Velayat-e Faqih*. As they became more confident, *Velayat-e Faqih* became their direct objective. The reformists argued that the conservatives had added a jurisprudential hypothesis to principles of religion in a manner unprecedented in Shi'a history. They accused the establishment of undermining traditional clergy and elevating *Velayat-e Faqih* to a divinely ordained truth.

Despite their mass popularity, the reformists were not successful in eroding the cohesion of the conservative incumbent, nor did they promote their own unity. Their news outlets relentlessly attacked figures within or on the margins of the establishment, some of whom were their new pragmatist allies. Instead of reinforcing their alliance with Rafsanjani to fight their mutual conservative enemies and fierce proponents of Absolute *Velayat-e Faqih*, the reformists targeted him, with some launching a massive media campaign to bar him from entering the legislative body. Their strategy was to eliminate him to isolate and thus extract more concessions from Khamenei, but their vicious attacks pushed their critical ally away, divided their own ranks, and emboldened the conservatives.

While serving as a political adviser to Khatami, *Sobh-e Emrouz*'s Hajjarian published critical comments, editorials, and articles against both Rafsanjani and the conservatives. The paper's investigative journalist and former IRGC commander, Akbar Ganji, ran a series of articles implicating Rafsanjani, whom he labeled "His Red Highness," and a number of conservative intelligence officials in the brutal killing of several intellectuals in the 1990s.[2] Others, including Abbas Abdi, a former leader of the hostage takers at the U.S. embassy in 1979, slammed Rafsanjani for failed economic policies, financial corruption, and his role in continuing the war with Iraq after the liberation of Khorramshahr. During the controversial parliamentary elections, reformist papers charged Rafsanjani with rigging the results.[3] In the end, the former president received only 25 percent of the vote and emerged as the winner of Tehran's last seat in parliament. The reformist candidates won 65 percent of the vote, including 90 percent of Tehran's seats. After such a dismal performance, Rafsanjani decided to withdraw his candidacy voluntarily before the official commencement of the Sixth Majles. This outcome served as a strong signal to Khamenei that the Guardian Jurist, too, could share the same fate if he entered an electoral contest. The allegations and statements profoundly alarmed the IRGC, the Supreme Leader, and other conservatives within the establishment and alienated Rafsanjani, whose initial support for the reformists was seen by many as critical to the movement's success in 1997. The frightened conservatives responded by taking advantage of the reformists' divisions and weak leadership and unleashing security forces to crack down on thinkers and journalists. Both camps moved further away from center and tilted toward their own hardliners.

In June 1999, the daily *Salam* published a classified document claiming that a new legislative bill to further restrict the Iranian press was the brainchild of a now-deceased top intelligence official who had masterminded the murder of several secular intellectuals the previous year.[4] *Salam*, a radical-turned-reformist paper, published the document a day before the bill was put to vote in the Majles. The conservative judiciary subsequently shut down *Salam* for publishing a classified document, a move that angered university students, unleashing a massive student protest that shook the foundations of the Islamic Republic for the first time since 1979. But security forces brutally put down the demonstrators, and the media paid dearly for its role in the unrest. In March 2000, Hajjarian, the "brain" of the reformists, political adviser to President Khatami, and managing editor of the daily *Sobh-e Emrouz*, was shot in the face by regime elements. Ganji, the investigative journalist who had accused several top officials of deadly plots against intellectuals, was imprisoned. One after another, editors, commentators, reporters, satirists, cartoonists, and activists experienced harassment, long periods of solitary confinement, and torture at the hands of intelligence and security agents.

Increasingly challenged by the media, the conservative establishment chose to demonstrate a typical characteristic of authoritarian states: rule by law rather than the rule of law. Article 24 of the Iranian constitution guaranteed freedom of the press "except when it is detrimental to the fundamental principles of Islam or the rights of the public."[5]

Many activists were speaking out against the parallel state because of their confidence in the mandate that twenty million voters had given to the reformists in the 1997 presidential election. However, they soon learned the fragility of that mandate, when an inexperienced, twenty-eight-year-old judge in Branch 1410 of the Press Court single-handedly put an end to the freedom of expression that they had briefly enjoyed. Saeed Mortazavi, who became known as the "Butcher of the Press," closed more than a hundred newspapers, blocked websites, and arrested journalists, bloggers, and student activists. Mortazavi reportedly even participated in the interrogation of Zahra Kazemi, the Iranian-Canadian photojournalist who died while in detention in 2003.[6] Vague and broadly defined provisions in the Islamic penal code and security laws allowed judges to charge anyone at any time with "insulting" religious or government figures, "acting against national security," or "planning for a soft [velvet] revolution."[7] Interpreted in religious terms, these laws were the regime's main tools to suppress freedom of expression.[8]

In response, the reformists argued that under these laws, even the publication of the Quran could be suspended and Prophet Mohammad could be put in prison for acting against the Islamic state! Recognizing the danger posed by the media law, one of the first priorities of the reformists after winning the Majles in 2000 was to change the legislation so that the judiciary could no longer stifle the press. The reformists introduced an amended media bill three weeks into the new Majles session. On August 6, 2000, before the Majles had begun debating the bill, Speaker Mehdi Karroubi read a letter he had received from Khamenei. Iran's Supreme Leader said that he could no longer remain silent because the new bill was "neither legitimate nor in the interest of the system and country." He warned, "If the enemies of Islam, the Revolution, and the Islamic System control the press or penetrate it, a grave danger will threaten the security, unity, and faith of the people."[9] It was the first time that Khamenei blatantly interfered in the affairs of the Majles. He had saved this extralegal act as a last resort for a crucial matter: the media. The bill was tabled.

U.S. Foreign Policy, the Decline of Reform, and the Ahmadinejad Era

From this point until 2005, pressure on the media and the declining reformists only increased. The political establishment became more sophisticated at cracking down on all forms of freedom of expression. After the Guardian Council disqualified most of their candidates, the reformists lost control of the Majles, and eventually the presidency. Despondent over the frailty of their internal political leverage, the reformists gradually shifted their focus to an external force—or threat—to use as an instrument for increasing their bargaining power against the conservative establishment. They argued that their reformist version of Islam would bring not just democracy but also security to the regime and the country.[10] This tactical shift coincided with a strategic shift in post-9/11 American foreign policy. The George W. Bush administration claimed that the undemocratic nature of regimes was relevant to U.S. national security.[11] Despite Iran's critical support in overthrowing the Taliban in Afghanistan, President Bush labeled Tehran a member of the "Axis of Evil." If during the Clinton administration the reformists had hoped that rapprochement with Washington would empower them domestically, under the Bush administration they tried to take advantage of America's foreign policy adventures in neighboring Afghanistan and Iraq, using the threat of U.S. action in Iran in an attempt to gain leverage over the conservatives. Their message was that internal unity could prevent external attacks.

Despite alleged orders by the Supreme National Security Council instructing the media to not report on U.S. threats against Iran, reformist newspapers widely covered any American statement that implicitly or explicitly isolated and threatened the country. Thus, their indirect message to the conservatives was that the only way to preempt the imminent threat of U.S. action was to unify behind the reformists' plan to liberalize Iranian society, democratize the political system, open up the electoral process, and establish a "religious democracy." By contrast, the conservatives argued that 9/11 was a project carried out by the U.S. government to justify a declaration of war against Muslims, and therefore Iranians needed to stand with the Guardian Jurist and defend their Islamic government. The conservatives also tried to minimize the American threat by portraying the United States as a paper tiger that was about to fall and bring about the inevitable end of Western civilization.

The reformists' tactic did not yield their desired results. In the end, Iran's conservatives proved to be the real winners. The Americans were now desperate for Iran's help in war-torn Iraq and Afghanistan. Khamenei also saw as a victory for Tehran the failure of Israel to defeat the Iranian proxies Hezbollah and Hamas in the 2006 and 2008 invasions of Lebanon and Gaza, respectively. On the newly opened nuclear front, Iran's defiance had also paid off politically, although not economically. Despite international pressure and U.S. threats since 2002 to end Iran's nuclear activities, Tehran continued to advance its technological capabilities and significantly expand its uranium enrichment facilities. As I will explain in the final chapter, Khamenei attributed this success to his resistance to the United States and his steadfast loyalty to political Islam.

Khamenei's international triumph coincided with and contributed to a domestic victory: the ascendance of Tehran's conservative mayor, Mahmoud Ahmadinejad, to the presidency in 2005. With the massive support of the IRGC, the Basij, and other conservative political and religious institutions, Ahmadinejad defeated Rafsanjani and the divided reformist candidates. The conservatives used tactics and allegations against Rafsanjani similar to those the reformists had employed to discredit and crush him. The centrist, pragmatic man who had betrayed the left in 1989 when he allied with the right and then subsequently defeated the right in 1997 when he allied with the left, was ultimately beaten by the left and the right in 2000 and 2005, respectively. Khamenei could now run the entire state through his new president and not worry about the reformists. Conservative media praised President Ahmadinejad's absolute loyalty to *Velayat-e Faqih* and called his controversial election the "miracle of the third millennium."[12] In this environment, the parallel state had even less tolerance for its critics. Khamenei repeatedly warned the media not to project a "black" image of the Islamic state but rather to support his narrative that political Islam had brought Iran power and prestige.

Many disillusioned voters, especially the youth who had boycotted the disputed 2005 election after eight frustrating years of attempted reform, suddenly realized that their situation could worsen dramatically. A new wave of emigration from the country began. Numerous dissidents, intellectuals, activists, journalists, and bloggers fled Iran and appeared in the capitals of Western countries. However, this exodus only vindicated the state's accusation that the U.S. Central Intelligence Agency (CIA) had been funding the reform movement. Some émigrés joined their Iranian colleagues at the London-based BBC Persian Service, the Washington-based Voice of America (VOA), the Prague-based and American-funded Radio Farda, and the Dutch-funded Radio Zamaneh. Others initiated their own sites and blogs. The new media brain drain profoundly enriched the aforementioned news services. A fresh, young, ambitious generation of journalists, trained during the reform movement and well versed in the nuances of Iranian society and politics, resumed their profession in these newfound media refuges. Now they could analyze and debate political and religious issues without worrying about the Islamic Republic's red lines. As many had lost hope that they would ever return to Iran, their critiques of *Velayat-e Faqih* became more radical and their advocacy for a secular government more blatant.

Those who stayed in Iran, however, had to improve their political gymnastics or pay the price for crossing the ever-multiplying red lines. Despite this pressure, young people continued to join the endangered profession in a country that had been repeatedly branded as the world's biggest prison for the media.[13] In contrast, the new political conditions provided a ripe environment for the growth of conservative media. Countless websites and blogs belonging to ultraconservative figures and groups emerged. They attacked the reformists and the reformist era for its contribution to the West's "cultural onslaught" against Iran. The reformists were repeatedly accused of collaborating with Hungarian-American investor George Soros, political scientist Francis Fukuyama, and other Westerners to undo *Velayat-e Faqih* and pave the way for a soft revolution in the country.[14] The conservative media quoted Fukuyama as saying that the only way to bring down the Islamic Republic was through "reverse engineering," that is, the process of disassembling *Velayat-e Faqih* through insiders, namely the reformists. Fukuyama's denial of the statement attributed to him did not soften the charge or the conservatives' appetite for the quote, the original source for which remains unclear.[15] Thus, the conservatives successfully mined the public sphere for any adventurist journalists, activists, and intellectuals who dared to question or criticize the establishment. Debate was either silenced or came from Iranian émigrés abroad.

The Birth of the Green Movement and the Advent of New Media

Iran's political landscape was about to change precisely at the time its leadership was at the zenith of its confidence. Domestically, the conservatives controlled all of the government's elected and appointed bodies. Regionally, Iran's proxies in Iraq, Afghanistan, Lebanon, and Palestine provided Tehran with strategic depth against the United States and Israel. Internationally, the United States was occupied with the 2008 financial crisis, while Iran was flush with unprecedented levels of oil cash. Meanwhile, Iran's nuclear program continued expanding despite mounting pressure from the United Nations Security Council. Khamenei and the IRGC concluded that Iran's rising status in the region was due to his wise and uncompromising leadership. It was time to translate that foreign policy success into preventing internal rivals from returning to power. It had taken Khamenei sixteen years since assuming Supreme Leadership to remove the reformists and the pragmatists from the political arena and replace them not just with conservatives, but with a loyal, ultraconservative faction consisting of a younger generation of revolutionary figures and IRGC members, such as Mahmoud Ahmadinejad. Just as his predecessor Khomeini had expunged the Marxists, nationalists, and other political groups after the revolution and then struck a balance between the two wings of his Islamist faction, Khamenei intended to remove the reformists and the centrists in order to strike a balance within his own faction between the traditional conservative right and the new "principlist" ultraconservative right. Therefore, he was determined to ensure that there were no further reformist or pragmatist obstacles during the upcoming 2009 presidential election. He publicly asked President Ahmadinejad to continue governing as though he were going to be president for a second term.[16]

The reformists, on the other hand, had begun to strategize for the 2009 election and ponder who would be the ideal candidate in light of this massive political shift to the right. They understood that their candidate must not only be popular but possess impeccable revolutionary credentials that could pass the Guardian Council's vetting process. They were enthusiastically aware of the traditional right's contempt for Ahmadinejad, who strove to marginalize other conservatives. Therefore, an ideal candidate was one who could exploit the new rift among the conservatives. However, a political platform that appealed to these "moderate" conservatives might alienate pro-reform young constituencies. In this climate, two candidates emerged: Mir-Hossein Mousavi, the former wartime prime minister, and Mehdi Karroubi, former speaker of the Majles. Mousavi was one of the few Islamist leftists who had stayed out of politics and his allies' reformist reinvention in the 1990s. He thus portrayed himself not as a reformist but as a "reformist-principlist" who did not intend to push for drastic reform within the system but rather to revive the "golden" years of the 1980s when he was the prime minister. To Khamenei's dismay, Mousavi's well-known loyalty to the original notion of *Velayat-e Faqih* and its author Ayatollah Khomeini appealed to the rank-and-file members of the IRGC and other revolutionary organizations. Karroubi, on the other hand, advocated for more changes, including reforms to the press law and even the constitution. His radical approach appealed to more restless voters, particularly students.

In addition to the reformists' private circles, the media remained one of the main venues for election-related deliberations. As usual, the conservative establishment demonstrated some limited tolerance for freedom of the press before the election in order to increase voter turnout and shore up the regime's legitimacy. What the conservative right could not foresee was the role that the new media would play in Iran's political scene. The 2009 presidential election brought the political factions' use of the media to an unprecedented level in the Iranian election cycle. While newspapers had played an important role during the 1997 election, in 2009, satellite television channels and the Internet accompanied the "old" media. The BBC Persian Television, VOA Persian News Network, and many other satellite channels provided millions of Iranian viewers with news and analysis that state-controlled television would not—and the reformist press could not—provide. Facebook became a place to debate and share the latest stories about the presidential candidates.

It brought video clips, audio files, newspaper articles, and blog pieces together into one easily accessible location. Millions of Iranians inside and outside the country found in Facebook a single forum in which to share and converse about nearly everything.

While the state was preoccupied with controlling and using the "old" media, the new media contributed critically to informing and politicizing a new generation of young Iranians. If the state-controlled media emphasized the "achievements" of the Ahmadinejad era, the new media pointed out the "lies," "religious superstitions," "hypocrisies," and "obtuse" management of this period. During the 2005 presidential campaign, Ahmadinejad had criticized the morality police for going after young girls over their dress. In a television debate, he asked, "Really, our people's problem is the style of our children's hair? . . . Is our country's problem really the clothes that such and such a girl wore?"[17] Despite these statements, attacks against "Westernized" youth only intensified during Ahmadinejad's presidency, a fact that the new media repeatedly brought to the public's attention. Similarly, after his first address to the United Nations General Assembly in 2006, Ahmadinejad told Ayatollah Abdollah Javadi-Amoli that there had been a divine "aura" around his head while he addressed the assembly and that world leaders "did not even blink" in his presence.[18] Despite Ahmadinejad's later denial of this statement, the video of his conversation with the aggravated cleric emerged on YouTube shortly thereafter. The aura story was never forgotten by the youth nor forgiven by the offended clergy. On another occasion, Ahmadinejad claimed that a sixteen-year-old girl "discovered nuclear energy" in her basement by acquiring some parts from the bazaar.[19] Now people were sharing Ahmadinejad's gaffes and discussing whether they could tolerate another four years of his leadership. Although one step behind the voters, the reformist candidates themselves also began to attack Ahmadinejad for relying on "lies" and "superstition" to manage the country. The overwhelming wave of criticism against Ahmadinejad in the virtual world was finding its way to the real world. Years after the election, the IRGC acknowledged the destructive power of the "new tools" of social media in that period.[20]

Failing to effectively employ the new media, Ahmadinejad's strategy was to counter through more traditional outlets. His plan was to rely on the support of the conservatives and the lower classes. In a series of highly rated TV debates, Ahmadinejad presented himself as Khamenei's candidate and accused his Rafsanjani-backed rivals of corruption, nepotism, and deviating from the values of the Islamic Revolution. His calm yet aggressive and sarcastic style angered his opponents and their supporters. He brought documents to "expose" Zahra Rahnavard, Mousavi's wife, for being admitted to a Ph.D. program without going through the normal procedures, and accused Karroubi of receiving money from an imprisoned embezzler.[21] In the end, these debates backfired for Ahmadinejad. He lost many fellow conservatives who were offended by his style. Later, even Khamenei criticized state-controlled TV for mismanaging the election debates properly. He saw that the establishment's sanctity was about to be lost.

A week before election day, throngs of people in major cities were turning out in green (the official color of the opposition) indicating that, as in 1997, the election was turning into a movement. The regime saw this looming revolt as potentially more damaging than the reform movement. Khamenei believed that the "cultural" avalanche he had first warned of nearly two decades earlier had finally arrived. His media mouthpieces, such as *Kayhan* and Fars News, repeated the old line that the reformist candidates were being backed by the United States and had no place in the hearts and minds of the Iranian people; that many of those who voted for them were deceived by the "seditionist" media; and that Ahmadinejad was going to be the clear winner by a large margin.[22] The Quranic term *fitna* (sedition) was used to refer to the climate created by the reformists, suggesting that people could not choose between right and wrong because the reformists relied on their revolutionary background and presented such a powerful religious discourse that voters were blinded by their hidden secular and subversive "plot."

While behind the scenes the entire parallel-state apparatus was preparing for the post-election unrest, conservative officials and commentators continued to predict an easy victory for Ahmadinejad. However, the pervasive expectation among Ahmadinejad's opponents was that he would lose if the votes were properly counted. Fears of election rigging rose among the reformists. On June 11, 2009, the eve of the election, Karroubi's paper, *Etemad Melli*, ran the headline "Tomorrow Night, We Are All Awake," implying that the people should be watchful against election irregularities.[23] It was also a reference to the rigging of the 2005 election that Karroubi alleged took place—during his nap on election night—against him and in Ahmadinejad's favor.

On election day, the conservative media reported that Ahmadinejad was in the lead while reformists projected that their candidates would win. A YouTube clip showed the angry wife of former president Rafsanjani, Effat

Mar'ashi, exiting a voting booth telling a reporter that election fraud was "highly likely" and that the people should "pour into the streets."[24] Hours before the voting ended, conservative news agencies declared Ahmadinejad the winner.[25] The twenty-four million (60 percent) votes that the parallel state reported Ahmadinejad had won were close to the twenty to twenty-two million votes that several conservatives had predicted for him. This, together with other circumstantial evidence, led many citizens to believe that the election was rigged.[26] Mousavi won only 33 percent of the vote, while Karroubi received 1 percent, even less than the number of discarded or blank ballots. Both candidates lost their home provinces. In some cities, there were more votes cast than registered voters. To many, the results were more like a clumsy joke or a political coup than a reflection of real numbers. Nevertheless, Khamenei rushed to congratulate Ahmadinejad on his victory before the Guardian Council had even confirmed the election results.[27] As the ultimate decision-maker, Khamenei's message was clear: the election was over.

In the following days, however, history unfolded under the watchful eyes of the media; rarely had the world witnessed such heartbreaking moments of humanity through the eyes of "citizen journalists." Millions of peaceful protesters poured into the streets throughout the country, capturing the movement with their own mobile phone cameras. According to Mohammad Bagher Qalibaf, the conservative mayor of Tehran and a former IRGC commander, three million protesters participated in one of the first demonstrations in the city.[28] The opposition's figures were higher. The initial slogan was one phrase: "Where Is My Vote?" The media broadcast hundreds of YouTube clips from peaceful protests mere hours—or in some instances minutes—after the marches took place. The parallel state responded with a violent crackdown. Newspapers and websites were shut down. Reformist figures, many of whom had been senior officials in the first decade of the revolution if not recently, were arrested overnight. Security forces, particularly the Basij, were deployed across the country. The disproportionate reaction was designed to quickly decapitate and stifle what had become known as the Green Movement.[29]

The state's brutality, however, radicalized the movement. The protesters were now targeting Khamenei instead of Ahmadinejad. "Death to the Dictator" and "Down with Khamenei" appeared on street walls, city buses, and banknotes and were chanted by the protesters. The demonstrations were no longer about the election but targeted the heart of the establishment. With the expansion of the uprising throughout the country, IRGC commanders took control of the situation. Gruesome images of security forces beating young protesters shocked not just the world but also many diehard supporters of the Islamic Republic. The last moments of Neda Agha-Soltan, a philosophy student shot during a protest, shook the world's conscience.[30] Within hours, the image was on YouTube, and from there it spread to hundreds of international media sites. Conservatives accused the BBC and foreign organizations of planning Neda's death.[31] They realized that the security forces' brutality was costly; nevertheless, they calculated that for the moment, their survival was more important than their image. As the crackdown intensified, so did its coverage. BBC Persian was receiving a stream of videos from inside Iran. Iranian monarchists had often accused the BBC Persian Service of fomenting the 1979 revolution because of its wide coverage of the demonstrations against the Pahlavi monarchy.[32] Now, once again, images of a massive movement were increasing domestic and international support for the protesters.

In an effort reminiscent of Khomeini's pledge to the Shah's army in 1979, the reformists sought to undermine the cohesion of the security forces by deploying a familiar narrative. The initially peaceful uprising already enjoyed the support of millions of restless young and female Iranians, many of whom hoped for radical change. But Mousavi and other top leaders were fixated on what they called the "gray area" made up of religious associations and traditional factions that did not quite support the Green Movement but were also quietly unhappy with the rise of Ahmadinejad. By pledging unconditional loyalty to the foundations of the Islamic Republic, the leaders of the Green Movement hoped to attract or at least neutralize these "moderate" conservatives along with many influential figures in various religious, political, and military institutions.

Mousavi, Karroubi, and other reformists asked their supporters to use the media to "inform" society of their religious and freedom-loving messages. Mousavi praised the IRGC senior commanders for their glorious and spiritual endeavor during the Iran–Iraq War and criticized them for their deviation from Khomeini's path into greed and power. Invoking the memories of Hassan Bagheri and other war heroes, Mousavi reached out to the brutal force of the regime, the Basij, on the thirtieth anniversary of its formation:

The *Basij* that the Imam wanted would not stand against the nation, but would stand behind them and with them. [He envisioned] A *Basij* whose actions would go beyond political factions and its broad shoulders would protect all, a *Basij* that would enjoy the friendship of the people, a *Basij* that would be seeking people's friendship and unity. A *Basij* that would overlook the differences of opinion and protect the life and liberty of the masses, that would see them all as brothers or one in creation. A *Basij* that would protect the privacy of people. The Imam did not want the *Basij* as a tool of authority, but a place for people to project their own power, a place that would allow them to have a part in their own future. It was supposed to be that the actions and behavior of the *Basij* would be an example to the people, not to have the power of the *Basij* crush the people. The *Basij* was not supposed to be on the government payroll and was not supposed to receive bonuses for arresting people for participating in demonstrations. It is a sad day if the *Basij* becomes just another political party. This is not what the Imam wanted for the *Basijis*. The *Basij* was not supposed to be an instrument to take away people's freedom in their votes.[33]

The Green Movement leaders also imbued the old revolutionary concepts and occasions with new meanings. As the regime refused to issue a legal permit for any opposition assemblies, the protesters resorted to using existing official political and religious occasions to stage demonstrations. Student Day, Ashura, and the anniversaries of the hostage crisis and victory of the revolution became the scenes of largely peaceful anti-Khamenei protests that were suppressed brutally by security forces. On the thirtieth anniversary of the occupation of the U.S. embassy, Mousavi provided a new reading of the hostage crisis in which Khomeini did not dictate but was guided by the nation's will:

On the surface, the students called themselves the followers of the Imam, but in reality, it was the Imam who followed what they did. None of the leaders and commanders of the revolution had a role in shaping what came to be that day. Even the students themselves thought that everything would be over in a few days and that they would return home. But the Imam followed the events and called it a revolution greater than the first revolution . . . He preferred to let people lead because he knew simply passing one historic milestone is not enough in the prosperity of a nation. The nation must have such knowledge and insight to be able to tell right from wrong in every day and age, and to be able to walk the right path. Today, our people are the leaders and this is the great wish that the Imam had for them.[34]

Similarly, the anti-Israeli Jerusalem [Quds] Day was "not only specific to Palestine, but was also the day of the oppressed and the day of Islam."[35] Mousavi warned, "After killing the republicanism of the regime on the altar, you [Khamenei loyalists] are now aiming to disgrace the Islamicness of it as well?"[36] These statements and letters soon appeared on opposition websites and were then picked up by the mainstream media. New reformist sites such as *Jaras* (run by reformist cleric Mohsen Kadivar), *Kalemeh* (close to Mousavi), and Saham News (close to Karroubi) emerged and became reliable sources for international media outlets such as the BBC, CNN, the *New York Times*, and the *Washington Post*.

The heads of the Basij, the Law Enforcement Forces, and the IRGC realized the deep split and crisis that the Green Movement's religious and revolutionary language was creating within their own rank and file. As these officials later acknowledged, they had to initiate internal briefings to protect the cohesion of the regime elites.[37] A leaked audiotape from one such session revealed the desperate techniques the establishment used to regain legitimacy and demonize its opponents. In his meetings with local officials around the country, the deputy minister of intelligence and IRGC general, Abdullah Zighami, also known by his pseudonym General Moshfeq, had a surprising narrative about the reformists that went back to the early days of the revolution. He claimed that the reformists had been directly connected to the CIA since 1979, when they "staged" the occupation of the U.S. embassy to undermine the newly born Islamic government.[38] He accused former president Khatami of being connected to Israel's Mossad and repeated claims that the reformists were following Fukuyama's advice to "reverse-engineer" the Islamic system by targeting *Velayat-e Faqih*.

However unbelievable these accusations sounded, even to the local religious and political elites across the country, Moshfeq perhaps unintentionally revealed the depth of the IRGC's involvement in the controversies surrounding the 2009 presidential election, including wiretapping the reformists. In response to these revelations, seven prominent reformists wrote an open letter from prison to Ayatollah Sadeq Larijani, the head of the judiciary, complaining of the politicization of the military and security forces and their illegal support of Ahmadinejad.[39] Other opposition figures and organizations pressured the Supreme Leader to prohibit the IRGC's interference in politics. The IRGC's only reaction came from its Political Office, which stated that the commanders would continue with their "enlightening" briefings.[40]

However, the efforts to protect the conservatives' unity were not completely successful. Despite the IRGC's massive crackdown and extensive briefing tours, many religious and military elites gradually distanced themselves from the conservative establishment. For example, Khamenei's longtime backer, the right-wing cleric Ayatollah Javadi-Amoli—a senior member of the Assembly of Experts who had once conveyed a message from Khomeini to Mikhail Gorbachev and later became agitated when Ahmadinejad claimed there was an aura around his head at the UN—resigned from his position of leading Friday prayers in the city of Qom. Javadi-Amoli's decision came a few months after Rafsanjani's pro-opposition statements in his last Friday prayer was followed by his permanent absence in leading this symbolically important ceremony in Tehran. Javadi-Amoli apologized to the people for failing to "fulfill his duties for the Friday prayer," indirectly referring to the rising political challenges.[41] Several other conservative clerics left or were ostracized in religious institutions and circles. Many of these figures had silently questioned Khamenei's dubious rise to marja'iyyah earlier, which posed a threat to their authority. Nonetheless, they remained allies of Khamenei until the rise of the Green Movement in 2009, at which point they began to distance themselves from the conservative establishment. They were already discontented with Khamenei's reliance on the IRGC and support of Ahmadinejad and implicitly objected to the brutality of the security forces and the crackdown on the 2009 protesters.[42] To compensate for the loss of these senior clerical figures, Khamenei pressed for the meteoric promotions of low- and mid-ranking clerics who were absolutely loyal and "dissolved" in his view of *Velayat-e Faqih*.

In response, more conservatives dissented. Mohammad Nourizad, a former columnist for the hardline *Kayhan* daily, was another figure who had a change of heart and was imprisoned. During the Green Movement, he wrote weekly letters to Khamenei in which he criticized the Supreme Leader and his security apparatus. Nourizad asked Khamenei to invite all current and former officials, security and IRGC authorities, members of the Majles, and religious judges to formally apologize to the people—the youth, women, students, religious and ethnic minorities, workers, farmers, the families of martyrs, and emigrants—for the "repression," "humiliation," and "ruination" of their country's resources and the "burning" of their homeland in the thirty-three years since the revolution.[43]

Nourizad called on other notables to join his campaign and write to Khamenei, specifically naming several prominent figures, including the former head of the IRGC's navy, General Hossein Alaie. On January 9, 2012, the general wrote a controversial piece coinciding with the thirty-fourth anniversary of the infamous and controversial article that had insulted Ayatollah Khomeini and sparked the movement that led to the fall of the Shah. Alaie's article appeared in the same newspaper, *Ettelaat*, that had published the aforementioned piece in 1978. Although Alaie's letter was addressed to the late Shah, it was widely interpreted as directed toward Khamenei. General Alaie stated that if the Shah had not "ordered [the soldiers to] fire at the protesters," "put prominent figures under house arrest," and "accused his opponents of acting against the country's national security," he would not have been overthrown.[44] Alaie's references and vocabulary left little doubt that he was drawing an allusion to Khamenei's suppression of the Green Movement.

Subsequent physical and verbal attacks by vigilantes, the conservative media, and IRGC leaders forced General Alaie to deny that he intended to compare the monarchy to the Islamic Republic. Without mentioning Khamenei's name, he stressed his loyalty to *Velayat-e Faqih*. Some interpreted this as questioning whether the current leader was the true follower of the founding father of the Islamic Republic. Further pressure led him to emphasize that he had continued to "obey" Khamenei since the days when the former seminarian was first preaching in the Keramat mosque in Mashhad before the 1979 revolution. The general stressed that the number of "pictures [of Khamenei] surpassed anyone else's" in his house.[45] However, when Hossein Shariatmadari, managing editor of *Kayhan* (a Supreme Leader–appointed position), attacked the general,[46] Alaie fired back by stating, "Respect people's intelligence and if someone does not think like you, do not call them the enemy's puppet or prey."[47] Javadi-Amoli, Alaie, and other quietly dissident religious and military elites, however, stayed in the "gray area" and did not defect to the reformist side. Neither camp managed to decisively win the war of narratives. Khamenei bitterly criticized "the imprudent elites' silence," an unequivocal reference to the centrist conservatives for refusing to bless the state's violence against the protesters. However, the net loser would be the reformists. As I will discuss in the next section, a number of discursive blunders, magnified by the media, contributed to the entrenchment of these moderate conservative elites in the gray area and divided the reformists.

The outcry of the international community and the media over the suppression of the Green Movement put the reformists in an awkward position. Two decades earlier, these former radicals had attacked dissidents and opposition groups by calling them subversive because of the sympathy they received from the "foreign media." Indeed, then–prime minister Mousavi and Speaker Karroubi themselves had often angrily criticized their "liberal" opponents and asked why the BBC and other "foreign radio stations" paid so much attention to them. Now they were being branded the "new liberals" and had to face the same question from the conservative establishment.

Moreover, the democratic nature of the new media and lack of centralized messaging on the part of the Green Movement soon became a double-edged sword, as it exposed and deepened divisions among various opposition groups, whose levels of religiosity differed. When exiled dissident Akbar Ganji told the BBC Persian Service that he did not believe in the Hidden Imam, other opposition figures had no choice but to condemn his statement. The state-controlled media opportunistically bombarded viewers with that clip to validate the regime's claim that the opposition consisted of secular, Westernized, and alienated figures who did not share the Shi'ites' fundamental beliefs.[48] Conversely, exiled dissident cleric Mohsen Kadivar's attempt to neutralize the establishment's secular accusations backfired within his own camp. He claimed on Voice of America that during demonstrations in Iran, people were chanting "Both Gaza and Lebanon, my life for Iran," thus expressing sympathies for the plight of their fellow Muslims. In response, many angry reformist activists attacked him on social media, charging that the slogan was, in fact, "*Neither* Gaza, *nor* Lebanon, my life for Iran." In the end, he was forced to "clarify" and partly acknowledge his error.[49]

These incidents, accompanied by the controversial support of sworn enemies of the regime in exile, such as the monarchists, former communists, banned pop singers, and others, increased the cost for moderate religious, political, and military elites to side with the protesters. They could not risk being associated with the old anti-Islamist forces without losing their own credibility. The government's tactic of questioning the opposition's religiosity by branding it an alliance of heretics and divas "from Soroush to [the Persian diva] Googoosh" prevented the conservatives in the gray area between the regime and the opposition from becoming Green. This was the same strategy that Khomeini and his Islamist allies used to prevent the clergy from siding with the Shah from 1963 until 1979.

At the same time, the regime inadvertently made controversial statements that were exploited and spread by the opposition. If the reformists stumbled upon people's religious beliefs, the incumbent's blunders occurred mostly over the citizens' fundamental rights. During a pro-regime rally, Ahmadinejad told his supporters that the Green Movement protesters were nothing but "dirt and dust."[50] His statement further aggravated the demonstrators and led even conservatives to attack the president for his use of insulting and provocative language. His attempt to "clarify" and "correct" the media coverage of his statement went only so far. Khamenei made a similar gaffe: a year after the controversial election, he stated, "The 1388 [2009] sedition vaccinated the country against social and political microbes."[51] In a rare moment, his website was forced to immediately defend the Supreme Leader against the overwhelming reaction of the diaspora media against this statement, stressing that Khamenei did not mean that all protesters were microbes.

In a sign of a serious crisis of legitimacy for the regime, dissidents, clerics, activists, and political prisoners increasingly addressed Khamenei himself through open letters, holding him directly accountable for the human rights violations committed by the Iranian security forces. In one of the first and most widely publicized letters, Abdolkarim Soroush joyfully predicted that "religious tyranny is crumbling." He addressed Khamenei:

I am most grateful to you. You said that "the ruling system's sanctity has been violated" and its integrity ravished. Believe me, I had never heard such good news from anyone in my life. Congratulations, you have acknowledged and announced the sordidness and wretchedness of religious tyranny . . .

You were prepared to shame God rather than to be shamed yourself. To have people turn their backs on religion and the prophethood rather than to turn their backs on your guardianship . . . I know that you are going through difficult and bitter days. You made a mistake. A grave mistake. I showed you the way out of this mistake twelve years ago. I told you to adopt freedom as a method. Never mind about its rightfulness and its virtue; you should use it to attain a successful state. Don't you want this? Why do you send out spies and informers to discover what is in the people's minds or to use tricks and ploys to make the people tell them something against their will? Why must you listen to reports that are based on information that is obtained by stealth and contains a mixture of truths, untruths, and half-truths? Allow newspapers, parties, associations, critics, commentators, teachers, writers, etc. to operate freely. The people will tell you what's on their minds plainly and in a thousand different ways. They will open the windows of news and views to you and help you run the land and the state. Don't strangle the newspapers. They are society's lungs.[52]

Although the level of brutality against Khomeini's disciples dismayed many diehard supporters of the regime, few defected to the other side, and the integrity of the political and security apparatus remained intact. As the regime finally managed to suppress the protesters and control the streets in the beginning of 2010, the government devised a multipronged approach to root out "sedition." In October of that year, Khamenei characterized the entire conflict as a "media war" and mobilized all of his resources to deal with it. He declared the media to be the most potent strategic weapon:

Today, the most effective international weapon against enemies and the opposition is the weapon of propaganda and the media. Today, this is the most powerful weapon and it is even worse and more dangerous than the atomic bomb. Didn't you see this weapon of the enemy during the post-election unrest? With this very weapon, the enemy was following our affairs second-by-second and giving advice to those who were evil [the opposition].[53]

Khamenei ordered the IRGC to mobilize its forces to focus on the "soft war" and prevent a "velvet revolution" from taking place in Iran. More newspapers, websites, and blog pages emerged to denounce the opposition and analyze and publicize its American roots. Heidar Moslehi, Iran's minister of intelligence, claimed that the "enemy" spent seventeen billion dollars on the soft war of the post-election demonstrations.[54] In response, the Iranian government reportedly allocated five billion dollars for this new battle.[55]

New laws were introduced to further limit the media, especially new media. After Facebook and Twitter, Google Plus was the latest social network to be banned, two weeks after it was introduced in the United States and months before it actually became available in Iran. The state acquired better technologies to jam satellite channels and monitor Internet activities. A "cyber army" was created to attack the websites of the "enemy," and a plan to create a "clean" Internet was revealed. Radio Zamaneh, VOA, and the personal sites of exiled dissidents such as Mohsen Sazegara were hacked by an entity calling itself the "Iranian Cyber Army."[56] The Iranian Cyber Army claimed that it was not connected to the Iranian government, but the praise that it received from official media suggested otherwise. In April 2011, Google announced that hackers impersonated the giant search engine to snoop on its Iranian users. In an interview with the *New York Times*, an Iranian hacker claiming to be a twenty-one-year-old university student operating independently from the government stated that he had decided to monitor the activities of what Google estimated to be three hundred thousand users.[57] In short, although the state was initially several steps behind the media-savvy opposition and protesters, it managed to catch up.

The Conservative Split

In the midst of the battle between the Guardian Jurist's conservative forces and their reformist-pragmatist rivals during the Green Movement, another conflict inside the conservative camp was in the making. The lame-duck President Ahmadinejad and his faction were in search of new leverage to secure their positions within the regime after the end of his second term. Predictably, he found himself in a conflict with the Supreme Leader similar to that experienced by his predecessors, Rafsanjani and Khatami. Relying on his "popular support," Ahmadinejad began to echo their words and reflect the public mood, and pursue corresponding policies. During his first term, he had vigorously promoted a Shi'a discourse to "expedite" the return of the Hidden Imam in an effort to consolidate his links with the parallel state by positioning himself as a foot soldier of the Supreme Leader. He was the "bulwark" protecting Khamenei against Rafsanjani, Khatami, Mousavi, and all other competing forces. Ahmadinejad claimed that the United States' invasion of Iraq in 2003 had little to do with 9/11 or Saddam Hussein's alleged weapons of mass destruction programs but rather aimed at preventing the imminent return of Mahdi.[58] Although his reference to the Hidden Imam dismayed the traditional clerical establishment, he remained the conservatives' ally. He provoked Israel and the United States by denying the Holocaust and implying that 9/11 was an "insider's" job in an attempt to generate popular support in the anti-Israel Arab streets. According to polls, at one point he was the third-most popular man in the Arab world after Iran's other allies, Hezbollah's Sheikh Hassan Nasrallah and Syrian president Bashar al-Assad.[59] With these controversial statements, he maintained close ties within the ever-expanding IRGC and other key institutions within the regime during his first term.

In his second term, however, Ahmadinejad transitioned from a messianic discourse to a Persian nationalist platform. As he saw the end of his presidency approaching, he calculated that a nationalistic and pro-American posture would bring many Green Movement supporters to his side, granting him and his circle leverage to bargain with the conservatives in the lead-up to the next election. Cyrus the Great replaced the Hidden Imam, and friendship with the United States and even the Israelis substituted his earlier anti-American and anti-Israeli statements. He praised Cyrus the Great as one of the "prophets," Iranian poet Ferdowsi as the "savior" of Islam, and *Velayat-e Faqih* as an "Iranian" reading of Islam.[60] In September 2010, he unveiled the 2,500-year-old Cyrus Cylinder (known as the first human rights declaration in history), which was on loan from the British Museum in Tehran, and took off his Palestinian-style Keffiyah scarf worn by Basiji militiamen and put it around the neck of a bowing symbolic Cyrus.[61] Conservatives, including those who had praised Ahmadinejad as the "miracle of the third millennium," ridiculed and attacked his nationalistic turn and invocation of pre-Islamic history.[62] They attributed his sudden shift to the "satanic" influence of his adviser and longtime friend, Esfandiar Rahim Mashaei. Mashaei was already a contentious figure due to his claimed "connection" to the Hidden Imam, which would by definition bypass the stature of not only the clergy but even the Supreme Leader. Additionally, Mashaei had expressed friendship toward the Israelis, to which Khamenei strongly reacted. Following the model of Russian president Vladimir Putin and his prime minister Dmitry Medvedev, Ahmadinejad seemed to be grooming Mashaei to run for president at the end of his second term and hold the office until he could reclaim it four years later. But Mashaei would soon spark a serious conflict between Khamenei and Ahmadinejad, which would play out in full display in the media—in real time. After his contentious reelection in June 2009, Ahmadinejad ignored the controversies surrounding Mashaei and appointed him as the first vice president. At a time when the ruling conservatives were facing the Green Movement, the most serious internal challenge since the 1979 revolution, Ahmadinejad's move put them in a difficult position. They could not attack him at the same time that they were brutally repressing the demonstrators who opposed his reelection. Understanding this conundrum, Ahmadinejad was determined to impose these concessions on Khamenei. Both figures intentionally brought the conflict to the media to induce the other to compromise through pressure from the public. Before any official reaction was issued, *Kayhan*'s Hossein Shariatmadari expressed frustration that the president, instead of dismissing Mashaei after his controversial statement over Israel a year earlier, was now promoting him to a higher position. Shariatmadari "predicted" that the president would dismiss Mashaei soon.[63] Religious and political figures echoed these sentiments. Conservatives such as Ayatollah Naser Makarem Shirazi, Mohammad Nabi Habibi (the secretary general of the conservative *Mu'talefe* coalition), and various members of the Majles likewise vociferously opposed Mashaei's appointment. In an attempt to increase the pressure on Ahmadinejad, some conservatives alleged that Khamenei had ordered Mashaei's dismissal in a private letter to Ahmadinejad, a claim that the Supreme Leader's office did not deny.

Nevertheless, Ahmadinejad remained defiant. In fact, he further publicized his deep friendship with Mashaei as "one of the honors and blessings that God" had bestowed upon him.[64] The presidential office continued its publicity campaign, announcing that Mashaei would "carry on his service in the position of the first vice president to the Islamic Revolution, the Iranian nation, and the country."[65] The statement was widely covered by the daily *Iran*, IRNA (the Islamic Republic News Agency), and other media outlets traditionally loyal to the president. Ahmadinejad's strategy was to increase the political cost of overriding him by positioning Khamenei against the elected president and thus the popular will. Would the nonelected Leader publicly oppose the man who had supposedly won a landslide election? Given Khamenei's ongoing violent battle against millions of Green Movement supporters, would he risk antagonizing more citizens? Ahmadinejad was willing to test these questions.

But he had overplayed his hand. In response, Khamenei published the aforementioned letter ordering Ahmadinejad to "cancel" Mashaei's appointment. Dated six days earlier, it demonstrated that not only had Ahmadinejad ignored Khamenei's direct order, he had in fact defiantly announced that Mashaei would remain the first vice president three days after receiving the letter. Now it was Khamenei who had upped the cost for Ahmadinejad. How could a fallible elected man oppose God's representative on earth? The parallel case of Iran's first president, Abolhassan Banisadr, who was dismissed by Khomeini's order and the Majles vote three decades earlier, had already set the precedent. The Supreme Leader had limitless constitutional and extrajudicial tools to undermine or even remove the president. Understanding the dire consequences, Ahmadinejad submitted to Khamenei's will and removed Mashaei from his post, only to immediately appoint him as his chief of staff. *Kayhan*'s Shariatmadari, who had initially "predicted" that Ahmadinejad would remove Mashaei, later said that he was aware of Khamenei's letter at the time of his previous column. He expressed disappointment that Ahmadinejad delayed following the order until after the letter became public.[66] Ahmadinejad, however, was remorseless, continuing to calculate that his new nationalistic, challenging, and pro-American posture would bring Green Movement supporters to his side.

The David Ignatius Affair

In March 2011, BBC Persian learned that an Iranian delegation led by Mashaei had applied for U.S. visas. The stated reason for the trip was to attend the United Nations' Earth Day, which coincided with the Persian New Year, Nowruz. But sources told the BBC that this might be a cover for the true motivation behind Mashaei's trip, which was to conduct meetings with intermediaries to improve relations with the United States.[67] Within hours, the story went viral in the Iranian media.[68] The Foreign Ministry's spokesperson was forced to confirm that U.S. visa applications for Iranian officials had been submitted but strongly denied that the president's adviser was to meet with U.S. officials:

> Unfortunately, because the UN General Assembly is based in the U.S., for any meeting that is going to be held at this organization, [one] inevitably needs to apply for a visa from this country. The fact that our delegations are granted U.S. visas in order to attend UN international meetings is within the defined frameworks of international norms . . . Every once in a while, we witness targeted interpretations and opinions that relate the trips of Iranian delegations for an active presence at the UN to other vague issues behind these trips.[69]

Four days later, the political deputy of the presidential office stated that UN secretary general Ban Ki-Moon had personally invited Mashaei, who was planning to celebrate Nowruz with local Iranians as well. The following day, Mashaei himself said that his trip had not been finalized.[70] But the conservative uproar did not abate. Finally, Mashaei was forced to cancel his trip to

New York. On March 19, 2011, the communication and information deputy of the presidential office said that Mashaei's trip had been canceled due to the "Secretary General's change of plans."[71] However, the semi-official Mehr News Agency announced that it had received information that certain "opposition to this trip" was the reason for its cancellation.[72] It implied that the Supreme Leader's intervention stopped the delegation's UN expedition. Mashaei continued to reach out to U.S. officials, only to be stymied again due to the media.

A few months after the UN trip was canceled, David Ignatius of the *Washington Post* wrote an op-ed column claiming that Mashaei was on a mission to message U.S. officials:

> Sources say Mashaei has sent multiple signals indicating that he wants to meet with American representatives. U.S. officials say there hasn't been a meeting, and that's probably because Washington isn't clear precisely who Mashaei represents or what his agenda for talks might be. Although President [Barack] Obama has never dropped his offer to talk with Iran, it would be risky for the United States to engage any single faction. That's likely one explanation for U.S. wariness about Mashaei's overtures.[73]

Two days later, Ignatius told BBC Persian Radio that Mashaei persisted in trying to meet with U.S. officials through a number of different channels, but since he was not backed by the highest powers in Iran, Washington was not willing to meet with him.[74]

Conservative media outlets reprinted the Ignatius story under provocative headlines such as "Mashaei's Futile Effort to Communicate with the U.S."[75] Soon after, pressure on Mashaei intensified. Dozens of individuals close to his circle were detained.[76] Rumors appeared that Mashaei was about to be arrested as well and that Ahmadinejad himself could be impeached. However, these pressures temporarily waned after Ahmadinejad threateningly defined his cabinet as his "red line," warning that he would publicly share certain "issues" with the Iranian people if his cabinet was attacked. This tactic of threatening to publicize classified documents containing unflattering information about his enemies was a favorite of his, and it worked. The daily *Iran* (affiliated with IRNA), run by the executive branch, once published a satirical poem claiming that the Ahmadinejad administration had 140,000 classified documents on 314 top conservative figures.[77] Although

Ahmadinejad's adviser and the managing editor of *Iran*, Ali Akbar Javan-
fekr, downplayed the threat as mere satire, the conservatives were careful not to cross Ahmadinejad's red line and touch Mashaei for the time
being.[78]

Knowing the power of blackmailing his rivals within the regime, the president now sought to bring the intelligence agency under his control. In
April 2011, the media reported that Iran's intelligence minister, Heydar
Moslehi, had resigned. Ahmadinejad accepted Moslehi's resignation, but
Khamenei issued an order asking Moslehi to remain in his position. In reaction, Ahmadinejad took refuge at home and did not appear at the office for
eleven days, expecting that either Khamenei would back down or his supporters would rise up. But with no reaction from Khamenei, the elite, or the
public, he returned to work. The conflict between Ahmadinejad and the
conservative establishment would reach its height during his final months
in office in February 2013.

At a fiery parliamentary session that was being broadcast live on state
radio, Ahmadinejad fought to prevent the removal of his labor minister by
threatening to expose corruption and nepotism on the part of the powerful
Larijani brothers, two of whom headed the judiciary and legislative bodies.
He ultimately played a video to prove the existence of a backroom deal that
involved the Larijani family. In response, the speaker of parliament, Ali Larijani, accused Ahmadinejad of mafia-type activities and did not allow him to
continue. Ahmadinejad angrily left the parliament, and moments later one
hundred ninety-two of two hundred seventy-two members of parliament
voted in favor of the minister's removal. The prospect of impeachment put
Ahmadinejad's remaining presidency in danger, since many of his allies in
the cabinet faced, if not experienced, similar fates.

But the more the parallel state pressured him, the more Ahmadinejad
endeavored to leverage his "popular mandate." During the impeachment
proceedings, Ahmadinejad told parliament that he came to "tell the people
that the president they have elected is under the power of the speaker of
the parliament." A few months earlier, he had asserted, "The only one who
is accountable [to the people] is us [the administration] . . . Is everything in
order in this country and only the administration has a weakness? . . . I am
probably the only official who is not afraid of going out to the people. I
have no fear. I swear to God I have no fear." In an implicit reference to
Khamenei, he said, "I, Ahmadinejad, am the only one in the country who you

[journalists] can talk to his face like this. If there is a second one, name them!"[79] His deployment of the narrative of popular legitimacy to claim the Green Movement mantle did little to garner public support—such support would have had to be massive to stand even a chance against the absolute power of Khamenei. A narrative was not enough. Given his recent associations with the parallel state and the tragedies of the 2009 election, his anti-establishment turn had little credibility.

His final act came in May 2013, when he daringly accompanied Mashaei to the Ministry of the Interior to register him as a candidate for the upcoming presidential race. During a press conference after the registration, he said, "Ahmadinejad means Mashaei and Mashaei means Ahmadinejad."[80] Despite his aggressive posture, after this point Ahmadinejad suddenly went mute. The Guardian Council's disqualification[81] of Mashaei's candidacy did not provoke any significant reaction by Ahmadinejad, nor did he make any other headlines in the last months of his presidency. There were rumors that soon after the announcement of Mashaei's candidacy, the IRGC had threatened to physically eliminate Ahmadinejad. A reported accident a few weeks later, which forced his helicopter to make an emergency landing, generated more unsubstantiated rumors in the same vein.[82]

The new media—especially social media—broke open the regime's monopoly on the deployment of religious and political narratives in the public sphere. In this period, powerful new ideas could be shared—not only about alternative readings of Islam and its relationship with the state, but narratives about the suffering of the people and the incompetence of the regime. It was no longer a taboo to call on Khamenei to take off his cloak of *Velayat-e Faqih* and return to his pre-revolutionary job as a preacher at the Keramat mosque.[83] But it was also evident that the opposition groups were widely fragmented on a variety of political and religious issues and had little tolerance for each other. The parallel state still had tremendous hard power to silence its opponents and enforce discipline on its own discourse; in contrast, the openness and democratic exchange of ideas on the part of the opposition resulted in an undisciplined deployment of narratives that fractured its ability to be effective.

TEN

Historical Revisionism and Regional Threats

IRAN'S POLITICAL LANDSCAPE in the aftermath of the Green Movement left the legitimacy of the Guardian Jurist—and indeed the *Velayat-e Faqih* system itself—in dispute. Nearly all post-revolutionary political and religious leaders had eventually clashed with the Guardian Jurist in one way or another. The list included Ayatollah Khomeini's appointed provisional prime minister Bazargan (February 1979 to November 1979), Iran's first president Banisadr (1980–1981), Prime Minister Mousavi (1981–1989), all of Ayatollah Khamenei's presidents, including Rafsanjani (1989–1997), Khatami (1997–2005), and Ahmadinejad (2005–2013), and even the theologian who dedicated his life to theorizing and instituting *Velayat-e Faqih* in the constitution, Ayatollah Montazeri. Yet conservative loyalists demonized these once-influential leaders as "seditionists," "deviants," "imprudent," "pro-U.S. infiltrators," or outright "anti-*Velayat-e Faqih*."

These figures had come to challenge both the Guardianship of the Jurist (*Velayat-e Faqih*) and the Guardian Jurist himself. The opposition's objective was to break the Guardian Jurist's monopoly over the use of religion and weaken his parallel state. Building on Khomeini's pragmatic elevation of the state over Islamic law, it wished to diffuse the expediency power of the Guardian Jurist to state institutions. To do so required these former defenders of *Velayat-e Faqih* to reframe it, replacing its previously claimed essential and timeless character with a politically contingent and fluid concept. Claiming that Khomeini's original *Velayat-e Faqih* doctrine was an unorthodox theological invention designed for a particular time and place, the leftist-centrist coalition effectively called for an overhaul of the system to increase its "efficiency." It should be noted, however, that they wanted to retain a nominal *Velayat-e Faqih* and a semi-"Islamic" state, which would allow them to keep the old and new secular nemeses out of the political process.

The Khamenei-led ultraconservatives were concerned that this competing coalition would reduce the Guardian Jurist to a ceremonial position similar to that of the British monarch. Additionally, the main two suppression tools of the Guardian Jurist—the IRGC and the Guardian Council—feared fading or merging into their counterpart institutions within the state, as voters' electoral behavior consistently signaled frustration with the parallel state comprising the Guardian Jurist, the Guardian Council, and the IRGC. So in response, the conservatives sought to develop new narratives and religious doctrines to maintain the Guardian Jurist's monopoly over the final interpretation of Islam, particularly *Velayat-e Faqih*. They reintroduced the concept not as Khomeini's revolutionary invention but as the most common denominator in the orthodox Shi'a clerical establishment since the First of the Twelve Imams. As I delineate in this chapter, state-funded religious circles and journals initiated a theological campaign to argue that even those clerics who opposed Khomeini's political blueprint never refuted in principle his overarching claim that governance was the exclusive right of the clergy. Khamenei and his allies thereby rejected any contingent nature of Khomeini's *Velayat-e Faqih*, reconstructing it as a consistent and given concept in Shi'a Islam. This was a uniquely formidable battle—to define and defend the reading of *Velayat-e Faqih*—between former allies who were equally well versed in its theological and political foundations.

Concurrently, Iran's conservatives were facing similar ideological competition from Turkey's Islamist-rooted Justice and Development Party (AKP) and Egypt's Muslim Brotherhood. These new external rivals promoted a "civil Islam" comparable to what Iran's reformists had developed two decades earlier. The second section of this chapter examines the strategies the conservative establishment adopted to counteract the ideological narratives of these rising rivals in the period before they declined in the tragedies of the post–Arab Spring Middle East.

The Expansion and Contraction of *Velayat-e Faqih*

Following the upheaval of the reforms and Green Movement, numerous academic and research institutions and journals were tasked with demonstrating that the clergy, mandated by a notion of *Velayat-e Faqih*, was an instrumental player in every major political event in Iran's history. Fearing the return of quietism and calls for the separation of mosque and state in the seminaries, Khamenei launched a new campaign to reinterpret Iranian and Islamic history in light of the post-revolutionary experience. Government-paid scholars discovered unknown clerics in all corners of the country who had led the people against oppressive rulers and foreign interventions. The anti-British uprisings in the early twentieth century in the southern province of Bushehr were led not only by the famous tribal leader Ra'is Ali Delvari (1882–1915) but also by Ayatollah Abdullah Mujtahid Beladi Bushehri (1874/1875–1952/1953), according to this new official narrative.[1] Grand Ayatollah Borujerdi was never a quietist figure but a true believer of *Velayat-e Faqih* who actively opposed the monarchy.[2] These writers claimed that all Shi'a clerics, even Khomeini's fierce opponents, believed the right to govern in the absence of the Hidden Imam belonged to an Islamic jurist, although for a variety of reasons (from people's apathy to fear of a bloodbath to their own individual flaws), some did not invoke *Velayat-e Faqih* in their lifetimes.[3] This account was in contrast to previous assertions by Khomeini's own acolytes and nemeses that *Velayat-e Faqih* in the absolute political sense was his extraordinary invention. In his original lecture in Najaf, Khomeini viciously attacked the ossified clergy for distorting the Prophet's political message for 1,400 years and limiting Islam to praying at cemeteries and other trivial affairs. But according to the new official narrative, there was no rupture, only continuity with regard to the inherently political role of the clergy.[4] Every single Imam and marja between the Prophet Mohammad and Ayatollah Khomeini took *Velayat-e Faqih* as a given;[5] Khomeini's genius was in its implementation, not invention, or so the argument went. With such a discourse, Khamenei's stated goal was to "completely root out" quietism and the idea of separation of religion and politics in the seminaries.[6] He insisted that political *feqh* in Shi'a Islam preceded other branches of *feqh*.[7] But now he sought to open new vistas for *Velayat-e Faqih* in an attempt to claim novel contributions to the doctrine, reinforce his own challenged marja'iyyah, and thus fortify his control over the state.

While Khamenei's opponents were fighting what Soroush called "the obesity of religion," the Supreme Leader went on to theorize a new *feqh*, which he called *hokoumati* or governmental *feqh*, distinguished from *siasi* or political *feqh*. It was an "advanced" branch of jurisprudence specific to the needs and necessities of the Islamic government. Now that such a government had finally emerged and was successfully consolidated after fourteen centuries, he called on seminarians to follow his path and develop a highly specialized jurisprudence to run the state, society, and literally the world.[8] This new *feqh* would address challenging concepts and institutions such as the source of sovereignty, citizens' rights, elections, popular votes, the constitution, the separation of powers, and even nuclear issues. This initiative was evidently intended to strengthen the "divine" source of sovereignty at the expense of its popular origins by either rejecting modern democratic institutions or robbing them of their original meaning.

Many heeded Khamenei's calls to construct a fresh jurisprudence and a new narrative about the history of Islam and Iran. Abbas-Ali Kadkhodaei, a former IRGC member and a lay Guardian Council jurist, argued in a piece he coauthored that Montesquieu and other modern philosophers misunderstood the principle of the separation of powers and built the notion on the mistaken assumption of the human greed for power.[9] An Islamic system, run by a pious and informed jurist, the authors added, necessitates an "organic" arrangement distinct from Western concepts. Others claimed that under *Velayat-e Faqih*, the three branches of government should be independent from each other but remain under the Guardian Jurist's direct control.[10] Responsibilities were delegated by him to various state institutions based on their expertise and then held accountable to *him*. Accordingly, the political participation of the people was not required to lend legitimacy to the "divine-based" system, although public participation was critical in demonstrating the government's popularity to its internal and external adversaries. It is in this context that conservative clerics, including Khamenei himself, considered voting a religious duty. Ayatollah Hossein Nouri-Hamedani even warned that not voting in an election constituted a "cardinal sin."[11]

But these narratives did not change the practical truth that elections could still provide candidates with popular mandates that were potentially at odds with *Velayat-e Faqih*. Khamenei had faced the danger of presidential elections-turned-political-movements in 1997 and then in 2009. He had also experienced the peril of a president-turned-rival (even if it was his own pick) in Mahmoud

Ahmadinejad. A president was simply too powerful because, unlike the Supreme Leader, he was elected directly by the people. To counter that threat, Khamenei suggested that the presidency might be weakened and replaced with a parliamentary system similar to what had existed in the first decade of the revolution. Throughout the 1980s, Khamenei had been the ceremonial, weak, and dutiful president under Khomeini. In October 2011, Khamenei announced the possible revival of the position of prime minister: "If one day, probably in the distant future, it is felt that it would be better for a parliamentary system to choose the head of the executive branch, there is no problem with changing the current mechanism."[12]

In fact, a year earlier Khamenei had reportedly tasked an expert legal team with examining "tens of clauses" in the constitution that needed to be revised. Article 107 of the Iranian constitution permits just such a review, authorizing the Supreme Leader to ask the heads of the three branches of the government, members of the Expediency Council, and others to study his recommendations on the "problems" of the constitution. A senior member of the Majles who was familiar with the debate pointed out that in order to "rejuvenate" the Islamic Republic's political system, "the second layer of the political structure" needed to be altered.[13] The goal was to modify the political structure from a presidential to a parliamentary system. Moreover, to further control the parliament itself, Khamenei asked the legislative body to pass a bill to "monitor" members of the parliament in 2010. The stated rationale for this shift was that Iran's political system in reality was not presidential: the head of the state was unmistakably the Supreme Leader, even though it was the president who was elected directly by the people.

Perhaps no one articulated the conservatives' deep fear of the popular vote better than Khamenei's own ally, conservative cleric Ayatollah Mesbah-Yazdi. He denounced democracy not just as a Western phenomenon, but also as a Sunni plot that stretched back to the first caliphs, who had not permitted the Prophet Mohammad's son-in-law, Ali, to succeed the Prophet after his death. According to Mesbah-Yazdi, even though the Prophet had designated Ali as his heir, others gathered at a place called the Saghifeh and selected Abu Bakr as the next leader of the Muslim community with the justification that "the people have to choose the government . . . Therefore, the foundation of democracy was laid in the Saghifeh . . . The foundation of secularism and the separation of religion and politics was laid in the Saghifeh as well."[14]

Khamenei likewise took a number of steps to redefine Khomeini's legacy of *maslahat* (expediency) as a jurisprudential and divine concept that must be under the Guardian Jurist's direct supervision and expertise. His aim was to counter the reformists and pragmatists, who sought to appropriate the concept of *maslahat* and delegate it to the state. The Expediency Council, the embodiment of the system's pragmatism, was increasingly neutralized, and there were even hints that it might be dissolved. In 2010, when the Expediency Council headed by Rafsanjani proposed to limit the vetting power of the Guardian Council over the elections, Khamenei put the pragmatic body in its place. He pointed out that the views of the Expediency Council were not binding but only "consultative." He warned that the electoral authority of the Guardian Council, including "monitoring and discerning the qualifications" of candidates, should not be "invaded."[15] Various state-funded scholars theorized the concept of expediency as the Supreme Leader's exclusive area of expertise that should not be extended to any other institution. In striving to put the genie of Khomeini's "pragmatism" back in the bottle (and safely under Khamenei's control), conservatives argued that Khomeini did not secularize the system; rather, his pragmatism was an inherent characteristic of *Velayat-e Faqih*.[16]

Meanwhile, Khamenei established new parameters for *Velayat-e Faqih*. In July 2010, Khamenei issued a fatwa to further undermine both popular sovereignty and the traditional independence of Shi'a clerics:

> *Velayat-e Faqih* is the ruling of the qualified *faqih* in the absence of the Infallible Imam. It is a branch of the guardianship and rule of the Prophet Mohammad and the Infallible Imams. You may ensure full commitment to the Guardian Jurist by obeying his administrative rulings.[17]

He stressed that all Muslims, including the "grand jurists, let alone their followers" must surrender to him, the Guardian Jurist. "We believe commitment to *Velayat-e Faqih* cannot be separated from commitment to Islam and the Guardianship of the Infallible Imams." Khamenei followed by emphasizing what many thought was a reference to the Green Movement, during which many senior clerics refused to lend legitimacy to the regime's brutality: "The decisions and authority of the Guardian Jurist, as far as it is pertinent to the public interests of Islam and Muslims, take precedence and prevail over the will of the masses, if they are in contradiction." Obeying the Guardian Jurist's political orders was compulsory for all people, even top jurists. The excuse that other jurists might be more qualified in different theological areas would not be accepted.

Widespread negative reactions, ridicule, and criticism by dissidents and the Iranian diaspora forced Khamenei's office to downplay his fatwa. His official website pointed out that the concept of *Velayat-e Faqih* had long been established and defined by the Prophet Mohammad, the Imams, and Khomeini. It added that in his fatwa, Khamenei simply clarified what commitment to *Velayat-e Faqih* entailed, interpreting it broadly according to his "maximum attraction, minimum repulsion [of supporters'] strategy" during the Green Movement.[18] Conservative clerics such as Mohammad Gharavi defended Khamenei's "minimalist" view, which stressed only a "practical" commitment to *Velayat-e Faqih*. Gharavi argued that, according to Khamenei's decree, citizens did not need to believe in *Velayat-e Faqih* in their hearts; they only needed to obey it.[19] However, the opposition continued to fiercely attack Khamenei's fatwa. With his usual candid tone, opposition leader Mehdi Karroubi stated that the power of *Velayat-e Faqih* had expanded and surpassed that of the Prophet Mohammad himself. He went on to state, "I do not believe that God has considered a right for such treatment of His creatures [by other creatures] even for Himself."[20]

Khamenei was derided for inflating his rule to include the most private aspects of people's lives. After the dissident cleric Montazeri passed away, Khamenei issued a statement saying that he hoped God would "forgive" Montazeri for his "worldly" mistakes. He also allowed Montazeri to be buried at a holy shrine next to his martyred son. Montazeri's student, Mohsen Kadivar, sarcastically reacted from exile to reports of Khamenei's statement:

Although I have studied various facets of the sphere of Absolute *Velayat-e Faqih* for years, I have to confess that I have never paid attention to this field of the sphere of Absolute *Velayat-e Faqih*: the Guardianship over graves. According to the theory of Absolute Appointed *Velayat-e Faqih*, the leader not only has guardianship over life, but death, not only one's worldly home, but one's other-worldly resting place . . . [The leader apparently has guardianship over] who is buried where and into which grave goes which dead.[21]

Shortly before his death, Montazeri inflicted what was perhaps the most powerful damage on *Velayat-e Faqih*. As one of the concept's original creators and implementers, Khomeini's most learned student apologized for his role in institutionalizing it:

> I am a firm defender of the rule of religion and one of the people who laid the foundations of *Velayat-e Faqih*—of course not under its current shape and form, but the one in which the people elect the leader and supervise his activities—and I made much scholarly and practical endeavor to implement it. Now, I feel humiliated before the informed Iranian people for the oppression that is being carried out in the name of *Velayat-e Faqih*. I feel responsible before God.

Montazeri also opposed Khomeini's famous old statement that the survival of the Islamic state was the utmost religious duty. He viewed this declaration as an excuse that could justify any political act:

> One of the points frequently mentioned these days is that safeguarding the system is an obligation. Safeguarding the system is not an [religious] obligation *per se*. This means that if we violate Islamic instructions, the system will not be secured. Securing the system is a prelude to safeguarding and carrying out Islamic instructions. If we take anti-Islamic actions with the excuse of safeguarding the system, neither the system nor Islam will survive.[22]

Despite this overt opposition, the conservative establishment continued to expand Khamenei's authority. Major General Hassan Firouzabadi, the armed forces chief of staff, stated, "*Velayat-e Faqih* is not simply an issue of governance and the preeminent power in the country, but rather the Guardianship of science, knowledge, and wisdom."[23] Mahdavi-Kani, a prominent conservative cleric, scorned opposition leader Mousavi for not believing in Khamenei's "holiness."[24]

These new official narratives did not go unchallenged as reformists worked relentlessly to demonstrate the contingent, political, and even conspiratorial nature of both *Velayat-e Faqih* broadly and Khamenei's own selection more specifically—in contrast to their officially divine roots. Mid-ranking cleric Mousavi Khoeiniha, a former radical mentor of the students who occupied the U.S. embassy, stepped back from his earlier beliefs and attacks, pointing out that many other jurists did not share Khomeini's view of Absolute *Velayat-e Faqih*. Khoeiniha contradicted Khamenei by arguing that since *Velayat-e Faqih* was in the constitution, it was a temporary "national contract, which only requires practical obedience, not belief in the heart, since many citizens are followers of the jurists who do not believe in this absolute juris-prudential view." According to Khoeiniha, the conservatives were trying to ensure that no one dared to pose the "least criticism toward the Leader's smallest deed."[25] Having once used "anti-*Velayat-e Faqih*" accusations to vanquish opponents in the early 1980s, he now accused the conservatives of reducing the "entire constitution, Islam, and that Islamic Republic to the articles that are pertinent to *Velayat-e Faqih*."[26]

The critics disputed not only the institution of *Velayat-e Faqih*, but Khamenei's legitimacy in holding that authority. They questioned his selection for the position and implicitly compared it to the aforementioned Sunni plot in the Saghifeh. Karroubi claimed that while Khomeini laid in a coma during the last hours of his life in June 1988, the Assembly of Experts convened to decide on the question of succession. He alleged that in an initial meeting of Khomeini's closest disciples, "no name was mentioned as a successor," and instead, those present supported the creation of a leadership council consisting of three or five clerics. However, in a subsequent meeting a week after Khomeini's death and Khamenei's selection, "there was a different atmosphere."[27] He claimed that Absolute *Velayat-e Faqih* was a post-Khomeini invention. The word "Absolute" was added to the authority of the Supreme Leader, although "this was not at all approved by the Imam." Karroubi argued that it was the IRGC that wanted the phrase inserted into the constitution. He also asserted that the Assembly of Experts initially voted to reduce the lifetime term for the Supreme Leader to ten years, stating, "The [Assembly of] Experts believed that the Imam [Ayatollah Khomeini] was a different personality because he was the founder of the system and he was old as well. But in the present time, the term of leadership should be limited." However, another right-wing cleric, this time Ayatollah Abolghasem Khazali, torpedoed this proposal and, hand-in-hand with other conservative clerics, blocked a final vote on this critical issue. The final obstacle to the ascendance of Khamenei had been the condition that the Supreme Leader must be a marja. Karroubi claimed that in a meeting of the Assembly of Experts, conservative cleric Ayatollah Mohammad Yazdi proposed that this condition should be removed, since *ijtihad* (the authority to interpret the Holy Text) was enough for *Velayat-e Faqih*.[28] As a result, the mantle of leadership was tailored to fit the mid-ranking Khamenei. Karroubi added that the conservative right wanted to change other republican institutions and democratic aspects of the constitution, including eliminating local elections, but they could not consider any steps beyond the cases that the late Supreme Leader had specified for revision. After that, Karroubi said, the meetings of the Assembly of Experts moved from the Majles to a building "next to the office of Mr. Khamenei," a clear political message to the leftist faction that the right was dominating the scene.

Despite these attacks, the regime emphasized the sacredness of Khamenei's position by arguing that he was appointed by God and not accountable to anyone. Head of the judiciary Ayatollah Sadeq Larijani unequivocally declared that no ordinary citizen, not even a member of the Assembly of Experts that had selected the Supreme Leader, could monitor his activities.[29] In the run-up to the Assembly of Experts elections in 2016 and in a clear reference to the increasing debates about the Supreme Leader's accountability, Larijani warned against "illegal" wishes and argued that "in the constitution, we don't have such a thing called monitoring the Leader."

Cultural Revolution 2.0

As the intra-clerical struggle over the authority of the Supreme Leader continued, Khamenei ordered a new cultural revolution to purge the academic curricula of anti–Velayat-e Faqih concepts. In the immediate aftermath of the Islamic Revolution, the new government shut down the universities, and a group of clerics and religious social scientists were handpicked by Khomeini to "Islamicize" the higher education system. Thirty years later, the universities became a hotbed of anti-establishment activities once more. A few months after the Green Movement emerged, Khamenei expressed concerns about the two to three million Iranian students studying the humanities and the social sciences, which he saw as "materialistic and [based on] a lack of belief in divine and Islamic teachings . . . and promoting skepticism."[30] Around the same time, Saeed Hajjarian, a leading reformist figure now in prison, was brought to court and later onto TV to "confess" that his praxis was erroneous because his theory was flawed. Hajjarian was forced to declare that Max Weber's theory of rationalization and model of charismatic leadership, which had influenced his own reformist thoughts, did not apply to Iran's Islamic government. Along with Weber, the government indicted other social scientists and philosophers such as Jürgen Habermas, Richard Rorty, and Karl

Popper.[31] Khamenei asked students and scholars to refrain from reading Popper, whose work, including *The Open Society and Its Enemies*, had brought the late British philosopher unmatched popularity among Iranian reformists.[32] In reaction to these Soviet-style show trials, many opposition activists and intellectuals targeted what they deemed to be the expanding interpretation of *Velayat-e Faqih*. Soroush, an original member of the Cultural Revolution Council and now a leading liberal and secular thinker in exile, warned that Khamenei's claim to be the Guardian of Islamic jurisprudence did not give him permission to assume the Guardianship of the humanities—an area that was "neither his expertise nor his responsibility."[33] Not surprisingly, Khamenei's allies blamed the failure of the first Cultural Revolution on Soroush, Mousavi, and other "deviants."[34]

The Iranian government took action to implement the Supreme Leader's view and "re-Islamicize" the educational system. In October 2010, Minister of Science and Higher Education Kamran Daneshjoo announced that twelve majors in the social sciences and humanities needed to be revised, as they were not compatible with Islamic principles. These fields of study included law, political science, sociology, philosophy, psychology, education, human rights, and management. His ministry prevented the expansion of these majors and promised "revisions of at least 70 percent" of their curricula within the next five years.[35] The second wave of "Islamization" was not limited to the universities. The Ministry of Education announced a new collaboration with the seminaries that entailed basing a cleric in every school across the country to provide religious consultation.[36] The return of ideology was compounded by the movement of the Basij militias, the guardians of ideology, to center stage. The Basij was to have a stronger presence in the schools, universities, mosques, and government offices. It would create both a façade of popularity and an effective tool of suppression, since the Basijis were the "ordinary people." Khamenei declared, "As long as there is the Basij, the Islamic System and the Islamic Republic will not be threatened by the enemy . . . The Basij's criterion is intuition and faith. Faith springs out of its heart and forces action."[37]

Khamenei characterized his battle against secularism as not only a matter of ideology but central to the material success of the Islamic Revolution. Rationalism, pragmatism, secularism, and de-ideologization were all terms that Khamenei used to describe the soft war that the "West" and its local agents were waging against Iran. He argued that since the 1979 revolution, the world had tried to overthrow the Islamic Republic through coups, ethnic conflicts, and war. These "hard" confrontations against Iran had failed. Now, the enemy was looking to wage a soft war, which, according to Khamenei, "means war with cultural tools; with influence, lies, and the spreading of rumors with the advanced tools that exist today. [These] communication tools did not exist ten, fifteen, and thirty years ago but have spread today. [This] soft war is creating doubt in the people's hearts and minds."[38] The popular protests in the aftermath of the controversial election in June 2009 were a result of the creation of a murky climate in which people could not distinguish truth from falsehood, hence the use of the term "seditionists" by the conservatives to describe the reformists, who had used powerful religious language to mobilize the people.

The Challenging Rise of Turkey's Islamists

In the midst of Khamenei's internal battle with the reformists over the parameters and legitimacy of *Velayat-e Faqih*, a similar group of religious political actors were coming to power next door in Ankara.[39] The ascendance of the AKP in Turkey in 2002 initially thrilled Khamenei, who hoped that as Ankara moved toward an Islamist government, it would become ideologically and strategically closer to Tehran. Iranian conservatives surmised that the AKP's goal was a similar Islamic republic, even if it was achieved through elections rather than revolution. They considered Turkey's special relationships with the West not as a threat but as an instrument to reduce Tehran's isolation and protect its interests. During meetings with then–prime minister Recep Tayyip Erdogan and President Abdullah Gul from 2006 to 2010, Khamenei congratulated Turkey for its economic and political achievements and stressed that the AKP's shift toward the Middle East would "strengthen" Muslim countries while further popularizing the AKP domestically and regionally.[40] He was also eager to use Turkey's new stance to his own advantage. Iran welcomed Turkey's mediation, along with Brazil's, on the nuclear issue in 2010, even though the gambit ultimately failed.

Much to the surprise of the Iranian government, however, Turkey became a regional competitor, and its secular model of "moderate" Islamic politics proved more popular than Iran's hardline "revolutionary" Islamist approach. The AKP's "social Islam" was a mirror image of the Iranian reformists' "civil

Islam" in advocating a minimalist reading of religion.[41] Although born in diametrically opposed political systems (Iran's theocracy and Turkey's secular republic), both Iranian and Turkish reformists sought to strike a balance between Islam and liberal democracy. The Iranian reformists' adherence to Islam helped their return to the electoral process in 1997 by increasing the cost of their disqualification by the Guardian Council. Similarly, the AKP's stated loyalty to Kemalism facilitated its victory in 2002 by overcoming the secular establishment's constraints against Islamist parties.

The AKP's success in Turkey had the potential to challenge the *Velayat-e Faqih* system in Iran, both regionally and internally. Aware of the ideological affinity between Iran's reformist opposition and the AKP, and mindful of the damage that ideology had caused them, Tehran's conservatives were concerned that the AKP's reformist approach to religion might reinvigorate their reformist rivals and create a crisis of legitimacy for the Iranian government on a regional level, weakening Iran's soft power, undermining its popularity in the Muslim world, and attracting its allies, such as Hamas. Indeed, Turkish policy toward Israel and the broader region during the Arab uprisings challenged Iran's status and Islamist message.

In May 2010, Israel attacked what was known as the Gaza Freedom Flotilla—Turkish-supported ships bound for Gaza on a humanitarian mission. In their condemnations of the Israeli attacks on the humanitarian ships, Iranian leaders expressed support for the Palestinians but remained nearly silent on the leading role of Turkey in the confrontation. Instead, the Iranian conservative media and officials expressed concerns that Iran's role in the incident was not prominent. Anxious to reassert Iran into the Palestinian issue, governmental organizations announced that Iran would soon send its own humanitarian ships to Gaza. Iran's Red Crescent Society even set the date of the departure, but the ships were never launched, for Iran was not really seeking a direct confrontation with Israel.[42] A commentator offered a suggestion that subsequently revealed Iran's ambivalence: Iran should grant citizenship to supporters of the Palestinians who died during such humanitarian incidents and provide compensation for their families. It would provide a compelling way of inserting Iran into the narrative, but it did not happen.[43]

The Arab Spring in the early 2010s brought the Islamists in Tunisia and Egypt to power. Iranian conservatives called it the "Islamic Awakening" and the fruit of their 1979 revolution. But it was Turkey, not Iran, that initially seemed to seize the moment. Iranian conservatives watched in horror as

Erdogan was received rapturously during his post-revolution trips to Arab countries. His advocacy of a secular model of government that respected Islam concerned conservative political and religious authorities in Tehran. Senior clerics attacked Turkey's "liberal" and "Western" interpretations of Islam and warned that Iran had fallen behind Turkey in the region.[44] What finally sent Iranian conservatives over the edge was Turkey's shift in relations with Syria. Prime Minister Erdogan went from being a staunch ally of Syrian president Bashar al-Assad to telling Assad to either reform or be ousted. With the Arab Spring in 2011 and the consequent civil war in Syria, Turkey hosted conferences for the Syrian opposition and sheltered anti-regime fighters. In response, Tehran sent several messages to Ankara, making it clear that Syria was its "red line" and warning Erdogan not to back the anti-Assad opposition.[45] Turkey did not heed Iran's warning. Conservative columnists opened fire and criticized Turkey for being a Sunni dictatorship. Pointing to Turkey's ethnic and religious fault lines, they added that its people yearned for the implementation of Islamic law but that the AKP provided them with only a veneer of Islam.

Moreover, the commentators argued that Turkey, unlike Iran and Egypt, lacked a long tradition of jurisprudential scholarship and therefore did not have nearly the intellectual heft necessary to lead the Islamic world. Finally, they argued that the Arabs would not forget their bitter memories of the Ottoman period and thus Ankara's euphoric moment would not last, as post–Arab Spring Egypt would once again reassert itself and balance Turkey. This meticulously constructed narrative pointed to Turkey as part of a bigger U.S.-Israeli-Saudi plot to derail the new wave of Islamic awakenings. It alleged that because the United States was losing its puppets (Hosni Mubarak, Zine El Abidine Ben Ali, etc.) in the region, it had decided to use the Turkish model as a damage control measure. The United States would also use the AKP as a tool to implement its regime change policy in Iran after the failure of the Green Movement in 2009, the argument continued.

In February 2013, President Ahmadinejad made a historic trip to Egypt.[46] He was the highest-ranking Iranian official to visit Cairo after the two countries broke diplomatic relations in 1979. Despite high hopes in Tehran, Egyptian religious and political groups across the spectrum were not eager to thaw relations with the Shi'a state. In a joint press conference with Ahmadinejad, the head of Al-Azhar, the most prominent religious institution in the Sunni world, criticized Iran for discriminating against its Sunni minority. The

Salafi members of Egypt's parliament declared Shi'ites "worse than naked women" and warned the country's Islamist president Mohamed Morsi against lifting visa restrictions for Iranian tourists.[47] Yet Iran continued to express readiness to share its "experience" with Morsi in making the transition from a secular state to a full-fledged Islamic one. Nevertheless, Morsi kept his distance from Iran. In his trip to Tehran for the summit of the Non-Align Movement, he began his speech by paying respects to the Prophet Mohammad's companions, namely Abu Bakr, Umar, and Uthman, historical figures disliked by many Shi'ites. To further infuriate his host, Morsi criticized Iran's ally, Bashar al-Assad, for killing Sunni protesters. Iran's state-controlled TV purposely mistranslated Morsi's live speech by replacing "Syria" with "Bahrain," making it seem that the Egyptian president was slamming the Persian Gulf monarchy for cracking down on its Shi'a population.[48]

To add salt to the wound, Morsi and Erdogan drove a wedge between Iran and the Palestinian militant group Hamas. The longtime ally of Iran closed its Political Bureau in Damascus and moved to align more with Cairo and Ankara. Hamas leader Khaled Meshaal and Morsi were special guests at the AKP's annual congress in September 2012. The event was highly choreographed to consolidate the AKP's position against both its domestic secular and religious rivals, and its Shi'a competitor in Tehran. Both figures praised Erdogan as the architect of a successful model to be emulated by others. Morsi declared AKP's achievements to be "followed with respect by the entire world," while Meshaal called Erdogan "not only a leader in Turkey now, [but] a leader in the Muslim world as well."[49] Evidently, the AKP was now operating on a transnational level—striving to become champion of Islamists in the region, directing them away from Iran's route toward its own model.

Iran quietly watched these developments and only hoped that the more conservative wings of the Brotherhood would eventually remove the "liberal" Morsi, just as the Iranian conservative clerics themselves brought down their own interim government after the 1979 revolution. In the end, it was the Egyptian army's coup against the democratically elected Morsi on July 3, 2013, that relieved the Iranian conservatives of the challenge of the Turkish–Egyptian Islamist alliance. Perhaps the Guardian Jurist hoped a similarly successful coup in Turkey would end the AKP's rule and bring back the friendlier, diehard secular—but less ideologically threatening—Kemalists. However, the Syrian civil war, Turkey's internal political instability, and

Erdogan's increasingly authoritarian actions ultimately reduced his model's appeal and thus his ideational threat to Iran.

Tehran's conservatives perceived the threats from internal and external religious actors as indistinguishable and thus prescribed comparable ideological discourses to counter them. In a meeting with the clerical members of the Assembly of Experts, Khamenei attacked those who spoke of "rationalizing" the Islamic Republic, as well as those who advocated less ideological domestic and foreign policies. He acknowledged that pursuing revolutionary principles created difficulties for the country's progress both domestically and internationally, referring to the Rushdie affair to note that some top officials had asked the late Ayatollah Khomeini not to issue the fatwa against Salman Rushdie because of its consequences for the country. However, "He [Khomeini] did not capitulate. He insisted. These challenges continue to this day." Not surprisingly, Khamenei did not mention that he himself tried to downplay Khomeini's fatwa by announcing that Rushdie could repent. According to Khamenei, if the state gave up on its principles and spiritual goals, its pragmatic goals would not be realized. At various times, revolutions deviated from their principles, and this was the beginning of their end. Therefore, Khamenei argued, one must remain true to their ideology in order to guarantee both spiritual and material success: "We tested and noticed that it is possible to keep [our] principles and reach [our] achievements as well."[50] Thus, he advocated continuing along the hardline ideological route, not despite but precisely because of the looming challenges. Conveniently, that hardline ideological route conferred to him unassailable authority and power.

That same year, Khamenei had a similar message for the regional Islamist leaders. In 2011, he was the keynote speaker at the First Islamic Awakening Conference organized by Tehran. Given his experience as both a political and religious leader in Iran, he provided the six hundred participants from reportedly eighty countries with an articulate roadmap based on the experiences of the Islamic Revolution.[51] Having emerged from a grave conflict with his old allies during the Green Movement, he warned against the temptation to make ideological deviations and compromises in response to promises or threats from the United States. He also cautioned his audience that "untrustworthy" factions would receive financial or media support from the United States in order to marginalize the "true" revolutionaries. Khamenei's solution was to "write down" the slogans and principles of the revolution and remain loyal to them; otherwise, the "seditionists" would undoubtedly hijack the movement and come to power again. Every downfall, he continued, started with ideological deviation, period. Khamenei later attributed Morsi's downfall to his pro-American shift. What he failed to share was that reserving the power to define that ideology in the first place was critical to this approach.

ELEVEN

The Domestic Sources of Nuclear Politics

IN THE CONTEXT of emerging and shifting internal and regional ideological fault lines, competition among Iran's political elites played out in the international arena over development of the nation's nuclear capabilities. Mounting international pressure on Iran since the revelation of its nuclear activities in 2002 threatened both the regime and the factions within it. Elites' jockeying to strike a balance between regime security and their respective political factions influenced the tumultuous nuclear negotiations, which lasted more than a decade until the 2015 agreement. An indispensable component of this rivalry was tapping into popular preferences and adopting a corresponding discourse. Nationalism was becoming the new game in town. This shift in political discourse would continue even after the accord with significant factional consequences.

Given the popular support for a rapprochement with the United States among Iranians in this period, various political groups competed to resolve the nuclear crisis and use it as a bridge to improve relations with Washington, although those who relied on popular votes had more incentive to achieve an agreement than the appointed Guardian Jurist. Presidents Khatami, Ahmadinejad, and Rouhani each displayed flexibility toward compromise during their tenures but undermined negotiations when their rivals held the executive branch. However, Ayatollah Khamenei and the IRGC would undercut any nuclear proposal and détente with the United States that rewarded these elected officials, thereby compromising their supreme authority. Instead they maintained their anti-American discourse, sought an alliance with Russia, and expanded their influence in Iraq and Syria. In the age of the Islamic State of Iraq and Syria (ISIS) and an unprecedented sectarian calamity throughout the Middle East, they increasingly framed *Velayat-e Faqih* and the IRGC as protectors of the nation's security and territorial integrity, and the defenders of the sacred Shi'a shrines in Iraq and Syria. From this cauldron, a sturdy leftist-centrist coalition emerged that further shaped the Iranian polity. The alliance challenged the conservatives' factional interests even as it boosted the regime's overall legitimacy and security.

This chapter relies primarily on Persian media to shed light on policy debates among the elites and specifically to demonstrate how the Iranian media often serve as an acute thermometer and even bellwether of Iran's foreign policy. The media reflect emerging consensus and conflict within the polity over major policy issues. Designed to advance competing factional interests and agendas, the media have more often been an accurate measure of Iran's foreign policy than the actual statements of officials, including the president and even the Supreme Leader.

Nuclear Negotiations

Iran's nuclear program was thrust into the international limelight in 2002 when the Iraq-based Iranian opposition group, the MKO, revealed to the world the activities at the Natanz and Arak facilities. With Khamenei's blessing, the Khatami administration agreed to suspend its uranium enrichment program in 2003 during negotiations with France, Germany, and the United Kingdom (EU3). The agreement was part of the larger reformist approach to reduce tensions with the United States in the post-9/11 environment. However, the failure of the Europeans to provide sufficient incentives for Iran to continue its suspension weakened Khatami's position internally. Combined with the declining threat posed by the United States as it became bogged down in Iraq and Afghanistan, this internal opposition prompted conservatives to subvert the voluntary suspension and resume nuclear activities.[1] Following the defeat of the reformists in the 2005 presidential election, Iran further expanded its enrichment program. President Ahmadinejad ridiculed the reformists, arguing that suspension would not bear any fruit: "A few years ago, three European countries came and sat in Sa'd Abad [the presidential palace] and said, 'You have to negotiate for ten years. After ten years, we may allow you to build a couple of research centrifuges.' "[2] Within a few years, however, the number of Iran's centrifuges jumped from twenty to nearly twenty thousand. Despite mounting UN and U.S. sanctions, Iran now claimed that its "indigenous" enrichment program was more advanced than the programs of other nuclear powers, such as Pakistan.[3] But Tehran remained engaged with the international community about the issue through diplomatic channels to prevent a sudden escalation of U.S. pressure.

In October 2009, the arduous negotiations over Iran's nuclear program seemed to have finally reached a breakthrough. During a meeting with the five permanent UN Security Council members and Germany (P5+1) in Geneva, Tehran agreed "in principle" to move most of its enriched uranium out of the country. In return, Iran would receive the nuclear fuel that it needed to power the Tehran Research Reactor (TRR). Moreover, Iran's nuclear negotiator, Saeed Jalili, and U.S. undersecretary of state William Burns talked directly and bilaterally, marking one of the highest levels of contact between the two countries in three decades.[4] The U.S. media reported that Washington and Tehran had agreed for the first time to one-on-one negotiations regarding Iran's nuclear program.

Then, just as everything seemed to be going well, Tehran rolled back the progress. A few days after the announcement, Iran dismissed the accord, refusing to ship its low-enriched uranium (LEU) to Russia in return for fuel rods from France as it had previously agreed.[5] Negotiations hoping to revive the agreement continued until the end of January, at which point Iran formally rejected the deal.[6] This puzzling incident frustrated P5+1 officials and Iran experts, who were confounded by what they viewed as Tehran's complicated, opaque, and unpredictable decision-making process. They were surprised by both the initial success and eventual failure of this round of nuclear talks. As I explain in the next section, the Geneva negotiations had the full support of the Supreme Leader. But a number of factors—including Ahmadinejad's eagerness to turn the accord into a bridge toward better relations with the United States; criticisms from the reformists, pragmatists, and moderate conservatives; and finally the international media's portrayal of the negotiations' outcomes—threatened the Guardian Jurist's position and uncompromising image that were so critical to his ability to maintain authority. So he changed course.

Iran had initially entered the Geneva talks with a different tone, signaling flexibility on a number of issues, including the nuclear fuel swap. On October 1,

2009, the first day of the negotiations, *Kayhan* ran an editorial with an unusually optimistic opening line: "The October negotiations can be the starting point for a fundamental change in the Western relationship with Iran."[7] The author, Mehdi Mohammadi, spoke of Iran's "new package that has provided an important opportunity" for the West. In the following issue, *Kayhan* portrayed the Geneva talks as a triumph. However, it focused primarily on what Iran would get from the deal, not what it had agreed to give. According to the story, Iran forced the P5+1 to drop the suspension of its enrichment program as a precondition for comprehensive negotiations. Moreover, Javier Solana, the European Union's foreign policy chief, was quoted as saying that Iran would acquire TRR fuel from other countries. *Kayhan* even quoted Fox News and acknowledged that William Burns held a forty-five-minute "negotiation" with Jalili on a "wide range of issues."[8] But the story took on a life of its own as other accounts became public; *Kayhan* was forced to backtrack and the government soon followed.

The opposition leader, Mir-Hossein Mousavi, attacked Ahmadinejad's negotiating team, and indirectly Khamenei, for giving away the "achievements" of the past years. Rouhani, the former chief nuclear negotiator under Khatami, said that Iran should simply purchase the fuel needed for the TRR and not give up its enriched uranium.[9] The reformists, who had been previously criticized by Ahmadinejad and other conservatives for suspending the enrichment program when they were in power in 2003, were now claiming that giving up the 3.5 percent enriched uranium the country had produced since 2005 was tantamount to a four-year suspension and not having achieved anything. The opposition was also relentless in publicizing and criticizing Jalili's meeting with Undersecretary Burns. These internal pressures were compounded by international media reports that Iran was giving up its enriched uranium in return for the ability to purchase fuel—which often portrayed the deal as far less favorable to Iran.

Kayhan struggled to convince its conservative elite audience that all major media outlets in the world had attested to Iran's victory in these negotiations, which had not compromised any aspects of its enrichment program. It quoted Israeli figures that had reportedly expressed disappointment over the Geneva talks.[10] Hossein Shariatmadari, the paper's managing editor, wrote an editorial article sarcastically titled "We Did Not Compromise, They Were Compromised!" He rejected the "Western officials' and media's claims" that Iran had agreed to the nuclear swap.[11] In fact, he argued, this proposal "did not have Iran's positive or negative response." The editorial continued to state that even if Tehran had agreed to ship its LEU stockpile, it would mean that the other side had effectively accepted Iran's low-enrichment program. Therefore, it was still a victory for the Islamic Republic. The next day, the Supreme Leader made a vague, short, but trendsetting statement that echoed *Kayhan*'s earlier backtracking. In an implicit reference to the international reaction to Iran's initial agreement, he said, "The excitement of the revolution's enemies is the sign of a deviant move."[12] The deal was effectively killed, although Ahmadinejad tried to keep it alive.

On the same day as Khamenei's speech, Ahmadinejad welcomed the results of the Geneva talks and hailed the bilateral meeting with Undersecretary Burns. In a marked move away from his master's anti-American rhetoric, the president said, "We have no limits for interactions, except with the Zionist regime. The U.S. representative wanted a negotiation and Mr. Jalili welcomed it as well and actually their negotiations were good negotiations."[13] His unwillingness to stay within Khamenei's red lines along with the unexpected change of policy and tone sparked a confrontation with key conservative figures, which was amplified in the right-wing media. Ayatollah Ahmad Jannati, the powerful head of the Guardian Council, attacked those who "misinterpreted" the talks, stating, "There is no negotiation with the United States. Some fantasize that the door for negotiations has opened and thus everything has changed."[14]

Kayhan, which had initially reported the "negotiations" between Jalili and Burns, reframed the meeting in an effort to tamp down both Ahmadinejad's excitement and the opposition's criticism. In a reference to Ahmadinejad's statement, *Kayhan*'s Shariatmadari alleged that what had happened in Geneva was not a negotiation but rather a "unilateral meeting" that the Americans had "planned and staged." According to Shariatmadari, when Jalili was about to leave the conference room after the multilateral talks adjourned, Burns walked toward him and expressed an interest in discussing a few important points. However, Jalili dismissed Burns and it all ended there, Shariatmadari claimed. Thus, what had taken place was an "anti-negotiation." *Kayhan*'s managing editor rejected every clause in Ahmadinejad's statement, saying, "It was neither welcomed [by Jalili], nor was it a negotiation in the first place whose result can be assessed as 'good.'"[15] In the editorial, Shariatmadari went even further in asking the president not to make statements about major foreign policy issues, which are the Supreme Leader's turf according to Article 110 of the constitution. Conservative members of the Majles eventually confirmed what many had suspected: Khamenei's objections had put an end to the deal.[16]

A few months later, after Iran officially rejected the proposal, Ahmadinejad criticized those who had derailed the negotiations. He regretfully added that the deal would have paved the way for a rapprochement with the United States. In an interview with a state-controlled television channel, he remained defiant in his interest in resolving the nuclear issue and opening a direct line with the United States. However, instead of blaming his internal enemies, he pointed to external actors, namely the United Kingdom and Israel: "They have said that if confrontation [between Iran and the United States] becomes interaction, the deal is done."[17] He claimed that the P5+1 was still sending messages that the agreement remained on the table and that there was even additional flexibility on the issue of the fuel swap. However, *Kayhan*'s Shariatmadari expressed anger over Ahmadinejad's eagerness for a compromise, which he characterized as a "trap" that had been neutralized by the Leader's astuteness.[18]

While many anticipated the continuation and expansion of the current enrichment level, *Kayhan* signaled that a significant shift might be coming: upping the level of enrichment. It claimed that the new policy was in response to a shift in the United States' approach to Iran in light of the Green Movement protests. The paper wrote, "Up until the election, the situation almost demonstrated that the Americans felt entering comprehensive negotiations with Iran to attract its participation in managing the regional issues was inevitable. The only problem [for the United States] was whether or not Iran would accept these negotiations."[19] However, following the election, the United States chose to invest in Iran's internal conflict instead of "accepting the realities of its nuclear program and its regional power." Khamenei, too, declared: "Some will have to answer to God for doing something that the enemy perceives as divisiveness in the country which makes [the enemy] more audacious."[20]

According to this narrative, there was a strategic shift in Western capitals to move the focus from compromising with the ruling faction to helping the opposition. The May 2010 Turkish- and Brazilian-brokered Tehran Agreement, of which the P5+1 disapproved and which was followed by more sanctions, only confirmed the perspective that the West was not interested in coming to a fair deal with the government. Therefore, in the eyes of the establishment, the new sanctions imposed by the UN Security Council and the unilateral U.S. and EU sanctions against Iran's energy sector and financial institutions were designed less in response to the nuclear program than to help the opposition topple the regime.

In light of this view and since Iran remained unable to purchase nuclear fuel without giving up its LEU stockpile, Tehran's nuclear strategy would be to move to a higher level of enrichment. Immediately after the passage of UNSC Resolution 1929 in June 2010, Tehran announced that it would end all voluntary cooperation with the International Atomic Energy Agency (IAEA), build ten new enrichment sites (in addition to the Natanz and Fordo facilities), and increase the level of enrichment from 3.5 to 20 percent.

Conservative commentators further argued that there were two reasons behind the decision to undertake 20 percent enrichment: first, to show that no one, including Ahmadinejad, could hijack the establishment's official and stated nuclear policy; and second, to prove that, counter to the claims of U.S. officials and experts, the post-election conflict did not affect Iran's foreign policy.[21] The conservatives soon claimed that the West dropped one of its preconditions as a result of Iran's resistance:

> Many may not know, but it has been years since the Westerners have inhumanely stopped selling radioisotopes, which have no use except for medical purposes, to Iran. Last Wednesday (21 Bahman), Philip Crowley, an aide [deputy spokesperson] to the U.S. secretary of state, unexpectedly announced that the U.S. is ready to sell isotopes to Iran [for the Tehran Research Reactor]. After that, in a letter to the head of the IAEA, three countries (the U.S., France, and Russia) stressed that even if Iran does not accept the Vienna proposal, it can buy radioisotopes from the international market and does not need the 20 percent enrichment [program]. Surely, Iran disregarded this proposal because it was clear that the Westerners only showed a kind of tactical flexibility in order to stop 20 percent enrichment in Iran.[22]

From 2009 onward, bilateral and multilateral sanctions on Iran mounted, effectively expelling the country from the international financial system. Iran faced various political, financial, and technological obstacles to exporting oil and bringing the revenues back home. Former president Rafsanjani and other marginalized figures warned the leadership "to take the sanctions seriously and not as a joke."[23] American officials, including Treasury Undersecretary for Terrorism and Financial Intelligence Stuart A. Levey, quoted Rafsanjani, claiming that this was evidence that the sanctions were working.[24] However, Rafsanjani, who had been accused by the ultraconservatives of masterminding the Green Movement, made such a statement to call for "unity" to counter the unprecedented sanctions.[25] Unity was a code word for reconciliation between the conservatives and the reformists, which Khamenei had so far resisted. Rafsanjani and other moderate conservatives tried to make a strong case to force Khamenei to move away from the far right to the center.

But Khamenei offered a different interpretation of the situation. He portrayed the sanctions as a sign of the growing power of Iran. In an apparent reference to Undersecretary Levey, he said, "The U.S. government has appointed one of its top economic and financial officials to . . . run committees, travel around the world, contact countries' leaders, and constantly force other countries to turn against Iran." He drew "several points" from this and claimed that the new U.S. pressures were precisely "because of the increasing power of awakening Islam."[26] Sitting next to Rafsanjani and before a large crowd of elderly clerical members of the Assembly of Experts, Khamenei argued that his two decades of leadership had paid off: "When you see the other side [the United States] is nervous and anxious, knocks on this door, knocks on that door, does this, sees that, meets this person—it shows that this side [Iran] has gained some power that he is fearful and anxious of. If we were weak, if we were vulnerable, if they could bring us to our knees with one blow, all of these attempts would have been unnecessary. This attempt is a sign of this side's authority. That is the truth of the matter." He reminded the very body that had selected him in 1989 that, as president in the early days of the revolution, he had to go around the world and beg for weapons ("i.e., 20–30 tanks") to continue the war against Iraq: "I went to Yugoslavia, which received us very well and with a lot of respect. Nevertheless, however much we insisted, they did not agree to give us these conventional weapons." Perhaps conscious of his unprecedented crisis of legitimacy since the presidential election in 2009, Khamenei concluded that those days were long gone and that under his leadership, the country had reached a prominent position in the Middle East. Today, it was the United States that was in the weak position of begging at the doorsteps of various countries to join the sanctions effort against Iran.

Despite his apparent defiance, Khamenei was careful not to cross certain red lines, such as leaving the Treaty on the Non-Proliferation of Nuclear

Weapons (NPT) or increasing Iran's stockpile of enriched uranium. He emphasized his "religious" opposition to the use of nuclear weapons as a confidence-building measure. He indicated that he had said "several times" that nuclear weapons were "forbidden and *haram.*"[27] This pronouncement did not receive a reaction from the international audience that accused Iran of being an ideological state. *Kayhan* complained about why the West had ignored this fatwa: "Up until today, the Westerners have consistently stressed that Iran's decisions in the foreign policy and national security arenas are ideological. That is fine. If the West truly believes that Iran is an ideological state, then why has its media boycotted the explicit and clear fatwa of the Supreme Leader of the Islamic Revolution on the use of the nuclear weapons being forbidden?"[28] However, as *Kayhan*'s Mehdi Mohammadi pointed out, the door was open for a deal: "The U.S.'s big problem is that it cannot conceive of the characteristics of a probable win-win deal with Iran. The Americans' reaction to the Tehran Declaration clearly demonstrated this."[29] Khamenei was searching for an approach to the nuclear situation that Rafsanjani, Khatami, Ahmadinejad, or outsiders could exploit. As a caveat, it is not my contention that none of these factions were genuinely concerned with broader geostrategic ramifications of the nuclear issue. On the contrary! Because they all perceived the sanctions as politically and economically consequential, they tied them to the internal dynamics as well. They were simultaneously pursuing factional, regime, and state interests.

The 2013 Presidential Election

At the end of Ahmadinejad's second term in 2012, the nuclear challenge remained unresolved, international sanctions had reached an unprecedented level, and the Iranian polity continued to be as fractured as ever. Khamenei looked to the upcoming presidential election as a means to manage the external and internal crises. A popular election could signal legitimacy to the world, enhance Iran's position in the nuclear negotiations, and help mend factional rifts. But once again, Rafsanjani challenged Khamenei by announcing his candidacy literally minutes before the registration deadline.[30] To the nation's surprise, the Guardian Council disqualified Rafsanjani and barred him from entering the race. Zahra Mostavafi, the daughter of Ayatollah Khomeini, wrote an open and blunt letter to Khamenei to intervene on Rafsanjani's behalf. She began the letter by referring to her father's alleged anecdote that groomed Khamenei to be his successor. She divulged that the "same day" Khomeini had privately declared Khamenei a potential Supreme Leader, he had also asserted Rafsanjani's qualification for that position. The letter effectively claimed that in the eyes of the founding father of the Islamic Republic, Rafsanjani was on par with Khamenei in terms of his qualifications to be the next Guardian Jurist. She unsuccessfully demanded that Khamenei use the power of *Velayat-e Faqih* to overrule the Guardian Council's decision and "avert a dictatorship."[31]

Despite mounting support from a number of other influential figures, Rafsanjani remained out of the race. But his shocking disqualification generated a polarized climate that helped his protégé, Hassan Rouhani, win the election with 51 percent of the vote in June 2013. Given Rafsanjani's uncompromising position against the ultraconservatives since the Green Movement, his possible victory would have constituted a referendum on Khamenei's legitimacy. However, Rouhani's victory would not have the same political connotation, which might explain why the Guardian Council approved Rouhani's candidacy but not his mentor's. Rouhani's centrist campaign to pledge to resolve the nuclear issue brought the reformists and moderate conservatives on board. The reformists remained marginalized since their only vetted candidate, Mohammad Reza Aref, dropped out to ensure Rouhani's victory, which they considered their potential bridge to the state. It is important to note that the election of the only cleric in the race once again demonstrated that voters did not necessarily associate "moderation" with non-clerics. Above all, the election helped repair the fissure within the elites that had appeared after the Green Movement. Although Khamenei's fellow conservative candidates were defeated, his regime as a whole was now more legitimate and cohesive after the election. He then called for a "heroic leniency" to resolve the nuclear issue.

Though early negotiations between Iran and the United States had started a few months before the presidential elections, it was the Rouhani administration that swiftly reached an interim agreement with the P5+1 in November 2013. Consequently, the president's conservative rivals faced a particularly complex challenge. They feared a nuclear deal with terms that would (in their estimation) undermine the regime as a whole and, at the same time, empower Rouhani's pragmatist faction by virtue of their achieving a popular agreement. Complete failure of the negotiations would likewise threaten the se-

curity of the regime and all factions; quick success even with the most favorable of terms would benefit pragmatist-reformists at the expense of the
conservatives. The question for both sides was how to strike the right balance between regime security and factional interests.

The conservatives were concerned that the nuclear agreement would undermine the regime by failing to recognize Iran's enrichment rights while
locking Tehran into a framework that would tie the removal of sanctions to
other issues such as human rights, terrorism, and, eventually, regime change.
In a much-misunderstood speech, Khamenei pointed out, "I am not optimistic about the negotiations and they will not lead anywhere, but I do not
oppose [them] either."[32] In Washington, many pundits interpreted this
statement as a cautious effort to back Rouhani while appeasing the skeptical ultraconservatives. However, Khamenei was expressing a deep-seated
concern built up through decades of interactions with the United States and
by observing the fates of other leaders who had negotiated with Washington,
from Mikhail Gorbachev to Muammar Qaddafi. Even if the talks succeeded,
Khamenei predicted, the sanctions against Iran would not be removed.
Rather, concessions would lead to more vulnerability. In Khamenei's view, the
nuclear challenge was only a pretext for the United States to put pressure
on Iran to pursue regime change.

Additionally, the conservatives worried that Rouhani's potential success
in sealing the nuclear deal would vindicate his pragmatic discourse and thus
further expand his constituency on both the elite and popular levels. Some
even accused the Rouhani and Obama administrations of collaborating
against the institution of *Velayat-e Faqih*. In this context, a public acknowledgment by the United States that the negotiations could lead to limited enrichment in Iran did not appease the conservatives; rather, it made them more
paranoid. After much effort to bury the U.S. statement, which was widely celebrated by the pragmatists, ultraconservative commentators close to the
Supreme Leader concluded that the United States was playing a sophisticated
game to engineer Iran's domestic political landscape two years before two
critically important elections: those of the parliament and of the Assembly
of Experts, the latter of which would choose the next Supreme Leader. In
other words, these ultraconservatives claimed that the nuclear negotiations
were specifically geared toward bolstering the pragmatists' domestic position, bringing the "liberal" reformists back in, and eventually fomenting
regime change through a soft revolution.

Nevertheless, Khamenei was careful not to declare the talks dead yet. In the same speech, he reportedly made a statement that was quickly removed from his official website: "As you saw, [the negotiations] did not lead anywhere." BBC Persian took a screenshot of that line on Khamenei's official website before it was taken out of the transcript, audio, and video versions of the speech.[33] If Khamenei had indeed said and then retracted these words, it could be yet more evidence that Khamenei was impatiently waiting for the talks to stall to prove his foresight. Still, for now, the Guardian Jurist carefully provided the negotiators enough time, support, and space so that if they failed, they would have no excuse other than their misguided trust of the mischievous Americans. For him, the best outcome would be a limited success that could be framed as an utter failure: success in the sense that the negotiations had forced the P5+1 to gradually recognize Iran's right to enrich uranium while removing some of the financial and energy-related sanctions, but failure in the sense that Rouhani could still be blamed for making too many concessions on the nuclear issue without leading to the lifting of all sanctions and other forms of U.S. pressure.

In April 2015, Iranian nuclear negotiators finally reached a tentative agreement with the P5+1 in Lausanne, Switzerland.[34] The conservatives adopted a strategy to deal with Rouhani's post-agreement popularity by encouraging a public debate to "educate" the elites on the nuclear deal's flaws. In a restless country where an election could split the elites and turn into an opposition movement, where a pop singer's death could spontaneously attract large crowds,[35] and where even a preliminary nuclear agreement that might signal a possible end to some sanctions could start an impromptu street party,[36] a final nuclear agreement, or lack thereof, could dangerously polarize both the society and the polity while fomenting instability. As a senior conservative cleric warned, "the product of the negotiations should not be a polarized society."[37] Many Iranians from all walks of life anticipated a different outlook after the final deal, from better laundry detergent and more advanced medical technology to easier access to U.S. and European visas and even swift social and political liberalization. Popular sentiments were perhaps best captured by the jokes that emerged soon after Lausanne, including this one: "What kind of deal is this?! I just saw two mullahs in the street [the clerics are still in charge]!"[38]

Under these circumstances and given the ongoing jubilation in Iran, accepting the deal might have weakened the regime externally, but rejecting it could have led to internal unrest. Consequently, maintaining societal and political cohesion superseded the nuclear negotiations, regardless of outcome. This unity could be achieved and fortified by continuing an orchestrated public discourse that managed popular expectations and revealed to the nation the extent of U.S. and European betrayal of Iranian dreams. In his first reaction to the April 2015 Lausanne framework, Khamenei urged the authorities to invite criticism and enlighten "the people, particularly the elites," about next steps.[39] His invitation's goal was to ensure that the negotiations maintained the conservative elites' cohesion and the internal stability of the regime. Khamenei pressed the Rouhani administration not to sideline the opponents of the deal but rather to cultivate a debate to inform the elites of the potential defects in the final agreement. This would either guarantee a "good" deal or ensure a united country in the case of a failed deal. Additionally, this would give more credit to the conservatives for "helping" the pragmatists secure a better deal and assist the former in avoiding blame if the deal failed to materialize. Ironically, both the regime and the conservatives within it would benefit from an open national debate on the country's most challenging issue, so the calculation went.

As usual, the conservative media was ahead of the leadership's public pronouncements. Since the beginning of negotiations in 2013, and particularly after Lausanne, conservative commentators and nuclear experts had been analyzing the declarations, statements, interviews, and fact sheets from all parties involved to reveal their discrepancies and the Western treachery behind them. They brought English dictionaries and compared these texts word by word to show that the "suspension of sanctions" indeed meant "suspension," not "termination" as Iran's foreign minister, Mohammad Javad Zarif, claimed. Critics pointed to the heated Iran debate in Washington, particularly on Capitol Hill, to demonstrate that the nuclear deal would never reduce U.S. pressure on the Islamic Republic. Zarif struggled to defend the preliminary agreement without divulging the details and resisted the call by 213 out of 290 members of parliament to release the "Iranian fact sheet."[40]

The final agreement could plausibly include elements absent in the Lausanne framework. For instance, the previous Joint Plan of Action (JPOA) signed by Iran and the P5+1 in November 2013 did not explicitly recognize Iran's right to enrich uranium. U.S. officials, including President Obama, stressed that the JPOA did not "grant Iran a right to enrich."[41] Even Khamenei reportedly expressed doubts about Rouhani's and Zarif's claims: "I am a jurist myself. I have read this [JPOA] text three times and I still do not see the right to enrich uranium coming out of it."[42] However, now both the Lausanne framework and even the U.S. fact sheet practically recognized Iran's enrichment program, but under extraordinary constraints and intrusive inspections. In commentaries and televised debates, the conservatives blamed Zarif for not properly capitalizing on Iran's regional ascension and "success" in Iraq, Syria, Lebanon, and Yemen. "I wish the nuclear negotiation room had one window: a window that would open to Sana'a, Beirut, Damascus, and Baghdad," lamented the conservative commentator and former nuclear negotiator under Ahmadinejad, Mehdi Mohammadi.[43] Mohammadi insisted that only 13 percent of all nuclear-related sanctions would be *suspended*, not even removed, all of which could be reimposed at any time under murky interpretations, devious mechanisms, and ceaseless accusations of Iranian violations of the deal. Moreover, Iran would lose 98 percent of its 12,000-kilogram stockpile of enriched uranium and cut down two-thirds of its nearly twenty thousand centrifuges, leaving only "enough to make carrot juice."[44] Additionally, under an unusual snapback provision, Iran's Russian and Chinese partners in the UN Security Council could not use their veto power to block the return of sanctions. The deal was so devastating, claimed a conservative member of the Iranian parliament, that even Ali Akbar Salehi, the head of Iran's atomic agency who had participated in the negotiations with the P5+1, asked others to "pray" for its collapse.[45] But what was worse, from their standpoint, was that the scope of the agreement far exceeded Iran's nuclear program. They warned that the final agreement, the Joint Comprehensive Plan of Action (JCPOA), and UN Security Council Resolution 2231, which endorsed the agreement, had all gone "kilometers beyond the Additional Protocol and opened a monitoring umbrella over Iran whose outcome will be to control all national security-related scientific, research, and development activities."[46] Putting the pragmatists in a defensive position, these critics even argued that it was better to give up the entire enrichment program than to let Western spies penetrate the country in the name of nuclear inspections. Mohammadi surmised that the actual objective of the deal was not to ensure that Iran's nuclear program remained peaceful but rather, to ensure the "long-term strategic containment" of the country.

According to this narrative, the United States was now moving to further weaken Iran's conventional military capability by imposing bans on arms imports and ballistic missiles.[47] Meanwhile, Washington was strengthening its presence in the Persian Gulf and promising even more modern advanced weapons to its Arab and Israeli allies, all of whom already enjoyed the American security umbrella. *Kayhan* summarized the deal in a headline: "The Vienna Agreement Is a Shot Aimed at Iran's Security."[48] Its Khamenei-appointed managing editor declared that the accord's final objective was to overthrow the Iranian government.[49] In the end, however, implementation of the deal began on January 16, 2016.

The Pragmatists' American and the Conservatives' Russian Turns

With the implementation of the nuclear agreement, the two factions' rivalry shifted once again to their orientation toward the United States. Iran's pragmatists had long pressed for their country to follow what they called the "China model": liberalizing the economy and opening up diplomatically to the United States while constricting a political space. The conservatives instead came to favor a "Russia model": securitizing the state and the economy and pursuing anti-Americanism to prevent a U.S.-supported regime change.[50] Iranian conservatives feared that pragmatists and reformists would now build on their foreign policy success to press for improved relations with the United States. They were concerned that this could eventually undermine the institution of *Velayat-e Faqih*, the IRGC, the Guardian Council, and other conservative organizations that fed off of anti-Americanism. A quarter of a century earlier, then-president Rafsanjani had pursued a rapprochement before newly appointed Supreme Leader Khamenei sidelined him. Presidents Khatami and even Ahmadinejad entertained the same idea in the late 1990s and 2000s. Both were also silenced and eventually settled for better relations with Europe, China, and Russia. In 2002, to the dismay of Iran's conservatives, a public poll revealed that the majority of Iranians backed normalizing ties with the United States.[51] Interestingly, the controversial poll was conducted by Abbas Abdi, one of the leaders of the radical students who seized the U.S. embassy in 1979. On November 4, 2002, on the twenty-third anniversary of the hostage crisis, Abdi was arrested for spying for the United States. Each time the issue was revisited, the pull became stronger as these elected leaders became aware of the potential of this unexploited and yet dangerous reservoir for leverage against the parallel state.

Ironically, the same internal political dynamic that led to the seizure of the U.S. embassy in Tehran thirty-five years before was now pushing the Islamist government toward a rapprochement with the reluctant United States. Just as the radical political elites had instrumentally used widespread anti-Americanism to consolidate their position after the 1979 revolution, a coalition of reformists, pragmatists, and moderate conservatives now cautiously hoped to capitalize on pro-American sentiments to weaken their ultraconservative rivals. After winning a surprising election in June 2013, Iran's pragmatic president Hassan Rouhani demonstrated his plan to go beyond Europe, China, and Russia. Too weak or too invested in the animosity between Iran and the United States, these "little satans" could neither replace nor serve as a bridge to Washington. It was time to talk directly with the "Great Satan," or the "Village Chief," as some argued. Riding the wave of his popular support, Rouhani moved quickly. His "Prudence and Hope" government took an audacious British turn to release the country from what he perceived to be a de facto network of hawks in Tehran and Washington. Within weeks following his election, Britain and Iran announced their plan to reestablish direct diplomatic ties, which had been severed after ultraconservative vigilantes stormed the British embassy in November 2011. Counting on the "special relationship" between Washington and London, Iranian lawmakers formed a parliamentary friendship group with Britain and, perhaps naively, hoped to eventually upgrade it to a parliamentary friendship group with the U.S. Congress. In September 2013, Foreign Minister Zarif met with his British counterpart, William Hague, and days later, Rouhani and Obama spoke on the phone to mark the first ever direct communication between the leaders of the United States and the Islamic Republic. The popular excitement in Iran (with the exception of conservative circles) did not end even after Khamenei called Rouhani's action "inappropriate."[52] The conservative establishment slowed Rouhani's overtures, but it failed to reverse them. Khamenei repeatedly warned against "putting make-up on the United States." Opposition to this line of thought among pragmatists, including former president Rafsanjani, was unprecedented. Rafsanjani explicitly said that the time was long overdue to put an end to anti-Americanism, and he claimed that even Iran's first Leader, Khomeini, was in favor of ending "Death to America" slogans.[53]

Playing along with much of the public's optimism about the nuclear agreement, Rouhani maintained that the deal was the first step to better relations with the international community. This was a calculated move to link the breakthrough in the negotiations to his 2013 election and sustain the support of the elites and public. More importantly, he hoped that this new tone would induce flexibility with regard to Iran's terms of the agreement in return for more substantial long-term gains. Hamid Aboutalebi—a political adviser to Rouhani who was allegedly involved in the seizure of the U.S. embassy in 1979—wrote unmistakably on Twitter that there was a bigger prize behind the nuclear negotiations: "The interaction between Iran and the U.S. is more valuable than the nuclear issue. We should not let it pass easily."[54] The pragmatists and their allies hoped to bring major American companies to Iran's thirsty eighty-million-strong market, which would drastically boost their popular support and weaken the conservative establishment.

But these actors were aware that their political competitors had long mastered the game of the instrumental use of foreign policy issues. The conservative head of the Guardian Council, Ayatollah Jannati, warned that the "seditionists" were plotting to turn a possible victory in the nuclear negotiations into an electoral success in 2016, when the fate of the Majles and the Assembly of Experts would be decided. Additionally, the conservative establishment turned toward Russia to compensate for its rival's pragmatic[55] and Anglo-American[56] turns. After the nuclear deal, rarely a week passed without the two countries announcing a long-term joint adventure in the sea, on land, or in space.[57] The IRGC forged an unparalleled partnership with the Kremlin in Iran's backyard in Syria while rapidly expanding a wide range of cooperative security, financial, and communication activities with Moscow.[58]

Concerned that the fall of the Assad regime in Syria would weaken both the Iranian regime as a whole and the IRGC's position in Iran's internal balance of power, Khamenei turned to Russia for help in Syria. The Quds Force commander, Qasem Suleimani, made a secret trip to Moscow in June 2015 to coordinate a new military operation with President Vladimir Putin.[59] Iran contributed its ideological might, deep intelligence, and Shi'a foot soldiers; Russia, its advanced military airpower. Putin had already worked with Iran to mediate a deal with Assad to dismantle Syria's chemical arsenals. That critical move in 2013 prevented U.S. military action against Damascus at the time and silenced Iranian pragmatists' calls for a compromise in Syria. Nevertheless, Russia had avoided direct involvement in Syria, even while Iran drastically stepped up its military presence there after the chemical agreement.

But now that the nuclear agreement was all but concluded, Khamenei and Putin seemed ready to jointly double down in support of Assad. The Kremlin may have grasped the internal dynamics in Iran and been concerned—as were Khamenei, the Arab monarchies, and Israel's Benjamin Netanyahu—perhaps prematurely, that Iran's Rouhani administration was ripe for a move toward the United States. To Khamenei, Putin was now a more reliable partner than ever after years of failed experiences with the United States. Both shared the same threat from "U.S.-initiated soft revolutions" at home. Moreover, Putin's anti-American policies were backed by reportedly solid approval ratings, which his new involvement in Syria only heightened. By contrast, Khamenei was struggling with a population that as late as 2013 voted overwhelmingly for a candidate that ran on a platform of cooperation on international issues rather than confrontation with the United States.

Iran's upcoming parliamentary and Assembly of Experts elections made matters worse for both Khamenei and the IRGC. The population seemed poised to reward Rouhani for the nuclear agreement despite increasing economic problems largely due to chronic mismanagement and corruption. All of this, combined with the diverging objectives of and historical mutual distrust between Tehran and Moscow, made Iran's turn to Russia more fragile. But if Putin's partnership in Damascus could help Khamenei maintain the current balance of power in Tehran in the short term, the conservatives could engineer the return of anti-Americanism to Iran in the long term. Just as the Russian population was disenchanted with the United States after the collapse of the Soviet Union, it was possible that the Iranian population, particularly the youth, would feel betrayed by the United States after the nuclear deal. Or so Khamenei hoped. His orders to test-fire ballistic missiles (with anti-Israeli slogans written on them) immediately after the nuclear agreement would further project an irrational image of the Guardian Jurist and invite more pressures and sanctions. With the U.S Congress preparing the next generation of anti-Iran bills and the Obama and subsequent Trump administrations arming Tehran's regional rivals, Khamenei anticipated that both elites and the population would eventually come to appreciate his anti-American "prudence."[60] Indeed, some polls suggested that the Iranian population became more skeptical toward the United States after implementation of the nuclear agreement began.[61]

For a regime that had come to power and remained there through the strategic development and deployment of ideological narratives, a renewed sense of anti-Americanism mixed with nationalism would be a rejuvenating elixir. With an anti-American population similar to that of the 1970s and

1980s, Khamenei could be an even more influential and powerful leader in the region than he would have been with even the most sophisticated of nuclear arsenals.

The 2016 Majles Elections

In the run-up to the February 26, 2016, parliamentary and Assembly of Experts elections, Khamenei's official website published his "special election ordinances," declaring voting a religious obligation.[62] The ordinances superseded traditional religious fatwas by stating that a woman did not need her husband's permission to leave home to vote. He also reiterated his appeal during the 2013 presidential election, asking even those who "don't believe in the system" to vote. Comparing the current stability in Iran to the bloody chaos in the post–Arab Spring region, Khamenei claimed that the *Velayat-e Faqih* system was at least providing the citizens with "security" in the war-torn Middle East. He was later forced to clarify—in response to the Guardian Council's mass disqualifications of the reformists—that what he meant was that those who did not believe in the system could only vote, but not run for an office.[63] State-controlled television channels aired nationalistic songs encouraging the people to vote while showing documentaries about the intelligence ministry's successful counter-terrorism efforts. Iranian officials claimed repeatedly that if the IRGC did not fight in Damascus, it would be fighting in Tehran.[64] This was part of a larger public relations campaign to frame the IRGC's involvement in Syria against ISIS as a preemptive national security strategy.

The reformists and pragmatists adopted a different strategy. Rafsanjani, Rouhani, and Khatami pushed Khamenei to accept a set of internal policy compromises they called "JCPOA 2.0."[65] They argued that although Iran had made painful concessions regarding the nuclear program, the agreement paved the way for the country to rejoin the international community. They insisted that the model that had led to a compromise on the nuclear issue externally could now lead to internal changes to bring about a factional reconciliation through a relatively free and fair election. Their goal was to remove the sharp edge of the Guardian Council's vetting knife.

Consequently, the same reformist-pragmatist coalition that had helped Rouhani win in 2013 came to work again. The reformists allied with the pragmatists, claiming that they did not have enough candidates because the Guardian Council had disqualified more than 90 percent of their members. Hassan Khomeini, a grandson of the founding father of the Islamic Republic, was among those disqualified candidates. He later said he had announced his candidacy knowing he would be barred from running.[66] Reminiscent of Rafsanjani's surprising disqualification in 2013, this was the coalition's strategy to impose a costly measure on the Guardian Council and thus polarize the election and further deepen the crack within the conservatives. Referring to the potential consequences of Hassan Khomeini's disqualification, Rafsanjani, too, stated that it was his initial candidacy in 2013 that had helped his protégé, the "less known" Rouhani, to win. Rafsanjani, Khatami, and Rouhani backed a joint "List of Hope." The list's names showed that the coalition's objective was not so much to win as to block the ultraconservatives from winning. Rouhani acknowledged the electorate's frustration by comparing voting to shopping: "Sometimes you don't find the ideal clothes for your children at the store. Nevertheless, you buy the clothes that are not your ideal just to prevent your child from catching a cold."[67]

Although he was banned from appearing on the media, Khatami posted a video from his virtual house arrest and appealed to the people to vote for "every single person on the two lists [List of Hope] for the Majles and the Assembly of Experts."[68] The video went viral on social media. Khatami, who had run on a civil society platform in 1997, was now backing a list that included merciless judges of military and revolutionary tribunals from the 1980s. In a letter from prison, a political activist described her pain in casting her votes for Khatami's lists.[69] Yet millions such as her responded to Khatami's call and delivered a historic victory, particularly in Tehran.

The popular response was astounding to all sides, including to the reformists. It was a test of popularity for Rafsanjani, Khatami, and Rouhani and a proxy election for Khamenei. The winners of Tehran's thirty seats in the Majles were the thirty candidates on the List of Hope. Mohammad Reza Aref, Khatami's vice president (2001–2005), won the majority of the votes in the capital. Similarly, the same coalition in Tehran won fifteen of the sixteen seats in the Assembly of Experts.[70] Rafsanjani and Rouhani, themselves candidates, came out as the first and third winners, respectively. Ayatollah Jannati, the head of the Guardian Council, the body that disqualified the vast majority of the reformists, barely won the sixteenth seat. Behind him, defeated, was the head of the Assembly of Experts, Ayatollah Mohammad Yazdi. Ultraconservative Ayatollah Mesbah-Yazdi was vanquished, too. Khamenei himself put aside his supposed impartiality and publicly described the defeat of Yazdi and Mesbah-Yazdi as "damag[ing]" to the system.[71]

The next day, Rafsanjani tweeted a sarcastic message claiming that Mesbah-Yazdi was a "ladder" through which the "deviant" Ahmadinejad had ascended to power in 2005.[72] Two days later, Mesbah-Yazdi unleashed verbal attacks against Rafsanjani's ally, President Rouhani, and the recent nuclear agreement without mentioning the latter's name. During a meeting at Jalili's office, Mesbah-Yazdi told the former presidential candidate and nuclear negotiator under Ahmadinejad, "Someone is ready to surrender seventy to eighty million people of his own country to an enemy in order to sit on this seat a few more days. What is more denigrating than this?"[73] Mesbah-Yazdi implied that Rouhani and his coalition had compromised the country's nuclear program to lift sanctions in order to win the elections. Behind these ceaseless, vicious accusations, there was a clear understanding that the recent elections were in fact a referendum on *Velayat-e Faqih*. An ultraconservative cleric lamented that the elections were like scissors that the disloyal people used on cardboard to cut around the Supreme Leader to take his allies out.[74] The particular concern was that the electoral outcome could influence the dynamics within the Assembly of Experts and backroom dealings to select Khamenei's successor after his death. At the time of the elections, he was seventy-six and rumored to have prostate cancer.

The 2017 Presidential Election and the Turn to Persian Nationalism

The stunning performance of the "moderate" coalition in the 2016 parliamentary and Assembly of Experts elections, preceded by the 2013 presidential election, revealed the emergence of a powerful new force.[75] The victors of these elections were a strong centrist coalition of pragmatists, reformists, and moderate conservatives; it aimed to narrow the ideological spectrum in Iran at the expense of both democracy and Islamism.[76] Headed by Rafsanjani and Rouhani, this coalition had been three decades in the making. In this final section of the final chapter, a recap of earlier chapters can help us understand the trajectory of this umbrella alliance and its ideational consequences.

As described throughout the book, Iranian Islamists split into the radical left and the conservative right after removing communist and nationalist rivals in the wake of the 1979 revolution. Khomeini struck a balance between the two Islamist factions until his 1989 death unleashed a vicious rivalry for power. Rafsanjani seized the opportunity and teamed up first with the conservative right against the radical left, but in 1997 shifted allegiances and partnered with the left against the right. The first alliance supported Khamenei's transition from a weak president to a weak Supreme Leader and Rafsanjani's from a powerful speaker of the Majles to a powerful president, both thanks to the recent constitutional amendments. The balance of power between the two figures, however, reversed, and they fell out in the mid-1990s over various domestic and foreign policy issues, culminating in Khamenei's blocking of Rafsanjani's efforts to change the constitution to allow a third term as president. To Khamenei's dismay, Rafsanjani then threw his political machinery behind the former radical left, now calling themselves "reformists," helping Mohammad Khatami secure the presidency in 1997.

In the following two decades, however, both left and right ensured that Rafsanjani paid a price for his treachery to his alliances. During a brief, more liberal period, the radical wing of the reformist camp accused him of masterminding the killings of dissidents and pushed him out of the parliamentary race in 2000. With Rafsanjani out of the picture, Khamenei easily ousted the divided reformists. Soon after, it was the radical wing of the conservatives, led by Ahmadinejad and blessed by Khamenei, that defeated Rafsanjani in the 2005 presidential race. Ahmadinejad's controversial reelection in 2009 and the bloody Green Movement brought Iran's political actors to a deadlock. The conservative establishment had the hard power but suffered from a lack of legitimacy, while the reformists had popular support with little access to the state.

Taking advantage of the deep fissures within each camp, Rafsanjani gradually reemerged as a political player by bringing the "moderate" side of each faction into a new coalition. But that required ideological concessions. The reformists downgraded their democratic and human rights priorities, while the moderate conservatives moved away from their anti-American and overtly Islamist rhetoric. Both inched closer to Rafsanjani's economic development and pragmatic foreign policy models. Reformists adamantly remained unified behind Rouhani and Rafsanjani by lowering their democratic demands. That even a moderate conservative such as Ali Larijani, speaker of the Majles, ended up on their list and enjoyed their popular support demonstrated how far both sides had moved toward the center. Perhaps the best indication of the durability of this alliance was that the very same reformists who spearheaded the campaign against Rafsanjani and Khamenei in the late 1990s were now calling for absolute restraint from any antagonizing behavior.[77] The Supreme Leader found himself in the position of either continuing to back the losing ultraconservatives or slowly shifting to the center as well. The second option could make him a less powerful leader in a more powerful regime. He preferred not to lose this personal battle to Rafsanjani; nevertheless, the net result could be positive for him.

While this sequence of events, options, and decisions, in the context of tremendous uncertainty, might seem to be consistent with emblematic democratic transition models, it can also be seen as an archetypal authoritarian strategy.[78]

The Islamic Republic owes much of its existence and survival to the clever use of "moderates." It was Khomeini's alliance with nationalist leader Mehdi Bazargan that projected a democratic vision for the upcoming revolution and helped delink the Shah from the United States and Iran's Imperial Army. Bazargan, who became the first prime minister subsequent to the revolution, was also the first moderate casualty after Khomeini turned anti-American in order to outbid his communist nemesis. But the regime began to generate its own moderates in the coming three decades. Each time, these emerging factions clashed with the conservative establishment while projecting a new face and hope, thus helping to resolve the regime's international or internal crises. By now, the regime has lost so many layers to the moderate camp that one wonders which group of Khomeini's disciples represented the real Islamic Republic.

On the one side, there was Khamenei; on the other, there were all of his presidents—except Ahmadinejad, a controversial figure disowned by all parties. The fault line similarly cut through key institutions such as the IRGC, and now reportedly even the Guardian Council.[79] Various members of the latter body expressed frustration with its head, Jannati, and the vetting process. The elections released centripetal forces to mend this internal fissure. Khamenei and his conservative but key minority constituency would have no choice but to come on board—or so Rafsanjani thought.

Similarly, the Iranian electorate saw no option but to vote for the candidates it had, not the candidates it wished for. To manage a restless young population, Rafsanjani and Rouhani came to realize that they must prepare for a major act. They sought to dilute the Islamist core of the state, release it from the self-inflicted anti-American trap, and set it on a nationalist path directed toward the United States. The pragmatists could present their liberalizing measures to the citizens as a bridge toward democracy while framing them for the conservative establishment as an authoritarian delaying tactic.

Rafsanjani's fatal heart attack in January 2017 further galvanized Rouhani's popularity and boosted his momentum in the short term, but it also deprived him of a potent ally in long-term, behind-the-scenes bargaining. Rouhani's landslide reelection (57 percent of the vote) in May 2017 further proved the effectiveness of the coalition's strategy. But more importantly, the election revealed how far the Islamic Republic as a whole had come. As religiously inspired ideologies seemed to have lost their mobilizing power in Iran, its leaders were increasingly adopting and manipulating nationalism as the next ideology of choice. Throughout the presidential campaign, contenders outbid each other in promising to bring glory to the motherland—an act the government previously despised and declared as "un-Islamic." Rouhani stressed "Everybody for Iran" and "Iran Again," while promising freedom from both excessive political and religious restrictions. He warned the voters that his conservative rivals would soon bring back the "executions" and "imprisonments" of the 1980s and separate men and women in the streets, an ironic statement from a national security official and in light of his previous self-declared leading role to force Iranian women to veil after the 1979 revolution.[80] The public's response to Rouhani's rhetoric of fear prompted his main opponent to strenuously deny any extremist plans. To further repudiate the accusation and cast his candidacy in a more moderate light, his main conservative rival—the black-turbaned, former hanging judge of political prisoners, Ibrahim Raisi—met with a controversial underground singer, while his supporters organized street parties with female DJs.[81]

As Raisi struggled to make the elections about economic issues and fixing potholes, he even resorted to playing Iran's pre-revolutionary nationalist anthem at his campaign rallies. At the same time, the Rouhani administration officially recognized the old nationalist anthem, which was banned until recently, as part of Iran's "national heritage."[82] Meanwhile, the state-controlled media closely tied to the office of the Supreme Leader worked to increase voter turnout by airing strongly worded nationalistic songs in the final weeks before the election, along with symbolic images such as the tomb of the ancient Persian king, Cyrus the Great. Calling on the masses to participate in the election, these video songs replaced the religious attributes of epic post-revolutionary scenes (such as those of the Iran–Iraq War) with emotional nationalistic narratives about defending the homeland. This, too, was ironic, as a year earlier, security forces had violently cracked down on chanting crowds around Cyrus's tomb.[83] Images of Cyrus's tomb and other symbols of Persian nationalism became ubiquitous in the official discourse throughout the election season.

The limited references to Islamist ideology in the official discourse during the election season signified the elites' recognition of a massive societal change in which the heyday of Islamism was perhaps over. Although religion was still a factor, the overriding power of religious ideology had receded. The nationalist provisional prime minister, Mehdi Bazargan, once bitterly complained that while he desired "Islam for Iran," Khomeini wanted "Iran for Islam." Four decades later, Khomeini's successors have begun to carefully invoke Persian nationalism.

This gradual turn, however, may put them in a challenging position in two ways. Religion has been a crucial tool of statecraft in post-revolutionary Iran. Khomeini's rise to power was due to his reconceptualization of the state as a monopoly over the legitimate use of religion. Incorporating nationalism may be potentially destabilizing since it might open the polity to secular actors more qualified to appropriate the discourse. Second, Iran owes much of its regional power to its ideological appeal. Adopting Persian nationalism could undermine Tehran's ties with its traditional allies in the region. Iran's Arab friends have already faced difficulties justifying their relations with the non-Arab Iran. Accused of being the pawn of the Persians, Hezbollah leader Hassan Nasrallah has pointed to Iran's Supreme Leader's black turban (signifying his lineage to the Prophet Mohammad) to argue that Tehran's leaders are in fact Arabs.[84] But despite these internal and external challenges, all political factions seemed to be cautiously absorbing nationalism into their religious framework. This was particularly important, given the expectation that the Islamic Republic is preparing for the selection of its next Supreme Leader. Both Rouhani and Raisi are seen as aspiring candidates to succeed Khamenei.

Rafsanjani's sudden death added more uncertainty to the future of *Velayat-e Faqih*. He had pushed to "democratize" the country's ultimate institution of religious and political authority by restricting it to a ten-year term limit or turning it into a council of jurists. He and other Islamist clerics had discussed both of these proposals immediately after Khomeini's death, too, but quickly concluded that appointing a supreme figure with no term limit would better serve the orderly transition to the post-Khomeini era. Rafsanjani's later proposal fell on the IRGC's deaf ears.[85] The IRGC and ultraconservative clerics intend to engineer their own smooth power transition to the post-Khamenei era by searching for a figure who meets their political criteria. The reformists and pragmatists can no longer hope that Rafsanjani will emerge from his shadows, reveal one of his secret but handy quotes from Khomeini, and keep the country in the "center." In the absence of such a strong power broker, the post-Rafsanjani era further obscures the direction of the country after Khamenei.

Velayat-e Faqih remains at the center of this reformist-pragmatist-conservative battle. The conservatives continue to define and deploy it in an absolute sense to maintain their monopoly over the use of religion. This protects three critical institutions: the office of the Guardian Jurist, the Guardian Council, and the IRGC. The pragmatist-reformist coalition, on the other hand, struggles to promote a limited form of religious pluralism and diffuse the power of *Velayat-e Faqih* from the parallel state institutions to the state. No one can afford to eliminate the nominal power of this ultimate religious authority altogether, for it could open the door for new political actors who might seize control of the state from all of the factions.

Conclusion

THE ISLAMIC Republic of Iran never fails to bemuse ordinary spectators, academic observers, policymakers, and even its own leaders. It has profoundly changed and yet remained constant; modern ideas are attributed to ancient personalities and ancient ideas are recycled by contemporary characters. The cast of political elites has hardly changed in four decades, but its ideological discourses are relentlessly altered. Rarely has a polity seen the infusion of such fluid ideas into the veins of such selfsame bodies. This makes Iran an ideal case with which to study the role of ideas in general and religious ideas in particular. In this book, I have brought in a wide array of debates, narratives, and events to explain the contingent nature of Islamist ideology. I have argued that Ayatollah Khomeini's *Velayat-e Faqih* (Guardianship of the Jurist) was not a fixed theological creed but a malleable, yet powerful, doctrine highly susceptible to the fickle circumstances of specific political contexts. Khomeini and his successors continually and strategically calibrated it to meet perceived threats and tap into emerging opportunities. I have also dissected Iran's seemingly monolithic Islamist clergy, identifying the shifting factions and alliances and tracing the various turns of their religious discourses. This book has demonstrated the critical importance of factional threat perceptions in explaining both the malleability and stickiness of religious doctrines, particularly the evolution of—and contest over—contradictory interpretations of Islam. As stated at the beginning of the book: there is no such thing as "political Islam." There is, however, a *politics* of

Islam—the complex, variable appropriation and application of a rich, religious tradition to serve the ever-changing political imperatives of those who vie for power.

Empirical Findings

As demonstrated in the preceding chapters, the religious doctrines promoted by the Islamists were not merely a reflection of their "moral system" or fixed determinants of their political actions. Rather, these doctrines were developed and deployed in response to the shifting political landscape at a given time.

Far from being Khomeini's ally, the Shi'a clerical establishment was at best lukewarm—but more often aggravated or even antagonistic—with regard to his religious and political positions. Nevertheless, they could not help but support his leap to the center of the political stage occupied by competing communist, nationalist, and Islamist opposition groups. His constitutionalist approach against the "un-Islamic" monarch throughout the 1960s and 1970s compelled the orthodox clergy to join his "limited" political movement, attracted well-established urban religious and nationalist opposition groups, neutralized the army, and cut the Shah's umbilical cord with the United States.

The post-revolutionary Islamist-nationalist coalition led by Khomeini faced challenges from the Marxist Left and ethnic minorities. Additionally, Khomeini's own Islamist deputies were in fierce competition with the nationalists within the regime. Each new challenge required a novel discourse. The Islamists' quick turn to implementing "shari'a laws" was a consolidation strategy aimed at increasing the cost of clerical opposition to the new Islamic Republic. The Shi'a establishment would find it difficult to dispute a regime that had removed the immoral Shah and revived the millennia-old "divine" rules, such as banning alcohol consumption and forcing women to veil. But the clergy's opposition to Khomeini's instrumental use of religion combined with the intense Islamist-nationalist competition ended the utility of his "moderate" constitutionalism. The sudden and quiet revival and institutionalization of Khomeini's doctrine of *Velayat-e Faqih* further ensured a monopoly over the use of religion. It stifled rising religious and political dissent in an uncertain and fast-paced political environment. *Velayat-e Faqih* blocked a potential coalition of orthodox clergy and nationalists that might have chipped away at the Islamists' religious—and thus political—power, particularly after Khomeini's death.

The book's empirical contribution also includes unearthing the communist root of the hostage crisis in Iran, revealing that Khomeini's anti-American turn was a response to the rapid expansion of leftist groups. His alliance with the U.S.-friendly nationalists, a critical asset before the revolution, had become a liability after the revolution. The Islamist students' occupation of the U.S. embassy established Khomeini's anti-imperialist credibility and disarmed the Left. Although the confrontation with the United States created an international threat to the new regime, it addressed the more immediate leftist menace to the Islamists.

The Iran–Iraq War, too, was influenced by Tehran's factional politics and the rivalry between the IRGC and the regular army. Saddam Hussein's invasion of Iran helped the Islamists expand the IRGC at the expense of the army, further isolate the nationalists, and eliminate Khomeini's archenemy, Ayatollah Shariatmadari. But when a rivalry between the Islamists' political leadership and its IRGC arm subsequently evolved, it was no longer useful for the war to drag on. In each phase of the conflict, a corresponding religious narrative (e.g., the battle of Karbala or the Prophet's peace treaty with the infidels) was articulated to facilitate escalating or terminating the war.

The addition of "Absolute" to *Velayat-e Faqih* allowed the Guardian Jurist to undertake government activities that would otherwise be considered "un-Islamic" and declare them fully consistent with the faith. So doing helped to preserve the *Islamic* state, a paramount duty suddenly placed above implementing other "secondary" *shari'a* laws.

The ideological compromises Islamists made to capture the state have prompted social scientists, including the French scholar Oliver Roy, to declare the "failure of political Islam" in creating a just society.[1] However, if we consider controlling the state—rather than perfecting human beings—as the Islamists' more immediate goal, "political Islam" has had a successful track record in Iran since 1979. In the Islamists' "worldview," the two are not mutually exclusive; Khomeini himself declared that without an Islamic government, no moral society could exist.

System effects[2] have continued to shape actors' preferences in the post-Khomeini era. The success of the Islamist right in removing the Islamist left from power—indeed from any meaningful role in the government—led to the reversal of the two factions' earlier positions. The right adopted anti-Americanism and resisted liberal economic policies, while the left advocated a rapprochement with the United States and opposed state control of the economy. The mutual attacks continued, except that they exchanged each other's "American Islam" and "communist Islam" accusations. They each developed readings of *Velayat-e Faqih* to match their specific objectives. The Islamist right's incumbency required preserving clerical sovereignty as well as keeping religious authority under its custody, while the Islamist left's marginalization necessitated reliance on popular sovereignty and religious pluralism. For the right, "Islamic democracy" ordained a divinely appointed system with popular *backing*. For the left, it implied popular *legitimacy* for an elected system run by Muslims. The adjective "Islamic" was simultaneously used by the incumbent right to *reduce* the cost of repressing their rivals and by the opposition left to *increase* the cost of that same repression.

Additional Empirical Reflections

Popular preferences play a critical role in the factional causes and ideational consequences of Iranian politics. Elites are manipulated by the very masses they are striving to manipulate; competing factions tap into existing popular preferences to gain advantages against each other. Sometimes strong public sentiments can limit political options. In the early days of the revolution, the prevalence of anti-American sentiments in Iran and fierce competition with the communists hindered Khomeini's secret communications with the United States. It brought him to an unwanted confrontation with Washington that culminated in the hostage crisis. Similarly, the decline of anti-Americanism in recent decades in Iran has placed the ruling conservatives in a new dilemma. If the Islamists in 1979 were struggling to maintain cordial relations with Washington in a highly anti-American climate, they are now hard-pressed to sustain animosity with the United States in a relatively pro-American context. If the communist Left's strategy was to bring down Khomeini's Islamists in an anti-American outbidding contest, the reformists' strategy is to win the elected bodies from Khamenei's conservatives through a subtle pro-American campaign.

Unlike Khomeini, who successfully prevailed in the anti-American competition with the communist Left, Khamenei fears the gamble of engaging in a pro-American match with the reformists. He views the United States as an existential threat with whom his conservative faction cannot establish normal ties. This is perhaps partly because the U.S. posture toward Iran has threatened the very concept of *Velayat-e Faqih* and its IRGC arm. Since the hostage crisis, U.S. politicians have increasingly outbid each other in taking measures against Iran. This predicament has compelled Khamenei to repeatedly claim that his negative view of the United States is by no means fanaticism or ideological but simply practical. Relations with the United States would not benefit the Iranian nation, Khamenei has stressed; otherwise, he claims, he would be the "first" to initiate the rapprochement.[3] By fanning anti-Iranian sentiments in the United States, Tehran's conservatives help derail any possible détente between the two countries—which serves their ends, since it would benefit only the reformists and pragmatists.

Another significant societal change is the declining role of religious authority. Long gone are the days when Iranian rulers and dissidents needed a marja to claim legitimacy and mobilize the masses. The absence of the senior clerics' leadership in Iran's political protests since the 1997 reform movement reveals that the clerics are no longer necessary or sufficient to incite mass uprisings. To be sure, the state's crackdown and co-optation have contributed to the dearth or invisibility of the clergy's dissidence. More importantly, the collective experience of the *Velayat-e Faqih* system may have entailed a learning process for both the opposition elites and society. Three decades after his famous call on the clergy to lead the anti-Shah opposition, Bazargan remorsefully urged the clergy to leave politics and return to their seminaries.[4] He presented a theological argument, made a case for a secular Islam, and called political Islam "Satan's commodity."[5]

That is not to suggest the decline of religion or the rise of anti-clericalism in Iran. Although the quality of people's religiosity may have changed,[6] religion remains a forceful channel through which to communicate with, cooperate with, and confront the Islamist government and its divine Leader. The empathetic voice of dissident clerics, including the late Grand Ayatollah Montazeri, has been an invaluable boost for opposition movements in the past. However, the fact that clerics are no longer a primary medium between the intellectuals and the masses, as they traditionally were, signals a societal turn and the transformation of what German philosopher Jürgen Habermas calls the "lifeworld."[7] The behavior of the Iranian electorate suggests that its votes are based on which candidate shares its preferences rather than whether or not he is a cleric. In recent years, reformist clerics have had more electoral success than Islamist lay figures, as evidenced by Khatami's unparalleled popularity since the 1997 landslide election and Rouhani's victory against his non-cleric conservative rivals in the 2013 and 2017 elections.

In his state-building project, Khomeini did not dissolve—but kept—the "wicked" Western-style state he had inherited from the Shah, and he built parallel institutions around it. For example, the IRGC, the Komiteh, the Revolutionary Courts, and the Guardian Council emerged in parallel with the army, police, judiciary, and parliament, respectively. Thousands of young, ambitious students, many with religious and traditional backgrounds, flooded these new institutions, where they were given weapons and a divine mandate to break the old state's monopoly over the use of force. Khomeini hoped his "Islamic" parallel state would over time replace the secular state as he and his Islamist faction took over the government. However, the end result was the devolution of these shadow institutions into the state structure in the decade that followed his death. The Komiteh militia merged with the police, the Reconstruction Jihad Ministry joined the old Ministry of Agriculture, and the Ministry of Cooperatives dissolved into the Ministry of Labor and Social Welfare. Despite its claims to the contrary, the IRGC was eventually institutionalized as a conventional army with "Western"-inspired hierarchies and doctrines, although it has remained separate from, and above, the regular army.

The Guardianship of the Jurist, once occupied by Khomeini, his son, and a handful of associates, is now anything but a typical Shi'a scholar's office. It has evolved into a complete mini-state shadowing the state with specialized military, foreign policy, intelligence, public relations, and clerical advisers along with other functionaries. Nevertheless, the institution of *Velayat-e Faqih* along with its two extralegal/extrajudicial arms (namely, the IRGC and the Guardian Council) have remained the three bodies most distinct from—and thus above—the state. The conflict between this parallel state and the official state will continue to define much of Iran's factional politics and war of religious narratives.

Broader Theoretical and Policy Implications

Macro-level studies often miss both the domestic sources and ideational consequences of politics. In this book, I have argued that political factions use multiple domestic and international levers to gain power and ensure survival. Security threats on the factional level are distinct from—and can trump—security threats on the state and regime levels. They include threats that undermine a political faction's actual or potential grip on the state's institutions and the regime's extra-state institutions.

A threatened faction will develop, among other things, its own ideological capabilities to ensure survival. Religion is an extraordinarily potent tool in an actor's power arsenal. Factions persistently shape ideas, including religious ideas, to project power. Here, ideas do not constitute interests or identities, but rather they are deliberately developed and deployed to gain political leverage. "Religious" political parties develop theological arguments for policy and ideological shifts so that they can retain their core supporters while creating political space, expanding their reach, and challenging their rivals. Both the incumbent and opposition factions may position themselves internationally to reduce the threat they are facing internally, with the interests of the state coming second. To engage in a macro-level analysis of international events is to miss the domestic origins of foreign policy behavior. Consider Iran's tumultuous relations with the Turkish ruling Justice and Development Party (AKP) in recent years, after decades of friendly ties between the Islamists in Tehran and the Kemalists in Ankara. The AKP's reformist "social" Islam initially generated ideological appeal in the region as well as affinities with the reformists in Iran, thus posing a real threat to Tehran's conservative establishment and its revolutionary Islam. This ideological rivalry contributed to a proxy war in the Syrian conflict.

In their quest for power, religious actors require theological latitude to utilize political opportunities. They seek to capitalize on the "norms" of the political establishment and shape them according to their interests. It is at this stage that ideas matter. Intellectual and jurisprudential circles and debates can be crucial to providing the necessary repertoire of ideas for religious parties. Although political actors cannot control the scope and consequences of their ideological trajectories, they can—for example—become friends or foes of democracy to the extent that democracy is in line with their political objectives. Moderation (or the lack thereof) is an integral component of strategic calculations by religious actors. As I demonstrated in the empirical chapters, behavioral change does not precede ideological change, as many rational choice theorists argue. Religious parties can moderate when they push to open the political process out of self-interest. Conversely, if these parties dominate the establishment, they can turn to more authoritarian readings of religion to limit electoral opportunities for others. (Turkey is a case in point of both scenarios.) Thus, factional politics can pave the way for both moderate and immoderate politics, depending on the political configuration and context. It is institutional political interests that influence religious doctrines, not the other way around.

Real-world events constantly test a narrative's strength and discourse's standing. Elites pursue policies with particular attention to the ideational consequences that each action may bring. Developing nuclear programs, sending monkeys to space, stationing satellites in orbit, testing ballistic missiles, and foreign policy adventures are all examples of costly initiatives carried out by Iran's Islamist government partially to prove to its own people and to others that, despite all social, economic, and political shortcomings, it was able to achieve prominence through "local" ideologies. In other words, disputes over meaning and interpretation often become so critical that elites may seek material power as hard evidence of ideological superiority or to salvage failed ideas. There was a time when Iran would rely on its revolutionary ideology to project power. Today, Iran uses its power to project ideology.

Yet scholarship often ascribes either overpredictive power to religious ideas or is dismissive of them. Some studies of religion approach their cases from a security perspective and search for potential links between adherents of a specific religion and conflict.[8] In this context, religion is a crucial factor (an independent variable) that can help shape worldviews as well as the behaviors of state and nonstate actors. Indeed, this is a microcosm of a larger continuing problem in the coverage and study of the Middle East, the latest example of which is ISIS. Those who declare this group to be "very Islamic"[9] fail to explain its alliance formations, its strategic use of violence, and its instrumental deployment of religion and the media. At the same time, no rationalist can simply dismiss ideology as a mere façade when increasingly violent groups whose actions are saturated with religion have engulfed the region. Religion must be "working" if it is so often used.

*   *   *

This book argued that religious ideas matter, not "all the way down," but *all along*. They are salient, and yet transformable. They empower, not just influence, elites and the masses. Actors' strategic interests shape ideas, which become institutionalized to create political opportunities, reduce threats, and facilitate political action. Ideas are not on the periphery or an accidental outcome. They are at the center of the political battlefield. They are at the service of individual, group, institutional, and state actors, who often disaggregate them, turn them upside down, and add elements from other religions or philosophies. Hand in hand with material factors, ideas are deployed in the combat zone according to the threats that political actors face. If the ideas withstand the clash, they are vindicated. If not, they may be repaired, changed, polished, or completely shelved and replaced. Institutions and intellectual circles arise or are created to produce ideational repertoires for actors. Independent intellectual salons are approached in an attempt to understand what went wrong, to help determine how to bounce back, and to return to the trenches. Actors invoke ideas to mobilize resources, deepen and expand their constituencies, disarm their rivals, aggravate or pacify crises, create new political cleavages, or establish fresh bonds. In short, ideas are part and parcel of the battles of factions, parties, regimes, and states. If we do not see them, it is because we do not look for them. If we do not observe theological changes, it is because we do not inspect the microfoundations of actors' daily interactions. Like a seismologist, we need to record every shockwave that politics sends through religious discourses. We should follow major tectonic shifts all the way to the small aftershocks that religious institutions and ideas experience and absorb. It is only then that we can faithfully account for the role and rope of religion.

Many have been led astray by the Quran:
by clinging to that rope many have fallen into the well.
There is no fault in the rope, O perverse man,
for it was you who had no will to ascend to the top.

—Rumi (1207–1273 A.D.)

Notes

Introduction: The Politics of Islam

1. I use the terms *ideologies, narratives, discourses,* and *rhetoric* interchangeably to mean a set of ideas with an objective whether it comes in the form of written or verbal statements offered formally or informally.
2. Clifford Geertz, " 'The Pinch of Destiny': Religion as Experience, Meaning, Identity, and Power," *Raritan* 18, no. 3 (1999): 7; see also Clifford Geertz, *The Interpretation of Cultures* (New York: Basic Books, 1973).
3. See Robert Jervis, *System Effects: Complexity in Political and Social Life* (Princeton: Princeton University Press, 1999).
4. David D. Laitin, *Identity in Formation: The Russian-Speaking Populations in the Near Abroad* (Ithaca: Cornell University Press, 1998), 24.
5. Quintan Wiktorowicz, "Introduction: Islamic Activism and Social Movement Theory," in *Islamic Activism: A Social Movement Theory Approach,* ed. Quintan Wiktorowicz (Bloomington: Indiana University Press, 2004), 16.
6. I am thankful to Reyko Huang for bringing this to my attention. Also, see Reyko Huang, "Religion, Tactics, and Violent Conflict," paper presented at American Political Science Association Annual Meeting in San Francisco, September 2015.
7. Laurence R. Iannaccone, "Religious Extremism: The Good, the Bad, and the Deadly," *Public Choice* 128, no. 1 (2006): 109–129.
8. See Hamid Dabashi, *Theology of Discontent: The Ideological Foundation of the Islamic Revolution in Iran* (New Brunswick, N.J.: Transaction, 1993), 39–101; Mehrzad Boroujerdi, *Iranian Intellectuals and the West: The Tormented Triumph of Nativism* (Syracuse, N.Y.: Syracuse University Press, 1996), 65–76.
9. See Dabashi, *Theology of Discontent,* 102–146; Boroujerdi, *Iranian Intellectuals and the West,* 105–120.

10. Hossein Bashiriyeh, *The State and Revolution in Iran* (New York: St. Martin's Press, 1984), 53–77.
11. For a critical analysis of the cultural explanations of the Iranian Revolution, see Charles Kurzman, *The Unthinkable Revolution in Iran* (Cambridge, Mass.: Harvard University Press, 2005), 50–76.
12. Henry Precht, "Ayatollah Realpolitik," *Foreign Policy*, no. 70 (Spring 1988): 109–128.
13. Kurzman, *The Unthinkable Revolution in Iran*, 44.
14. On this idea, see Dan Slater, *Ordering Power: Contentious Politics and Authoritarian Leviathans in Southeast Asia* (New York: Cambridge University Press, 2010).
15. Robert D. Putnam, "Diplomacy and Domestic Politics: The Logic of Two-Level Games," *International Organization* 42, no. 3 (1988): 427–460.
16. On the role of the new media in Iran, see Annabelle Sreberny and Gholam Khiabany, eds., *Blogistan: The Internet and Politics in Iran* (London: I.B. Tauris, 2010).
17. Bernard C. Cohen, *The Press and Foreign Policy* (Princeton: Princeton University Press, 1963), 13 (emphasis in original).
18. Recent studies do not view the state and the media as a unitary player but rather as a set of actors who are in a "tug of war" to compete over the formulation of policy. See Ole R. Holsti, *Public Opinion and American Foreign Policy* (Ann Arbor: University of Michigan Press, 1996); Matthew Baum and Philip Potter, "The Relationships Between Mass Media, Public Opinion, and Foreign Policy: Towards a Theoretical Synthesis," *Annual Review of Political Science* 11 (2007): 39–65. Moreover, these studies have demonstrated that even in nondemocracies, the media is a critical tool that both the regime and the opposition employ to shape public opinion; see Roya Akhavan-Majid, "Mass Media Reform in China: Toward a New Analytical Framework," *Gazette* 66, no. 6 (2004): 553–565; Marc Lynch, *Voices of the New Arab Public: Iraq, Al-Jazeera, and Middle East Politics Today* (New York: Columbia University Press, 2006); Marc Lynch, "After Egypt: The Limits and Promise of Online Challenges to the Authoritarian Arab State," *Perspectives on Politics* 9, no. 2 (2011): 301–310.
19. As George and Bennett explain, through process tracing "the researcher examines histories, archival documents, interview transcripts, and other sources to see whether the causal process a theory hypothesizes or implies in a case is in fact evident in the sequence and values of the intervening variables in that case," in Alexander L. George and Andrew Bennett, *Case Studies and Theory Development in the Social Sciences* (Cambridge, Mass.: MIT Press, 2005), 6.
20. Michael Coppedge, *Democratization and Research Methods* (New York: Cambridge University Press, 2012), 118; Barbara Geddes, *Paradigms and Sand Castles: Theory Building and Research Design in Comparative Politics* (Ann Arbor: University of Michigan Press, 2003).

1. The Factional Causes and Religious Consequences of Politics

1. Samuel P. Huntington, "The Clash of Civilizations?," *Foreign Affairs* 72, no. 3 (1993): 22–49; Bernard Lewis, "The Roots of Muslim Rage," *Atlantic Monthly* 266, no. 3

(1990): 47–60; Michael Cook, *Ancient Religions, Modern Politics: The Islamic Case in Comparative Perspective* (Princeton: Princeton University Press, 2014).

2. Stathis N. Kalyvas, *The Rise of Christian Democracy in Europe* (Ithaca: Cornell University Press, 1996); Stathis N. Kalyvas, "Unsecular Politics and Religious Mobilization: Beyond Christian Democracy," in *European Christian Democracy: Historical Legacies and Comparative Perspectives*, ed. Thomas Kselman and Joseph A. Buttigieg (Notre Dame, Ind.: Notre Dame Press, 2003), 293–320; Seyyed Vali Reza Nasr, "The Rise of 'Muslim Democracy,'" *Journal of Democracy* 16, no. 2 (2005): 13–27.

3. Alexander L. George and Andrew Bennett, *Case Studies and Theory Development in the Social Studies* (Cambridge, Mass.: MIT Press, 2005), 17–18. George and Bennett define a "class of events" as "a phenomenon of scientific interest, such as revolutions, types of governmental regimes, kinds of economic systems, or personality types that the investigator chooses to study with the aim of developing theory (or 'generic knowledge') regarding the causes of similarities or differences among instances (cases) of that class of events."

4. Talcott Parsons, "Introduction" in *The Sociology of Religion*, by Max Weber, trans. Ephraim Fischoff (Boston: Beacon Press, 1963), xxix–lxxvii.

5. Mancur Olson, *The Logic of Collective Action* (Cambridge, Mass.: Harvard University Press, 1971 [1965]).

6. Clifford Geertz, *The Interpretation of Cultures* (New York: Basic Books, 1973).

7. Ann Swidler, "Culture in Action: Symbols and Strategies," *American Sociological Review* 51, no. 2 (1986): 273–286.

8. David D. Laitin, *Hegemony and Culture: Politics and Change Among the Yoruba* (Chicago: University of Chicago Press, 1986).

9. Lisa Wedeen, "Conceptualizing Culture: Possibilities for Political Science," *American Political Science Review* 96, no. 4 (2002): 714; see also Lisa Wedeen, *Ambiguities of Domination: Politics, Rhetoric, and Symbols in Contemporary Syria* (Chicago: Chicago University Press, 1999).

10. Sheri Berman, *The Social Democratic Movement: Ideas and Politics in the Making of Interwar Europe* (Cambridge, Mass.: Harvard University Press, 1998) (emphasis in original).

11. Theda Skocpol, *States and Social Revolutions: A Comparative Analysis of France, Russia and China* (Cambridge: Cambridge University Press, 1979).

12. Theda Skocpol, "Rentier State and Shi'a Islam in the Iranian Revolution," *Theory and Society* 11, no. 3 (1982): 275.

13. Daniel Philpott, "Explaining the Political Ambivalence of Religion," *American Political Science Review* 101, no. 3 (2007): 505–525.

14. Monica Duffy Toft, "Getting Religion? The Puzzling Case of Islam and Civil War," *International Security* 31, no. 4 (2007): 97–131.

15. Monica Duffy Toft, "Religion and Civil Wars: Next Steps?," in *Religion and International Relations: A Primer for Research*, Working Group Paper on International Relations and Religion, Mellon Initiative on Religion Across the Disciplines, University of Notre Dame, 142, http://rmellon.nd.edu/assets/101872/religion _and_international_relations_report.pdf.

16. Ibid.

17. See David D. Laitin, *Identity in Formation: The Russian-Speaking Populations in the Near Abroad* (Ithaca: Cornell University Press, 1998).
18. Ibid., 24, n. 39.
19. Occultation is a Shi'a concept that refers to an era during which the messianic figure, the Mahdi, has disappeared from earth.
20. Berman, *The Social Democratic Movement.*
21. See, for example, Ali Mirsepassi, *Political Islam, Iran, and the Enlightenment: Philosophies of Hope and Despair* (Cambridge: Cambridge University Press, 2011); for a constructivist argument applied to the Muslim Brotherhood, see Carrie Wickham, *The Muslim Brotherhood: Evolution of an Islamist Movement* (Princeton: Princeton University Press, 2013).
22. Wickham, *The Muslim Brotherhood.*
23. Berman, *The Social Democratic Movement*, 32–33.
24. James D. Fearon and David D. Laitin, "Violence and the Social Construction of Ethnic Identity," *International Organization* 54, no. 4 (2000): 845–877.
25. Stathis Kalyvas, "Ethnic Defection in Civil War," *Comparative Political Studies* 41, no. 8 (2008): 1046.
26. Kalyvas, *The Rise of Christian Democracy*, 25, 45, 261.
27. Ibid., 262.
28. Guillermo Trejo, *Popular Movements in Autocracies: Religion, Repression, and Indigenous Collective Action in Mexico* (Cambridge: Cambridge University Press, 2012); Karrie J. Koesel, *Religion and Authoritarianism: Cooperation, Conflict, and the Consequences* (Cambridge: Cambridge University Press, 2014); Anthony Gill, *The Political Origins of Religious Liberty* (Cambridge: Cambridge University Press, 2008).
29. Nasr, "The Rise of 'Muslim Democracy,'" 15.
30. Ibid.
31. Jillian Schwedler, *Faith in Moderation: Islamist Parties in Jordan and Yemen* (Cambridge: Cambridge University Press, 2007); see also Stacey Philbrick Yadav, "Understanding 'What Islamists Want': Public Debate and Contestation in Lebanon and Yemen," *Middle East Journal* 64, no. 2 (2010): 199–213.
32. Nathan J. Brown, *When Victory Is Not an Option: Islamist Movements in Arab Politics* (Ithaca: Cornell University Press, 2012); Nathan J. Brown, *Arguing Islam After the Revival of Arab Politics* (New York: Oxford University Press, 2016).
33. Tarek Masoud, *Counting Islam: Religion, Class, and Elections in Egypt* (Cambridge: Cambridge University Press, 2014), 41 (emphasis in original).
34. See Jillian Schwedler, "Can Islamists Become Moderates? Rethinking the Inclusion-Moderation Hypothesis," *World Politics* 63, no. 2 (2011): 347–376; Güneş Murat Tezcür, *Muslim Reformers in Iran and Turkey: The Paradox of Moderation* (Austin: University of Texas Press, 2010); Carolyn M. Warner, "Christian Democracy in Italy: An Alternative Path to Religious Party Moderation," *Party Politics* 19, no. 2 (2013): 256–276; Sumita Pahwa, "Pathways of Islamist Adaptation: The Egyptian Muslim Brothers' Lessons for Inclusion Moderation Theory," *Democratization* 24, no. 6 (2017): 1066–1084, http://dx.doi.org/10.1080/13510347.2016.1273903.
35. For a critical analysis of secularization literature, see Elizabeth Shakman Hurd, *The Politics of Secularism in International Relations* (Princeton: Princeton Univer-

sity Press, 2008); see also Elizabeth Shakman Hurd, *Beyond Religious Freedom: The New Global Politics of Religion* (Princeton: Princeton University Press, 2015).

36. Ali Ansari, "Civilization Identity and Foreign Policy: The Case of Iran," in *The Limits of Culture: Islam and Foreign Policy*, ed. Brenda Shaffer (Cambridge, Mass.: MIT Press, 2006), 241–263.

37. Mahmood Sariolghalam, "Iran in Search of Itself," *Current History* 107, no. 713 (2008): 425.

38. Suzanne Maloney, "Identity and Change in Iran's Foreign Policy," in *Identity and Foreign Policy in the Middle East*, ed. Shibley Telhami and Michael N. Barnett (Ithaca: Cornell University Press, 2002), 114.

39. See Farhad Khosrokhavar, "Neo-conservative Intellectuals in Iran," *Critique: Critical Middle Eastern Studies* 10, no. 19 (2001): 5–30.

40. Bari Weiss, "The Tyrannies Are Doomed," *Wall Street Journal*, April 2, 2011, http://www.wsj.com/articles/SB10001424052748703712504576234601480205330.

41. Homeira Moshirzadeh, "Discursive Foundations of Iran's Nuclear Policy," *Security Dialogue* 38, no. 4 (2007): 521–543.

42. Anoushiravan Ehteshami, "The Foreign Policy of Iran," in *The Foreign Policies of Middle East States*, ed. Raymond A. Hinnebusch and Anoushiravan Ehteshami (Boulder, Colo.: Lynne Rienner, 2002), 283–309.

43. Trita Parsi, *Treacherous Alliance: The Secret Dealings of Israel, Iran, and the United States* (New Haven, Conn.: Yale University Press, 2007).

44. Brenda Shaffer, "The Islamic Republic of Iran: Is It Really?," in *The Limits of Culture: Islam and Foreign Policy*, ed. Brenda Shaffer (Cambridge, Mass.: MIT Press, 2006), 219–239.

45. Stephen M. Walt, *The Origins of Alliances* (Ithaca: Cornell University Press, 1987).

46. F. Gregory Gause III, "Balancing What? Threat Perception and Alliance Choice in the Gulf," *Security Studies* 13, no. 2 (2004): 273–305; see also Curtis R. Ryan, *Inter-Arab Alliances: Regime Security and Jordanian Foreign Policy* (Gainesville: University Press of Florida, 2009).

47. Gause, "Balancing What?," 274.

48. F. Gregory Gause III, *The International Relations of the Persian Gulf* (Cambridge: Cambridge University Press, 2009), 10.

49. Gause, "Balancing What?," 278.

50. Kanchan Chandra, "Introduction," in *Constructivist Theories of Ethnic Politics*, ed. Kanchan Chandra (New York: Oxford University Press, 2012): 1–47; Stathis N. Kalyvas, "Ethnic Defection in Civil War," *Comparative Political Studies* 41, no. 8 (2008): 1043–1068; Reyko Huang, "Religion, Tactics, and Violent Conflict," paper presented at American Political Science Association Annual Meeting in San Francisco, September 2015.

51. Brown, *When Victory Is Not an Option: Islamist Movements in Arab Politics*; Anna Grzymala-Busse, "Why Comparative Politics Should Take Religion (More) Seriously," *Annual Review of Political Science* 15 (2012): 421–442; see also A. Kadir Yildirim, *Muslim Democratic Parties in the Middle East: Economy and Politics of Islamist Moderation* (Bloomington: Indiana University Press, 2016). On audience cost theory, see James D. Fearon, "Domestic Political Audiences and the Escalation of International Disputes," *American Political Science Review* 88, no. 3 (1994): 577–

592; Jessica L. Weeks, "Autocratic Audience Costs: Regime Type and Signaling Resolve," *International Organization* 62, no. 1 (2008): 35–64; Jessica Chen Weiss, "Authoritarian Signaling, Mass Audiences, and Nationalist Protest in China," *International Organization* 67, no. 1 (2013): 1–35.

52. Robert Jervis, *System Effects: Complexity in Political and Social Life* (Princeton: Princeton University Press, 1999).

53. Ibid., 5.

54. Alexander Wendt, *Social Theory of International Politics* (Cambridge: Cambridge University Press, 1999), 331.

55. Susan D. Hyde, *The Pseudo-Democrat's Dilemma* (Ithaca: Cornell University Press, 2011), 19.

56. Wedeen, *Ambiguities of Domination*.

57. Benedict Anderson, *Imagined Communities: Reflections on the Origin and Spread of Nationalism* (London: Verso, 1991).

58. Michael N. Barnett, *Dialogues in Arab Politics: Negotiations in Regional Order* (New York: Columbia University Press, 1998); Ronald R. Krebs, *Narrative and the Making of US National Security* (Cambridge: Cambridge University Press, 2015).

2. A Shi'a Theory of the State

1. Max Weber, *Essays in Sociology*, trans. and ed. H. H. Gerth and C. Wright Mills (New York: Oxford University Press, 1946), 77–128.

2. See, for example, Baqer Moin, *Khomeini: Life of the Ayatollah* (London: I.B. Tauris, 1999), 68.

3. Timur Kuran, *Private Truths, Public Lies: The Social Consequences of Preference Falsification* (Cambridge, Mass.: Harvard University Press, 1995).

4. On state–clergy relations in Iran, see Michael M. Fischer, *Iran: From Religious Dispute to Revolution* (Cambridge, Mass.: Harvard University Press, 1980); Roy Mottahedeh, *The Mantle of the Prophet: Learning and Power in Iran* (London: Oneworld Publications, 2014); Said Amir Arjomand, *The Turban for the Crown: The Islamic Revolution in Iran* (New York: Oxford University Press, 1988).

5. Fischer, *Iran: From Religious Dispute to Revolution*, 11.

6. Mottahedeh, *The Mantle of the Prophet*, 229.

7. See Habib Ladjevardi, *Khaterat-e Mehdi Ha'eri Yazdi: Faqih Va Ostad-e Falsafeh Islami* (Cambridge, Mass.: Harvard University Press, 2001).

8. Mottahedeh, *The Mantle of the Prophet*, 230.

9. Seyyed Mohammad Taghi Khansari, Seyyed Sadr al-Din al-Sadr, and Seyyed Mohammad Hojjat Kooh Kamari were known as the "Triangle of Ayatollahs," in Hossein-Ali Montazeri, *Khaterat* (Los Angeles: Ketab Corp., 2001), 37.

10. For a similar point in a different context, see Anna Grzymała-Busse, *Nations Under God: How Churches Use Moral Authority to Influence Policy* (Princeton: Princeton University Press, 2015).

11. Ehsan Naraghi, *From Palace to Prison: Inside the Iranian Revolution* (London: I.B. Tauris, 1994), 8.

12. Mohsen M. Milani, *The Making of Iran's Islamic Revolution*, 2nd ed. (Boulder, Colo.: Westview Press, 1994), 47.

13. Montazeri, *Khaterat*, 61–90.

14. "Aya Shah ba Imam Molaghat Dasht?," Khomeini's official website, January 22, 2014, http://www.imam-khomeini.ir/fa/76_15203/پرسش_و_پاسخ/ امام/آیا_امام_با_شاه_ملاقات_داشت؟.

15. Ladjevardi, *Khaterat-e Mehdi Ha'eri Yazdi*, 92–93.

16. Ruhollah Khomeini, *Velayat-e Faqih* (Tehran: Amir Kabir and Namayesh-gah-e Ketab, 1979), 197.

17. Montazeri, *Khaterat*, 66–67.

18. Ali Rahnema, *Nirou-ha-ye Mazhabi bar Bastar-e Harekat-e Nehzat-e Melli* (Tehran: Gam-e No, 2005), 58–59.

19. Ibid.

20. Montazeri, *Khaterat*, 61–62.

21. *Ettelaat*, June 7, 1988; reprinted in "Sahar-gah-e Khoonin," *Mashregh News*, January 16, 2013, http://www.mashreghnews.ir/news/186500/مواضع-سحرگاه-خونین- امام-خمینی-ر ه-در خصوص-فدائیان-اسلام-چه-بود.

22. "Rahbar-e Mo'azzam-e Enghelab: Nokhostin Jaraghe-ha-ye Enghelabi-ye Islami be Vasile-ye Navvab dar Man be Vojood Amad," Fars News, January 3, 2010, http://www.farsnews.com/newstext.php?nn=8810120844; "Goft-o-Gou ba Ayatollah Khamenei Darbare-ye Shakhsiat-e Shahid Navvab-Safavi," Khamenei's official website, January 12, 1985, http://farsi.khamenei.ir/speech-content?id=1231.

23. "Ali Davani" in *Khaterat-e 15 Khordad*, ed. Ali Bagher, vol. 1 (Tehran: Hoze-ye Honari-ye Sazaman-e Tablighat-e Islami, 1995), 86.

24. Montazeri, *Khaterat*, 80–81.

25. Ibid., 81.

26. Ibid.

27. "Further Development on the Question of a Successor to Ayatollah Borujerdi," Foreign Service Dispatch from the U.S. Embassy in Tehran to the Department of State, Washington, D.C., April 4, 1961, National Archives.

28. Montazeri, *Khaterat*, 91.

29. Ibid.

30. "Azerbaijani Reaction to the Death of Ayatollah Borujerdi," Foreign Service Dispatch from the U.S. Consulate in Tabriz to the Department of State, Washington, D.C., April 8, 1961, National Archives.

31. Mehdi Bazargan, "Entezarat-e Mardom az Maraje'," in *Bahsi Darbare-ye Marja'iyyat va Rohaniyat* (Tehran: Enteshar, 1962), 103–127.

32. Ladjevardi, *Khaterat-e Mehdi Ha'eri Yazdi*, 100–101.

33. Hassan Rouhani, *Khaterat-e Doctor Hassan Rouhani: Enghelab-e Islami (1341-1357)*, vol. 1 (Tehran: Majma'-e Tashkhis-e Maslahat-e Nezam), 83.

34. Montazeri, *Khaterat*, 92, 100.

35. "Ebrahim Amini," in *Khaterat-e 15 Khordad*, ed. Ali Bagher, vol. 6, (Tehran: Hoze-ye Honari-ye Sazaman-e Tablighat-e Islami, 1997), 61.

36. Fakhreddin Azimi, "Khomeini and the 'White Revolution,'" in *A Critical Introduction to Khomeini*, ed. Arshin Adib-Moghaddam (Cambridge: Cambridge University Press, 2014), 19–42.

37. Montazeri, *Khaterat*, 102.
38. Ibid.
39. Hamid Rouhani, *Barresi va Tahlili az Nehzat-e Imam Khomeini*, vol. 1 (Tehran: Ente-sharat-e Rah-e Imam, 1982), 151.
40. Ibid., 255.
41. For more on *taqiyya*, see Hamid Enayat, *Modern Islamic Political Thought* (Austin: University of Texas Press, 1982), 175–181.
42. Mehdi Araghi, *Nagofte-ha: Khaterat-e Shahid Haj Mehdi Araghi* (Tehran: Rasa, 1991), 165.
43. Montazeri, *Khaterat*, 100.
44. *Ghiyam-e 15 Khordad be Revayat-e Asnad-e Savak*, vol. 2, (Tehran: Markaz-e Barresi-e Asnad-e Tarikhi-e Vezarat-e Ettelaat, 1999), 195.
45. Ibid., 249.
46. "Ebrahim Amini," 49.
47. Rouhani, *Barresi va Tahlili az Nehzat-e Imam Khomeini*, vol. 1, 212; "Mohammad Mo'men," in *Khaterat-e 15 Khordad*, ed. Ali Bagher, vol. 6 (Tehran: Hoze-ye Honari-ye Sazaman-e Tablighat-e *Islami*, 1997), 396–397; Emad Baghi, *Foroudastan va Faradastan: Khaterat-e Shafahi-e Enghelab* (Tehran: Jame'ye Iranian, 2000), 15.
48. "Dar Arz-e 20 Daghigheh Bi-pedar Shodim," *Etemad*, January 12, 2017, 2.
49. Montazeri, *Khaterat*, 104.
50. Araghi, *Nagofte-ha*, 167.
51. Montazeri, *Khaterat*, 103.
52. Rouhani, *Barresi va Tahlili az Nehzat-e Imam Khomeini*, vol. 1, 224.
53. Montazeri, *Khaterat*, 112.
54. "Mohammad Mo'men," 397.
55. Rouhani, *Khaterat*, vol. 1, 145–146.
56. Montazeri, *Khaterat*, 115.
57. "Religious Opposition to Shah's Reform Program: Extent and Significance," cable from U.S. Embassy in Tehran to Department of State, Washington, D.C., May 1, 1963, Pol 15-6 Iran, National Archives.
58. Ibid.
59. Montazeri, *Khaterat*, 114.
60. Ibid.
61. Rouhani, *Khaterat*, 160–161.
62. Ibid., 162–163.
63. Araghi, *Nagofte-ha*, 169.
64. Montazeri, *Khaterat*, 125.
65. Araghi, *Nagofte-ha*, 183–184.
66. Ibid., 175–176.
67. Ruhollah Khomeini, *Sahife-ye Imam*, vol. 8 (Tehran: Mo'asseseh Tanzim va Nashr-e Asar-e Imam Khomeini, 1999), 53; Moin, *Khomeini*, 111–114; Milani, *The Making of Iran's Islamic Revolution*, 51–52.
68. Said Barzin, *Zendeginame-ye Siasi-e Mohandes Mehdi Bazargan* (Tehran: Nashr-e Markaz, 1995), 161–165.
69. *Ghiyam-e 15 Khordad be Revayat-e Asnad-e Savak*, vol. 2, 283.

70. Bijan Jazani, *Teory-e Jam'-bandi-ye Mobarezat-e Si-sale Akhir dar Iran*, 1974, 83, http://www.iran-archive.com/sites/default/files/sanad/jazani-vaghayee-si-saale.pdf.

71. Montazeri, *Khaterat*, 121.

72. Rahim Rouḥbakhsh, *Naghsh-e Bazaar dar Ghiyam-e 15 Khordad* (Tehran: Markaz-e Asnad-e Enghelab-e Islami, 2002), 75–76.

73. See, for example, "Vakonesh-e Saleh be Ezharat-e Ansari Darbare-ye Naghsh-e Jame'-e Modarresin dar Marja'iyyat-e Imam Khomeini," Fars News, October 10, 2017, http://www.farsnews.com/newstext.php?nn=8907250486.

74. "Aftermath of Riots," cable from U.S. Embassy in Tehran to Secretary of State, Washington, D.C., July 6, 1963, Pol 25-1 Iran, National Archives.

75. *Ghiyam-e 15 Khordad be Revayat-e Savak*, vol. 2, 246, 291; Rohani, *Barresi va Tahlili az Nehzat-e Imam Khomeini*, vol. 1, 74–76.

76. "Significance of Muharram's Riots of June, 1963 for Iran's Future," cable from U.S. Embassy in Tehran to Department of State, Washington, D.C., July 19, 1963, Pol 15-7 Iran, National Archives.

77. Ibid.

78. Ibid.

79. Ibid.

80. Telegram on Khomeini's release, from U.S. Embassy in Tehran to Department of State, Washington, D.C., April 6, 1964, Pol 23-9 Iran, National Archives.

81. Moin, *Khomeini*, 119.

82. Telegram on Khomeini's speech, from U.S. Embassy in Tehran to Department of State, Washington, D.C., September 10, 1964, Pol 23-9 Iran, National Archives.

83. Montazeri, *Khaterat*, 128.

84. Ibid., 134.

85. Asghar Heidari, *Ayatollah Shariatmadari be Revayat-e Asnad* (Tehran: Markaz-e Asnad-e Enghelab-e Islami, 2010), 269, 318.

86. Ibid., 295.

87. Ibid., 272.

88. "Islam in Iran: A Research Paper," Foreign Assessment Center, March 1980, 67, RAC Project, NLC-25-43-7-2-8, Jimmy Carter Presidential Library; "Alleged Views of Ayatollah Khomeini," cable from U.S. Embassy in Tehran to Department of State, Washington, D.C., November 6, 1963, Pol 15-7 Iran, National Archives.

89. "Significance of Khomeini's September 9th Speech," cable from U.S. Embassy in Tehran to Department of State, Washington, D.C., September 22, 1964, Pol 23-9 Iran, National Archives.

90. Moin, *Khomeini*, 121.

91. Morteza Pasandideh, *Khaterat-e Ayatollah Pasandideh* (Tehran: Hadith, 1995), 112.

92. Khomeini, *Sahife-ye Imam*, vol. 1, 415.

93. Ibid. 416.

94. Araghi, *Nagofte-ha*, 170; Montazeri, *Khaterat*, 130.

95. Montazeri, *Khaterat*, 135.

96. Sadeq Tabatabaei, *Khaterat-e Siasi Ejtema'ie Doctor Sadeq Tabatabaei*, vol. 1 (Tehran: Orouj, 2008), 198.

97. See Moin, *Khomeini*, 129–159.

98. Quoted in Hossein Ahmadi, *Tactic-ha-ye Mobarezati-ye Imam Khomeini* (Tehran: Markaz-e Asnad-e Enghelab-e Islami, 2012), 237.

99. Akbar Fallahi, *Tarikh-e Shafahi-e Zendegi va Mobarezat-e Imam Khomeini dar Najaf* (Tehran: Markaz-e Asnad-e Enghelab-e Islami, 2012), 73–79.

100. Heidari, *Ayatollah Shariatmadari be Revayat-e Asnad*, 341.

101. Mohammad Reza Mahdavi-Kani, *Khaterat-e Ayatollah Mahdavi-Kani* (Tehran: Markaz-e Asnad-e Enghelab-e Islami, 2006), 144; Tabatabaei, *Khaterat-e Siasi Ejtema'ie Doctor Sadeq Tabatabaei*, vol. 2, 173, 197.

102. Ruhollah Khomeini, *Velayat-e Faqih* (Tehran: Mo'asseseh Chap va Nashr-e Asar-e Imam Khomeini, 1999), 19.

103. *Seyr-e Mobarezat-e Imam Khomeini dar Ayeneh Asnad be Revayat-e Savak*, vol. 7 (Tehran: Mo'asseseh Tanzim va Nashr-e Asar-e Imam Khomeini, 2008), 220.

104. Ibid.

105. Ibid.

106. Ibid., 224.

107. Ibid., 226.

108. See Mohsen Kadivar, *Siyasatnameh-ye Khorasani* (Tehran: Kavir, 2008).

109. See Mohsen Kadivar, *Nazariyyeh-ha-ye Dolat dar Feqh-e Shi'a* (Tehran: Nasani, 1997).

110. Mohsen Milani, "Shi'ism and the State in the Constitution of the Islamic Republic of Iran," in *Iran: Political Culture in the Islamic Republic*, ed. Samih K. Farsoun and Mehrdad Mashayekhi (London: Routledge, 1992), 136.

111. Ruhollah Khomeini, *Kashf al-Asrar* (Tehran: Nashr-e ZAfar, 1970), 185.

112. Ruhollah Khomeini, *Islam and Revolution: Writings and Declarations of Imam Khomeini*, trans. Hamid Algar (Berkeley: Mizan Press, 1981), 37.

113. Ibid.

114. Ibid., 78.

115. Ibid., 62.

116. Ibid., 54.

117. Moin, *Khomeini*, 158; Mohsen Kadivar, "Monker-e Velayat-e Faqih Hatta dar Omour-e Hasbiyeh," Kadivar's website, June 1, 2016, http://kadivar.com/?p=15327; http://kadivar.com/?p=15506.

118. Tabatabaei, *Khaterat-e Siasi Ejtema'ie*, vol. 2, 182.

119. *Seyr-e Mobarezat-e Imam Khomeini dar Ayeneh Asnad be Revayat-e Savak*, vol. 7, 219.

120. Montazeri, *Khaterat*, 99.

121. *Seyr-e Mobarezat-e Imam Khomeini dar Ayeneh Asnad be Revayat-e Savak*, 275–284.

122. Ibid., 295.

123. Ibid.

124. Ibid., 380.

125. Ibid., 383.

126. Ibid., 382.

127. Ibid., 394, 409.

128. Ibid., 388.

129. Jalal Al-e Ahmad, *Gharbzadegi* (Tehran: Ravagh, 1962), 77.

130. Ali Shariati, *Shi'a Yek Hezbe Tamam* (Tehran: Hosseini-ye Ershad, 1977).

131. For more on Shariati and Al-e Ahmad, see Hamid Dabashi, *Theology of Discontent: The Ideological Foundation of the Islamic Revolution in Iran* (New Brunswick, N.J.: Transaction, 1993).
132. Ervand Abrahamian, "The Crowd in the Iranian Revolution," *Radical History Review* no. 105 (2009): 13–38.
133. Khomeini, *Sahife-ye Imam*, vol. 1, 262.
134. Khomeini, *Sahife-ye Imam*, vol. 3, 249.
135. Ibid., 211–212.
136. Ibid., 227.
137. Ibid., 238.
138. Ibid., 245.
139. Ibid., 248.

3. The "Islamic" Revolution

1. Ahmad Rashidi-Motlagh, "Iran va Este'mar-e Sorkh va Siah," *Ettelaat*, January 7, 1978, 7.
2. *Seyr-e Mobarezat-e Imam Khomeini dar Ayeneh Asnad be Revayat-e Savak*, vol. 6 (Tehran: Mo'asseseh Tanzim va Nashr-e Asar-e Imam Khomeini, 2008), 167.
3. Ibid., 168.
4. Ibid.
5. Ibid., 172.
6. Ibid., 200–203.
7. Ibid., 173.
8. Ibid., 180.
9. Ibid., 193.
10. Ruhollah Khomeini, *Sahife-ye Imam: Majmou'e-ye Rahnemoud-ha-ye Imam Khomeini*, vol. 3 (Tehran: Mo'asseseh Tanzim va Nashr-e Asar-e Imam Khomeini, 1999), 446.
11. For example, see "Gozaresh-e Mosavvar az Tazahorat va Rah-peymaee-ye Azim-e Tehran," *Kayhan*, September 5, 1978, 5.
12. Quoted in Janet Afary and Kevin B. Anderson, *Foucault and the Iranian Revolution: Gender and the Seductions of Islamism* (Chicago: University of Chicago Press, 2010), 253.
13. See Ebrahim Yazdi, *Shast Sal Sabouri va Shakouri: Khaterat-e Doctor Ebrahim Yazdi*, vol. 3, 446–450, http://www.nedayeazadi.net/media/up/book/Ebrahim_Yazdi/YAZDI_3_jeld%203%20.pdf.
14. Fatemeh Tabatabaei, *Eghlim-e Khaterat: Khaterat-e Hamsar-e Ahmad Khomeini*, (Pazhuheshkade-ye Imam Khomeini va Enghelab-e Islami, 2011), 418; see also Sadegh Tabatabaei, *Khaterat-e Siyasi Ejtema'ie*, vol. 3 (Tehran: Nashr-e Orouj 2008), 12–17.
15. Yazdi, *Shast Sal Sabouri va Shakouri*, vol. 3, 54.
16. Ibid.
17. Ibid.
18. Khomeini, *Sahife-ye Imam*, vol. 3, 481.
19. Tabatabaei, *Eghlim-e Khaterat*, 428–429.

20. Ibid., 429.
21. Ibid.
22. Yazdi, *Shast Sal Sabouri va Shakouri*, vol. 3, 449.
23. Ibid., 65.
24. Tabatabaei, *Eghlim-e Khaterat*, 442.
25. Ibid., 440.
26. Ibid., 442.
27. Yazdi, *Shast Sal Sabouri va Shakouri*, vol. 3, 100.
28. Ibid., 99.
29. Tabatabaei, *Khaterat-e Siyasi Ejtema'ie*, vol. 3, 57.
30. Yazdi, *Shast Sal Sabouri va Shakouri*, vol. 3, 214.
31. Tabatabaei, *Khaterat-e Siyasi Ejtema'ie*, vol. 3, 41.
32. Yazdi, *Shast Sal Sabouri va Shakouri*, vol. 3, 152.
33. David Frost's Interview with the Shah of Iran in Panama, *ABC News*, January 17, 1980, posted on July 21, 2015, https://www.youtube.com/watch?v=a2BY7Z_QbdI.
34. Ibid.
35. Kambiz Fattahi, "Posht-e Sahne-ye Mosahebe-ye PBS ba Ayatollah Khomeini," *BBC Persian*, February 15, 2015, http://www.bbc.com/persian/iran/2015/02/150204 _u01-maneil-khomeini.
36. Khomeini, *Sahife-ye Imam*, vol. 3, 373.
37. Ibid., 250.
38. Ibid., 482.
39. Ibid.
40. Ibid., 247.
41. Ibid., 38.
42. Ibid., 548.
43. Ibid., 418.
44. Ibid.
45. Khomeini, *Sahife-ye Imam*, vol. 4, 334.
46. Tabatabaei, *Khaterat-e Siyasi va Ejtema'ie*, vol. 3, 18. The veracity of this report has been widely questioned by Khoei's family and students. See "Aya Ayatollah Khoei ba Farah Pahlavi Didar Kard va az Vey Hediye Gereft?," *Khabar Online*, June 26, 2011, http://www.khabaronline.ir/print/159630/history/history?model=WebUI .Models.Details.DetailsPageViewModel.
47. Abbas Gharabaghi, *Haghayegh Darbareh-e Bohran-e Iran* (Paris: Soheil, 1981), 19, 36.
48. "Toufanian/Von Marbod Conversation," cable from American Embassy in Tehran to Secretary of State, Washington, D.C., February 4, 1979, NLC-16-47-5-31-4, Jimmy Carter Presidential Library.
49. Hossein-Ali Montazeri, *Khaterat* (Los Angeles: Ketab Corp., 2001), 229–230.
50. Gharabaghi, *Haghayegh Darbareh-e Bohran-e Iran*, 24.
51. Khomeini, *Sahife-ye Imam*, vol. 5, 289.
52. Richard W. Cottam, "The Shah and the Opposition," *Washington Post*, October 2, 1978. Cottam later regretted his optimism about Khomeini's movement, particularly on human rights issues. See Kambiz Fattahi, "Richard Cottam, Halghe Etesal-e America ba Enghelab-e Iran," *BBC Persian*, February 2, 2015, http://www .bbc.com/persian/iran/2015/02/150201_u01-revolution-cottam.

53. Khomeini, *Sahife-ye Imam*, vol. 3, 303.
54. Ibid., 304.
55. Ibid., 371.
56. *Sahife-ye Imam*, vol. 4, 3.
57. Kambiz Fattahi, "Two Weeks in January: America's Secret Engagement with Khomeini," *BBC News*, June 3, 2016, http://www.bbc.com/news/world-us-canada-36431160.
58. Khomeini, *Sahife-ye Imam*, vol. 3, 473.
59. "Iran," Mini-Special Coordination Committee Meeting, January 11, 1979, NLC-15-20-6-14-2, Jimmy Carter Presidential Library.
60. William Sullivan, *Mission to Iran* (New York: Norton, 1981), 199–213.
61. "Cottam on Khomeini, Liberation Movement (LM), and National Front (INF)," cable from American Embassy in Tehran to Secretary of State, Washington, D.C., January 2, 1979, Jimmy Carter Presidential Library.
62. "Iran: Khomeini's Prospects and Views," Intelligence Memorandum, January 19, 1979, National Foreign Assessment Center, Central Intelligence Agency, National Security Archives.
63. Robert Jervis, *Why Intelligence Fails: Lessons from the Iranian Revolution and the Iraq War* (Ithaca: Cornell University Press, 2010), 39–40.
64. Khomeini, *Sahife-ye Imam*, vol. 5, 377.
65. Ibid., 431.
66. "Cable to U.S. NATO," RAC Project, January 3, 1979, NLC-23-2-4-16-3, Jimmy Carter Presidential Library.
67. Gary Sick, *All Fall Down: America's Tragic Encounter with Iran* (New York: Random House, 1985), 150–153.
68. Ibid., 153.
69. Sullivan, *Mission to Iran*, 230.
70. "USG Policy Guidance," cable from American Embassy in Tehran to Secretary of State, Washington, D.C., January 10, 1979, NLC-6-29-3-50-6, Jimmy Carter Presidential Library.
71. Sullivan, *Mission to Iran*, 233.
72. Sick, *All Fall Down*, 1985.
73. "Notes, Iran-Meetings," folder 2/1/79–2/17/79, container 12, Zbigniew Brzezinski Collection, February 1–17, 1979, Jimmy Carter Presidential Library.
74. Mohammad Reza Pahlavi, *Answer to History* (New York: Stein and Day, 1980), 173.
75. Ibid., 172.
76. Sullivan, *Mission to Iran*, 231–232.
77. The Shah accuses General Gharabaghi of betraying him and claims that he was the only general who was not executed because Bazargan was his "savior." See Pahlavi, *Answer to History*, 173.
78. Ibid.; a year later, *New York Times* columnist William Safire leaked government reports and officials' statements that Huyser's trip aborted military action by the Iranian army. Safire wrote, "[O]ne year ago, our intelligence agents in Tehran were reporting that a military coup was imminent. Huyser arrived in Tehran with the new year. He met with the generals who wanted to take power from the benumbed Shah and deny power to the mullahs. After the U.S. general

spoke with them, the Iranian generals decided 'not to resist.' Cause and effect? We don't know" (William Safire, "The Huyser Mission," *New York Times*, January 17, 1981). In June 1981, Huyser testified on the House's Committee on Foreign Affairs' Subcommittee on Europe and the Middle East. He denied that his mission was to neutralize the Iranian Army and claimed that by the time he was in Tehran, the Shah's generals had lost their capability to restore order and thus capitulated. His task, Huyser pointed out, was simply to protect the unity of the army; see "General Huyser's Mission to Iran, January 1979," hearing before the Subcommittee on Europe and the Middle East of the Committee on Foreign Affairs, House of Representatives, Ninety-seventh Congress, first session, June 9, 1981, https://www.loc.gov/resource/conghear09.0018624865A /?st=gallery; see also his book, Robert E. Huyser, *Mission to Tehran* (New York: Harper & Row, 1986).

79. Mehdi Bazargan, *Enghelab-e Iran dar do Harekat* (Tehran: Nehzat-e Azadi, 1984), 71.
80. Shaul Bakhash, *The Reign of the Ayatollahs: Iran and the Islamic Revolution* (New York: Basic Books, 1984), 50.
81. Bazargan, *Enghelab-e Iran dar do Harekat*, 71.
82. "Message to USG from Khomeini," cable from American Embassy in Paris to Secretary of State, Washington, D.C., RAC Project, January 27, 1979, NLC-16-25-4-9-9, Jimmy Carter Presidential Library.
83. "Yazdi's Response to USG Questions," cable from Secretary of State, Washington, D.C., to American Embassy in Tehran, January 19, 1979, National Archives, https:// aad.archives.gov/aad/createpdf?rid=117110&dt=2776&dl=2169.
84. William Branigin, "Top Moslem Leader in Iran Withholds Support of Khomeini," *Washington Post*, January 20, 1979.
85. Shahpour Bakhtiar, *Khaterat-e Shahpour Bakhtiar: Akharin Nokhost Vazir-e Regim-e Pahlavi*, ed. Habib Ladjevardi (Cambridge, Mass.: Harvard University Center for the Middle East, 1996), 108.
86. Khomeini, *Sahife-ye Imam*, vol. 5, 538.
87. Quoted in Fattahi, "Two Weeks in January."
88. Khomeini, *Sahife-ye Imam*, vol. 6, 18.
89. Abbas Gharabaghi, *Haghayegh dar bare-ye Bohran-e Iran* (Paris: Sazman-e Chap va Entesharat-e Sohayl, 1981), 108.
90. *Kayhan*, February 8, 1979, 1.
91. See Gharabaghi, *Haghayegh Darbareh-e Bohran-e Iran*. Iranian agents killed Bakhtiar in 1991 for his alleged collaboration with Saddam Hussein to attack Iran.
92. "Ayatollah Khalkhali: Az Enghelabi-gari ta Enzeva," *BBC Persian*, November 27, 2003, http://www.bbc.co.uk/persian/iran/story/2003/11/031127_a_khalkhali .shtml.
93. "Mehdi Bazargan, Pirouzi-e Ghiyam-e Por-shokouh-e Bahman ra 'Mosibat-e Bozorg' Midanad," *Kar*, December 26, 1979, Appendix, 2.
94. Khomeini, *Sahife-ye Imam*, vol. 6, 155.
95. Bazargan, *Enghelab-e Iran dar do Harekat*, 90.
96. Khomeini, *Sahife-ye Imam*, vol. 3, 431.
97. Bazargan, *Enghelab-e Iran dar do Harekat*, 116.

98. Ibid., 78.

99. "Bazargan Bozorg-tarin Kolahi Boud ke Imam be Sar-e America Gozasht," Fars News, January 16, 2011, http://www.farsnews.com/printable.php?nn=891026 1425.

100. Akbar Hashemi Rafsanjani, *Dowran-e Mobareze*, vol. 1 (Tehran: Daftar-e Nashr-e Ma'aref-e Islami, 1997), 329.

4. Institutionalizing *Velayat-e Faqih*

1. Ruhollah Khomeini, *Sahife-ye Imam: Majmou'e-ye Rahnemoud-ha-ye Imam Khomeini*, vol. 6 (Tehran: Mo'asseseh Tanzim va Nashr-e Asar-e Imam Khomeini, 1999), 54.

2. "Lahze be Lahze: 22 Bahman 1357 Chegoune Gozasht?," *Tasnim News*, February 10, 2014, http://www.tasnimnews.com/Home/Single/278913.

3. "Hezb-e Jomhuri Islami," *BBC Persian*, February 6, 2009, http://www.bbc.co.uk /persian/iran/2009/02/090206_ir_islamic_republic_party.shtml.

4. "Ta'sis-e Hezb-e Jomhuri Islami," *Markaz-e Asnad-e Jomhuri Islami*, http://www .irdc.ir/fa/calendar/180/default.aspx.

5. Sadeq Tabatabaei, *Khaterat-e Siasi Ejtema'ie Doctor Sadeq Tabatabaei*, vol. 3 (Tehran: Orouj, 2008), 258–259.

6. Ervand Abrahamian, *The Iranian Mojahedin* (New Haven, Conn.: Yale University Press, 1989), 45.

7. William Branigin, "Many in New Iran Resent Clergy's Growing Authority," *Washington Post*, May 14, 1979.

8. Jonathan C. Randal, "Khomeini Returns Triumphantly to Home in Qom, Attacks the West, Leftists," *Washington Post*, March 1, 1979.

9. "Vezarat-e 'Amr be Ma'rouf va Nahy az Monkar' Tashkil Mishavad," *Ayandegan*, March 3, 1979, 1.

10. "Nemikhahim Begouyim Zanan be Edareh Naravand," *Ayandegan*, March 11, 1979, 1; "Hejab-e Khanoum-ha Elzami Nist," *Ayandegan*, March 12, 1979, 1.

11. "In Dowlat Olgou-ye Hokoumat-e Islami Nist," *Ayandegan*, March 15, 1979, 2.

12. *Ayandegan*, May 17, 1979, 1.

13. "Pakhsh-e Mousighi az Radio Televizion Ghat' Shod," *Ayandegan*, July 24, 1979, 1.

14. For more, see Mirjam Keunkler, "The Special Court of the Clergy (Dadgah-e Vigeh-ye Ruhaniyyat) and the Repression of Dissident Clergy in Iran," in *The Rule of Law, Islam, and Constitutional Politics in Egypt and Iran*, ed. Said Amir Arjomand and Nathan J. Brown (Albany: State University of New York Press, 2013): 57–100; Majid Mohammadi, "Special Court for the Clergy: Raison d'être, Development, Structure and Function," *Iran Human Rights Documentation Center*, August 2010, http://www .iranhrdc.org/files.php?force&file=pdf_en/LegalCom/Special_Court_for_the _Clergy_854451794.pdf.

15. "Bayan va Ghalam dar Islam Azad Ast," *Ettelaat*, September 30, 1979.

16. Seyyed Reza Sadr, "Dar Zendan-e Velayat-e Faqih," Mohsen Kadivar's website, November 2, 2016, http://kadivar.com/?p=15651.

17. See, for example, "9 Rouhani-nama dar Shiraz Khal'e Lebas Shodand," *Ayandegan*, April 8, 1979, 4; "Tir-baran-shode-gan-e Mashhad," *Kayhan*, April 24, 1979, 1.
18. "Tote'e Owqaf Alayh-e Ayatollah Khomeini," *Ayandegan*, March 18, 1979, 3.
19. "Hich Yek az Aghshar Nemitavanad be Tanha-ee in Viraneh ra Besazad," *Ayandegan*, March 27, 1979, 10.
20. "Hashemi Rafsanjani: Pedar Basham, Pedar-e Hame Ahzabam," Iranian Students' News Agency, March 18, 2016, http://www.isna.ir/news/8709-01408/ ‫.ابم-انتخابات‌هاشمي-ر‌فسنجاني-كامل-پدر-باشم-پدر-همه-احز‬
21. *Ayandegan*, May 13, 1979, 1.
22. *Ayandegan,* April 26, 1979, 1.
23. *Ayandegan*, April 24, 1; *Ayandegan*, April 25, 1979, 1, 3.
24. "Bayaniyeh Ayatollah Khalkhali Darbare Maghaleh Khod dar Ettelaat," *Ettalaat*, April 25, 1979.
25. "Ayatollah Taleqani be Safar-e E'teraz-amiz Raft," *Tarikh-e Irani*, http://tarikhirani .ir/fa/events/3/EventsDetail/138.
26. Ibid.
27. "Ayatollah Taleqani: be Estefade-ha-ye Bija az Quran Payan Dahim," *Kayhan*, May 6, 1979, 1.
28. "Enzabat be Ja-ye Entegham," *Kayhan*, May 29, 1979, 2.
29. "Dowlat ba Khatar-e Dekhalat-ha-ye Beja va Bija Movajeh Ast," *Kayhan*, April 25, 1979, 1.
30. "Dowlat va Showra-ye Enghelab dar ham Edgham Shod," *Ayandegan*, July 21, 1979, 1, 12.
31. Tabatabaei, *Khaterat-e Siasi Ejtema'ie*, vol. 3, 276.
32. Khomeini, *Sahife-ye Imam*, vol. 6, 433.
33. "Qom, Moshtaghaneh be Pishvaz-e Refrandom Raft," *Ayandegan*, March 31, 1979, 4.
34. "Jomhuri Islami Mafahim-e Ghabel-e Ghabool-e Donya ra dar bar Darad," *Ayandegan*, March 29, 1979, 1–2.
35. Khomeini, *Sahife-ye Imam*, vol. 6, 435.
36. Ibid., 471.
37. Ali Rahnema, "Ayatollah Khomeini's Rule of the Guardian Jurist: From Theory to Practice," in *A Critical Introduction to Khomeini*, ed. Arshin Adib-Moghaddam (New York: Cambridge University Press, 2014), 108.
38. Khomeini, *Sahife-ye Imam*, vol. 7, 282.
39. Ibid., 282.
40. "Baki Nadarim ke dar Gharb Darbare-ye Ma Che Migouyand," *Ayandegan*, April 3, 1979, 1.
41. "Ra'is-e Jomhuri Ghat'an Yek Siasatmadar Khahad Boud Na Yek Faqih," *Ayandegan*, April 5, 1979, 1–2.
42. "Showra-ye Enghelab Naghsh-e Velayat-e Faqih ra Ifa Khahad Kard," *Ayandegan*, March 31, 1979, 1.
43. Some lawyers objected that Khomeini could not relegate the power of *Velayat-e Faqih*, which was exclusive for a marja, to local clerical judges. See "Velayat-e Faqih Ghabel-e Towkil Nist," *Ayandegan*, April 16, 1979, 4.
44. Hossein-Ali Montazeri, *Khaterat* (Los Angeles: Ketab Corp., 2001), 486.

45. Ibid., 489.
46. "Homafaran be Tahasson-e Khod Payan Dadand," *Ayandegan*, July 24, 1979, 2.
47. Khomeini, *Sahife-ye Imam*, vol. 13, 46–47.
48. Ibid., 46.
49. "Pishnahad-e Ayatollah Shariatmadari," *Kayhan*, May 13, 1979, 1.
50. "Baray-e Maraje' Ghaboul-e Post-e Dowlati Salah Nist," *Ettalaat*, June 4, 1979, 8.
51. "In Refrandom Ghanoun-e Asasi-e Ma ra Bi-e'tebar Mikonad," *Ayandegan*, June 17, 1979, 1; "Sherkat-e Hezb-e Jomhuri-e Khalq-e Mosalman dar Seminar-e Hoghoughdanan," *Ayandegan*, June 17, 1979, 1.
52. "Imam: Ehsas-e Khatar va Tote'e Mikonam," *Ayandegan*, June 17, 1979, 1, 12.
53. See, for example, *Ettalaat*, June 20, 1979, 1.
54. Asghar Schirazi, *The Constitution of Iran: Politics and the State in the Islamic Republic* (London: I.B. Tauris, 1997), 32.
55. *Sourat-e Mashrouh-e Mozakerat-e Majles-e Barresi-ye Naha'i-ye Ghanoun-e Asasi-ye Jomhuri-ye Islami-ye Iran*, vol. 1 (Tehran: Edareh-ye Koll-e Omour-e Farhangi va Ravabet-e Omoumi-ye Majles-e Showra-ye Islami, 1985), 5–6.
56. Ibid., 7.
57. Schirazi, *The Constitution of Iran*, 47–48.
58. *Sourat-e Mas Sourat-e Mashrouh-e Mozakerat-e Majles-e Barresi-ye Naha'i-ye Ghanoun-e Asasi-ye Jomhuri-ye Islami-ye Iran hrouh*, vol. 1, 73.
59. Ibid., 72–73.
60. Ibid., 74.
61. Ibid., 104.
62. Ibid., 90–91.
63. Schirazi, *The Constitution of Iran*, 45.
64. *Sourat-e Mashrouh-e Mozakerat-e Majles-e Barresi-ye Naha'i-ye Ghanoun-e Asasi-ye Jomhuri-ye Islami-ye Iran*, vol. 1, 107.
65. Ibid., 384.
66. Ibid.
67. Schirazi, *The Constitution of Iran*, 55.
68. *Sourat-e Mashrouh-e Mozakerat-e Majles-e Barresi-ye Naha'i-ye Ghanoun-e Asasi-ye Jomhuri-ye Islami-ye Iran*, 561.
69. Mehdi Bazargan, *Enghelab-e Iran dar do Harekat* (Tehran: Nehzat-e Azadi, 1984), 124.
70. "Pishnevis-e Ghanoun-e Asasi ba Ekhtiarat-e Fowgh al-'Ade'ie ke be Ra'is Jomhur Dad-e Ast Dictatori-ye Jadidi dar Astin Miparvaranad," *Kar*, July 30, 1979, 1.
71. "Bedonbal-e Tasvib-e Velayat-e Faqih Kheyme Shab Bazi dar Majles-e Khobergan Vaz'e Mozheki be Khod Gerefteh Ast," *Kar*, October 1, 1979, 7.
72. Quoted in Jonathan C. Randal, "Iran Anti-U.S. Campaign Used to Offset Opponents of Proposed Constitution," *Washington Post*, November 28, 1979.
73. Jonathan C. Randal, "Bloody Attack Stirs Rivals of Khomeini; Killing in Qom Angers Anti-Khomeini Faction," *Washington Post*, December 7, 1979.
74. Stuart Auerbach, "Khomeini's Rival Bars Talks on Tabriz Conflict," *Washington Post*, December 11, 1979.

75. Michael Weisskopf, "Waldheim Going To Iran for Talks On U.S. Hostages; Tabriz Rally Backs Key Khomeini Rival; Tabriz Rally Threatens Death to Khomeini Aides," *Washington Post*, December 30, 1979.
76. Hashemi Rafsanjani, *Dowran-e Mobareze*, vol. 1, 334.

5. The Hostage Crisis: The Untold Account of the Communist Threat

1. See, for example, James A. Bill, *The Eagle and the Lion: The Tragedy of American-Iranian Relations* (New Haven, Conn.: Yale University Press, 1988), 293–304; Mark Bowden, *Guests of the Ayatollah: The First Battle in America's War with Militant Islam* (New York: Atlantic Monthly Press, 2006); Blake W. Jones, "How Does a Born-Again Christian Deal with a Born-Again Moslem? The Religious Dimension of the Iranian Hostage Crisis," *Diplomatic History* 39, no. 3 (June 2015): 423–451; David P. Houghton, "Explaining the Origins of the Iran Hostage Crisis: A Cognitive Perspective," *Terrorism and Political Violence* 18, no. 2 (2006): 259–279.
2. Barry Rubin, *Paved with Good Intentions: The American Experience in Iran* (New York: Penguin, 1981), 303.
3. See, for example, L. Bruce Laingen, *Yellow Ribbon: The Secret Journal of Bruce Laingen* (New York: Brassey's, 1992); Rocky Sickmann, *Iranian Hostage: A Personal Diary of 444 Days in Captivity* (Topeka, Kans.: Crawford Press, 1982); Charles W. Scott, *Pieces of the Game: The Human Drama of Americans Held Hostage in Iran* (Atlanta: Peachtree Publishers, 1984); Barbara and Barry Rosen, *The Destined Hour* (New York: Doubleday, 1982); John Limbert, *Negotiating with Iran: Wrestling the Ghosts of History* (Washington, D.C.: United States Institute for Peace, 2009).
4. Gary Sick, *All Fall Down: America's Tragic Encounter with Iran* (New York: Random House, 1985); Zbigniew Brzezinski, *Power and Principle: Memoirs of the National Security Advisor* (New York: Farrar, Straus, and Giroux, 1983); Cyrus R. Vance, *Hard Choices: Critical Years in America's Foreign Policy* (New York: Simon & Schuster, 1983).
5. Rubin, *Paved with Good Intentions*, 280.
6. Stephanie Cronin, "Introduction," in *Reformers and Revolutionaries in Modern Iran: New Perspectives on the Iranian Left*, ed. Stephanie Cronin (New York: Routledge, 2013), 1.
7. Ali Mirsepassi, "The Tragedy of the Iranian Left," in *Reformers and Revolutionaries in Modern Iran: New Perspectives on the Iranian Left*, ed. Cronin, 230.
8. Mohammad Amjad, *Iran: From Royal Dictatorship to Theocracy* (Westport, Conn.: Praeger, 1989), 14; see also Valentine Moghadam, "Socialism or Anti-Imperialism? The Left and Revolution in Iran," *New Left Review* 166 (1987): 5–28; Said Amir Arjomand, *The Turban for the Crown: The Islamic Revolution in Iran* (New York: Oxford University Press, 1988), 139; Ervand Abrahamian, *Khomeinism: Essays on the Islamic Republic* (Berkeley: University of California Press, 1993); Ali M. Ansari, *Confronting Iran: The Failure of American Foreign Policy and the Next Great Crisis in the Middle East* (New York: Basic Books, 2007), 88–89.

9. Emadeddin Baghi, *Enghelab va Tanazo'-e Bagha* (Tehran: Nashr-e 'Orouj, 1997), 14–15, 95.

10. In "Siasat-e Khareji-e Iran az 1357 ta Konoun; Charkhesh-ha va Chalesh-ha, Bakhsh-e Nokhost," *BBC Persian,* April 4, 2004, http://www.bbc.com/persian /iran/story/2004/03/printable/040323_a_amini_revo_aniv25.shtml.

11. "Kodam Gerogan? Kodam Gerogangiri?," *Andishe-ye Pouya,* no. 21 (November 2014); also reprinted in "Goftogu-ye Gerogangir va Gerogan-e Sabegh; Asgharzadeh va Limbert," *Tarikh-e Irani,* November 24, 2014, http://tarikhirani.ir/fa /news/30/bodyView/4835/گفتگوی.گروگانگیر.و.گروگان.سابق؛.اصغرزاده.و.لیمبرت .html.

12. Zeinab Safari, "Reghabat ba Gorouh-ha-ye Chap dar Taskhir-e Sefarat-e Amrica Mo'asser Boud," *Tarikh-e Irani,* November 6, 2011, http://tarikhirani.ir/fa/files /38/bodyView/370/امام.پژوهشکده.در.ابتکار.از.سخنرانی.ایرانی.تاریخ.گزارش بود.موثر.آمریکا.سفارت.تسخیر.در.چپ.گروه‌های.با.رقابت:.خمینی.html.

13. Ibid.

14. "Vakonesh-e Mousavi Khoeiniha be Edde'a-ye Hozour-e Monafeghin dar Eshghale Sefarat-e Amrica: Rajavi va Khiabani Ejazeh Nayaftand be Dakhel-e Lane-ye Jasousi Biyayand," *Tarikh-e Irani,* November 4, 2011, http://tarikhirani.ir /Modules/News/Phtml/News.PrintVersion.Html.php?Lang=fa&TypeId =9&NewsId=1481.

15. "Revayat-e Tosifi-Tahlili-ye Ayatollah Mousavi Khoeinha az Taskhir-e Sefarat-e Amrica," *Tarikh-e Irani,* November 19, 2011, http://tarikhirani.ir/fa/files/38 /bodyView/377/تسخیر.از.خوئینی‌ها.موسوی.آیت‌الله.تحلیلی.توصیفی.روایت آمریکا.سفارت.html.

16. "Asgharzadeh: Gerogan-e an Gerogangiri Shodim," *Ghanoon,* November 4, 2013.

17. "Bazargan Siastmadar Nabood, Goftogooy-e Reza Khojaste-Rahimi ba Abbas Abdi," *Sharvand-e Emruz,* January 2008, reprinted in *Gooya,* January 6, 2008, http://news.gooya.com/politics/archives/2008/01/066705.php.

18. Asieh Bakeri, "Taskhir-e Sefarat Comonist-ha ra Khal'e Selah Kard: Goft-o Gou ba Mohammad Moslehi and La'ia Pour-Ansari, az Zowj-ha-ye Gerogangir-e Sefarat," *Tarikh-e Irani,* November 14, 2011, http://tarikhirani.ir/fa/files/38 /bodyView/375/کرد.سلاح.خلع.را.کمونیست‌ها.آمریکا.سفارت.تسخیر.html.

19. According to Charles Nass, deputy ambassador and chargé d'affaires at the U.S. Embassy in Tehran, it was Ayatollah Beheshti, not Mahdavi Kermani, who accompanied Yazdi to deliver General Gast. However, Yazdi himself claimed that it was Mahdavi Kermani. See "Ebrahim Yazdi: Payam-e Ayatollah Khomeini Pasokh be Payam-e Carter Bood," *BBC Persian,* November 9, 2015, http://www.bbc .com/persian/iran/2015/11/151108_l10_khomeini_carter_yazdi_reax.

20. Kambiz Fattahi, "Maghamat-e Amrica-ee az Didarha-ye Mahraman-e ba Beheshti Migouyand," *BBC Persian,* November 2, 2014, http://www.bbc.com/persian /iran/2014/11/141101_u01-beheshti-main.

21. Kambiz Fattahi, "Majara-ye Didar-e Safir-e America ba Mousavi-ye Ardebili," *BBC Persian,* June 7, 2016, http://www.bbc.com/persian/iran/2016/06/160607_kf _mousaviardebili_us; Kambiz Fattahi, "Aya Akharin Arteshbod be Shah Khianat Kard?," *BBC Persian,* June 11, 2016, http://www.bbc.com/persian/iran/2016/06

/160611_l13_shah_betrayed; Kambiz Fattahi, "Chera Brzezinski bi Saro Seda Don-bal-e Beheshti Bood?," *BBC Persian*, February 4, 2015, http://www.bbc.com/persian/iran/2015/02/150203_u01_beheshti_americans.

22. "Jimmy Carter Oral History, President of the United States," Miller Center, University of Virginia, November 29, 1982, https://millercenter.org/the-presidency/interviews-with-the-administration/jimmy-carter-oral-history-president-united-states.

23. Cable from U.S. Embassy in Tehran to Secretary of State, Washington, D.C., June 4, 1979, RAC Project, NLC-16-49-3-3-5, Jimmy Carter Presidential Library.

24. Mark Gasiorowski, "US Intelligence Assistance to Iran, May–October 1979," *Middle East Journal* 66, no. 4 (2012): 613–627.

25. Ibid; also in James G. Blight et al., *Becoming Enemies: U.S.-Iran Relations and the Iran-Iraq War, 1979-1988* (London: Rowman & Littlefield, 2012), 71, 245.

26. "Current Situation in Iran," cable from the Situation Room to Camp David, February 19, 1979, RAC Project, NLC-16-122-1-35-0, Jimmy Carter Presidential Library.

27. Ibid.

28. "Iran: Recent Tudeh Party Activity," National Foreign Assessment Center, April 1980, RAC Project, NLC-25-43-8-7-2, Jimmy Carter Presidential Library; "Iran: Growing Leftist Influence Among Minorities," National Foreign Assessment Center, January 1980, RAC Project, NLC-25-43-5-1-1, Jimmy Carter Presidential Library.

29. "Current Situation in Iran."

30. "Looking Ahead," cable from Ambassador Sullivan to Secretary Vance, January 12, 1979, Document Number: 1979TEHRAN00589, National Archives.

31. "Iran: The Leftist Challenge to the Bazargan Government," National Foreign Assessment Center, March 5, 1979, RAC Project, NLC-25-42-10-9-8, Jimmy Carter Presidential Library.

32. "Meeting with Islamic Leader Mohammed Beheshti," cable from U.S. Embassy in Tehran to U.S. Secretary of State, March 20, 1979, National Archives, https://aad.archives.gov/aad/createpdf?rid=205264&dt=2776&dl=2169.

33. John Limbert, "Death to America? Or a Life Sentence?," *LobeLog*, August 3, 2015, http://lobelog.com/death-to-america-or-a-life-sentence.

34. "Meeting with Ayatollah Montazeri," cable from U.S. Embassy in Tehran to U.S. Secretary of State, October 26, 1979, National Archives, https://aad.archives.gov/aad/createpdf?rid=287982&dt=2776&dl=2169.

35. Maziar Behrooz, *Rebels with a Cause: The Failure of the Left in Iran* (London: I.B. Tauris, 1999), 105.

36. Jonathan C. Randal, "Khomeini Warns Leftist Guerrillas Against 'Uprising,'" *Washington Post*, February 20, 1979.

37. William Branigin, "Radical Iranian Groups Acquire More Members and Arms," *Washington Post*, February 13, 1979.

38. Ervand Abrahamian, "Iran in Revolution: The Opposition Forces," *MERIP Report*, no. 75/76 (1979): 8.

39. See Ervand Abrahamian, *Tortured Confessions: Prisons and Public Recantations in Modern Iran* (Berkeley: University of California Press, 1999).

40. For more on the Iranian Left, see Behrooz, *Rebels with a Cause*; Sepehr Zabir, *The Left in Contemporary Iran* (Stanford: Hoover Institution, 1986); Ervand Abrahamian, *Iran Between Two Revolutions* (Princeton: Princeton University Press, 1982); Ervand Abrahamian, *The Iranian Mojahedin* (New Haven, Conn.: Yale University Press, 1989); Ali Banuazizi, *Darbareh Siasat va Farhang: Ali Banuazizi dar Goft-o Gou ba Shahrokh Meskoub* (Paris: Khavaran, 1994).

41. "Iran: The Leftist Challenge to the Bazargan Government," 5.

42. Farrokh Negahdar, "Dastan-e Nameh be Bazargan va Sarnevesht-e Ma," *Kar*, February 25, 2010, http://new.kar-online.com/node/1676.

43. Nozar Alaolmolki, "The New Iranian Left," *Middle East Journal* 41, no. 2 (1987): 218; Baqer Moin, *Khomeini: Life of the Ayatollah* (New York: St. Martin's Press, 1999), 240.

44. "Iran: The Leftist Challenge to the Bazargan Government."

45. Peyman Vahabzadeh, *A Guerilla Odyssey: Modernization, Secularism, Democracy, and the Fadai Period of National Liberation in Iran* (Syracuse, N.Y.: Syracuse University Press, 2010), 67.

46. "Name-ye Sargoshade-ye Cherik-ha-ye Khalq be Ayatollah Khomeini Mobareze-e Alighadr and Pishva-ye Bozorg-e Shi'ayan," February 17, 1979, *Arshiv-e Asnad-e Opozosion-e Iran*, http://www.iran-archive.com/node/5781.

47. Formerly known as the Baghdad Pact, CENTO was an anti-Soviet security treaty composed of Iran, Turkey, Pakistan, and the United Kingdom. The United States was an associate member. It dissolved in 1979 after Iran ended its membership.

48. Ruhollah Khomeini, *Sahife-ye Imam: Majmou'e-ye Rahnemoud-ha-ye Imam Khomeini*, vol. 7 (Tehran: Mo'asseseh Tanzim va Nashr-e Asar-e Imam Khomeini, 1999), 410.

49. Khomeini, *Sahife-ye Imam*, vol. 8, 138–139.

50. *Entekhab Daily*, August 22, 2015, http://www.entekhab.ir/fa/news/222078/ احمدی-نژاد-گفت-برویدبه-رئیس-دولت-اصلاحات-و-بقیه-را-دستگیر-کنید-و-شر-همه-را-کم-کنید-گفتم-مرد-حسابی-چه-می‌گویی-می‌روی-می‌گویی-خس-و-خاشاک-و-آت-و-آشغال-و-حالا-می‌گویی-بگیرید-ببرید-و-تمام.

51. Quoted in "Siasat-e Khareji-e Iran az 1357 ta Konoun; Charkhesh-ha va Chalesh-ha, Bakhsh-e Nokhost."

52. "Artesh-e Vabaste Hafez-e Manafe'e Amperialism Ast," *Kar*, March 22, 1979, 1; "Farmandehan-e Artesh Tajarob-e Artesh-e Amrica dar Vietnam ra dar Kordestan be Kar Migirand," *Kar*, April 23, 1980, 4.

53. *Kar*, September 3, 1979, 1.

54. "Gharardad-ha-ye Esarat-avar-e Iran ba Amrica va Sayer-e Keshvar-ha-ye Amperialist Bayad Laghv Shavad," *Mardom*, May 26, 6; 1979; *Kar*, May 26, 1979.

55. "Ehdas-e Nirougah-e Atomi Yek Khianat-e Digar-e Pahlavi," *Mardom*, June 23, 1979, 6.

56. "Yekbar-e Digar Ma va Refrandom," *Mardom*, March 28, 1979, 1.

57. "Iran dar Hafteh-ee ke Gozasht," *Mardom*, April 4, 1979, 2.

58. "Hezbe Tudeh-ye Iran va Mazhab," *Mardom*, May 12, 1979, 1, 4.

59. "Hamleh be Daftar-e Mardom dar Rasht," *Mardom*, June 27, 1979, 1; "Zedde Enghelab Yek Ketabforoushi ra dar Shabestar Gharat Kard," *Mardom*, July 25, 1979, 8.

60. "Rafigh Noureddin Kianouri, Dabir-e Avval-e Komiteh-ye Markazi-ye Hezb-e Tudeh-ye Iran dar Conferanc-e Matbou'ati Goft: Hezb-e Tudeh-ye Iran Azadaneh va Betor-e Ghanouni Fa'aliyyat Mikonad, Vali in Azadi-ye Fa'aliyyat Hanouz dar Tamam-e Noghat-e Keshvar Ta'min Shodeh Nist," *Mardom*, October 10, 1979, 3.
61. "Khatar-e Besiar Jeddi Dastavard-ha-ye Enghelab ra Tahdid Mikonad," *Mardom*, July 25, 1979, 1–5.
62. "Sarmaghaleh: Doroud bar Dadgah-ha-ye Enghelabi," *Mardom*, April 11, 1979, 1.
63. Mohsen Milani, "Harvest of Shame: Tudeh and the Bazargan Government," *Middle Eastern Studies* 29, no. 2 (1993): 312.
64. "Chera Candida-ha-ye Hezb-e Jomhuri Islami az Sandough Biroon Amadand," *Kar*, August 9, 1979, 1–2.
65. "Iran dar Hafteh-ee ke Gozasht," *Mardom*, April 25, 1979, 2.
66. "Chera ba Yaman-e Democratic va Cuba hanouz Rabeteh-ye Siasi Bargharar Nakardim?," *Mardom*, April 11, 1979, 1.
67. "Iran dar Hafteh-ee ke Gozasht," *Mardom*, May 3, 1979, 2.
68. "Iran dar Hafteh-ee ke Gozasht," *Mardom*, April 25, 1979, 2.
69. Kambiz Fattahi, "Avvalin E'dam-e Khalkhali ke Sedash be Goush-e Congere-ye America Resid," *BBC Persian*, February 6, 2016, http://www.bbc.com/persian/iran/2015/02/150206_u01-revolutioin-elghanian.
70. "E'lamieh Komiteh Markazi-ye Hezb-e Tudeh Iran," *Mardom*, May 24, 1979, 1.
71. "Az Rasoul-e Ranj be Imam-e Khalq," *Mardom*, June 30, 1979, 6.
72. "Chetor 'Ghahremanan-e Mobareze-ye Zedde Amperialisti Dast-e Hamdigar ra Roo Mikonand," *Kar*, October 16, 1980, 5.
73. "Karshenas-e Nezami va Aslahe-ye Amricaee," *Mardom*, July 11, 1979, 4.
74. Ibid.
75. "Chera Nokhost Vazir az Bordan-e Nam-e Amperialism-e Amrica be 'Onvan-e Doshman-e Asli-ye Enghelab-e Iran Eba Darad?,"*Mardom*, August 6, 1979, 1.
76. "Dowlat Pareh-ee az Gharardad-ha-ye Nezami ba Amrica ra Ebgha Kard," *Kar*, July 30, 1979, 1–2.
77. Ibid.
78. "Sar Maghaleh: Mohandes Bazargan Ebgha'e Gharardad-ha-ye Esarat-bar ba Amperialist-ha ra be Naf'e Mamlekat va Mardom Midanad," *Kar*, August 6, 1979, 7.
79. "Chera Farmandehan-e Artesh Mikhahand Jenayat-e Rejim-e Sabegh Faramoush Shavad?," *Kar*, June 14, 1979, 1; "Tajdid-e Sazman-e Artesh be Yari-e Mostasharan-e Amricaee," *Kar*, July 23, 1979, 8.
80. "Chera Gharardad-e Dojanebe-ye Nezami ba Amrica Molgha Nemishavad?," *Mardom*, May 3, 1979, 1.
81. "Esteghlal-e Iran Ijab Mikonad ke Gharardad-e Dojanebeh Nezami ba Amrica Foran Laghv Gardad," *Mardom*, June 25, 1979, 4.
82. "Navgan-e Panjom-e Amrica Kabous-e Jadidi Baray-e Mantagheh Ma," *Mardom*, April 18, 1979, 4.
83. "Derang dar Laghv-e Gharardad-e Dojanebeh Nezami ba Amrica Gostakhi-e Amperialism-e Amrica ra Sheddat Mibakhshad," *Mardom*, August 11, 1979, 1.
84. During the revolution and amid violence and strikes, all schools were shut down throughout the winter and spring of 1979.

85. "Bazgosha'i-ye Daneshgah-ha va Madares va Safbandi-ye Jadid-e Nirou-ha," *Kar*, September 17, 1979, 1.
86. "Shah's Illness," cable from U.S. Embassy in Tehran to U.S. Secretary of State, Washington, D.C., October 21, 1979, RAC Project, NLC-16-50-6-2-1, Jimmy Carter Presidential Library.
87. Ibid.
88. Ibid.
89. "Mah-ha Entezar Baray-e Safar be Yengeh Donya," *Ettelaat*, September 13, 1979, 5.
90. Rosen, *The Destined Hour*, 103 (emphasis in original).
91. "Shah-e Makhlou' be New York Raft: Mohammad Reza Baray-e Mo'alejeh Bimari-hayash vared-e Amrica Shod," *Kayhan*, October 23, 1979, 1.
92. "Iran dar Mored-e Fa'aliyyat-ha-ye Shah-e Makhlou' be Amrica Hoshdar Dad; Shah-e Makhlou' dar Astaneh-ye Marg Gharar Gereft," *Kayhan*, October 24, 1979, 1.
93. *Jomhuri Islami*, October 24, 1979, 1.
94. Khomeini, *Sahife-ye Imam*, vol. 10, 336.
95. "Paziresh-e Shah-e Makhlou' az Taraf-e Amrica Yek Amal-e Siasi Ast bar Zedde Enghelab-e Iran," *Mardom*, October 27, 1979, 1; "Shah-e Makhlou' ra Mitavan va Bayad az Amrica Pas Gereft," *Mardom*, October 29, 1979, 1.
96. "Anti-U.S. Demonstration in Iran Scheduled for November 1," cable from NEA—Harold H. Saunders to Newsom—Deliver to Robert Gates for Zbigniew Brzezinski, October 31, 1979, RAC Project, NLC-4-40-2-17-3, Jimmy Carter Presidential Library.
97. Bakeri, "Taskhir-e Sefarat Comonist-ha ra Khal'e Selah Kard."
98. *Kayhan*, October 25, 1978, 5.
99. Massoumeh Ebtekar, *Takeover in Tehran: The Inside Story of the 1979 U.S. Embassy Capture* (Burnaby, Canada: Talonbooks, 2000), 54.
100. Ibid., 59.
101. Ibid.
102. Bakeri, "Taskhir-e Sefarat Comonist-ha ra Khal'e Selah Kard."
103. Ibid.
104. Ebtekar, *Takeover in Tehran*, 70.
105. Mohammad Reza Mahdavi-Kani, *Khaterat-e Ayatollah Mahdavi-Kani* (Tehran: Markaz-e Asnad-e Enghelab-e Eslami, 2006), 223.
106. Ibid., 180 (emphasis added).
107. Mehdi Bazargan, *Enghelab-e Iran dar do Harekat* (Tehran: Nehzat-e Azadi, 1984), 92–101.
108. Ibid.
109. Telegram from U.S. Embassy in Stockholm to U.S. Secretary of State, Washington, D.C., September 17, 1980, RAC Project, NLC-128-2-7-1-9, Jimmy Carter Presidential Library.
110. "(Tasavir-e) Taskhir-e Sefarat-e America dar Tehran," *Fararu*, November 4, 2015, http://fararu.com/fa/news/251742/تصاویر-تسخیر-سفارت-امریکا-در-تهران.
111. Khomeini, *Sahifeh-ye Imam*, vol. 10, 519.
112. "Chera Markaz-e Jasousi-ye Amrica Taskhir Shod?," *Kar*, November 12, 1979, Appendix, 3.

113. Ibid., 2.
114. "Siasat-e Amperialism-e Amrica va Hakemiyyat-e Siasi-ye Novin dar Yek Sal-e Gozashteh," *Kar*, February 20, 1980, 17.
115. Ebtekar, *Takeover in Tehran*, 174.
116. "Hamleh-ye Mosallahaneh be Tazahorat-e Zedde Amperialisti," *Kar*, December 19, 1979, 12.
117. "Ettela'i-ye Daftar-e Imam dar Qom," *Mardom*, November 24, 1979, 3.
118. "Chera Markaz-e Jasousi-ye Amrica Taskhir Shod?," *Kar*, November 12, 1979, Appendix, 1.
119. Ibid.
120. "Chera Sokhangoo-ye Dowlat-e Bazargan Jasous-e Amperialism-e Amrica az Ab dar Amad," *Kar*, December 26, 1979, Appendix, 3.
121. "Bazargan va Yazdi az Raftan-e Shah be Amrica Hemayat Kardand," *Kar*, December 19, 1979, 1–2.
122. "Chera Sokhan-goo-ye Dowlat-e Bazargan Jasous-e Amperialism-e Amrica az Ab dar Amad," 3.
123. "Naghdi bar Saf-'araaee-ha-ye Jahani," *Kar*, December 19, 1979, 1, 8–9.
124. " 'Vahdat-e Kalemeh' va Vahdat-e Amal-e Showra-ye Enghelab ba Amperialism-e Amrica," *Kar*, January 30, 1980, 1–2.
125. Ibid.
126. See front pages of *Mardom*, November 5, 1979; *Mardom*, November 6, 1979; *Mardom*, November 7, 1979; *Mardom*, November 8, 1979; and *Mardom*, November 18, 1979.
127. See front pages of *Mardom*, November 6, 1979; and *Mardom*, November 7, 1979.
128. "Mosahebeh Agha-ye Doctor Beheshti Dabir-e Showra-ye Enghelab," *Mardom*, November 19, 1979, 2.
129. Sick, *All Fall Down*, 241.
130. Jimmy Carter, *White House Diary* (New York: Macmillan, 2010), 368.
131. Cited in Jones, "How Does a Born-Again Christian Deal with a Born-Again Moslem?," 433.
132. Ruhollah Khomeini, *Islam and Revolution: Writings and Declarations of Imam Khomeini*, trans. Hamid Algar (Berkeley: Mizan Press, 1981), 284.
133. Ibid., 283.
134. "From Attorney General to the President," Zbigniew Brzezinski Collection; Series: Subject File; Folder: Meetings: SCC 199, Container 30, November 12, 1979, Jimmy Carter Presidential Library.
135. "Siasat-ha-ye 'Gam be Gam' Gam be Gam Shah ra be Iran Nazdiktar Mikonad," *Kar*, April 2, 1980, 14.
136. Ibid.
137. "Chera A'za-ye Showra-ye Enghelab az Mohakemeh Gerogan-ha Tafreh Miravand," *Kar*, January 16, 1980, 2.
138. Ibid.
139. Ibid.
140. "Toudeh-ha va Refrandom," *Kar*, December 12, 1979, 2.
141. Ibid.
142. "Ba Sherkat dar Entekhabat-e Riasat-e Jomhuri Saf-e Nirou-ha-ye Moteraghi ra Taghviat va Liberal-ha ra Monfared Konim," *Kar*, January 16, 1980, 5.

143. Ibid.

144. Ibid.

145. Khomeini, *Sahife-ye Imam*, vol. 12, 119.

146. Ibid.

147. "Chegouneh Marz-e Doustan va Doshmanan-e Mardom ra dar Ham Mirizand!!," *Kar*, January 23, 1980, 1–2.

148. Ibid.

149. "Salamati-ye Ayatollahi Khomeini ra Arezou Mikonim," *Kar*, January 30, 1980, 2.

150. "Timsar Madani Khastar-e Arteshi Ast ke Zir-e Nazar-e Amrica Bashad," *Kar*, January 16, 1980, Appendix, 2.

151. *Kar*, January 23, 1980, 8.

152. "Natayej-e Avvalin Entekhabat va Avvalin Khatabeh-e Ra'is-e Jomhur," *Kar*, January 30, 1980, 7.

153. "Rahnemoud-e Hashemi Rafsanjani be Amperialist-ha," *Kar*, March 18, 1981, 10.

154. "Regim-e Jomhuri Islami dar Jahat-e Bazsazi-ye Sanaye'-e Vabasteh Gam Barmidarad," *Kar*, April 8, 1981, 1–2.

155. "Banisadr dar Fekr-e Ettehad ba Amperialism-e Oroupa va Japon," *Kar*, April 16, 1980, 2.

156. "'Vahdat-e Kalemeh' va Vahdat-e Amal-e Showra-ye Enghelab ba Amperialism-e Amrica," *Kar*, January 30, 1980, 1–2.

157. "Chamran Istgah-ha-ye Jasousi-ye Amrica ra Dobareh be Kar Andakhteh Ast," *Kar*, February 6, 1980, 2.

158. "Naghsh-e Timsar-ha-ye Artesh dar Amaliyyat-e Nezami-ye Amrica," *Kar*, April 30, 1980, 1–2.

159. Abrahamian, *The Iranian Mojahedin*, 201.

160. Bahman Baktiari, *Parliamentary Politics in Revolutionary Iran: The Institutionalization of Factional Politics* (Gainesville: University Press of Florida, 1996), 67–68.

161. Sepehr Zabih, *The Left in Contemporary Iran* (Stanford: Hoover Institution, 1986), 37.

162. Ibid., 32. The Tudeh Party was tolerated for a few more years before it was banned in 1983. The Islamist government arrested and tried about one hundred members of the "military wing" of the Tudeh Party, including former navy commander Bahram Afzali. He was executed along with several other senior and junior officers. See Farhang Jahanpour, "Iran: The Rise and Fall of the Tudeh Party," *World Today* 40, no. 4 (1984): 152. Tudeh sources claimed that Islamist militant forces arrested about eight thousand of the party's members (see Zabih, *The Left in Contemporary Iran*, 56). Various sources have estimated the number of its members and sympathizers before its dissolution in 1983 to be between ten thousand and fifty thousand or much higher; see Fred Halliday, "Iran's Revolution Turns Sour," *Marxism Today*, December 1983, 32.

163. In Zabih, *The Left in Contemporary Iran*, 107.

164. "Dar Barkhord ba Mas'aleh Gerogan-ha Jasousan-e Amricaee Bayad Mohakemeh Shavand," *Kar*, September 30, 1980, 1, 6.

165. Bakeri, "Taskhir-e Sefarat Comonist-ha ra Khal'e Selah Kard."

6. Religion and Elite Competition in the Iran–Iraq War

1. Amatzia Baram, *Saddam Husayn and Islam, 1968-2003: Ba'thi Iraq from Secularism to Faith* (Baltimore: Johns Hopkins University Press, 2014).
2. For example, Ray Takeyh, "The Iran-Iraq War: A Reassessment," *Middle East Journal* 64, no. 3 (2010): 365–383.
3. See, for example, Williamson Murray and Kevin M. Woods, *The Iran-Iraq War: A Military and Strategic History* (Cambridge: Cambridge University Press, 2014); Rob Johnson, *The Iran-Iraq War* (London: Palgrave Macmillan, 2010); Trita Parsi, *Treacherous Alliance: The Secret Dealings of Israel, Iran, and the United States* (New Haven: Yale University Press, 2007); Gary Sick, "Trial by Error: Reflections on the Iran–Iraq War," *Middle East Journal* 43, no. 2 (1989): 230–245; Anthony H. Cordesman and Abraham R. Wagner, *The Lessons of Modern War: The Iran-Iraq War* vol. 2 (Boulder, Colo.: Westview Press, 1990).
4. For example, see Anoushiravan Ehteshami, "The Foreign Policy of Iran," in *The Foreign Policies of Middle East States*, ed. Raymond A. Hinnebusch and Anoushiravan Ehteshami (Boulder, Colo.: Lynne Rienner, 2002), 299; Stephen M. Walt, *Revolution and War* (Ithaca: Cornell University Press, 1996), 264–265.
5. Stephen M. Walt, *Revolution and War*; F. Gregory Gause III, "Balancing What? Threat Perception and Alliance Choice in the Gulf," *Security Studies* 13, no. 2 (2004): 273–305; Arshin Adib-Moghaddam, "Inventions of the Iran–Iraq War," *Critique: Critical Middle Eastern Studies* 16, no. 1 (2007): 63–83; Mark L. Haas, *The Clash of Ideologies: Middle Eastern Politics and American Security* (Oxford: Oxford University Press, 2012); Lawrence Rubin, *Islam in the Balance: Ideational Threats in Arab Politics* (Stanford: Stanford University Press, 2014).
6. See, for example, Murray and Woods, *The Iran-Iraq War*; Kevin Wood, David Palkki, and Mark E. Stout, eds., *The Saddam Tapes: The Inner Workings of a Tyrant's Regime, 1978-2001* (Cambridge: Cambridge University Press, 2011).
7. Akbar Hashemi Rafsanjani, *Enghelab va Pirouzi* (Tehran: Daftar-e Nashr-e Ma'aref-e Enghelab, 2004), 435.
8. Ibid., 440.
9. Bahman Baktiari, *Parliamentary Politics in Revolutionary Iran: The Institutionalization of Factional Politics* (Gainesville: University Press of Florida, 1996), 67–68.
10. Abolhassan Banisadr, *Rouz-ha bar Ra'is-e Jomhur Chegouneh Migozarad*, vol. 1 (Tehran: Entesharat va Amuzesh-e Enghelab-e Islami, 1980), 134–135.
11. Ibid., 205.
12. See Mark J. Gasiorowski, "The Nuzhih Plot and Iranian Politics," *International Journal of Middle East Studies* 34, no. 4 (2002): 645–666.
13. The commander of the air force complained to Banisadr that although the army itself neutralized the coup plot, the media reported it as though the outsiders, meaning the IRP and IRGC elements, stopped the coup. See Banisadr, *Rouz-ha bar Ra'is-e Jomhur Chegouneh Migozarad*, vol. 1, 46–47.
14. Banisadr, *Rouz-ha bar Ra'is-e Jomhur Chegouneh Migozarad*, vol. 2, 141.
15. Ibid., 199.

16. Ruhollah Khomeini, *Sahife-ye Imam: Majmou'e-ye Rahnemoud-ha-ye Imam Khomeini*, vol. 19 (Tehran: Mo'asseseh Tanzim va Nashr-e Asar-e Imam Khomeini, 1999), 116.
17. *Ettelaat*, September 22, 1980, 3.
18. Khomeini, *Sahifeh-ye Imam*, vol. 14, 164.
19. "Million-ha Nafar dar Namaz-e Doshman-shekan-e Jom'e Sherkat Kardand," *Ettelaat*, September 27, 1980, 6.
20. Khomeini, *Sahifeh-ye Imam*, vol. 13, 233.
21. "Dar Ra's-e Hame Omour, Tahzib-e Nafs Ast," *Jomhuri Islami*, January 21, 1982, 12.
22. "Namayandegan-e Majles Mozakereh ba Aragh ra Nemipazirand," *Ettelaat*, September 30, 1980, 3.
23. Khomeini, *Sahifeh-ye Imam*, vol. 13, 267.
24. Ibid., 225.
25. Khomeini, *Sahifeh-ye Imam*, vol. 16, 281.
26. Baram, *Saddam Husayn and Islam*, 162–163.
27. Loren Jenkins, "Fighting Rages Inside Port City; Iranian, Iraqi Units Battle for Port City," *Washington Post*, October 4, 1980.
28. Loren Jenkins, "Iraq Presses War in South, Seeks a Decisive Victory Over Iranians," *Washington Post*, October 14, 1980.
29. Loren Jenkins, "Khomeini Rejects New Truce Offer, Calls for Victory; Iraq Renews Truce Offer; Khomeini Calls for Final Victory," *Washington Post*, October 14, 1980.
30. William Claiborne, "Iraqi Troops Tightening Grip Around Iranian Oil Center of Abadan," *Washington Post*, October 17, 1980.
31. "Zipori: Israel Would Aid Iran in War Against Iraq if Iran Ends Anti-Israel Policy, Support of Terror," *Jewish Telegraph Agency*, September 29, 1980, http://www.jta.org/1980/09/29/archive/zipori-israel-would-aid-iran-in-war-against-iraq-if-iran-ends-anti-israel-policy-support-of-terror.
32. Bernard Gwertzman, "Israel Is Said to Have Sold Iran F-4 Tires," *New York Times*, August 21, 1981.
33. Bruce Riedel, "Has US Forgotten Lessons of Its First War with Iran?," *Al-Monitor*, April 10, 2012, http://www.al-monitor.com/pulse/originals/2012/bruce-riedel/has-us-forgotten-lessons-of-its.html.
34. "Hashemi Mokhalef-e Basij-e Emkanat-e Jang Boud," *Mashregh*, July 17, 2010, http://www.mashreghnews.ir/fa/news/475/هاشمی-مخالف-بسیج-امکانات-برای-جنگ-بود.
35. Sadegh Shafi'i and Asghar Montazer al-Qa'em, "Goft-o Gou ba Baradar Aziz Jafari," *Faslname-ye Takhassosi-ye Motale'at-e Defa'-e Moghaddas* 10, no. 37 (2011): 84.
36. "Revayat-e Shamkhani az Fathe Khorramshahr," Fars News, May 24, 2013, http://www.farsnews.com/newstext.php?nn=13920303000518.
37. Sepehr Zabih, *The Iranian Military in Revolution and War* (London and New York: Routledge, 1988), 109, 210.
38. See "Goft-o Gou ba Amir Hassani Sa'di," *Faslname-ye Motale'at-e Jang-e Iran va Aragh* 3, no. 9 (2004): 9–40.
39. Ibid.
40. Shafi'i and Montazer al-Qa'em, "Goft-o Gou ba Baradar Aziz Jafari," 82.

41. Mohammad Doroudian, "Tarikh-e Shafahi; Goft-o Gou-ye Sardar Gholam-Ali Rashid ba Doctor Mohsen Rezaei," *Faslname-ye Takhassosi-ye Motale'at-e Defa'-e Moghaddas* 12, no. 46 (2013): 63–66.

42. Mohsen Ardestani, "Tarikh-e Shafahi: Doctor Mohsen Rezaei dar Dowran-e Defa'-e Moghaddas," *Faslname-ye Takhassosi-ye Motale'at-e Defa'-e Moghaddas* 12, no. 46 (2013): 23; "Goft-o Gou ba Amir Daryaban Ali Shamkhani," *Faslname-ye Motale'at-e Jang-e Iran va Aragh* 3, no. 10 (2004): 19; "Bazdarandegi-ye Gorouh-bandi-ha-ye Ejetema'ie va Moghavemat: Goft-e Gou Ba Sar-lashkar Gholam-Ali Rashid," *Faslname-ye Takhassosi-e Jang-e Iran va Aragh* 4, no. 14 (2005): 23.

43. "Goft-o Gou be Amir Daryaban Ali Shamkhani," 14.

44. Banisadr, *Rouz-ha bar Ra'is-e Jomhur Chegouneh Migozarad*, vol. 3, 54.

45. Banisadr, *Rouz-ha bar Ra'is-e Jomhur Chegouneh Migozarad*, vol. 4, 127.

46. Banisadr, *Rouz-ha bar Ra'is-e Jomhur Chegouneh Migozarad*, vol. 3, 62.

47. Banisadr, *Rouz-ha bar Ra'is-e Jomhur Chegouneh Migozarad*, vol. 3, 96; Banisadr, *Rouz-ha bar Ra'is-e Jomhur Chegouneh Migozarad*, vol. 4, 139.

48. Banisadr, *Rouz-ha bar Ra'is-e Jomhur Chegouneh Migozarad*, vol. 2, 168; Banisadr, *Rouz-ha bar Ra'is-e Jomhur Chegouneh Migozarad*, vol. 3, 50–51.

49. Banisadr, *Rouz-ha bar Ra'is-e Jomhur Chegouneh Migozarad*, vol. 3, 136.

50. "Gelayeh Hashemi Rafsanjani az Ayatollah Khomeini dar Mored-e Ekhtelafat ba Banisadr," *BBC Persian*, June 20, 2011, http://www.bbc.com/persian/iran/2011/06/110615_l10_30khordad60_rafsanjani_letter_khomeini.shtml.

51. Akbar Hashemi Rafsanjani, *Obour az Bohran: Karnameh va Khaterat-e Hashemi Rafsanjani, Sal-e 1360* (Tehran: Daftar-e Nashr-e Ma'aref-e Islami, 1997), 106.

52. Ibid., 97.

53. Ibid., 124.

54. Banisadr, *Rouz-ha bar Ra'is-e Jomhur Chegouneh Migozarad*, vol. 2, 168.

55. "Revayat-e Ashk-e Hashemi va Azl-e Banisadr," Rafsanjani's website, December 4, 2013, hashemirafsanjani.ir/fa/content/روایت-اشک-هاشمی-و-عزل-بنی-صدر.

56. Rafsanjani, *Obour az Bohran* 42.

57. Ibid., 60.

58. Ibid., 66.

59. Ibid., 90.

60. Ibid., 82.

61. Ibid., 129.

62. Ibid., 131.

63. Ibid., 152.

64. Ibid., 153, 189.

65. Ibid., 189.

66. Ibid., 145.

67. Ibid., 153.

68. Rafsanjani had previously survived an attempted assassination by Furqan after his wife saved him from two armed men. She survived too.

69. Rafsanjani, *Obour az Bohran*, 181.

70. Ibid., 277.

71. Ibid.

72. Ibid.

73. Ibid., 278.
74. Ibid., 279.
75. Ibid., 318.
76. Ibid., 317.
77. Ibid., 305.
78. Ibid., 309.
79. See Doroudian, "Tarikh-e Shafahi; Goft-o Gou-ye Sardar Gholam-Ali Rashid ba Doctor Mohsen Rezaei," 72.
80. "Estefadeh az Tajrobeh Jang Pas az Jang," *Faslname-ye Takhassosi-ye Jang-e Iran va Aragh* 4, no. 15 (2006): 17; "Bazdarandegi-ye Gorouh-bandi-ha-ye Ejetema'ie va Moghavemat," 22.
81. Ibid.
82. "Na-gofteh-ha-ye Haj Sadegh Ahangaran az 8 Sal Defa'-e Moghaddas," *Pajouhesh-gah-e Oloum va Ma'aref-e Defa'-e Moghaddas*, October 19, 2011, http://www.dsrc.ir /Contents/view.aspx?id=6635.
83. "Goft-o Gou-ye Ekhtesasi ba Haj Sadegh Ahangaran," *Teyban*, May 19, 2008, http:// article.tebyan.net/66767/آهنگران-صادق-حاج-با-گفتگو-غلطان-خون-به-شهیدان-ای-.
84. "Nagofteha-ye Haj Sadegh Ahangaran," *Dez News Network*, July 15, 2010.
85. "Monazereh Saeed Hadadian va Sadegh Ahangaran dar Shabakeh 3," uploaded on December 8, 2013, https://www.youtube.com/watch?v=V77hA8_IC-c.
86. Doroudian, "Tarikh-e Shafahi; Goft-o Gou-ye Sardar Gholam-Ali Rashid ba Doctor Mohsen Rezaei," 73.
87. Gholam-Ali Rashid, "Fath-ol Mobin, Chera? Amaliyyat-e Tarikhi," *Faslname-ye Motale'at-e Jang-e Iran va Aragh* 5, no. 19 (2006): 126; Ahmad Dehghan, *Nagofteh-ha-ye Jang: Khaterat-e Sepahbod-e Shahid Ali Sayad-Shirazi* (Tehran: Sureh Mehr, 2009), 266.
88. Akbar Hashemi Rafsanjani, *Pas az Bohran: Karnameh va Khaterat-e Hashemi Rafsanjani, Sal-e 1361* (Tehran: Daftar-e Nashr-e Ma'aref-e Enghelab, 2007), 38.
89. Ibid., 43.
90. "Bazkhani-ye Amaliyyat-e Ramazan," *Faslname-ye Takhassosi-ye Motale'at-e Defa'-e Moghaddas* 6, no. 25 (2008): 64.
91. Gholam-Ali Rashid, "Fath-e Khorramshahr: Molahezat-e Neami, Payamad-ha-ye Strategic," *Faslname-ye Motale'at-e Jang-e Iran va Aragh* 6, no. 21 (2007): 90.
92. "Nagofte-ha-ee az Ekhtelafat-e Artesh va Sepah," an interview with General Seyyed Torab Zakeri, Iranian Students' News Agency, May 23, 2016, http://www .isna.ir/news/95030301290/جنگ-در-سپاه-و-ارتش-اختلافات-از-هایی-ناگفته.
93. See "Nameh Mahramaneh Mohandes Bazargan be Agha-ye Khomeini Darbareh Edameh Jang," *Neda-ye Azadi*, May 24, 2014, http://www.iranchamber.com /calendar/converter/iranian_calendar_converter.php.
94. See "Rouhani: Artesh Mokhalef-e Edame Jang Ba'd az Khorramshahr Boud," *Tarikh Irani*, August 1, 2014, http://www.tarikhirani.ir/fa/news/۴/body View/4553/0/روحانی:-ارتش-مخالف-ادامه-جنگ-بعد-از-خرمشهر-بود-نظر.م.بر-پایان-جنگ-بعد-از -خواست-کل-دولت-نظامی-شود C8%80%E2%فاو-بود-سپاه-می.html.
95. Hossein-Ali Montazeri, *Khaterat* (Los Angeles: Ketab Corp., 2001), 321.
96. "Nagofte-ha-ye Mohtashamipour: Imam Khomeini Mokhalef-e Edame Jang ba'd az Fath-e Khorramshahr Boud," *Parsineh*, November 20, 2013, http://www.parsine

پور-امام-C8%80%2Eهای-محتشمی‌C8%80%2E%ناگفته/167739/news/fa/com.
بود-مشهر-خر-فتح-از-بعد-جنگ-ادامه-مخالف-خمینی; "Mohsen-e Rezaei va Tadavom-e Jang ba'd az Khorramshahr," *Jaras*, October 8, 2011, http://www.rahesabz.net/story /43620/; "Revayat-e Ayatollah az Noushidan-e Jam-e Zahr," Rafsanjani's website, July 20, 2013, http://www.hashemirafsanjani.ir/content/-حاصل-قطعنامه-قبول اعتدال-امام-بود.

97. Rafsanjani, *Pas az Bohran*, 100.
98. *Ettelaat*, September 30, 1980.
99. *Jomhuri Islami*, April 22, 1982.
100. *Jomhuri Islami*, September 5, 1982, 11.
101. *Ettelaat*, April 24, 1982, 15.
102. "Aragh Bayad Baray-e Enteghal-e Nirou-ha-ye Zerehi-ye Iran be Souriyeh Rah Bedahad," *Jomhuri Islami*, June 12, 1982.
103. "Mosahebeh Mohem-e Ra'is-e Jomhur," *Ettelaat*, April 5, 1982, 13; "Nokhost Vazir Khastar-e Tashkil-e Artesh-e Beyin-al-melali-ye Islami-ye Ghods Shod," *Jomhuri Islami*, June 14, 1982, 4.
104. *Jomhuri Islami*, June 15, 1982, 1.
105. "Vaz'-e Mowjoud-e Jang," *Jomhuri Islami*, April 22, 1982.
106. *Jomhuri Islami*, July 10, 1982, 1.
107. *Jomhuri Islami*, July 7, 1982, 1.
108. Ibid.
109. "Iran Mohemtarin Markazi Ast ke Mitavanad Israel ra Naboud Konad," *Jomhuri Islami*, May 22, 1982, 12.
110. Ibid.
111. *Jomhuri Islami*, July 10, 1982, 2.
112. *Jomhuri Islami*, February 12, 1984, 4.
113. "Ma Mikhahim Qods ra Nejat Bedahim Laken Bedoon-e Nejat-e Aragh Nemitavanim," *Jomhuri Islami*, June 22, 1982, 12.
114. Rafsanjani, *Pas az Bohran*, 113.
115. "Bazkhani-ye Amaliyyat-e Ramazan," 69.
116. Ibid.
117. Rafsanjani, *Pas az Bohran*, 127.
118. "The Iranian Threat to American Interests in the Persian Gulf," cable from the National Intelligence Council to the National Security Council, July 20, 1982, The CIA Electronic Reading Room, https://www.cia.gov/library/readingroom /docs/DOC_0000763462.pdf.
119. Montazeri, *Khaterat*, 326; "Jang-e Iran va Aragh; Dorough-gouyi va Siasat-bazi," *Radio Zamaneh*, September 15, 2013, http://www.radiozamaneh.com/98435.
120. Ibid.
121. Malcolm M. Byrne, *Iran-Contra: Reagan's Scandal and the Unchecked Abuse of Presidential Power* (Lawrence: University Press of Kansas, 2014), 194.
122. Ibid.; James G. Blight, Janet M. Lang, Hussein Banai, Malcolm Byrne, and John Tirman, *Becoming Enemies: US–Iran Relations and the Iran–Iraq War, 1979-1988* (Lanham, Md.: Rowman & Littlefield, 2012), 125–150.
123. Akbar Hashemi Rafsanjani, *Owj-e Defa': Karnameh va Khaterat-e Hashemi Rafsanjani, Sal-e 1365* (Tehran: Daftar-e Nashr-e Ma'aref-e Enghelab, 2009), 338, fn. 1.

124. Joyce Battle, Malcolm Byrne, and Devin Kennington, "Iran-Iraq War Timetable," Woodrow Wilson International Center for Scholars, no date, 36, https://www.wilsoncenter.org/sites/default/files/Iran-IraqWar_Part1_0.pdf.

125. "Hoghough-e Khod ra be Har Gheymati az Hezb-e Ba'ath-e Aragh Khahim Gereft," *Kayhan*, June 4, 1988, 3.

126. Rafsanjani, *Pas az Bohran*, 278.

127. Saeed Sarmady, "Tardid va Ebham Darbareh Amaliyyat-e Valfajr," *Faslname-ye Takhassosi-ye Motale'at-e Defa'-e Moghaddas* 39, no. 10 (2011–2012): 41.

128. "Rouhani: Artesh Mokhalef-e Edameh Jang Ba'd az Khorramshahr Boud."

129. "Majara-ye Gharardad-e 450 Million Poundi ke Mir-Hossein Jelo-ye An-ra Gereft," *Kalemeh*, October 11, 2015, http://www.kaleme.com/1394/07/19/klm-226604/.

130. Mohsen Rafighdoost, *Bara-ye Tarikh Migouyam* (Tehran: Sureh Mehr, 2013), 198; "'Koudeta-ye Sepah Eshkali Nadarad, Ja-ye Douri Nemiravad,'" *Radio Farda*, May 3, 2016, https://www.radiofarda.com/a/27713925.html.

131. Bob Woodward, "CIA Aiding Iraq in Gulf War; Target Data From U.S. Satellites Supplied for Nearly 2 Years," *Washington Post*, December 15, 1986.

132. Elaine Sciolino, "Soviet Tie to Iraq Seems to Increase," *New York Times*, January 12, 1987.

133. Rafsanjani, *Owj-e Defa'*, 423.

134. Thomas L. Friedman, "Israel Sorts Its Interests in Outcome of Gulf War," *New York Times*, November 23, 1986.

135. Rafsanjani, *Owj-e Defa'*, 591.

136. Ibid., 594-595.

137. Ibid., 596.

138. Ibid.

139. Ibid., 604.

140. Ibid.

141. Battle, Byrne, and Kennington, "Iran-Iraq War Timetable."

142. Mohammad-Mehdi Raji, *Aghaye Safir* (Tehran: Ney, 2013), 77–83.

143. "Rou-namaee-ye Televisioni az Nameh Serri-ye Moshen Rezaei dar Payan-e Jang," *BBC Persian*, September 30, 2014, http://www.bbc.com/persian/iran/2014/09/140930_l39_mohsen_rezaei_secret_letter_war.

144. "Hashemi: Doroughi Bozorg Goftand," *Entekhab*, June 12, 2011, http://www.entekhab.ir/fa/news/28284/هاشمی-درونی-بزرگ-گفتند-نامه-ی-محسن-رضایی-به-امام-محرمانه-نبود-اختلافات-داخلی-سپاه-در-جنگ-روند-را-کند-کرد-شمخانی-با-شجاعت-می-گفت-نمی-توانیم-بجنگیم.

145. Ibid.

146. "Az Tafavot-e 'Paziresh-e Ghat'nameh' ba 'Payan-e Jang' ta Nameh be Hashemi va Khatami," *Tabnak*, May 1, 2011, http://www.tabnak.ir/fa/news/162151.

147. "Chera Ayatollah Khomeini Khastar-e E'dam-e Farmandehan-e Moghasser-e 'Shekast' dar Jang Shod?," *BBC Persian*, September 23, 2014, http://www.bbc.com/persian/iran/2014/09/140923_l39_file_iran_iraq_war.

148. "Khomeini Accepts 'Poison' of Ending the War with Iraq," *New York Times*, July 21, 1988.

149. "Ezharat-e Janeshin-e Farmandeh Koll-e Ghova Darbareh Elal-e Paziresh-e Ghat'nameh 598 Tavassot-e Iran va Nataye-je Hasel az Ejra-ye An," *Kayhan*, July 19, 1988, 16.
150. "Noushidan-e Jam-e Zahr bar Imam Tahmil Nashod," *Entekhab*, July 20, 2013, http://www.entekhab.ir/fa/news/121643/نوشیدن-جام-زهر-بر-امام-تحمیل نشدقبول-قطعنامه-نتیجه-اعتدال-امام-بود.
151. Ibid.; "Rafsanjani: Nagofte-ha-ye Ghat'name-ye 598 ra Hanooz Nabayad Be-gouyam," *BBC Persian*, June 2, 2015, http://www.bbc.com/persian/iran/2015/06/150 602_l39_rafsanjani_diaries_khomeini; "Didgah-e Imam Darbare-ye Ghat'name-ye 598 ra Nagofteh-am va Fe'lan Nemigouham," Iranian Students' News Agency, June 1, 2015, http://www.isna.ir/news/94031107030/نگفته-ام-و-فعلا-نمی-گویم 598 دیدگاه-امام-ر-ه-درباره-قطعنامه-.

7. The Metamorphosis of Islamism After the War

1. "Naft ra Vasileh-ee Baray-e Ta'aali-ye Farhang-e Ensani Gharar Dahim," *Jomhuri Islami*, November 13, 1982, 12.
2. "Jame'e Varzesh-e Ma Bayad Sarnevesht-e Khod ra ba Harekat-e Ommat-e Hez-bollah Peyvand Dahand," *Jomhuri Islami*, November 13, 1982, 10.
3. Ruhollah Khomeini, *Sahife-ye Imam: Majmou'e-ye Rahnemoud-ha-ye Imam Khomeini* 18 (Tehran: Mo'asseseh Tanzim va Nashr-e Asar-e Imam Khomeini, 1999), 434.
4. On the "Islamic banking" debate, see *Jomhuri Islami*, June 11, 1983, 9.
5. *Jomhuri Islami*, May 29, 1982, 12.
6. *Jomhuri Islami*, December 17, 1983.
7. Mehdi Moslem, *Factional Politics in Post-Khomeini Iran* (Syracuse, N.Y.: Syracuse University Press, 2002), 75.
8. Khomeini, *Sahife-ye Imam*, vol. 20, 170.
9. Oliver Roy, "The Crisis of Legitimacy in Iran," *Middle East Journal* 53, no. 2 (1999): 206.
10. Quoted in Moslem, *Factional Politics in Post-Khomeini Iran*, 74.
11. "Fatva-ye Rahbar-e Enghelab Darbareh Eltezam be Velayat-e Faqih," *Raja News*, July 20, 2010, http://www.rajanews.com/news/39957.
12. Ibid.
13. Ahmad Ashraf, "Theocracy and Charisma: New Men of Power in Iran," *International Journal of Politics, Culture and Society* 4, no. 1 (1990): 113–152. Ashraf used the term specifically to describe the fatwa against Rushdie.
14. Ayatollah Javadi-Amoli, "The Story of Delivering Imam Khomeini's Letter to Gor-bachev," Khomeini's official website, July 25, 2015, http://en.imam-khomeini .ir/en/n3770/The_ideas_of_the_Imam/Imam%E2%80%99s_Prediction/The _story_of_delivering_Imam_Khomeini%E2%80%99s_letter_to_Gorbachev.
15. Quoted in "Ayatollah Khomeini's Only Written Message to a Foreign Leader," *The Iran Project*, January 2, 2017, http://theiranproject.com/blog/2017/01/02 /ayatollah-khomeinis-written-message-foreign-leader/.

16. Abu Jafar Muhammad ibn Al-Tabari, *Tahdhib Tarikh al-Tabari: Tarikh al-Umam wal-al-Muluk* (Beirut, Lebanon: Dar al-Fikr, 1992).

17. Baqer Moin, *Khomeini: Life of the Ayatollah* (London: I.B. Tauris, 1999), 275.

18. Peter Murtagh, "Rushdie in Hiding after Ayatollah's Death Threat," *Guardian*, February 15, 1989.

19. Jonathan C. Randal, "Iran Hints at Death Reprieve If 'Verses' Author Apologizes," *Washington Post*, February 18, 1989.

20. Youssef M. Ibrahim, "Teheran Qualifies Threat to Author," *New York Times*, February 18, 1989.

21. Ibid.

22. Jonathan C. Randal, "Novelist Apologizes to Moslems; Iranians Issue Conflicting Replies About Death Order," *Washington Post*, February 19, 1989.

23. "Khomeini Spurns Rushdie Regrets and Reiterates Threat of Death," *New York Times*, February 20, 1989.

24. Ibid.

25. "Payam-e Hazrat-e Imam be Rouhaniyan, Maraje', Modarresan, Tollab, va A'emme Jom'e va Jamaa'aat," Khamenei's official website, February 22, 1989, http://farsi.khamenei.ir/special?id=3937.

26. Quoted in Moin, *Khomeini*, 276.

27. Ibid.

28. Moslem, *Factional Politics in Post-Khomeini Iran*, 81.

29. "Bimari-ye Ayatollah Khomeini Che Boud va Chegoune Dargozasht," *BBC Persian*, June 2, 2012, http://www.bbc.com/persian/science/2012/06/120602_l23_khomeini_lealth_report.

30. Ibid.

31. Ibid.

32. Akbar Hashemi Rafsanjani, *Bazsazi va Sazandegi: Karnameh va Khaṭerat-e Hashemi Rafsanjani, Sal-e 1368* (Tehran: Daftar-e Nashr-e Ma'aref-e Enghelab, 2012), 151.

33. Quoted in Mohsen Kadivar, "Momane'at-e Rahbari az Raf'-e Hasr-e Bimar-e Salmand-e Mobtala be Saratan," *Jaras*, July 3, 2013, http://www.rahesabz.net/story/72451/.

34. On Azari-Qomi, see Jalal Yaqubi, "Azari-Qomi: az Nazariye Pardazi-e Velayat-e Faqih ta Marg dar Hasr-e Khanegi," *BBC Persian*, February 11, 2014, http://www.bbc.com/persian/mobile/iran/2014/02/140211_l39_azari-qomi_yaghoobi.shtml; Moshen Kadivar, *Faraz va Foroud-e Azari-Qomi*, Kadivar's wesbsite, 2014, http://kadivar.com/wp-content/uploads/2014/03/آذری‌قمی-فرود-و-فراز.pdf.

35. Mohsen Kadivar, *Ebtezal-e Marja'iyyat va Shi'a Estizah-e Marja'iyyat-e Magham-e Rahbari*, Kadivar's website, 2015, 50–54, Kadivar.com/wp-content/uploads/2014/03/شیعه‌مرجعیت-ابتذال.pdf.

36. See, for example, Maureen Dowd, "Bush Says 'Clear Signal' from Iran on Hostages Could Reopen Ties," *New York Times*, August 16, 1989.

37. Rafsanjani, *Bazsazi va Sazandegi*, 162, n. 1.

38. Ibid., 162–164.

39. Ibid., 162.

40. Ibid., 171.

41. Ibid., 205.
42. Ibid., 332.
43. Ibid., 174.
44. See Reza Arjmand, "Inscription on Stone: Islam, State and Education in Iran and Turkey," PhD Dissertation (Umeå, Sweden: Pedagogiska Institutionen, 2008).
45. *Entekhab Daily*, August 22, 2015, http://www.entekhab.ir/fa/news/222078/ احمدی-نژاد-گفت-بروید-رئیس-دولت-اصلاحات-و-بقیه-را-دستگیر-کنید-و-شر-همه-را-کم-کنید-گفتم مرد-حسابی-چه-می-گویی-می-روی-می-گویی-خس-و-خاشاک-و-آت-و-آشغال-و-حالا-می-گویی-بگیرید ببرید-و-تمام.

8. The Factional Battle Over Khomeini's *Velayat-e Faqih*

1. Ahmad Ashraf and Ali Banuazizi, "The State, Classes and Modes of Mobilization in the Iranian Revolution," *State, Culture, and Society* 1, no. 3 (1985): 3–40; Ali Banuazizi, "Faltering Legitimacy: The Ruling Clerics and Civil Society in Contemporary Iran," *International Journal of Politics, Culture and Society* 8, no. 4 (1995): 563–578; Bahman Baktiari, *Parliamentary Politics in Revolutionary Iran: The Institutionalization of Factional Politics* (Gainesville: University Press of Florida, 1996); Mehdi Moslem, *Factional Politics in Post-Khomeini Iran* (Syracuse, N.Y.: Syracuse University Press, 2002); Daniel Brumberg, *Reinventing Khomeini: The Struggle for Reform in Iran* (Chicago: University of Chicago Press, 2001).
2. Quoted in Baktiari, *Parliamentary Politics in Revolutionary Iran*, 92.
3. Ibid., 121.
4. Moslem, *Factional Politics in Post-Khomeini Iran.*
5. FBIS-NES-89-023, February 6, 1989.
6. Anoushiravan Ehteshami, *After Khomeini: The Iranian Second Republic* (New York: Routledge, 1995).
7. Brenda Shaffer, *The Limits of Culture: Islam and Foreign Policy* (Cambridge, Mass.: MIT Press, 2006).
8. Ibid.
9. See Ehteshami, *After Khomeini*; Jahangir Amuzegar, *The Islamic Republic of Iran: Reflections on an Emerging Economy* (New York: Routledge, 2014); Suzanne Maloney, *Iran's Political Economy Since the Revolution* (Cambridge: Cambridge University Press, 2015).
10. Akbar Hashemi Rafsanjani, *Bazsazi va Sazandegi: Karnameh va Khaterat-e Hashemi Rafsanjani, Sal-e 1368* (Tehran: Daftar-e Nashr-e Ma'aref-e Enghelab, 2012), 406.
11. Ibid., 266.
12. Ibid., 280.
13. Maureen Dowd, "Bush Says 'Clear Signal' from Iran on Hostages Could Reopen Ties," *New York Times*, August 16, 1989.
14. Alan Cowell, "Iran's Top Cleric Rejects Talking to Washington," *New York Times*, August 15, 1989.
15. Ataollah Mohajerani, "Mozakere-ye Mostaghim," *Ettelaat*, April 26, 1990.

16. "Nameh be Aghaye Ataollah Mohajerani Darbareh Maghale-ye 'Mozakere-ye Mostaghim,' " Khamenei's official website, May 2, 1990, http://farsi.khamenei .ir/message-content?id=2305.

17. Akbar Hashemi Rafsanjani, *E'tedal va Pirouzi: Karnameh va Khaṭerat-e Hashemi Rafsanjani, Sal-e 1369* (Tehran: Daftar-e Nashr-e Ma'aref-e Enghelab, 2013), 93.

18. See, for example, "Kharej-e Feqh/Hokm-e Gheybat ba Abzar-e Ghalam va Resane-ha-ye Jadid," Khamenei's official website, December 28, 2010, http://farsi .khamenei.ir/speech-content?id=10770.

19. Ali Mirsepassi, *Political Islam, Iran and Enlightenment* (New York: Cambridge University Press, 2010); Ali Mirsepassi, *Democracy in Modern Iran* (New York: New York University Press, 2010); Naser Ghobadzadeh, *Religious Secularity: A Theological Challenge to the Islamic State* (New York: Oxford University Press, 2015); Nader Hashemi, *Islam, Secularism, and Liberal Democracy: Toward a Democratic Theory for Muslim Societies* (Oxford: Oxford University Press, 2009); Laura Secor, *Children of Paradise: The Struggle for the Soul of Iran* (New York: Penguin Random House, 2016).

20. Ali Paya, "Karl Popper and the Iranian Intellectuals," *The American Journal of Islamic Social Sciences* 20, no. 2 (Spring 2003): 50–79.

21. Mirsepassi, *Democracy in Modern Iran*, 125–147.

22. Mahmoud Sadri, "Sacral Defense of Secularism: The Political Theologies of Soroush, Shabestari, and Kadivar," *International Journal of Politics, Culture and Society* 15, no. 2 (Winter 2001): 257–270. See also Mohsen Kadivar, *Naẓriyyeh-ha-ye Dowlat dar Feqh-e Shi'a* (Tehran: Nasani, 1997); and Mohsen Kadivar, *Ḥokoumat-e Velayee* (Tehran: Nashr-e Ney, 1998).

23. Mohammad Mujtahid Shabestari, *Naghdi bar Ghara'at-e Rasmi az Din: Bohran-ha, Chalesh-ha, Rah-e Hal-ha* (Tehran: Tarh-e No, 2000).

24. These articles were later reprinted in Saeed Hajjarian, *Az Shahed-e Ghodsi ta Shahed-e Bazaari* (Tehran: Tarh-e No, 2001).

25. Ibid., 96.

26. Ibid., 84.

27. Ibid., 85.

28. Ibid., 87.

29. Ibid., 91.

30. Ibid., 145.

31. Ibid., 147.

32. See José Casanova, *Public Religions in the Modern World* (Chicago: University of Chicago Press, 1994).

33. Hossein-Ali Montazeri, *Hokoumat-e Dini va Hoghough-e Ensan* (Qom: Arghavan Danesh, 2007), 23.

34. Ibid., 24.

35. Sadri, "Sacral Defense of Secularism."

36. Mohsen Kadivar, interview with *Rah-e No*, 15.

37. See Abdolkarim Soroush, *Farbeh-tar az Ideologi* (Tehran: Mo'assese-ye Farhangi-ye Serat, 1995); Abdolkarim Soroush, *Ghabz va Basṭ-e Te'oric-e Shariat: Naẓariyeh Takamol-e Ma'refat-e Dini* (Tehran: Mo'assese-ye Farhangi-ye Serat, 1991); Abdolkarim Soroush, *Serat-ha-ye Mostaghim* (Tehran: Mo'assese-ye Farhangi-ye Serat, 1998);

Abdolkarim Soroush, *Modara va Modiriyyat* (Tehran: Mo'assese-ye Farhangi-ye Serat, 1997); Abdolkarim Soroush, *Siyasat-nameh* (Tehran: Mo'assese-ye Farhangi-ye Serat, 1999).

38. Abdolkarim Soroush, *The Expansion of Prophetic Experience*, trans. Nilou Mobasser, ed. Forough Jahanbakhsh (Leiden: Brill, 2009); Abdolkarim Soroush, *Reason, Freedom and Democracy in Islam*, trans. and ed. Ahmad Sadri and Mahmoud Sadri (Oxford: Oxford University Press, 2000), 131–155.

39. Soroush, *Reason, Freedom and Democracy in Islam*, 151.

40. Ibid., 66.

41. Ibid., 68.

42. Ibid., 64.

43. Ibid., 131.

44. Ibid., 63.

45. Ibid., 133.

46. Ibid., 194.

47. Needless to say, within this minimalist perspective of religion, there is a wide variety of views and arguments.

48. Casanova, *Public Religions in the Modern World*, 6–7.

49. Ali-Reza Alavi-Tabar, "Din dar 'Arseh Omoumi," *Kalemeh*, November 11, 2011, http://www.kaleme.com/1390/08/20/klm-79840/?theme=fast.

50. Asef Bayat, *Post-Islamism: The Many Faces of Political Islam* (Oxford: Oxford University Press, 2013).

51. Stathis N. Kalyvas, *The Rise of Christian Democracy in Europe* (Ithaca: Cornell University Press, 1996).

52. "Chera Hashemi dar Dahe 90 Ra'iy-e Khod be Nategh-Nouri ra Fash Mikonad?," *Khabar Online*, June 18, 2016, http://www.khabaronline.ir/detail/547479/Politics/parties.

53. "Transcript of Interview with Iranian President Mohammad Khatami," *CNN*, January 7, 1998, http://www.cnn.com/WORLD/9801/07/iran/interview.html.

54. It is crucial, however, to note that the reformists' own blunders, as mentioned, were an important factor that kept many disillusioned voters at home and mobilized many conservatives to vote against them. The reformists' lack of consensus on a single candidate divided their supporters and contributed to their defeat. It is also worth noting that the political landscape moved so much to the right that many of the old conservatives, including the right's candidate in the 1997 presidential election, Ali Akbar Nategh-Nouri, were now centrists and potential allies of the left.

55. *Sobh-e Emrouz*, January 19, 2000.

56. Farhad Khosrokhavar, "Neo-conservative Intellectuals in Iran," *Middle East Critique* 10, no. 19 (2001): 6.

57. Ibid., 20.

58. Nader Hashemi, "Religious Disputation and Democratic Constitutionalism: The Enduring Legacy of the Constitutional Revolution on the Struggle for Democracy in Iran," *Constellation* 17, no. 11 (2010): 50–60; Mohammad Taghi Mesbah-Yazdi, *Selsele-ha-ye Mabahes-e Islam, Siasat va Hokoumat* (Tehran: Daftar-e Motale'at va Barresi-ha-ye Siasi, 1999).

59. Khosrokhavar, "Neo-conservative Intellectuals in Iran," 16.
60. Ibid.
61. Ibid., 18.

9. Media, Religion, and the Green Movement

1. For more on the role of the media in contemporary Iranian politics, see David M. Faris and Babak Rahimi, eds., *Social Media in Iran: Politics and Society After 2009* (Albany: State University of New York Press, 2015).
2. Akbar Ganji, *Alijenab-e Sorkh-poush va Alijenaban-e Khakestari: Asib-shenasi-ye Gozar be Dowlat-e Democratic va Towse'-e-gara* (Tehran: Tarh-e Now, 2000).
3. *Sobh-e Emrouz*, February 24, 2000, 1; *Sobh-e Emrouz*, February 26, 2000, 1.
4. The agent was Saeed Emami. He was arrested but later "committed suicide." Many reformists believe that he was killed by the conservative security agents to prevent the investigators from tracing his actions up his chain of command.
5. *Constitution of the Islamic Republic of Iran*, adopted October 24, 1979, amended July 28, 1989, Article 24.
6. For more information about Saeed Mortazavi, see "Iran: Prosecute Mortazavi for Detention Deaths," *Human Rights Watch*, January 13, 2010, http://www.hrw.org/news/2010/01/13/iran-prosecute-mortazavi-detention-deaths.
7. *Islamic Penal Code*, Book Five, State Administered Punishments and Deterrents, ratified May 9, 1996.
8. See "You Can Detain Anyone for Anything: Iran's Broadening Clampdown on Independent Activism," *Human Rights Watch*, January 6, 2008, http://www.hrw.org/reports/2008/01/06/you-can-detain-anyone-anything.
9. "Nameh be Namayandegan-e Majles-e Showra-ye Islami dar Khosous-e Ghanoun-e Matbou'aat," Khamenei's official website, August 5, 2000, http://Farsi.khamenei.ir/message-content?id=3019.84.
10. Mohammad Ayatollahi Tabaar, "The Beloved Great Satan: The Portrayal of the US in the Iranian Media Since 9/11," *Vaseteh: Journal of the European Society for Iranian Studies* 1, no. 1 (2005): 63–78.
11. Francis Fukuyama, *America at the Crossroads: Democracy, Power, and the Neoconservative Legacy* (New Haven, Conn.: Yale University Press, 2007), 83.
12. Fatemeh Rajabi, who runs the ultraconservative site *Raja News*, published a book titled *Ahmadinejad, The Miracle of the Third Millennium* (Tehran: Nashr-e Danesh Amouz, 2006).
13. "Iran Is World's Biggest Prison for Journalists Again," *Reporters Without Borders*, January 6, 2010, http://en.rsf.org/iran-iran-is-world-s-biggest-prison-for-06-01-2010,35838.
14. See, for example, "Shariatmadari: Servic-ha-ye Ettelaati-e Gharb Mousavi, Khatami va Karroubi ra 'Fossil-e Zendeh' Midanand," *Kayhan*, July 9, 2011, 10.
15. "Fukuyama Parandeh Shi'a ba Bal-e Sorkh-o Sabz Nadideh Ast," *Jaras*, May 18, 2010, http://www.rahesabz.net/story/15680/.

16. "Bayanat dar Didar-e Ra'is-e Jomhuri va A'za-ye Hey'at-e Dowlat," Khamenei's official wesbite, August 23, 2008, http://farsi.khamenei.ir/speech-content?id=3661.
17. "kam hejabi dar iran," posted on January 24, 2009, https://www.youtube.com/watch?v=8YtMIMRqOok.
18. "Navad-e Siasi, Haleh Nour," posted on June 4, 2009, https://www.youtube.com/watch?v=IbbQeZDbSMo.
19. "Ahmadinejad: Dokhtar-e 16 Saleh too Zirzamin Energy Hasteh-ie," posted on October 12, 2012, https://www.youtube.com/watch?v=swDMY5-bEMk.
20. "9 Dey Payan Bakhsh-e Jang-e Ahzab: Fetne 88 Faz-e Dovvom-e Amaliyyat-e Alayh-e Nezam-e Islami Boud," *Mehr News,* January 2, 2012, http://www.mehrnews.com/fa/NewsDetail.aspx?NewsID=1498713.
21. "Matn-e Monazereh Ahmadinejad va Karroubi," *Hamshahri,* June 7, 2009, http://hamshahrionline.ir/details/83025.
22. "An-ha Midanestand," *Radio Farda,* June 18, 2009, http://www.radiofarda.com/a/RM_Ahmadinejad_Victory_in_News/1756572.html.
23. *Etemad Melli,* June 11, 2009, 1.
24. "Rafsanjani's wife after voting June 12 2009," posted on July 2, 2009, https://www.youtube.com/watch?v=llhECZTJ-Jk.
25. "An-ha Midanestand."
26. Hossein Bastani, "Aya dar Entekhabat-e Riasat-e Jomhuri Taghallob Shod?," *BBC Persian,* June 6, 2010, http://www.bbc.com/persian/iran/2010/06/100603_l39_elec_anniv_vote_rigging.
27. Parsa Piltan, "Gah-shomar-e Sad Rooz E'teraz-e Entekhabati dar Iran," *BBC Persian,* September 22, 2009, http://www.bbc.com/persian/iran/2009/09/090920_bd_pp_ir88_timeline_election.shtml.
28. "E'teraf-e Sepah be Hozour-e Millioni-e Mo'tarezan dar Rouz-e Qods," *Jaras,* September 29, 2009, http://www.rahesabz.net/story/2096/.
29. See Negin Nabavi, ed., *Iran: From Theocracy to the Green Movement* (New York: Springer, 2012); Nader Hashemi and Danny Postel, eds., *The People Reloaded: The Green Movement and the Struggle for Iran's Future* (Brooklyn, N.Y.: Melville House, 2010).
30. "A Death in Tehran," *PBS Frontline,* November 17, 2009, http://www.pbs.org/wgbh/frontline/film/tehranbureaudeathintehran/.
31. "Khanevadeh Neda Agha Soltan Namayesh-e Koshteh Shodan-e Ou ra Mahkoum Kard," *BBC Persian,* December 4, 2009, http://www.bbc.com/persian/iran/2009/12/091204_he_neda_show.shtml.
32. See Massoumeh Torfeh and Annabelle Sreberny, "The BBC Persian Service and the Islamic Revolution of 1979," *Middle East Journal of Culture and Communication* 3, no. 2 (2010): 216–241.
33. "Mousavi's 15th Statement: 30th Anniversary of the Formation of the Basij," *Khordad 88,* November 25, 2009, http://khordaad88.com/?p=790#more-790.
34. "Mousavi's 14th Statement," *Khordad 88,* October 31, 2009, http://khordaad88.com/?p=738.
35. "Mousavi's 13th Statement: Violence Is Not the Solution," *Khordad 88,* September 28, 2009, http://khordaad88.com/?p=671#more-671.

36. "Mousavi's 10th Statement: Trial of Green Movement Activists," *Khordad 88*, August 4, 2009, http://khordaad88.com/?p=94.

37. Bahram Rafi'i, "Negarani-ye Sepah az Kamboud-e Sarbaz va Nirou-ye Mosallah," *Rooz Online*, August 11, 2011, http://www.roozonline.com/english/news3/newsitem/article/-23a3161827.html.

38. "Matn va File Sowty-e Kamel-e Sokhanan-e Sardar Moshfegh," *Peyk-e Iran*, August 9, 2010, http://www.peykeiran.com/Content.aspx?ID=20280.

39. "Shekayat-e Haft Chehre-ye Eslah-talab az Ba'zi az Farmandehan-e Sepah-e Pasdaran," *BBC Persian*, August 8, 2010, http://www.bbc.co.uk/persian/iran/2010/08/100808_l01_election_fraud_mosavi.shtml.

40. "Defa'-e Edare-ye Siasi-ye Sepah az Ezharat-e Sardar Moshfegh," *BBC Persian*, August 14, 2010, http://www.bbc.co.uk/persian/iran/2010/08/100814_l10_reformists_complaint_against_sepah_javani_reax.shtml.

41. "Kenareh-giri-ye Ayatollah Javadi-Amoli," *Radio Farda*, November 28, 2009, http://www.radiofarda.com/a/f35_Javadi_Amoli_Resigned/1890061.html.

42. Mohammad Ayatollahi Tabaar, "Iran's Green Movement and the Grey Strategy of Patience," *Foreign Policy*, April 30, 2010, http://foreignpolicy.com/2010/04/30/irans-green-movement-and-the-grey-strategy-of-patience/.

43. "Mohammad Nourizad be Rahbari: az Mardom Pouzesh Bekhahid," *Kalemeh*, January 28, 2012, http://www.kaleme.com/1390/11/08/klm-88460/?theme=fast.

44. "Alaie: Nemikhastam Nezam-e Shahanshahi ra ba Nezam-e Jomhuri-ye Islami Moghayeseh Konam," *BBC Persian*, January 25, 2012, http://www.bbc.co.uk/persian/iran/2012/01/120115_ka_alaei_hossin.shtml.

45. *Ghanoon*, January 16, 2012.

46. Hossein Shariatmadari, "Ghatreh Daryast Agar ba Daryast," *Kayhan*, January 16, 2012, 2.

47. "Pasokh-e Sardar 'Alaie be Shariatmadari," *Entekhab*, January 17, 2012, http://www.entekhab.ir/fa/news/50384.

48. "Akbar Ganji dar BBC," January 14, 2010, posted on March 17, 2012, http://www.aparat.com/v/JYIP0/اکبر_گنجی_در_بی_بی_سی_(امام_زمان_وجود_ندارد).

49. Mohsen Kadivar, "Olaviyyat-e Iran bar Felestin Strategy-e Jonbesh-e Sabz Ast," *Jaras*, June 24, 2010, http://www.rahesabz.net/story/18104/.

50. "Ahmadinejad 'Khas-o Khashak' ra Takzib Kard," *Tabnak*, June 18, 2009.

51. "Website Ayatollah Khamenei: Hameye Mo'tarezan Microb-e Siasi Nistand," *BBC Persian*, October 25, 2010, http://www.bbc.co.uk/persian/iran/2010/10/101025_u03_khamenei_website_microbe_vaccine.shtml.

52. Abdolkarim Soroush, "Religious Tyranny Is Crumbling: Rejoice!," Abdolkarim Soroush's website, September 13, 2009, http://www.drsoroush.com/English/By_DrSoroush/E-CMB-20090913-ReligiousTyrannyisCrumblingRejoice.html.

53. "Bayanat dar Didar ba A'zay-e Majles-e Khobregan," Khamenei's official website, September 24, 2009, http://Farsi.khamenei.ir/speech-content?id=8094.

54. "Vazir-e Ettelaat: Hazine-ye 17 Milliard Dollar Baray-e Fetne-ye Parsal," President's official website, August 9, 2010, http://dolat.ir/NSite/FullStory/?id=191870.

55. A week into the June 2009 unrest, U.S. Secretary of State Hillary Clinton asked Twitter to delay its maintenance so the Iranian protesters could use it to communicate and organize. However, there is no evidence to show that Twitter had many users inside Iran at the time. Instead, it seems that other sites such as Facebook and YouTube played a critical role in informing the people of the latest events. See Golnaz Esfandiari, "The Twitter Devolution," *Foreign Policy*, June 8, 2010, http://foreignpolicy.com/2010/06/08/the-twitter-devolution/.

56. "Artesh-e Cyberi-e Sepah-e Pasdaran ya Hacker-ha-ye Ejare'ee," *Deutsche Welle Persian*, September 14, 2010, http://www.dw.com/fa-ir/ارتش-سایبری-سپاه-پاسداران-یا-هکرهای-اجارهای/a-5992646.

57. Somini Sengupta, "Hacker Rattles Security Circles," *New York Times*, September 11, 2011, http://www.nytimes.com/2011/09/12/technology/hacker-rattles-internet-security-circles.html?pagewanted=all.

58. "Ahmadinejad: Bozorgtarin Mane'e Zohour-e Imam Zaman Amrica Ast," *Kalemeh*, February 23, 2010, http://www.kaleme.com/1388/12/04/klm-12145/.

59. Shibley Telhami, "2008 Annual Arab Public Opinion Poll," Brookings Institution, March 2008, http://www.brookings.edu/~/media/events/2008/4/14%20middle%20east/0414_middle_east_telhami.

60. "Hoshdar-e Motahari be Ahmadinejad dar Mored-e 'Maktab-e Irani va Hejab," *BBC Persian*, March 9, 2011, http://www.bbc.com/persian/iran/2011/03/110309_l44_motahari_hejab_iranism.shtml.

61. Golnaz Esfandiari, "Historic Cyrus Cylinder Called 'A Stranger in Its Own Home,'" *Radio Free Europe/Radio Liberty*, September 14, 2012, http://www.rferl.org/content/Historic_Cyrus_Cylinder_Called_A_Stranger_In_Its_Own_Home/2157345.html.

62. "Vakonesh-ha be Ezharat-e Ahmadinejad Darbare-ye Manshour-e Kourosh," *BBC Persian*, September 20, 2010, http://www.bbc.com/persian/iran/2010/09/100920_l38_iran_cyrus_ahmadinejad.shtml.

63. *Kayhan*, July 19, 2009, 2.

64. "Ahmadinejad Dousti ba Mashaei ra Yek 'Ne'mat' Khand," *BBC Persian*, January 22, 2009, http://www.bbc.co.uk/persian/iran/2009/07/090722_si_ahmadi_mashaei.shtml.

65. "Khabar-ha-ye Zeddo Naghiz dar Mored-e Barkenari-ye Rahim Mashaei," *BBC Persian*, January 21, 2009, http://www.bbc.co.uk/persian/iran/2009/07/090721_op_mashai_contradictions.shtml.

66. *Kayhan*, July 25, 2009, 2; *Kayhan*, July 26, 2009, 2.

67. "Hey'at-e Siasi-ye Iran Darkhast-e Viza-ye Amrica Kardeh Ast," *BBC Persian*, March 8, 2011, http://www.bbc.co.uk/persian/iran/2011/03/110307_u03_delegation_trip.shtml.

68. "Darkhast-e Viza az Amrica Tavasot-e Hey'at-e Siasi-ye Iran? / Mashaei Nowruz be Amrica Miravad?," *Khabar Online*, March 8, 2011, http://www.khabaronline.ir/detail/135766/.

69. "Chera Safar-e Mashaei be Amrica Laghv Shod?," *Fararu*, March 19, 2011, http://fararu.com/fa/news/71565/چرا-سفر-مشایی-به-آمریکا-لغو-شد.

70. Ibid.

71. "Safar-e Mashaei be New York Laghv Shod," *Fars News*, March 19, 2011, http://www.farsnews.com/newstext.php?nn=8912280460.

72. "Safar-e Mashaei be New York Laghv Shod," Mehr News, March 19, 2011, http://www.mehrnews.com/news/1276762/شد-لغو-آمریکا-به-مشایی-سفر.

73. David Ignatius, "Internal Strife Emerges as Tehran Looks Westward," *Washington Post*, May 5, 2011, http://articles.washingtonpost.com/2011-05-05/opinions/35264246_1_esfandiar-rahim-mashaei-iranian-nation-iranian-presidential-elections.

74. *BBC Persian Radio*, May 8, 2011, The Morning Program.

75. "Talash-e Naa-farjam-e Mashaei Baray-e Rabete ba Amrica," *Jahan News*, May 8, 2011, http://www.jahannews.com/vdcfxtdy1w6dvea.igiw.html; "*Washington Post*: Talash-e Naa-farjam-e Mashaei bara-ye Rabete ba Amrica," *Fararu*, May 8, 2011, http://fararu.com/fa/news/76549/مشایی-جام-نافر-تلاش-پست-واشنگتن برای-رابطه-با-آمریکا.

76. Ibid.; "Dalil-e Bazdasht-e Yar-e Ghar-e Mashaei," *Tebyan*, May 4, 2011, http://www.tebyan.net/newindex.aspx?pid=164066.

77. "Naghsh-e Jaryan-e Enherafi dar Biroun Keshidan-e Parvandeh-ha az Vezarat-e Ettelaat," *Shafaf*, October 24, 2011, http://www.shafaf.ir/fa/pages/?cid=80446.

78. But a year later, the president showed that there was some truth in *Iran*'s parody. Retaliating against the impeachment of one of his ministers, Ahmadinejad revealed classified documents accusing the heads of the other two branches of the government of massive corruption. See Mohammad Ayatollahi Tabaar, "Supreme Showdown in Tehran," *Foreign Policy*, February 4, 2013, http://foreignpolicy.com/2013/02/04/supreme-showdown-in-tehran/.

79. Ibid.

80. "Hashemi Rafsanjani, Rahim Mashaei va Saeed Jalili Baray-e Entekhabat Sabt-e-nam Kardand," *BBC Persian*, May 11, 2013, http://www.bbc.com/persian/iran/2013/05/130511_ir92_election_regestering_last_day.

81. "Hashemi Rafsanjani va Mashaei Radd-e Salahiyyat Shodand," *BBC Persian*, May 21, 2013, http://www.bbc.com/persian/iran/2013/05/130521_l10_ir92_rafsanjani_mashai_disqualified.

82. "Helicopter-e Ahmadinejad Dochar-e Sanehe Shod; be Sarneshinan Asibi Naresid," *Radio Farda*, June 2, 2013, http://www.radiofarda.com/content/f12_ahmadinejad_not_hurt_helicopter_incident/25004498.html.

83. "Soroush: Farman-e 'Hobout-e' Ayatollah Khamenei Sader Shod-e Ast," *BBC Persian*, June 20, 2010, http://www.bbc.co.uk/persian/iran/2010/06/100619_u03-soroush-khamenei.shtml.

10. Historical Revisionism and Regional Threats

1. Ali Reza Kamari, "Barresi-e Andishe-ha-ye Nezami-e Ayatollah Seyyed Abdullah Mujtahid Beladi Bushehri," *Faslnameh-ye Motale'at-e Tarikhi* 6, no. 26 (Fall 2009): 10–25.

2. Arya Bakhshayesh and Moslem Tahavvori, "Ayatollah Ozma Borujerdi dar Tehran," *Faslnameh-ye Motale'at-e Tarikhi* 8, no. 31 (Winter 2010/2011): 151–183.

3. Bahram Akhavan Kazemi, "Ta'ammolat-e Siasi-ye Imam Khomeini va Maraje' dar Jaryan-e Enghelab-e Islami," *Islamic Revolution Studies* 9, no. 31 (Winter 2013): 107–124; Ismael Hassanzadeh and Mohammad Kazem Shafa'i Harissi, "Mavaze' va Eghdamat-e Ayatollah Golpayegani dar Ghebal-e Siasat-ha-ye Hokoumat-e Pahlavi," *Islamic Revolution Studies* 11, no. 37 (Summer 2013): 83–104.

4. Mehdi Aboutalebi, "Seyr-e Takomli-ye E'mal-e Veleyat-e Foqaha dar Tarikh-e Mo'aaser-e Iran," *Islamic Government* 18, no. 2 (Summer 2013): 6–32.

5. Asghar Montazer-al-Gha'em, "Seyr-e Tahavol-e Naghsh-e Imaman-e Shi'a dar Ehya'-e Te'ori-ye Imamat-e Elahi," *History of Islamic Culture and Civilizations* 5, no. 14 (Spring 2014): 51–70.

6. "Bayanat dar Aghaz-e Dars-e Kharej-e Feqh," Khamenei's official website, September 22, 1991, http://farsi.khamenei.ir/speech-content?id=2491.

7. "Bayanat dar Didar-e A'za-ye Majles-e Khobregan-e Rahbari," Khamenei's official website, September 8, 2011, http://farsi.khamenei.ir/speech-content?id=17226.

8. "Bayanat dar Aghaz-e Dars-e Kharej-e Feqh"; Seyyed Sajjad Izadehi, "Imam Khomeini va Ertegha'-e Jaygah-e Feqh-e Hokoumati," *Islamic Government* 17, no. 2 (Summer 2012): 57–86; Abass-Ali Meshkani-Sabzevari and Abolfazl Sa'adati, "Feqh-e Hokoumati; Narm-afzar-e Tose'-e Enghelab-e Islami," *Islamic Revolution Studies* 10, no. 32 (Spring 2013): 97–118; Mohammad Javad Arasta and Kamal Akbari, "Ta'sir-e Ta'sis-e Jomhouri Islami Iran bar Feqh-e Siasi," *Oloum-e Siasi* 14, no. 55 (Fall 2011): 23–56.

9. Abbas-Ali Kadkhodaei and Mohammad Javaheri-Tehrani, "Tafkik-e Ghova; Roya-ye Taghdis Shode," *Islamic Government* 17, no. 1 (Spring 2012): 99–122.

10. Abuzar Rajabi, "Tahlil-e Enteghadi-ye Nazari-ye Hokoumati-ye Sonnat-garayan dar Asr-e Gheybat," *Islamic Revolution Studies* 9, no. 30 (Autumn 2012): 155–176.

11. "Sherkat Nakardan dar Entekhabat Gonah-e Kabireh Ast," Fars News, May 17, 2009, http://www.farsnews.com/newstext.php?nn=8802270765.

12. "Hazrat-e Ayatollah Khamenei: Tagheer-e Nezame Riasati be Parlemani dar Ayandeh Dour Ehtemalan Moshkeli Nadarad," Mehr News, October 17, 2011, http://www.mehrnews.com/news/1435167/حضرت-آیت-الله-خامنه-ای-تغییر-نظام-سیاسی-از-ریاستی-به-پارلمانی.

13. "Ma'mouriyyat-e Daftar-e Rahbar-e Mo'azzam-e Enghelab be Yek Teem-e Takhassosi-e Hoghoughi Baray-e Barrasi-e Iradat-e Ghanoun-e Asasi," *Khabar Online*, November 7, 2011, http://www.khabaronline.ir/detail/183369.

14. Mohammad Taghi Mesbah-Yazdi, "Democracy Rah-avard-e Batel-e Saghifeh," *Kayhan*, March 10, 2011, http://kayhanarch.kayhan.ir/891219/8.htm#other801.

15. "Defa'-e Rahbar-e Iran az Ekhtiyarat-e Entekhabati-ye Showra-ye Negahban," *BBC Persian*, March 10, 2010, http://www.bbc.co.uk/persian/iran/2010/03/100310_u01-khamenei.shtml.

16. Seyyed Mahmoud Alavi, "Mahiyat-e Ahkam-e Hokoumati," *Islamic Government* 17, no. 3 (Autumn 2012): 5–36. Mr. Alavi became Iran's minister of intelligence in 2013.

17. "Fatva-ye Rahbar-e Enghelab Darbare-ye Eltezam be Velayat-e Faqih," *Raja News*, July 20, 2010, http://www.rajanews.com/news/39957; "Daftar-e Ayatollah Khame-

nei az Fatva-ye Eltezam be Velayat-e Faqih Defa' Kard," *BBC Persian*, July 26, 2010, http://www.bbc.co.uk/persian/iran/2010/07/100726_l03_velayat_faqih.shtml.

18. "Darbare-ye Fatva-ye Chegounegi-e Eltezam-e Amali be Velayat-e Faqih," Khamenei's official website, July 25, 2010, http://farsi.khamenei.ir/others-report?id=9774.

19. "Nazar-e Rahbar-e Enghelab Hadde-aghall-e Eltezam be Velayat-e Faqih Ast," Khamenei's official website, July 26, 2010, http://farsi.khamenei.ir/others-page?id=9787.

20. "Daftar-e Ayatollah Khamenei az Fatva-ye Eltezam be Velayat-e Faqih Defa' Kard."

21. Mohsen Kadivar, "Paksazi-ye Jomhuri Islami az Velayat-e Ja'er," *Jaras*, December 25, 2009, http://www.rahesabz.net/story/6204.

22. "Safeguarding system, no obligation - Iran dissident cleric," *BBC Monitoring Middle East*, October 14, 2009.

23. "Velayat-e Faqih Serfan Bahs-e Hokoumati Nist," Iranian Labour News Agency, February 4, 2010, http://www.ghatreh.com/news/nn4679583/متی-نیست-ولایت-فقیه-صرفا-بحث-حکو .

24. "Ayatollah Mahdavi-Kani: Mousavi Socialist Ast va be Agha-ye Khamenei E'teghad-e Velayee Nadarad," *Khabar Online*, December 4, 2011, http://www.khabaronline.ir/detail/187913/.

25. "Mousavi Khoeiniha Sanad-e bi E'teghadi-e Khodash va Mousavi be Asl-e Velayat-e Motlaghe-ye Faqih ra Rou Kard," *Raja News*, December 15, 2011, http://rajanews.com/Detail.asp?id=110949.

26. Ibid.

27. "Tahrif-e Nashianeh Enghelab Tavassot-e Mehdi Karroubi," *Raja News*, November 10, 2011, http://www.rajanews.com/news/90742.

28. "Nagofte-ha-ye Karroubi az Baznegari dar Ghanoun-e Asasi va Entekhab-e Dovvomin Rahbar-e Jomhuri Islami," *Kalemeh*, November 5, 2011, http://www.kaleme.com/1390/08/14/klm-79302/.

29. "Ra'is-e Ghove Ghazaiyye: Bayad az Pardakhtan-e be Maghoule-ye Entekhabat dar Chahar-choub-e Ghanoun Esteghbal Konim," *Tasnim News*, December 14, 2015, http://www.tasnimnews.com/fa/news/1394/09/23/942668/رئیس-قوه-قضاییه-نظارت-مجلس-خبرگان-بر-رهبری-سخنی-غیرقانونی-است.

30. "Ebraz-e Negarani-ye Ayatollah Khamenei az Amouzesh-e Oloum-e Ensani dar Daneshgah-ha," *BBC Persian*, August 31, 2009, http://www.bbc.co.uk/persian/iran/2009/08/090830_si_khamenei_universities.shtml.

31. Charles Kurzman, "Reading Weber in Tehran," *Chronicle of Higher Education*, November 1, 2009, http://chronicle.com/article/Social-Science-on-Trial-in-/48949/.

32. "Bayanat dar Didar-e Javanan va Daneshjooyan-e Daneshgah-ha-ye Ostan-e Hamedan," Khamenei's official website, July 7, 2004, http://farsi.khamenei.ir/speech-content?id=3243.

33. "Abdolkarim Soroush: Oloum-e Ensani Khoonin-tarin Shahid-e Pas az Enghelab Boodeh Ast," *Jaras*, January 14, 2010, http://www.rahesabz.net/story/7848/.

34. *Kayhan*, October 30, 2010.

35. "Asami-e 12 Reshteh Oloum-e Ensani Baray-e Baznegari," *Jaras*, October 24, 2010, http://www.rahesabz.net/story/25985/.

36. "Vorud-e Rouhaniyoun be Madares Baray-e Tarbiyat-e Dini-ye Danesh-amouzan," *Mardomsalari*, October 23, 2010, http://www.mardomsalari.com/template1/News .aspx?NID=88933; *Khorasan*, March 3, 2011, http://www.khorasannews.com/News .aspx?id=620396&type=2&year=1389&month=12&day=12.

37. Ibid.

38. "Bayanat dar Didar-e Jam'e Kasiri az Basijian-e Keshvar," Khamenei's official website, November 25, 2009, http://farsi.khamenei.ir/speech-content?id=8430.

39. Mohammad Ayatollahi Tabaar, "How Iran Sees Turkey," *Foreign Policy*, November 3, 2011, http://foreignpolicy.com/2011/11/03/how-iran-really-sees -turkey/.

40. "Didar-e Ra'is Jomhur-e Turkey-e ba Rahbar-e Mo'azzam-e Enghelab," Khamenei's official website, March 10, 2009, http://farsi.khamenei.ir/news-content?id =5986; "Didar-e Ra'is Jomhur-e Turkey-e va Hey'at-e Hamrah," Khamenei's official website, February 15, 2011, http://farsi.khamenei.ir/news-content?id=11144; "Didar-e Rajab Tayyeb Erdoghan Nokhost Vazir-e Turkey-e va Hey'at-e Hamrah ba Rahbar-e Enghelab," Khamenei's official website, October 28, 2009, http://farsi .khamenei.ir/news-content?id=8293; "Didar-e Nokhost Vazir-e Turkey-e ba Rahbar-e Enghelab," Khamenei's official website, December 3, 2006, http://farsi .khamenei.ir/news-content?id=1453; "Didar-e Nokhost Vazir-e Turkey-e ba Rahbar-e Enghelab," Khamenei's official website, March 29, 2012, http://farsi.khame nei.ir/news-content?id=19342.

41. See Güneş Murat Tezcür, *Muslim Reformers in Iran and Turkey: The Paradox of Moderation* (Austin: University of Texas Press, 2010); A. Kadir Yildirim, *Muslim Democratic Parties in the Middle East: Economy and Politics of Islamist Moderation* (Bloomington: Indiana University Press, 2016).

42. "E'zam-e Keshti Komak-resani-ye Iran be Ghazzeh Montafi E'lam Shod," *Radio Farda*, June 25, 2010, http://www.radiofarda.com/content/f10_Iran_aid_flotilla _ship_not_sending_Israel_Gaza_Turkey_Sheikholeslam/2082195.html.

43. *Kayhan*, June 8, 2010, 2.

44. "Ayatollah Shahroudi: Turkey-e dar Tahavvolat-e Mantaghe be Naf'-e Islam-e Liberali Naghsh-afarini Mikonad," Fars News, August 24, 2011, http://www .farsnews.com/newstext.php?nn=13900602182517.

45. "Hoshdar-e Jeddi be Turkey-e Darbareh Dekhalat dar Souriyeh," *Farda News*, June 12, 2011, http://www.fardanews.com/fa/news/151077/به-جدی-هشدار-سوریه ترکیه-درباره-دخالت-در.

46. "Iran President Ahmadinejad Begins Historic Egypt Visit," *BBC News*, February 5, 2013, http://www.bbc.com/news/world-middle-east-21336367.

47. Rania Rabih al-Abd, "Egypt: Salafis and Brotherhood Squabble Over Iranian Tourism," *Al-Akhbar English*, May 27, 2013, http://english.al-akhbar.com/node /15924; "Salafists to Hold Conference Against 'Spread of Shia Doctrine in Egypt,'" *Ahram Online*, April 4, 2013, http://english.ahram.org.eg/NewsContent/1/64 /68461/Egypt/Politics-/Salafists-to-hold-conference-against-spread-of-Shi .aspx; "Shias Are More Dangerous Than Naked Women: Salafist MPs," *Ahram Online*, May 13, 2013, http://english.ahram.org.eg/News/71355.aspx.

48. Saeed Kamali Dehgan, "Bahrain Attacks Iran Over Mistranslating Morsi's Speech on Syria," *Guardian*, September 3, 2012, http://www.theguardian.com/world /iran-blog/2012/sep/03/bahrain-iran-mistranslating-morsi-syria-speech.

49. "Leaders of the Region Meet at AKP Congress," *Hurriyet Daily News*, October 1, 2012, http://www.hurriyetdailynews.com/Default.aspx?pageID=549&nID=31356 &NewsCatID=359; Sami Kohen, "AKP Convention Spells Out Turkey's Foreign Policy Platform," *Al-Monitor*, October 5, 2012, http://www.al-monitor.com/pulse /politics/2012/10/akp-foreign-policy-congress.html.

50. Ali Khamenei, "Bayanat dar Didar-e A'za-ye Majles-e Khobregan-e Rahbari," Khamenei's official website, September 8, 2011, http://farsi.khamenei.ir/speech -content?id=17226.

51. "Bayanat dar Ejlas-e Bein al-Melali-ye Bidari-ye Islami," Khamenei's official website, September 17, 2011, http://farsi.khamenei.ir/speech-content?id=17269.

11. The Domestic Sources of Nuclear Politics

1. Seyyed Hossein Mousavian, *The Iranian Nuclear Crisis: A Memoir* (Washington, D.C.: Carnegie Endowment for International Peace, 2012), 193–207.

2. "Dastour-e Aghaz-e Ghani-sazi-ye 20 Darsadi-e Uranium dar Keshvar az Souy-e Ra'is-e Jomhur," *Aftab Yazd*, February 8, 2010, 2.

3. Javad Larijani, head of the Human Rights Council and international affairs deputy of the judiciary, argued that Iran was stronger than some other nuclear powers "because many of these countries got their atomic bombs from their heavy water reactors, which are not advanced compared to Iran." See *Aftab Yazd*, February 10, 2010.

4. Steven Erlanger and Mark Landler, "Iran Agrees to Send Enriched Uranium to Russia," *New York Times*, October 1, 2009, http://www.nytimes.com/2009/10/02 /world/middleeast/02nuke.html?pagewanted=all&_r=0.

5. Steven Erlanger, David E. Sanger, and Robert F. Worth, "Tehran Rejects Nuclear Accord, Officials Report," *New York Times*, October 29, 2009, http://www.nytimes .com/2009/10/30/world/middleeast/30nuke.html.

6. "Iran 'Formally Rejects Nuclear Fuel Deal,'" *BBC News*, January 20, 2010, http:// news.bbc.co.uk/2/hi/8469332.stm.

7. Mehdi Mohammadi, "Hich Gozineh-ee Rou-ye Miz Nist," *Kayhan*, October 1, 2009, 2.

8. "Tavafogh-e Iran va 5+1 Baray-e Edameh Goft-o Gou-ha," *Kayhan*, October 3, 2009, 2.

9. "Baray-e Soukht-e Reactor-e Tehran Bayad Poul Bedabim na Soukht," *Etemad*, February 21, 2010, 1.

10. *Kayhan*, October 4, 2009, 2.

11. Hossein Shariatmadari, "Koutah Nayamadim, Koutah Shodand!," *Kayhan*, October 6, 2009, 2.

12. "Rahbar-e Mo'azzam-e Enghelab dar Jam'e Mardom-e Por-shour-e Chalous," *Kayhan*, October 7, 2009, 3.

13. "Ahmadinejad: Mozakere-ye Jalili va Burns Mozakere-ye Khoubi Boud," *BBC Persian,* October 7, 2009, http://www.bbc.co.uk/persian/iran/2009/10/091007 _op_us_iran_ahmadinejad.shtml.

14. "Ayatollah Jannati dar Khotbe-ha-ye Namaz Jom'e Tehran: Siasat-e Edam-e Mozakereh ba Amrica Tagheer-Na-pazeer Ast," *Kayhan,* October 17, 2009, 3.

15. Hossein Shariatmadari, "Mozakereh bi Saghf-o Kaf!," *Kayhan,* October 18, 2009, 2.

16. *Aftab Yazd,* November 26, 2009.

17. Hossein Shariatmadari, "Chegouneh Motma'en Shodid?," *Kayhan,* February 6, 2010, 2.

18. Ibid.

19. *Kayhan,* November 15, 2009.

20. "Bayanat dar Didar-e Mardom be Monasebat-e Qadir," Khamenei's official website, December 6, 2009, http://farsi.khamenei.ir/speech-content?id=8485.

21. Mehdi Mohammadi, "Dobareh Negah Konid," *Kayhan,* February 9, 2010, 2.

22. Mehdi Mohammadi, "Vaghti Amrica Asabani Mishavad," *Kayhan,* February 18, 2010, 2.

23. Thomas Erdbrink, "Cleric Says Sanctions in Iran Are a Threat," *Washington Post,* September 15, 2010, http://www.washingtonpost.com/wp-dyn/content/article /2010/09/14/AR2010091406402.html.

24. "Can Sanctions on Iran Create the Leverage We Need?," Center for Strategic and International Studies, September 20, 2010, http://csis.org/event/can -sanctions-iran-create-leverage-we-need.

25. Mohammad Ayatollahi Tabaar, "How Iran Sees the Sanctions," *Foreign Policy,* September 22, 2010, http://foreignpolicy.com/2010/09/22/how-iran-sees-the -sanctions/.

26. "Bayanat dar Didar-e A'za-ye Majles-e Khobregan-e Rahbari," Khamenei's official website, September 8, 2011, http://farsi.khamenei.ir/speech-content?id =10141.

27. "Bayanat dar Didar-e Dast-andar-karan-e Sakht-e Nav-shekan-e Jamaran," Khamenei's official website, February 19, 2010, http://farsi.khamenei.ir/speech -content?id=8906.

28. *Kayhan,* October 21, 2010.

29. *Kayhan,* September 13, 2010, 2.

30. "Hashemi Rafsanjani dar Entekhabat-e Riasat-e Jomhuri Sabt-e-nam Kard," *Radio Farda,* May 11, 2013, http://www.radiofarda.com/a/f9_hashemi_registering _for_iran_presidential_election/24983195.html.

31. "Khaheshmand Ast Dekhalat Farmayeed va Neshan Daheed Velayat-e Faqih Mikhahad Jelo-ye Dictatori ra Begirad," *Jamaran,* May 22, 2013, http://www ی-را-بگیرد-بخش-سیاست-خواهشمند-است-دخالت-فرمایید-نشان-دهید-ولایت-فقیه/ jamaran.ir. .می-خواهد-جلوی-دیکتاتور

32. "Rahbar-e Iran: Mozekerat-e Hasteh-ee be Ja'ie Nemiresad," *BBC Persian,* February 17, 2014, http://www.bbc.com/persian/iran/2014/02/140217_l39_khamenei _nuclear_usa.

33. Ibid.

34. Carol Morello, "Iran Agrees to Nuclear Restrictions in Framework Deal with World Powers," *Washington Post,* April 2, 2015, https://www.washingtonpost.com

/world/negotiators-hold-marathon-all-night-session-in-last-ditch-effort-for
-agreement/2015/04/02/68334c88-d8b2-11e4-bf0b-f648b95a6488_story.html.

35. Thomas Erdbrink, "Public Grieving for Pop Singer Is Startling for Iran," *New York Times*, November 16, 2014, http://www.nytimes.com/2014/11/17/world/public
-grieving-for-pop-singer-is-startling-for-iran.html?_r=0&mtrref
=undefined&gwh=281E063198A7069E0F12ECE69B3BC9B4&gwt=pay.

36. Robert Mackey, "Iranians Celebrate Agreement Online and in the Streets," *New York Times*, April 3, 2015, http://www.nytimes.com/2015/04/03/world/middle
east/iranians-celebrate-agreement-online-and-in-the-streets.html?_r=0&
mtrref=undefined&gwh=B7700880E55E87849B7366DF025A22C5&gwt=pay.

37. "Montazer-e Ashadd-e Mojazat Baray-e Arazel-e Saudi Hastim," *Jam News*, April 10, 2015, http://www.jamnews.ir/detail/News/465532.

38. Golnaz Esfandiari, "Iranians Exchange Jokes About Tentative Nuclear Deal," *Radio Free/Europe Radio Liberty*, April 3, 2015, http://www.rferl.org/content
/iran-nuclear-deal-jokes/26937520.html.

39. "Bayanat dar Didar-e Maddahan-e Ahl-e Beyt," Khamenei's official website, April 9, 2015, http://farsi.khamenei.ir/speech-content?id=29415.

40. "Bish az 200 Namayandeh Majles-e Iran Khastar-e Enteshar-e 'Fact Sheet-e' Irani-e Tafahom-e Lowzan Shodand," *BBC Persian*, April 14, 2015, http://www.bbc
.com/persian/iran/2015/04/150414_l12_iran_nuclear_factsheet_lausanne
_majlis.

41. "Remarks by the President in a Conversation with the Saban Forum," White House Office of the Press Secretary, December 7, 2013, https://www.whitehouse
.gov/the-press-office/2013/12/07/remarks-president-conversation-saban
-forum.

42. Niloufar Zare', "Hamle-ye Sarih-e Rahbari Alayh-e Tavafogh-e Atomi; Mozakerat Rouy-e Labe-ye Tigh," *Jaras*, January 18, 2014, http://www.rahesabz.net/story
/79655/.

43. Mehdi Mohammadi, "Kash Otagh-e Mozakerat-e Hasteh-ie Panjareh-ie be Bagh-dad, San'aa, Beirut, va Dameshgh Dasht," *Vatan-e Emrouz*, February 16, 2015.

44. Thomas Erdbrink, "Iran's Leaders Begin Tricky Task of Selling Nuclear Deals at Home," *New York Times*, April 3, 2015, http://www.nytimes.com/2015/04/04
/world/middleeast/iran-nuclear-deal.html?_r=0&mtrref=undefined&gwh=A2
C68150C29ADF0998BAE2E5CFD955BB&gwt=pay&assetType=nyt_now.

45. "Salehi Migoft Beravid Do'aa Konid Tavafogh Beham Bokhorad," Fars News, January 25, 2016, http://www.farsnews.com/newstext.php?nn=13940511000167.

46. Mehdi Mohammadi, "Kilometr-ha Fara-tar az Protocol-ha," *Vatan-e Emrouz*, July 29, 2015, 1.

47. "IRGC Rejects Any Resolution Violating Iran's Red Lines," Tasnim News Agency, July 20, 2015, http://www.tasnimnews.com/en/news/2015/07/20/805111/irgc
-rejects-any-resolution-violating-iran-s-red-lines.

48. *Kayhan*, August 1, 2015, 1.

49. "Ansou-ye Tavafogh-e Vian," *Kayhan*, August 2, 2015, 2.

50. Mohammad Ayatollahi Tabaar, "Iran's Russian Turn: The Start of a New Alliance," *Foreign Affairs*, November 12, 2015, https://www.foreignaffairs.com
/articles/iran/2015-11-12/irans-russian-turn.

51. "Abbas Abdi Bazdasht Shod," *BBC Persian*, November 4, 2002, http://www.bbc
.com/persian/iran/021104_mf-abdi.shtml.

52. "Vakonesh-e Khamenei be Safar-e New York," *Radio Farda*, October 5, 2013,
https://www.radiofarda.com/a/f9_khamenei_remarks_rowhani_diplomatic
_efforts_newyork/25127669.html.

53. "Imam Movafegh-e Hazf-e Marg bar Amrica Boudand," Rafsanjani's website,
September 27, 2013, http://hashemirafsanjani.ir/fa/content/امام-موافق-حذف-
مرگ-بر-آمریکا-بودند.

54. Hamid Aboutalebi, Twitter post, April 10, 2015, 12:37 P.M., https://twitter.com
/DrAboutalebi/status/586613973597978624. Aboutalebi's controversial nomination to the UN ambassadorship was rejected by the United States due to his alleged role in the hostage crisis. See "US Refuses Visa for Iran's UN Envoy Choice
Hamid Aboutalebi," *BBC News*, April 11, 2014, http://www.bbc.com/news/world
-us-canada-26994936.

55. Mohammad Ayatollahi Tabaar, "Iran's Pragmatic Turn," *Foreign Policy*, September 12, 2013, http://foreignpolicy.com/2013/09/12/irans-pragmatic-turn/.

56. Mohammad Ayatollahi Tabaar, "Strategic Anti-Americanism in Iran from the
Hostage Crisis to Nuclear Talks," Monkey Cage, *Washington Post*, November 4,
2014, https://www.washingtonpost.com/blogs/monkey-cage/wp/2014/11/04
/strategic-anti-americanism-in-iran-from-the-hostage-crisis-to-nuclear
-talks/.

57. "Iran Navy Fleet Docks at Russia's Astrakhan Port," *Press TV*, October 23, 2015,
http://www.presstv.ir/Detail/2015/10/23/434673/Iran-Russia-Navy-fleet
-Damavand-destroyer-Astrakhan; "Russia and Iran Defense Ministers to Have
Talks in Tehran," *TASS*, January 20, 2015, http://tass.ru/en/russia/772043; "Russia
to Help Iran Build Own Satellite Observation Systems," *Russia Today*, August 25,
2015, https://www.rt.com/news/313410-Russia-Iran-space-cooperation/.

58. "Tehran and Moscow Vow to Bolster Ties," Mehr News, October 22, 2015,
http://en.mehrnews.com/news/111290/Tehran-Moscow-vow-to-bolster-ties;
"Russia and Iran Consider Bank to Finance Joint Projects," *Russia Today*, October 21, 2015, https://www.rt.com/business/319282-russia-iran-bank-energy
-novak/; "Russia's Yandex Iran Gambit to Counter 'US-Imposed Search Engines,'"
Russia Today, October 26, 2015, https://www.rt.com/business/319705-yandex
-iran-search-engine-russia/.

59. Laila Bassam and Tom Perry, "How Iranian General Plotted Out Syrian Assault
in Moscow," *Reuters*, October 6, 2015, http://www.reuters.com/article/us
-mideast-crisis-syria-soleimani-insigh-idUSKCN0S02BV20151006.

60. Karoun Demirjian, "The Next Generation of Iran Bills Is Cropping Up in Congress," *Washington Post*, October 1, 2015, https://www.washingtonpost.com
/news/powerpost/wp/2015/10/01/the-next-generation-of-iran-bills-are
-cropping-up-in-congress/.

61. "New Poll of the Iranian People on the Anniversary of Nuclear Deal (JCPOA),"
Iran Poll, July 7, 2016, https://www.iranpoll.com/blog/jcpoa.

62. "Ahkam-e Vijeh Entekhabat," Khamenei's official website, February 16, 2016,
http://farsi.khamenei.ir/package?id=31893&news_id=32304.

63. "Kasani ke Nezam ra Ghaboul Nadarand Ra'y Bedahand, Na Kasi ke Nezam ra Ghaboul Nadarad Befrestand Majles," Iranian Students' News Agency, January 20, 2016, http://www.isna.ir/news/94103018332/ایراندنندارانقبول-راهنظام-کهسانیک‍
بدهندنهکسیک‍هنظام-راقبول.

64. "Ayatollah Khamenei: Agar Jelo-ye Bad-khahan dar Souriyeh Gerefteh Nemishod Bayad dar Tehran va Khorasan Mijangidim," *BBC Persian*, January 5, 2017, http://www.bbc.com/persian/iran-38519790.

65. "Barjam-e Do," *BBC Persian*, March 24, 2016, http://www.bbc.com/persian/interactivity/2016/03/160324_l38_yt_nowruz_speechs.

66. "Jelogiri az Mosadereh Imam," *Shargh*, March 10, 2016, 2.

67. Morteza Kazemian, "Kelid-e Rouhani Ghofl-e Entekahbat ra Baz Nakard," *Radio Zamaneh*, February 11, 2016, http://www.radiozamaneh.com/260269.

68. *Khatami Media*, posted on February 21, 2016, https://www.youtube.com/watch?v=lcSYNfNpDZw.

69. "Gozaresh-e Bahare Hedayat az Entekhabat dar Zendan-e Evin," *Kalemeh*, February 29, 2016, http://www.kaleme.com/1394/12/10/klm-238541/.

70. Farzan Sabet, "Why Iran's Assembly of Experts Election Is the Real Race to Be Watching," *Washington Post*, February 24, 2016, https://www.washingtonpost.com/news/monkey-cage/wp/2016/02/24/why-irans-assembly-of-experts-election-is-the-real-race-to-be-watching/.

71. "Bayanat dar Didar-e A'za-ye Majles-e Khobregan-e Rahbari."

72. "Ta'ne-ye Twitteree-ye Hashemi be Mesbah-Yazdi," *Paytakht Press*, March 11, 2016, http://vazeh.com/nf/13504414.

73. "Enteghad-e Tond-e Mesbah-Yazdi az 'Taslim Shodan dar Barabar-e Doshman,'" *BBC Persian*, March 13, 2016, http://www.bbc.com/persian/iran/2016/03/160313_l26_mesbah_rouhani_nuclear_deal.

74. "Alam ol-Hoda: Atraf-e Rahbari ra Gheiychi Kardand," *Entekhab*, March 12, 2016, http://www.entekhab.ir/fa/news/257803.

75. Thomas Erdbrink, "Iranian President and Moderates Make Strong Gains in Elections," *New York Times*, February 29, 2016, http://www.nytimes.com/2016/03/01/world/middleeast/iran-elections.html?_r=0&mtrref=undefined&gwh=7DEDFF6C6778D7EE4E77C1DB9457BC4F&gwt=pay; "Why Iran's Elections Matter," Council on Foreign Relations, February 24, 2016, http://www.cfr.org/iran/why-irans-elections-matter/p37573.

76. Shervin Malekzadeh, "How Iran's Elections Marginalized Radicals and Consolidated a New Political Center," Monkey Cage, *Washington Post*, February 29, 2016, https://www.washingtonpost.com/news/monkey-cage/wp/2016/02/29/how-irans-elections-marginalized-radicals-and-consolidated-a-new-political-center/; Mohammad Ayatollahi Tabaar, "Why the Triumph of Moderates Is a Setback to Iranian Democracy," Monkey Cage, *Washington Post*, March 9, 2016, reprinted in *Iran's 2016 Election*, Project on Middle East Political Science (POMEPS) Studies, vol. 29, March 15, 2016.

77. Abbas Abdi, "Pasa Entekhabat Chegouneh Bashad," *Etemad*, February 27, 2016, 2.

78. See Guillermo O'Donnell, Philippe C. Schmitter, and Laurence Whitehead, eds., *Transitions from Authoritarian Rule: Tentative Conclusions About Uncertain Democracies*

(Baltimore, Md.: Johns Hopkins University Press, 1986); Andreas Schedler, *The Politics of Uncertainty: Sustaining and Subverting Electoral Authoritarianism* (Oxford: Oxford University Press, 2013); Jason Brownlee, *Authoritarianism in an Age of Democratization* (Cambridge: Cambridge University Press, 2007); Beatriz Magaloni, *Voting for Autocracy: Hegemonic Party Survival and Its Demise in Mexico* (Cambridge: Cambridge University Press, 2008); Jennifer Gandhi and Ellen Lust-Okar, "Elections Under Authoritarianism," *Annual Review of Political Science* 12 (2009): 403–422; Milan W. Svolik, *The Politics of Authoritarian Rule* (Cambridge: Cambridge University Press, 2012).

79. "Sokout-e Sokhangouy-e Showra-ye Negahban Shekast," Iranian Students' News Agency, March 1, 2016, http://isna.ir/fa/news/94121106963/ای-نگهبان-شکست سکوت-سخنگوی-شور.

80. Erin Cunningham, "Iran's Rouhani Lashes Rivals with Rare Criticism of Security Forces, Ruling Clerics," *Washington Post*, May 9, 2017, https://www.washingtonpost.com/world/middle_east/irans-rouhani-lashes-rivals-with-rare-criticism-of-security-forces-ruling-clerics/2017/05/09/6ba34d5a-34bd-11e7-ab03-aa29f656f13e_story.html?utm_term=.24d65006f226; Rohollah Faghihi, "Iran's Rouhani Shifts Strategy in Presidential Race," *Al-Monitor*, May 9, 2017, http://www.al-monitor.com/pulse/originals/2017/05/iran-rouhani-change-tactics-presidential-election.html; Hassan Rouhani, *Khaterat-e Doctor Hassan Rouhani: Enghelab-e Islami (1341-1357)*, vol. 1 (Tehran: Majma'-e Tashkhis-e Maslahat-e Nezam), 519–520.

81. Hossein Noush-Azar, "Rast-e Erati dar Boht-e Shekast," *Radio Zamaneh*, May 21, 2017, https://www.radiozamaneh.com/341966.

82. "Soroud-e 'Ey Iran' Sabt-e Melli Shod," Islamic Republic News Agency, May 15, 2017, http://www.irna.ir/fa/News/82530658/.

83. "Tajammo'-e Mardom dar Pasargad be Monasebat-e 'Rooz-e Kourosh,'" *BBC Persian*, October 28, 2016, http://www.bbc.com/persian/interactivity-37805667.

84. "Hassan Nasrallah: Iran Yek Keshvar-e Arabi Ast," *Aparat*, posted on November 22, 2016, http://www.aparat.com/v/MHupP/3%نصرالله حسن A_ایران_یک_کشور_عربی_است.

85. "Aya Khobregan Mitavanand Showra-ye Rahbari Entekhab Konand," *Mashregh News*, February 27, 2015, http://www.mashreghnews.ir/news/393158/آیا-خبرگان-می-توانند-شورای-رهبری-انتخاب-کنند; Hossein Bastani, "Aya Tashkil-e Showra-ye Rahbari Ba'd az Ayatollah Khamenei Gheir-e Momken Ast," *BBC Persian*, December 13, 2015, http://www.mashreghnews.ir/news/393158/آیا-خبرگان-می-توانند-شورای-رهبری-انتخاب-کنند.

Conclusion

1. Oliver Roy, *The Failure of Political Islam* (Cambridge, Mass.: Harvard University Press, 1994).

2. Robert Jervis, *System Effects: Complexity in Political and Social Life* (Princeton: Princeton University Press, 1999).

3. "Rabeteh ba Amrica Fe'lan Naf'ie Nadarad," Mehr News, January 3, 2008, http://www.mehrnews.com/news/615584/رابطه-با-آمریکا-فعلا-نفعی-ندارد.

4. Mehdi Bazargan, "Akherat va Khoda Hadaf-e Be'sat-e Anbia," *Kian* 5, no. 28 (1995–96): 46–61.

5. Ibid., 59.

6. Farhad Khosrokhavar, "The New Religiosity in Iran," *Social Compass* 54, no. 3 (2007): 453–463.

7. Jürgen Habermas, *The Theory of Communicative Action*, vol. 1, trans. Thomas McCarthy (Boston: Beacon, 1984); Jürgen Habermas, *The Theory of Communicative Action*, vol. 2, trans. Thomas McCarthy (Boston: Beacon, 1985).

8. See Sultan Tepe and Betul Demirkaya, "(Not) Getting Religion: Has Political Science Lost Sight of Islam?," *Politics and Religion* 4, no. 2 (2011): 203–228; Kenneth D. Wald and Clyde Wilcox, "Getting Religion: Has Political Science Rediscovered the Faith Factor?," *American Political Science Review* 100, no. 4 (2006): 523–529.

9. Graeme Wood, "What ISIS Really Wants," *Atlantic* 315, no. 2 (2015): 78–94.

Index

Abadan, 64, 154–155, 164

Abdi, Abbas, 116, 231, 287

Aboutalebi, Hamid, 289, 356n54

Abrahamian, Ervand, 120

Afghanistan, 121, 143, 233, 236

Afshar, Amir Khosrow, 65, 67

Afzali, Bahram, 333n162

Agha-Soltan, Neda, 241

Ahangaran, Sadegh, 166

Ahmadi-Moghaddam, Ismail, 123, 203

Ahmadinejad, Mahmoud: 2005
    presidential election, 206, 223, 234,
    294; 2009 presidential election, 223,
    238–239, 240, 294; blackmail tactics,
    253–254, 349n78; conflict with
    conservative elites, 237, 254–255,
    256; Egypt trip, 269–270; gaffes,
    238; on Green Movement, 247;
    ideological positioning, 2, 6, 25,
    249–250, 295; Mashaei issue,
    250–252; nuclear program, 273,
    274–275, 277, 278; U.S. relations, 2,
    252–254, 287

AKP (Justice and Development Party;
    Turkey), 257, 267–268, 269, 270, 305

Alaie, Hossein, 245

Alam, Assadollah, 41–42, 46–47

Alavi-Tabar, Ali-Reza, 221

Al-e Ahmad, Jalal, 4, 56

Algiers Agreement (1975), 65, 152, 196

Amir-Entezam, Abbas, 127, 137

anti-Americanism: Islamist/Khomeini
    appropriation from leftists, 8–9, 97,
    112, 113, 123, 130, 135, 141;
    Khamenei use of, 210–212, 274,
    290–291; leftist use of, 122–123,
    126–128, 129–130. *See also* hostage
    crisis

Arab Spring, 268–269

Araki, Mohammad Ali, 201, 212

Ardebili, Abdulkarim Mousavi, 81, 91,
    116, 150–151, 199, 200, 209

Aref, Mohammad Reza, 282, 292

Armenia, 26, 209

army: Banisadr and, 152; Iran-Iraq
    War, 157–158, 164–165, 177, 181; in

Khamenei, Ali: 1981 presidential election, 164; 2009 presidential election, 239, 240; 2013 presidential election, 281–282; 2016 parliamentary elections, 291, 293; anti-Americanism, 210–212, 274, 290–291; army control, 86, 163; ascendency, 10; assassination attempts, 163; clergy relations, 244, 258; conflict with Khomeini, 150–151, 160; constitutional amendment proposals, 197, 259–260; Cultural Revolution, 265–267; current situation, 295; Green Movement, 244–245, 247–248; hostage crisis, 133, 141, 143; Iran-Iraq War, 154, 158, 175, 184; IRGC control, 92–93; Islamic Republican Party founding, 91; leftist purge, 209–210, 223; legitimacy as Supreme Leader, 201–202, 209, 210, 264–265; Mashaei issue, 251–252; on *maslahat* (expediency), 261; on media, 233, 234–235, 248; on Montazeri, 262; Navvab-Safavi's influence on, 37; neoconservative shift, 223–225; nuclear program, 6, 234, 273, 275, 277, 278, 280–281, 283–284, 285; on oil, 187; political approach, 25, 202, 204, 223, 234, 236, 271–272; proposed invasion of Israel, 172; in Provisional Government, 96; Rafsanjani and, 202, 213–214, 294; religious authority, 212–213; Rushdie fatwa and, 194, 195, 271; Russian relations, 289–290; on sanctions, 280; Supreme Leader election,

199–201; on U.S. relations, 129, 234, 288, 302–303; on *Velayat-e Faqih*, 2, 25, 190–191, 258–259, 261–262; on voting, 259, 291

Khansari, Ahmad, 42, 62, 63

Khatami, Mohammad: 1997 presidential election, 24–25, 206, 222, 294, 304; 2016 parliamentary elections, 291, 292; Iran-Iraq War, 182; media freedom and, 230; nuclear program, 273, 274; as reformist, 2; U.S. and, 222, 287

Khazali, Abolghasem, 264

Khoei, Abolghasem, 49, 50, 53, 71, 93, 320n46

Khoeiniha, Mohammad Mousavi, 92, 115, 131, 207, 210, 263–264

Khomeini, Ahmad, 66, 67, 92, 95–96, 132–133, 164, 167, 173, 196, 199, 209–210

Khomeini, Hassan, 292

Khomeini, Mostafa, 50, 196

Khomeini, Ruhollah: introduction, 1–2, 3–4; 15th of Khordad Movement, 45; 1980 presidential election, 142; anti-Americanism, 123, 130; anti-Shah activism, 36, 41–45, 48–49, 53–55, 55–56, 59, 74–75; ascendency, 32–33, 40–41, 42, 45–47, 60–61; background, 40; Banisadr's impeachment, 162; on banking system, 188; Borujerdi and, 35, 36, 37–38; Carter message, 81–82; clergy relations, 9, 10, 47–48, 93–94, 108, 195–196, 197; on clerical role in politics, 10, 57–59, 69–70, 87, 101–102; on communism, 75; conflict with disciples over government, 110, 150–151, 159–160, 160–161, 163–164;

CPSIA information can be obtained
at www.ICGtesting.com
Printed in the USA
LVHW111102021019
632887LV00002B/2/P